MW01250657

ACKNOWLEDGEMENTS

I would like to express my profound gratitude to all of the researchers and writers from whose work I have drawn. In particular, I would like to acknowledge the following names listed in alphabetical order: Alan F. Alford, José Argüelles, Michael Baigent, Carlos Barrios, Itzhak Bentov, Gregg Braden, William Bramley, Rufus Camphausen, Fritjof Capra, Carlos Castaneda, Gina Cerminara, James Churchward, David Hatcher Childress, Joy Collier, Maurice Cotterell, Eric Von Däniken, Richard Dannelley, Ignatius Donnelly, Christopher Dunn, Ralph Ellis, George Feuerstein, Israel Finkelstein, Frater U∴D∴, Timothy Freke, Bob Frizell, Peter Gandy, Laurence Gardner, Brian Greene, George Gurdjieff, Graham Hancock, Michael Harner, Michael Hesseman, Eltjo Haselhoff, Richard Hoagland, John Hogue, Murry Hope, Leonard Horowitz, J. J. Hurtak, David Icke, Anodea Judith, Kurt Kaltreider, Robert Lenarden, Barbara Marciniak, Mark Morford, Jean Markale, Drunvalo Melchizedek, Ajit Mookerjee, Peter Moon, P. D. Ouspensky, Lynn Picknett, Clive Prince, Trevor Ravenscroft, James Redfield, Gordon-Michael Scallion, Phyllis Schlemmer, Lewis Spence, Rupert Sheldrake, Zecharia Sitchin, Jess Stearn, Rudolph Steiner, Robert Temple, Barbara Thiering, Willian Thomas, Neale Donald Walsh, John White, Collin Wilson, Gary Zucav.

I would also like to thank all those who have read for me and offered editorial comment, in particular, Enza Gaumond, Chris Dupont and Sandy Watson.

Thank you to Mike Montuori of Saturn Graphics, Peter Germain, Bea Benian, Anthony Dela Croce and Denis Laforge.

Special thanks to my sacred circle for guidance and inspiration.

CONTENTS

SYNOPTIC TABLE OF CONTENTS

CHAPTER 2—ANOTHER MODEL
Gaia; from a five-sensory personality to a multi-sensory personality; external power; authentic power

CHAPTER 3—REALITY ACCORDING TO ANCIENT MYSTICISM
What is a mystic?; Hinduism; Tantra; history of Tantra, male/female dualism, cosmogenesis, the power of sound; Buddhism; Chinese philosophy; Confucianism; Taoism; Zen Buddhism; Shamanic mysticism; Psychedelic plants; Egyptian Mystery Schools; Greek Mystery Schools; Qabala; Christian Mysticism; Sufism

CHAPTER 4—THE ATHEIST AND THE BEAR

CHAPTER 5—REALITY ACCORDING TO MODERN SCIENCE
History of physics; mechanistic view; matter as it appears at the sub-atomic level; *THE SPECIAL THEORY OF RELATIVITY:* Albert Einstein; space and time; space-time continuum; $E=mc^2$; *THE GENERAL THEORY OF RELATIVITY:* gravity; black holes; the Big Bang; *QUANTUM MECHANICS:* photo-electric effect; double slit experiments; wave-particle duality; equation of wave function; principle of uncertainty; quantum foam; quantum field theory; standard model; Bell's Theorem; consciousness; *STRING THEORY:* theory of everything; supersymmetry; more than three spatial dimensions

CHAPTER 6—THE PARALLELS BETWEEN MYSTICISM AND PHYSICS
Unity of all things; dualities; space and time; constant motion; emptiness and form; collective consciousness; usefulness of the scientific method

CHAPTER 7—CHAKRAS AND THE TREE OF LIFE
The chakra system; definition of a chakra; the non-physical bodies; the causal body; the astral body; the etheric body; nadi; kundalini; liberating current; manifesting current; sickness and disease; basic principles of healing; *FIRST: BASE/ROOT CHAKRA; SECOND: SACRAL CHAKRA; THIRD: SOLAR PLEXUS CHAKRA; FOURTH: HEART CHAKRA; FIFTH: THROAT CHAKRA; SIXTH: BROW CHAKRA; SEVENTH: CROWN CHAKRA; THE TREE OF LIFE;* Sepher Yetzirah; the ten Sephiroth; Qabalistic cosmology; the path of the serpent; abyss; thirty-two paths of wisdom; Tetragrammaton; Shekinah; four levels of meaning

CHAPTER 8—CONSCIOUSNESS
Reality is equivalent to consciousness; system of systems; pantheons of gods; hierarchy of angels; consciousness creates reality; seminars and conferences

Part Two—The Big Shift
End of the world

CHAPTER 9—GLOBAL CHANGES
Global warming; climatic change; pole shifts; collision with some celestial body; solar flares; the Big Shift;

BOOK 2

Part Six—Bible Roots and the History of Western Religion

THE NEW TESTAMENT

BOOK 3

I BELIEVE
or
'I Think I Believe'

INFORMATION BOXES

In presenting this type of information, it is very easy to digress. It's almost impossible to proceed in a direct, linear fashion. There are so many interrelated topics that it can be difficult to maintain a steady flow. It's often necessary to refer to some relevant sub-topic which would take several paragraphs to explain, so that by the time we return to the first line of thought, the original point becomes harder to grasp. To avoid this, I have decided to use information boxes, which will present self-contained mini-essays of related side issues. Thus, hopefully, the main text can proceed in a reasonably linear, fluid manner.

DIAGRAMS

INTRODUCTION

AWAKENING

When I awoke, I was in Australia at a spiritual retreat called Gunnebah, nestled in the rainforest near a sacred mountain called Wollumbin. It's not like I had been sound asleep. I wasn't awoken from a deep slumber by some sort of alarm. For years I'd been drifting in the twilight zone, that dreamy netherland between 'sound asleep' and 'wide awake'. I had been hiding out in limbo, aware of the path that I would soon take, but reluctant to make the commitment.

For most of my life I had been a blues musician, playing in smokey bars and nightspots across Canada, trying to deal with the confusion that seemed to be my constant companion. Since as long as I could remember, I'd been grappling with the mysteries of life, questioning the meaning of existence, trying to determine what was real and what wasn't. Why was I here, trying to run like the wind when it seemed like I was wading in the swamp, knee deep in mud? What was I doing here on the physical plane?

For a couple of years during my twenties I actually had a 'real job', but for the most part I found it very difficult to play the game, to be part of 'normal life'. It all seemed so trivial and pointless. In my late teens I had sought meaning by reading about Buddhism, Taoism and other world religions. At one point I found myself in a room full of spaced out hippies chanting 'nam yoho renge kyo' for what seemed like hours. I tried to make my way into the 'separate realities' that I had been reading about in the newly emerging works of Carlos Castaneda. When I was nineteen, I hitchhiked through Europe for six months, alone with my backpack, meeting a wide array of strange folk. It seemed like everyone I met had something to say regarding the questions that haunted me. In my mid-twenties I met a gentle woman who offered me great insight and wisdom; I have been with her for over twenty-five years. Ever since, I have been going about my business as a husband, father and working musician.

Then one day the universe decided to pull the rug out from under me. I began to suffer from a condition known as CFIDS—chronic fatigue immune deficiency syndrome. It was difficult to get out of bed, to continue on the current track. For several years the confusion around my musical career had been growing. Something had not felt right about this direction in my life. I now believe that the universe had been trying to gently nudge me off my track for years before it resorted to a major derailment. In my fatigued state I began to meditate more regularly and to pray. I began to devour books of all kinds that could give me more insight into the secrets of life. I began to more openly acknowledge and explore my spiritual side.

Over the next few years I worked at overcoming my illness and it slowly improved. I continued to work sporadically as a musician until my wife and I decided to spend a year on the east coast of Australia, near a small town called Murwillumbah. Day by day the fog in my mind began to lift. That day at Gunnebah it dawned on me that I was wide awake. The maniacal laugh of that infamous Australian bird, the kookaburra, seemed to be coming from deep within my own heart. It was hilarious. I could suddenly see more clearly than ever before.

Upon awakening, I began to understand my true identity. I could clearly see **who I am.** I am an incredibly beautiful being who exists simultaneously in a great many dimensions and time frames. I am an amazingly powerful entity with an enormous storehouse of information, capable of extraordinary feats of creative genius. I am, in fact, God. Like most Earthlings, however, I have forgotten much of this knowledge and am currently capable of only the feeblest of tasks. I am subject to the laws and limitations of life in the third realm; the physical plane. I am somewhat dense. Soon, however, all that will change.

Upon awakening, I also began to understand **why I am here.** I am here to remember. I am here to achieve a certain 'state of being'—to learn to accept any circumstance, no matter how difficult, with joy and gratitude. I am here to learn to set all judgement aside, to treat all beings, all things, with love and compassion. Inevitably, I will learn to see through the illusions, to realize that we are all cells in the same universal body, to reclaim the incredible creative power that is my birthright. I will inevitably remember more and more of my godliness. **I am God. So is everybody else.**

Upon awakening I understood that, from that moment on, every action I took would be motivated by the intent to facilitate this process of remembering. Guided by my 'higher self', I would consciously work at arriving at the state of being described above. This state of being has been given many names by many different cultures and traditions, such as: Christ-consciousness, Nirvana, Heaven, etc. In this book I will call it **enlightenment.** To be awake is to realize that everything we do is designed to bring us closer to the light, that any action that does not assist us along the path to enlightenment is not worth pursuing. I now knew that, in order to facilitate my own process of enlightenment, in order to heal, I needed to write a book.

I would write a book to celebrate my own awakening. It would help me to sort things out for myself, it would keep me focussed on the light. The 'big picture' would become clearer and clearer. Digging up relevant information, chewing it over and exposing it to my inner guides is a useful methodology for me—that's just the kind of guy I am. Some people don't need such a cerebral, left-brained process of accessing information in order to stay focussed on the path. But not me. I need to understand with my brain. Then that understanding will find its way to my bone marrow. I suspect that, in this modern world dominated by left-brained consciousness, there are many people who feel this way.

For me, writing this book is a method for moving toward enlightenment—it is a healing tool. It can be a great adventure, discovering the tools best suited to assist one in this healing process. For some, meditation is a tool, for others, working on the car is a tool. Praying, chanting, going to church, gardening and having sex; all can be useful on the mystical path. Hopefully, one learns to listen to one's higher self or inner voice, which will help to guide one to whichever paths seem most beneficial.

I have no intention to try to win you over to my way of thinking or to sign you up to some weird cult where you'll be asked to give up all your money or to prepare to board a space-ship to paradise. I claim no psychic abilities; I am not a medium for any particular angel or race of ET's; I have not been recently abducted and brought to another planet, nor am I the reincarnation (as far as I know) of some Atlantean king. This book simply represents my attempt at sharing my own process with the reader, at presenting some of the information I've come across, the thoughts, questions, opinions and beliefs I've had, the feelings and emotions I've encountered as I fumble my way along the path to enlightenment. While acknowledging that I've come a long way on that path, I am certainly aware that I still have a long way to go. This book is not designed to 'sell' you, the reader, a particular set of beliefs but rather, to encourage you to ask your own questions and find your own answers. Maybe, by bearing witness to my processes of discovery, you can help yourself with your own.

*I firmly believe that we are entering a new era—**the age of non-dogma**—in which it is becoming preferable to work things out for oneself, rather than adhere blindly to preconceived doctrine or the opinions of others.* What if I tell you that the purpose of life on the physical plane is to reach enlightenment? Now that you know that, you can go and watch 'The Simpsons' to learn about human foibles and the workings of life. Wait a minute—you're still reading. Don't you believe me? Don't you trust me?

For most people, the difficulty in accepting or even considering possible answers to questions of such enormity is that one needs evidence, one needs convincing. Questions of this nature are very difficult to address and possible answers can be very complex or very simple, and come in all shapes and sizes. Some people require solid, scientific answers. Others need to hear 'the message' from someone special—perhaps someone with a great talent, a member of a particular bloodline, a performer of miracles or maybe just a great orator.

For some it is enough to know that many other people find a particular message to be satisfactory, and therefore "what's good enough for them is good enough for me". Often a huge institution grows around such messages, complete with rules and regulations, rituals and traditions, preconceived doctrine, and officials who enforce and interpret it all for you. Many, especially in the past two thousand years, have been content to be a part of such an institution, faithfully accepting whatever is offered.

Some people, however, need to try to figure out the answers for themselves. I feel that seekers of this nature are on the increase, relying less and less on preconceived doctrine and more on their own inner voices. I believe that 'the message' resides deep within each and every one of us. Some modern spiritual leaders are encouraging people to trust their innate knowledge and to follow their hearts. Some gurus have even disbanded their followings. I truly believe that we are entering an era of renewed personal power in which we are capable of recognizing truth wherever or however it is encountered.

ABOUT THIS BOOK

The information that I'm presenting in this book is based on much reading, investigating, meditating and ruminating. The sources from which I've drawn run the gamut from pure science to ancient mystical wisdom to modern channeled information. (See BOX 1—CHANELLED INFORMATION) I offer my deepest gratitude to all the writers, researchers and resources from whom I have gathered much of this information. I have listed many of them in the 'Acknowledgements' section just before the Introduction. This book represents a *synopsis* of many points of view on many related topics. Any page in this book could probably be expanded into a book unto itself. My aim was to present a book with **a broad scope, rather than a deep scope**.

Many of the concepts in this book, especially in the first part, are very abstract and difficult to articulate. There are several *inherent hardships* in writing about this type of subject matter:

1) The English language has not yet developed words to deal with some of these concepts.

2) Some of it cannot be understood in the linear, logical way in which we have become accustomed to discussing things. Linear thinking can be defined as a tendency to explain things rationally, so that cause seems to precede effect in a flowing, linear way. Even science agrees with mysticism in acknowledging that rational thought and its accompanying verbal language is an inadequate way to perceive and discuss reality.

3) There are many concepts which are either strange dichotomies, or which are simply difficult to understand. For example, there is no beginning and no end; there is no such thing as time; there is no matter; we have free will,

and yet we are all part of the 'predetermined' divine will; we are both every-thing and nothing. It is very difficult to speak of the nature of the universe without encountering many inherent contradictions and paradoxes. Such things are ineffable, beyond words. They can only truly be understood by direct experience. As we shall see, modern science is also arriving at this perspective.

4) It is often difficult to find an analogy, metaphor or other explanatory device that can explain every aspect of a particular topic, sometimes forcing me to mix metaphors or combine several different explanations. I sometimes use several 'models' to try to explain something. There is no intention to inte-grate these different models into some sort of unified theory, but rather, to shine different lights from different perspectives on a particular issue.

Trying to explain reality using words and linear logic is very difficult, if not impossible. Many are of the opinion that such an endeavor is truly futile. *I dis-agree. I believe that **any** effort to expand one's awareness constitutes a good start and is thus useful and worthwhile.* It has been said that trying to describe the mysti-cal experience is like trying to describe color to someone who is colorblind.

> **BOX 1—CHANNELED INFORMATION:** Channeling is the process whereby a person, usually in a state of trance, acts as a 'channel' or 'medium' for some other entity. This other entity could be referred to as a god, an angel, an extra-terrestrial, a disembodied spirit, etc. The entity 'speaks' through the medium in various ways and the resulting chan-neled information can be in the form of spoken language (sometimes a language unfa-miliar to the medium), in written words or drawn pictures. Sometimes this happens as a form of 'automatic' writing or drawing, whereby the medium may not even be looking at his own hand, yet the hand is furiously scratching down information as if possessed by a will of its own. There is a wide variety of channeled information, some of it seeming to be more authentic and some of it more suspect. Many people feel inclined to discredit such info, yet most of the Bible, if it is accepted as the 'word of God' would qualify as hav-ing been channeled. Most Biblical prophets would fit the definition of a channel. Mme Blavatsky and Edgar Cayce are two well-known examples of modern channels.

Imagine a teacher who sees only in black and white trying to describe the multi-colored universe to others with the same visual impediment. Perhaps this teacher may try to gather varying descriptions from varying sources, all of whom have had a brief glimpse of this multi-colored reality. From this, the teacher may try to piece together a vague understanding of what color looks like and then convey it to the students. Even if only a vague understanding could be achieved, it could possibly be enough to convince both teacher and students that a deeper, more experiential understanding is well worth pursuing.

No matter how careful one is in choosing the words, analogies and various devices to try to discuss the nature of reality, it is inevitable that they will be less than perfect. All words are ultimately inadequate. This is especially so if the reader adheres too closely to the literal meaning of words and does not read with a genuine desire to understand. Having acknowledged the pitfalls and difficulties involved in a book of this nature, I will courageously stumble forth, confident that you will embrace the spirit, rather than the actual letter of what I am attempting to say. Please read with your heart.

What is this book about? It is about the evolution of the universe. It is about 'the journey to enlightenment', both in regards to us as individuals and to the human collective. It is about some of the established bodies of knowledge, both past and present, that have existed here on Earth. *I believe that these paradigms and the attitudes to which they have given birth, have a great effect on the journey. Are they impairing humanity's progress toward enlightenment? I believe it is time to re-examine our belief systems.*

I've presented this book in seven 'parts' which are divided into three 'books'. BOOK ONE, if I may be so bold, will be an effort to explain my understanding of how the universe works. It is expressed in two parts. Part One represents an effort to understand the nature of reality. It asks, 'Who are we?' It entails new ways of looking at things in terms of energy and the evolution of energy. It describes this evolution using the analogy of a great 'Game'. This new way of looking at things will take into account some of the perspectives arrived at by modern physics and other sciences, as well as those arrived at by the 'mystical' approach. The similarities between the mystical models and the scientific models will be discussed. The final chapter of Part One suggests that reality is the creation of 'consciousness'—that it actually 'is' consciousness.

Part Two goes on to discuss the question, 'Where are we going?' Many people both past and present believe that the planet is headed for enormous change. Some call it 'the Big Shift'. Part Two talks about this change and the huge role that collective humanity has to play in it.

BOOK TWO will question the ruling paradigms—taking a new look at old, established schools of thought and re-examining them in terms of the evolution of energy, and in light of newly emerging information. It asks, 'Where do we come from? Where do our attitudes and paradigms come from? Why do we think what we think? Are these paradigms serving humanity or are they impeding our progress toward the light?'

Throughout the book I use the term *'established information'*. By this I mean information that is widely accepted and dispensed by the major, established institutions of our society (usually western society unless otherwise noted). The military-industrial complex, and the power structure surrounding it, is the main institution. Within this wide and powerful web of influence are other institutions such as the major religions, academia and the mainstream media. Although there are parts of these three institutions that are involved with information that is not embraced by the ruling establishment, for the most part they toe the line of the power structure. The information generated by these establishments over the centuries has become part of our common knowledge and much of it is rarely questioned.

Part Three questions our paradigms regarding human origins, looking at the concept of natural selection and other possible evolutionary mechanisms. It also addresses the mythology of Atlantis and Lemuria and the notion that our history has been shaped by extra terrestrial life forms. Part Four playfully presents an alternative history of life on Earth; a compilation of non-conventional views that paint a picture very different from the 'accepted' version that we've been taught. Part Five looks at the many mysteries that continue to defy our ability to explain, including the Pyramids and other ancient enigmas, the crop circle phenomenon and UFO reports. Part Six examines the Bible and the religions that grew up around it. This powerful book has significantly influenced our past and continues to shape our present. Does it continue to serve us, or is it holding us back? How has it been manipulated and distorted? Are the attitudes that it spawned threatening our very existence? Book Two closes out with Part Seven, which deals with our attitudes toward the feminine half of humanity and toward human sexuality. Have we been overlooking a beautiful and very useful way of approaching the light?

Most of the established information that we have been fed is, I believe, greatly incomplete and often inaccurate. Some of it fosters attitudes that keep us disempowered and easy to manipulate. There is a great deal of compelling information that the mainstream schools and the mass media do not present, either because they don't have a good grasp of it, or because it's stuff that the establishment does not want us to see. I like to call this **alternative information**, or alterinfo. We will take a look at many controversial topics, bearing in mind that there is so much information on so many such topics, that even an enormous work of many volumes would not completely cover it.

Most books are concerned with presenting an argument, postulating a thesis and then going about the business of trying to convince the reader of the validity of the thesis. This book is not like that. **I didn't write this book to impose my views upon anyone**, but rather to encourage the reader to continue the search for his/her own understanding long after this book has been read. I am stressing this because I feel it's important. If you are interested in trying to figure out who we really are, where we came from, why we're here and where we're going, then I believe this book can be of assistance.

Even if you don't believe all the information that this book presents, I am sure that the process of considering such information will help you to refine your awareness and bring you closer to the answers you seek. Personally, much of the material in this book I neither believe nor doubt. Often I am just presenting what seems to be relevant information as food for thought. In most cases, when I am clearly presenting my own views, they will appear in italics.

Again, this book is a synopsis of a large body of information. If you wish to delve more deeply into any particular area of interest, this book suggests some sources and means by which to do so.

BELIEFS

I feel it is important to end this section by saying something about beliefs. Some people wear their beliefs like a badge, as a way to identify themselves. They cling to them in a sort of desperation and will argue red-faced with anyone who believes otherwise. One cannot help but have beliefs. Even the mildest opinion is a form of belief, which serves the believer by offering a foothold from which to negotiate through life. But when beliefs become 'written in stone', when they solidify into an impregnable fortress, then they succeed in blocking inner truths from surfacing into consciousness. They no longer serve the believer, succeeding only in blurring vision and impairing understanding.

There is a famous Zen Buddhist story of a university professor who went to visit a Zen master, asking to be taught the wisdom of Zen. As the master was pouring a cup of tea, the professor noticed that he filled the cup to overflowing and kept pouring till it was spilling out onto the table. When he was asked about this strange behavior, the Master said, "You are like this cup. You too are full of your own opinions and speculations. How can I show you Zen unless you first empty your cup?" Our cup is full of 'common sense', preconceived ideas about how things work. Our knowledge base, our everyday perceptions are deeply ingrained and based largely on information that originates with the five senses. However, both modern science and ancient mystical teachings tell us that these deeply ingrained perceptions are part of a complex illusion, which is obscuring the true nature of reality. To gain a better understanding of how the universe works, we cannot rely solely on our senses; we must see past our common sense beliefs.

At this point in my life, my beliefs no longer define me. The process of writing this book was an exercise in **liquefying my beliefs**, allowing them to flow. This allows me to evaluate new information in a more open way. Some beliefs will come and go according to whatever new information I am exposed to. Most of the 'nitty gritty' of what happened when, who did what and why, etc, is ultimately of no great concern to me. Sorting out all of these details is only useful if it assists my progress toward enlightenment. It is useful to me to see that the old paradigms of reality are becoming less and less capable of explaining the growing number of mysteries that are entering our collective field of vision. We need new, bigger paradigms. If we think of the old paradigms as being a box into which we are trying to cram ideas, observations and phenomena that just don't fit, then it is evident that we need a bigger box. A box, however, is still a box. The truth cannot be confined to any box. It cannot be described by any language. It can only be experienced.

Finally, I would like to say a few words about *skepticism*. I consider myself to be a skeptic, which may raise the eyebrows of other self-proclaimed skeptics reading this book, given the unusual range of topics and unorthodox opinions expressed herein. I believe that would result from an inaccurate idea of what 'skepticism' is. According to Webster's Dictionary, a skeptic is 'a person who questions the validity, authenticity or truth of something purporting to be factual'. The modern usage of the word comes from a school of philosophers from ancient Greece called the Skeptics who maintained that real knowledge of things is impossible. This ancient usage of the word derives from the Greek verb, 'skeptesthai', which means 'to consider or examine'.

It seems that a skeptic would apply an attitude of scrutiny to any and all information encountered. But too often, someone referring to themselves as 'skeptical' applies very little scrutiny to established information and scoffs at anything else. If anything needs to be closely scrutinized, it is established information and the beliefs and attitudes that go along with it, as it is these that underlie almost all of our actions, our history and our future. Considering the planet's current dire situation, shouldn't we be examining the validity of these old mind-sets? Shouldn't we be keeping an open mind about new ways of understanding reality? Let us not confuse skepticism with close-mindedness.

One of my greatest heroes, Albert Einstein, also considered himself to be a skeptic. As a youth, he was greatly interested in the work of Austrian physicist, Ernst Mach, who advocated 'intellectual skepticism'. Einstein questioned all information, including the staunchest, most established science. He subsequently revolutionized our notions of how the universe works. In the latter half of his life, Einstein applied his skepticism to his political mind as well, refusing to accept the propaganda of the time. He spoke out radically against violence, publicly taking a stand against both Nazi aggression and Allied attempts to develop nuclear weapons.

I have been interested in alternative information since my teen years, all the while maintaining what I believe to be a healthy skepticism. I remember rolling my eyes at many 'far out' ideas in the past, only to reassess those feelings many years later. I've always had an averse reaction to the term 'new age', and although I've come to embrace much of the information under that umbrella heading, I still feel that much of it is off the mark. At the same time, I've always had an instinctive mistrust of what could be called 'established information', much of which is offered in schools and by the media. A lot of it just doesn't add up. The more I look at various alternative notions and ideas, the more they start to make sense. Cross examination of information from a wide variety of sources, some of which seems unrelated, starts to yield a picture that makes much more sense. This picture began to resonate with feelings deep in my gut. Concepts that had formerly seemed 'wacky', are making more and more sense within the context of this growing picture.

To this day I greet any new information with a grain of salt, clinging tenaciously to nothing. *One thing I can say with any certainty is that I believe the 'established' view to be somewhat shallow and inadequate. Without being able to conclusively define reality, I believe it is safe to say that there is much more to it than meets the eye.* The examination of the information presented in this book, along with a good deal of meditation and rumination, has helped me to make sense of things, to accumulate a body of beliefs that I hope will always remain 'liquid'. Throughout the book, and especially in the final section called BOOK 3, I try to share some of these beliefs with the reader.

The continuing accumulation of information helps me to more fully appreciate the beauty of the great mystery, to be able to more readily see through the illusion of chaos and to recognize the order, the intelligent design that underlies everything. It fills me with awe and strengthens my core beliefs. *I have **seven core beliefs** that are very strong with me. It would be very difficult for these beliefs to be shaken by any new information that might cross my path. I would like to share them with you now.*

1. *Most of what we refer to as reality is an illusion.*
2. *We are not just clever naked apes designing better mousetraps— humanity is much more than we tend to believe.*
3. *An incredibly glorious, beautiful and exciting destiny awaits us all.*
4. *We are the creators.*
5. *We, and all things in all universes, are one.*
6. *There is absolutely nothing to fear.*
7. *Love is the master key to all doors.*

"Believe nothing, no matter where you read it, or who said it, no matter if I have said it, unless it agrees with your own reason and your common sense."
—*Gautama Buddha*

"So you will see how absurd is the whole structure you have built, looking for external help, depending on others for your comfort, for your happiness, for your strength. These can only be found within yourself."
—*J. Krishnamurti*

"The church is within yourself and not in any pope nor preacher, nor any building, but in self."
—*Edgar Cayce, No.5125-1*

"No man can reveal to you aught but that which already lies half asleep in the dawning of your knowledge."
—*Kahlil Gibran, from The Prophet*

"Be a light unto yourself."
—*the last words of Gautama Buddha*

"Admit that you do not know what you do not know— that is knowledge"
—*Confucius*

"Existence is beyond the power of words to define"
—Lao Tse

"The religion of the future will be a cosmic religion. The religion which is based on experience, which refuses dogma."
—*Albert Einstein*

BOOK 1

GOD = mc^2

or

'Well Then,
That Explains It!'

Albert Einstein introduced us to the famous equation, $E = mc^2$. The amount of energy (E) in a piece of matter is equal to its mass (m) multiplied by the speed of light (c) squared. When translated from the language of mathematics into the language of words, this means that matter is equivalent to energy. Matter, which has mass, is a manifestation, a state of energy. Einstein was bringing to the scientific world a piece of the knowledge that mystics have had for thousands of years—*all aspects of reality, everything in the universe, consists of different manifestations of the same substance.* For the purposes of this book, we will call this substance 'energy'. *Everything is energy, the Divine Consciousness.* By 'divine consciousness' we mean the 'intelligence' of the source of all things.

Continually changing and evolving, Energy twirls and whirls in a grand dance of creation and destruction, a cosmic journey, an eternal series of expansions and contractions. Consisting of countless systems and sub-systems, all inextricably linked and interconnected, Energy entertains itself with endless tragedies and comedies. It laughs and laughs and laughs in a state of eternal joy. Energy plays the divine Game, spiraling upward to macro-infinity and downward to micro-infinity. God is Energy is Consciousness, 'thinking' our 'reality' into existence. As individuals we are components or particles of Consciousness. We perceive only as much of 'reality' as our expanding awareness will allow. Someday, when enough experiences have been gathered, all obstacles to perception will dissolve and we will once again know unity with Consciousness, seeing everything, understanding everything, being everything.

Book One, as the title implies, will try to explain who we are and where we're going. In trying to understand who we really are, the first part deals with the nature of reality. Knowing our true identity involves having a better understanding of what the universe is. We will attempt to gain a better understanding of reality and our place in it. We will attempt to deal with questions that have always baffled mankind. Why is life? Why are we here?

The second part will take a look at where we are going. Life on this planet is currently in a precarious position, teetering on the brink of enormous change. What will be the nature of this change? Is it Armageddon? Is it a new beginning? Will we undergo a complete change of consciousness? Many opinions, including prophecies old and new from every corner of the globe, contend that we are experiencing a cosmic 'opportunity' that happens very rarely. Some people refer to this opportunity as The Big Shift. This moment in time is very special—we are truly living in exciting times.

Part One

The Nature of Reality

In order to tackle the question, 'why is life?', it is important to try to understand the nature of reality. What is real and what isn't? This next chapter will try to explain how the universe works and why we are all here!! No small task. One might even say, an impossible task. While I'm well aware that any word-bound solutions to such enormous puzzles will ultimately prove to be inadequate, the following explanatory models have helped me to make some sense of it all. The mystical traditions have their way of dealing with reality. Modern science uses a totally different method in an attempt to come to grips with reality. Interestingly, these diametrically opposed methodologies have yielded startlingly similar information. There have been many attempts made to illuminate various aspects of reality, so that by understanding its parts, we can better grasp the whole.

I have found no single explanation to be satisfactory. There are so many different perspectives, terminologies, analogies and metaphors. In this section I have offered several different perspectives or explanatory models. Each of these models can be delved into at greater length if the reader desires and I have offered references by which to do so. Each of these models, although related, are not interdependent. One does not need to understand the first model before going on to the next. This is important to point out because some of the models are more technical than others and may appeal to those with a more technical type of understanding. Others may prefer explanations that are more whimsical or allegorical. In any case, it is important to me that the reader not feel frustrated or bogged down by information. If that should happen, try closing your eyes and imagining something ludicrous, something that makes you laugh. Life is a sitcom.

The first section deals with reality using the analogy of a Game in which we are all involved. The terminology established in this first section will appear throughout the book. I'll try to paint an overview of the Game and, as the section proceeds, to explain aspects in more detail. Most of the concepts will appear again in other forms in subsequent sections. Hopefully, by the end of Part One, all of the different models will have come together to provide some insight into the great mystery of reality. Have fun!

Chapter 1

THE GLORIOUS GAME

To presume the motives of the Divine is to walk on very thin ice indeed. Like much of humanity, however, I can't seem to resist the temptation to attempt to explain why and how God created the universe. And so, across the frozen pond I scuttle, aware that any moment I may become very wet and very cold.

Once upon a time, God decided to create the universe. Wait a minute. It's probably not a great idea to use the word 'God'. It has such enormous baggage attached to it. So many people have mental pictures or preconceived notions that they associate with that word; lets try and start with a clean slate. Other words have been used as well, such as the Force, the Creator, etc. I think, in this section of the book at least, I prefer to call him The Source. Hold on a second! Did I say 'him'? Maybe I should just refer to The Source as an 'it'. Anyway, it's probably safe to say that The Source is a gender-less phenomenon.

Let's start again. Once upon a time, The Source decided to create the universe. It did so because it needed to 'know' its own glorious perfection 'experientially'. Or maybe, as some have suggested, it was bored. In any case, The Source put into place an elaborate 'Game', complete with laws, tendencies and systems, much of which is illusory by design. It then divided itself (while at the same time remaining whole) into countless sub-entities, each a perfect parcel of Divine Energy. These innumerable parcels were then sent out into 'the Game' with the mission of *experiencing all that could possibly be experienced*. Energy was thus set on a course of evolution through the many levels of 'the Game'; incrementally accumulating more and more experiences. Eventually, when all that could possibly be experienced was experienced, all the separate aspects of energy would come together again to re-experience the whole. This occurs over a vast amount of time, yet it also happens in the twinkling of an eye. Confused yet?

Let's try to get a better understanding of how the universe is put together. Both modern science and ancient mysticism have observed very similar phenomena in trying to answer this question. We'll explore this in some detail in subsequent sections of Part One. For now, however, let's just cut to the quick and say that all of creation consists of different manifestations of the same thing. All components of the Game, all aspects of creation are made of the same substance. This substance has been called different things by different people, such as akash and spirit. For the purposes of this book, we'll just refer to this substance as *energy*.

In the old classical physics it was believed that matter was composed of solid, irreducible particles upon which separate forces acted. The new physics, however, has observed that, at a sub-atomic level, the differences between the forces and the particles dissolve. In other words, matter and energy are different manifestations of the same thing. A particle represents an 'interaction' of different force fields. Although it constantly changes form, the ultimate cause or identity of this energy remains unknown to science.

Everything in the totality of creation is a different manifestation of energy, including sound, light, matter and even thought and emotion. Every form or manifestation has its own signature rate of vibration or frequency. Some frequencies are such that the energy manifests as matter, perceivable by the five senses. Different forms of matter have different frequencies or densities. The energy that makes up oxygen, for example, vibrates at a higher rate than lead and is thus less dense. The type of energy that is carried by electro-magnetic waves vibrates at much higher frequencies. This range of frequencies is called the electro-magnetic spectrum, and within this range there is a narrow band of frequencies representing visible light, which breaks down into the seven colors of the spectrum. (See DIAGRAM 1—THE ELECTRO-MAGNETIC SPECTRUM) Some of the frequencies slightly lower than visible light, such as radio waves and infrared light, are invisible to our naked eye, but we have instruments that can detect them. Electro-magnetic waves higher than light, such as x-rays and gamma rays are also invisible, but detectable with instrumentation. According to the mystics, however, some frequencies are vibrating so quickly that they are beyond the range of any type of human sensory perception. At thislevel of vibration, not even our instruments can detect them. In other words, there are aspects of reality that are beyond beyond the physical, material plane, existing at vibrations undetectable by the five senses.

DIAGRAM 1 • THE ELECTRO-MAGNETIC SPECTRUM

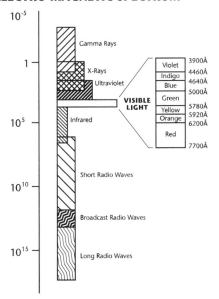

Although the Game is like an interdependent, interconnected web with all parts intrinsically related, it may be helpful to break it into its component parts—in order to better understand. I'll describe the Players, explain the layout of the Gameboard and outline the Objectives. We'll start with a sketchy overview and then we'll narrow in on the level of the Game, the physical plane, in which humanity currently finds itself.

The Gameboard on which the Game takes place is a vast, multi-leveled, multi-faceted set of constructs designed to facilitate the process of accumulating experiences. Each level of the Game has its own peculiarities and characteristics, which correspond to the different levels of consciousness of the Players. Each level and sub-level has inherent 'lessons' available to Players according to their level of accumulated expertise in the workings of the universe. In other words, Players become increasingly familiar with the subtle details of the Game, seeing through illusions to the underlying realities. Different illusions correspond to different levels. Eventually, all the illusions are unveiled, revealing the ultimate 'truth'.

The various levels of the Game are referred to by many names, including 'realms' or 'dimensions'. For our purposes at this moment, we'll call them *realms*. At this point, let's pause for a brief piano lesson. Each string on the piano vibrates at a specific frequency in order to produce the desired note. C, C#, D, E, etc.—each is a distinct note produced by a distinct speed at which the string vibrates. The higher the number of vibrations per second, the higher the pitch of the note. There are, in any given octave (i.e. the distance between middle C and treble C), twelve individual notes or semi-tones. Probably there are twelve micro-tones that exist between these notes, although they are not represented on the piano. Let us pretend that there are twelve octaves on the piano and that the combined 144 notes (instead of the usual 88) now represent the entire range of frequencies at which energy can possibly vibrate. Each octave on the keyboard is analogous to a realm, a level of reality. According to most channeled information, there are twelve major realms, each with twelve smaller levels or intervals or overtones. Thus, in the third realm, the physical plane, there are twelve sub-realms. Energy, for some reason, likes to break down into groups of twelve and, within the twelve, it likes to form into patterns of 7. (See BOX 2—THE LAW OF OCTAVES)

In this context then, a realm is a level of reality, or maybe 'perceived' reality. It is said that, in the exact time and space where you are now sitting, there are many other realities that exist simultaneously. We cannot perceive them because they vibrate at different frequencies and we are not 'tuned in' to those frequencies. Like a radio receiver, which can only access the information carried by the radio-wave frequencies to which it is 'tuned', we can only access the information or the reality carried by the frequencies to which we are tuned. Most of us are only tuned to the frequencies that define our physical reality, that of the third realm. The energy vibrating within the parameters of this realm interacts with our collective and individual consciousness to create the reality that we perceive.

The lower notes of a piano vibrate more slowly than do the higher notes. The third realm is denser than the fourth, that is, the range of vibration that we choose to call the third realm, is slower than the range of frequencies that we call the fourth realm. Souls incarnating into a particular realm are 'subject' to the conditions, to the 'realities' that belong to that range of frequencies. In other words, each range of frequencies has its own set of natural laws, ways in which energy likes to behave within the parameters of that range. The reality that one would perceive at the fourth level is different than that of the third level.

BOX 2—THE LAW OF OCTAVES; At all levels of the Game, there are specific laws and patterns according to which energy must behave. I have not encountered much information about the ways that energy behaves in the higher realms or in the first and second realms, but there are many laws with which we are becoming familiar here in the third realm, the physical plane. Some of these, such as inertia, refraction, etc., we learned in our high-school physics class. Other natural laws are in the domain of more sophisticated science. There are many other ways in which energy likes to behave and science is beginning to discover them. Also, there are those that are outside the current realm of science. Many of these laws have been referred to in ancient writings and traditions such as Tantra, alchemy, Hermetic magic, Qabala, shamanic rituals, etc. One of these is sometimes called the Law of Octaves. For some reason, energy likes to break down in divisions of twelve. In fact, twelve is a very significant number that appears over and over in many contexts throughout history. We have twelve months in the year and twelve signs of the Zodiac, twelve hours on a clock-face, twelve tribes of Israel, twelve gods in the Greek pantheon, twelve apostles surrounding Jesus who would be the thirteenth, etc. There are far too many examples to list here. In geometry it is noted that if a sphere had other equal sized spheres perfectly packed around it, each of them touching its surface, there would be twelve such spheres. The one in the center would be the thirteenth. The number thirteen represents Christ consciousness, the start of the next octave. Further to that, within the twelve, energy likes to arrange itself into patterns of seven. There are also countless examples of seven in our Earth culture, i.e. seven days, seven notes in the scale, seven colors in the spectrum, seven chakras, seven deadly sins, and many manifestations of seven in sacred geometry. The behavioral pattern of energy described in this paragraph is sometimes called the Law of Octaves, and is sometimes called the Second Fundamental Law of the Universe. The First Fundamental Law is sometimes called the Law of Three. It basically says that all actions and phenomena are the result of the simultaneous action of three forces:
1. positive/active/mental/male/electric/etc.,
2. negative/passive/emotional/female/magnetic/etc.,
3. a neutralizing or catalyzing agent.
Trilogies and trinities are present in many forms, in many cultures. Even atoms consist of electrons, protons and neutrons.

In order to get our linear minds to grapple with these notions of realms, they inevitably get presented with descriptions of realms as distinct 'bands' of frequency with definite, concrete boundaries. Although this may facilitate the understanding process, it is important to note that no such boundaries exist. The edges between realms are blurry. The frequencies that constitute a realm are in a constant state of flux, being affected by many factors. Some of these factors will be discussed later in the book. Possibly the most important of these factors is our awareness, our ability to perceive the higher frequencies.

The *density* of our circumstances, of our environment, affects our awareness, our ability to think and feel. The denser the environment in which we live, the more difficult it is to access or to interact with higher, less dense vibrations. What we think and feel, in turn affects the density of our environment. That is because, in truth, we are inseparable from our environment. Our consciousness is our environment. Our reality affects the way we think and feel, and the way we think and feel affects our reality.

As I've said, even thought and emotion are forms of energy vibrating at specific frequencies. 'Higher thoughts', those based in love, have a higher frequency. 'Lower thoughts', those based in fear, have a lower frequency. When we feel a particular emotion, think a thought or perform any action of any kind, we are emitting a vibration of energy. Depending on the 'quality' of our thoughts, i.e. whether they're based in love or fear, this adds a vibration of a certain frequency to the collective pool of vibrations in which we live. We thus create our own reality according to the level or 'quality' of our own individual consciousness. We do this both individually and collectively. Our thoughts literally become manifest. These are the laws of karma, which we'll expand upon in a moment.

Let's now describe *the Players of the Game*. As mentioned before, the Source divided itself up into countless perfect parcels of divine energy, vibrating at different frequencies. Although there may be many different types of energy parcels who play the Game in their own mysterious way, let's just talk about those manifestations that eventually evolve into common, individual human souls. (At this point it may be wise to acknowledge that the notion of individuality is actually an illusion, which we'll discuss later.) These individual souls are sent out into the Game to gather experiences by *evolving* through the various levels, a process that takes a great deal of time. (Time is also an illusion.)

A Player, then, is a soul. A soul is an entity that exists in all realms and time frames simultaneously. Only part of the soul is limited to the experiences of a particular realm. The part of the soul that is busy proceeding through the Game gathering experiences and expanding its awareness is sometimes called the 'ordinary consciousness' or 'personality'. In our analogy we've chosen to call it the Player. The part of the soul that perceives at all levels at once is sometimes called the 'meta-consciousness' or 'higher self'. As the Game proceeds, the ordinary consciousness expands until it merges with the higher self, becoming aware of the entire soul. (We will also refer to the soul as a genderless 'it'.)

This is *the Game Objective* of a Player as it negotiates its way through the many levels. It is to eventually arrive at a complete awareness of its own divinity and all that that entails. The collective objective of all the components of the entire Game is to experience all there is to experience. As components of the collective, the individual souls are guided by their 'higher selves' or their 'meta-consciousness' to accumulate whatever experiences are deemed necessary to expand their awareness to the point of making it to the next level of the Game. Each Player must arrive at more or less the same level of awareness or state of being before they are capable of proceeding to the next level, however they may not need to have experienced the same things.

The interesting thing about this game is that there are no losers. Everybody wins. Every Player eventually and inevitably arrives at the divine awareness, knowing that they are part of the indivisible whole that is The Source. They reclaim their power as creators of the universe. It is not a race. It may be that some take longer than others to reach this point, but as time is illusory, it becomes a moot point. Eventually we all remember our innate divinity.

As this description of the Game proceeds, it becomes more obvious that our efforts to understand are somewhat restricted by our current perspective in the third realm. I have been asked, "what about the first and second realms?" Although there is some information describing the higher realms, I have encountered none regarding these lower realms. I could only guess that the first and second realms are 'regions' or 'experiences' of very low density, where consciousness is very slow and limited to one-dimensional or two-dimensional realities. In these realms, manifestations of energy would get to experience what it is like to be confined to whatever conditions exist there. Perhaps they would need to 'learn lessons' before they were ready to experience three-dimensional physical form, and subsequently, life.

It is very difficult (and somewhat futile) to try to understand the nature of realms other than our own, so let's now try to narrow our discussion in an attempt to understand some of the conditions and workings of **the Game at the third level**—the physical plane. By doing so we may get a better grasp of the whole. Of course such an endeavor is a highly complex affair and it is not our task to thoroughly explore its many nuances in the context of this book. (For other, more detailed explanations of the workings of the Game at this level, please see; The Qabala, The Tantra, The Vedas, The Emerald Tablets of Thoth, the works of Heraclitus, Socrates, Plato, Aristotle, Pythagorus, Lao-Tse, Confusius, Gautama Buddha, Jesus the Nazorene, Mohammed, H.P. Blavatsky, Edgar Cayce, Rudolph Steiner, George Gurdjieff, Albert Einstein and many, many more.)

We'll proceed, at this point, by first giving an overview of the process of the Game at this level. Then we'll move on to discuss certain aspects of the Game in more depth. Let's first start by saying that the objective of a Player at this level is to get to the next level. Entry into the next level, however, is restricted to those who are **completely fearless and who react to every and all circumstances with nothing but love and compassion**. This is very important. The first, most obvious question then becomes, 'how does a Player arrive at this special state of consciousness?' A Player must learn, incrementally, a series of lessons, which bring an ever-expanding body of knowledge. It must become aware of the following incomplete list of things: all Players are part of the same whole; that whole is divine; we create our own reality; most of what we deal with is an illusion; beyond the illusion there is endless joy and love.

We'll now take a look at some of the characteristics of the Gameboard at the third level. There are many 'places' in the third realm, many different schools of learning. We'll only be talking about the one called *Earthschool*. Although we'll not be able to look at every aspect of the Game at this school, we'll try to touch on some that are quite important. To a great extent, much of the nature of things in this realm is some type of *illusion*. Time, space, matter and the notion that we are all separate entities are all illusions of a sort. One of the greatest illusions is the one surrounding what we call 'death'. These illusions are not only types of 'obstacles', they are key components by which the Players learn their lessons. By interacting with them Players experience 'life' and thus come to acquire ever-growing amounts of knowledge.

Probably the type of illusions most integral to the learning of lessons are those that have been set up as polarities or *dualities*—spectrums of possibilities, if you like, with one pole of the duality at each extreme, and an infinite number of possibilities in between. There are many such dualities; light/dark, happy/sad, female/male, etc. Many of these dualities, such as good/bad, right/wrong, smart/stupid, etc, belong to the category of positive/negative and underlie the attitudes and belief systems of most Players. In other words, most Players judge the things and people around them according to where they fit in the positive/negative spectrum. The actions of Players are usually based on such attitudes. However, even though these dualities are key components of the Game, a Player must eventually come to the awareness that they are illusions and to see through to the 'truth' that lies beyond.

Seeing past the illusion involves moving away from the idea that each player and indeed all the micro-components of the game are separate, individual entities. The trick is, they are all the same! They are all parts of a whole, made from the same substance. Each soul is ultimately neither good nor bad, male nor female, right nor wrong, etc. In fact it is all these things. There really are no dualities. Once this is realized, then the player sees the futility in deeming anything or anyone to be right or wrong, smart or stupid, better or worse, etc. There is no need for judgement. No soul is better than another, we are all just evolving at different levels, learning whatever lessons we need in the process of relearning or remembering our true natures. In other words, although different Players may be at different levels of evolution, no one is better than any-one else. We are all equal parts of a collective soul; equal parts of an even larg-er divinity. With this awareness comes **love and compassion**. There is no need for ruthless competition of the uncompassionate kind if ultimately we are only competing with ourselves. When we harm others, whether by acts of commis-sion or omission, we harm ourselves. It makes more sense to treat all factions of the whole with love and compassion.

Probably the greatest lesson to be learned here on Earthschool is the lesson of love. It is part of the love/fear duality. The opposite of love is **fear**. Hatred, anger, envy, greed and all such feelings of negativity are aspects of fear. Atrocious behavior, which is based on greed for example, may come from the fear that there is not sufficient abundance for all. Although this example is somewhat oversimplified, a thorough analysis of any negativity will find some sort of fear at its base. Love/fear is probably the most important duality. It too is an illusion. One might ask, "how can love be an illusion?" Like all the dual-ities, one must be able to experience one of the poles in order to know the other. One could not recognize cold if there was not heat; one could not expe-rience up if there were no down; without female there is no male. This is the basis of the Chinese concept of yin/yang. Likewise, without the contrast of fear, love could not be experienced. Beyond the illusions of duality, there are certain constants, which in the absence of a contrasting opposite, become the 'only way'. These constants thus become unrecognizable or 'taken for grant-ed'. Love is one such constant. Beyond the illusion of duality, love is all that is left. It is the only way, the default setting, the constant state.

Here on Earthschool a Player is continually being offered opportunities to learn the lesson of love. A Player, confronted with any set of circumstances, can choose to react with total love, which is at one extreme of the spectrum, or with total fear, which is at the other extreme. Most often it is with some mixture, which may lie anywhere between the two. Over the course of many lifetimes, lesson by lesson, a Player learns to see through more and more illu-sions and thus to realize that there is absolutely nothing to fear. At the same time, it learns that reacting to a situation with actions based in love always brings about more joy. Eventually it learns to greet all circumstances with love and gratitude, without a trace of fear. This state of consciousness, this state of being is what we call **enlightenment**. At this point the Player no longer needs to come to Earthschool and is ready to graduate to the next level, where new experiences await. This next realm, the fourth, is sometimes referred to as the realm of Christ-consciousness.

Lets back up and take a closer look at this business of lesson learning. In the process of becoming a better lover, a particular Player is presented with the cir-cumstances that belong to whatever lesson it needs to learn at that particular point in its development. Variations of these circumstances will keep reappearing until the current lesson is learned, even if it takes many lifetimes. For example, if one tends to react to life's situations with anger, then similar 'anger-eliciting' situations will keep recurring until one learns to respond differently. Once the lesson is learned, new circumstances will manifest to provide the opportunity for further lessons. In other words, if a Player emits positive energy in the form of a positive thought, word or deed (the cause), then the universe will send positive energy to that Player (the effect). If one reacts to certain circumstances with negative energy, the lower vibration output of that reaction will attract similar low-frequency energy, which in turn creates similar circumstances providing yet another opportunity to respond in a balanced, loving way. In this way we create our own reality.

To receive love, one must give love. To receive money, one must give money or some equivalent form of energy. Every event in the universe is a type of energy exchange. There is ample abundance in the universe for every soul, unless our thoughts, words and deeds, both individually and collectively, block the flow of abundance. There is an endless supply of energy, which can be manifested by consciousness into various forms of abundance. These laws of cause and effect, of give and take, are some of the **laws of karma**. We thus create our own reality according to the quality of our energy emissions, which are the results of our actions. All thoughts, words and deeds are types of actions. We can see that our belief systems are very powerful in their ability to shape our circumstances, as they underlie most of our actions.

Our collective reality is also created by the collective attitudes of all of mankind as we respond to various circumstances. As mentioned earlier, all actions—thoughts and emotions, words and deeds—are manifestations of energy with their own signature frequencies. The positive, love-based emotions vibrate at a higher frequency than the negative, fear based emotions. Thus, the more we choose to react to circumstances with vibrations of fear, the more we will pump lower vibrations into the collective 'vibe-pool'. The more we choose to react to circumstances with vibrations of love, the more we will pump higher vibrations into the collective vibe-pool. This vibe-pool has recently been referred to as the morphogenetic grid, or the matrix. The matrix generates the illusion. The actions of all of humanity, of which each of us is a part, bring forth circumstances or consequences which affect us all. The mistreatment of our planet, for example, brings about conditions to which we are all subject, even if we are staunchly against such mistreatment. We must all breath the same polluted air. Lessons must be learned by the collective soul, the greater system as well as the sub-systems that we call individuals.

When the collective human consciousness is more loving, the planet becomes less dense; when it is more fearful, the planet becomes more dense.

This density affects us. It would be more accurate to say that we affect the density, which in turn affects us. The density affects our consciousness, our ability to think and perceive clearly and fully. The denser the environment, the more difficult it is for an entity living in it to access the higher frequencies. In other words, if the range of frequencies of energy vibration which define our reality are lower, then the consciousness of the Players residing here will tend to resonate with these dominant frequencies. On the other hand, if the dominant frequencies are higher, then we will resonate with them, which will mean that we will have increased access to the information carried by these higher vibrations. In other words, we would have increased access to the light. There is growing awareness of this phenomenon on the planet at the present time. Many projects or movements are consciously trying to raise the planet's vibratory rate by collective praying, meditating, etc. They are purposefully trying to use consciousness to affect positive change in our environment. (More on this in a subsequent chapter.)

We now have a better idea of how the Game works at our physical, material level—the third realm. Having looked at an overview of it, we can see that it is a relatively complex affair involving many aspects, and the whole thing still probably seems somewhat confusing. I'll now attempt to shine the spotlight on some of these aspects of the game to try to get a better handle on how the whole thing works. Bear in mind that we are looking at these aspects separately only to facilitate understanding, but actually these aspects are all intricately connected to each other. I thought it might be useful to do this in a question and answer format.

QUESTION # 1: *Can you shed some light on the concept of enlightenment?*
The objective of a Player at the third level is to learn all the lessons needed to arrive at a certain state of mind, which is required to be able to negotiate the next level. This is the objective even though a Player may not be aware of it. This state of mind has been given many names by many different traditions, but in this book we will call it enlightenment. The root meaning of the verb 'to enlighten' can be viewed as the act of moving from the dark into the light, or as the act of becoming less heavy. The modern dictionary meaning of enlighten is 'to give intellectual or spiritual meaning to'. All of these interpretations apply in the spiritual context which we are exploring, but it also incorporates much more, and hopefully this will become clearer as we move through the various aspects.

For now, let's just reiterate that someone who is enlightened is able to exist in a sustained state of love and joy, with no trace of fear. This ability comes about in conjunction with a growing enlightening, with an increased awareness of the true nature of things. For example, realizing that death is an illusion quickly leads to a loss of the fear of death. Fear of failure, fear of rejection, fears of all kinds fall away as our perceptions become clearer. In other words, an enlightened Player reacts to all circumstances with love and gratitude because it is completely unaffected by any form of fear or anxiety. Underlying this unflappable inner tranquility is knowledge; the awareness that we are all sub-systems within a larger system; that everything is one; that all components of life and death are parts of a complex illusion; that we have the power to create our circumstances; that the essence of our being is divine. When all these memories have been rekindled, one's awareness is flooded with the bliss of endless joy and love. One is then ready for the next level, confidently in control of all thoughts and emotions, joyfully awaiting whatever new adventures the Game can provide.

Why must an enlightened Player be in total control of all thoughts? This ability is necessary in order to graduate to the next level because existence at the fourth level has some distinct features that are very different than those at this level. Whereas here in the third realm reality manifests 'slowly' as a result of the actions of the individual and collective consciousness, in the fourth realm thoughts instantly manifest into reality. In environments of lesser density, the barriers or edges between reality and consciousness break down. In other words, consciousness **IS** reality. All thoughts are real. Nothing can impede the being's ability to go anywhere, do anything, because all it needs do is imagine it. For a being to exist in the fourth realm it must be have complete and constant willful control over the mind. Will and imagination become unified. There is no room for fear of any kind, as it would quickly manifest into reality.

QUESTION # 2: *What are the differences between the third and fourth realms?*

There is not a lot of clear information that I've encountered to describe life in the fourth realm. What does the landscape looks like? What are the unique characteristics of the Gameboard at that level? What are the main lessons to be learned? These are questions that can only be partially addressed. Most sources agree that the fourth realm is no longer involved with physicality, that it is a 'spiritual' or 'ethereal' existence. The lessons at that level probably have something to do with the prudent exercising of the greatly increased power that one acquires. A certain amount of educated guessing would suggest that many more decisions are made collectively and that individual souls feel much more connected to the group soul. Some sources claim that the fourth level is actually a brief transitory phase, a place where one would get used to their 'space legs', and that the features I'm describing actually belong more to the fifth realm. For our purposes here, however, I'll continue to refer to it as the fourth realm.

Although many psychics, mystics and channels or mediums have reported on what they have observed at higher levels, I find it difficult to be confident of such descriptions unless they seem to make a lot of sense and to resonate with other information that I do feel comfortable with. The aspects of the fourth realm mentioned in the preceding paragraph seem to make sense, yet it doesn't feel to me that they are important to my current position in the Game. An understanding of them will not really serve my Game objectives here in the physical realm. The following aspects, however, do seem to be relevant to the understanding we're attempting to gain with this book.

At the next level, energy is vibrating more quickly, at frequencies that are beyond the physical or material. As the mystics have always said, which modern physics is beginning to realize, consciousness is inseparable from reality. In fact it is reality. In the fourth realm, the spiritual plane, the Gameboard is much different. Matter, time, the dualities and other illusions are no longer necessary for the ongoing learning of lessons; the illusions of the third realm are absent. Thus the power of consciousness to create is much greater, much more immediate. Also, our conception of time at that level is very different. A being of the fourth realm has the ability to affect its position in time as well as in space. The understanding of these last two concepts are useful to our quest here in the physical plane, so the next two questions will deal with them.

QUESTION # 3: *Can you elaborate on the 'power of consciousness to create'?*

As we have already noted, our consciousness is instrumental in shaping the circumstances of our environment. Our thoughts, words and deeds, our actions, literally create our reality. This happens at an individual as well as a collective level. An individual's success at bringing about a desired set of circumstances becomes greatly enhanced if s/he has an incredibly strong will. This means that, amongst other things, there is not a shred of doubt or fear of failure and that there is only the strongest, most fervent conviction. Even with this, however, success is much more difficult when one's creative powers are interfered with by the creative powers of others.

Let me try to explain this another way. Every realm has its own set of Laws, or parameters within which certain things are possible, or more accurately, probable. Here in the physical world we create our own reality, but it must happen according to the laws of this realm; within the parameters of this range of frequencies. Many things are possible at this level, but they may not be very probable. For example, it is possible to decide to live for 500 years, but it is not all that probable. It is possible to raise a bus ten feet in the air using only mind-power, but it is not that probable. An individual can shape his reality using his own thoughts and beliefs, (his will), only if they are completely pure and free from even the slightest doubts and are not being affected by the fears and doubts of those around us. In other words, the consciousness of those around us also affect the raising of the bus and the longevity of one's life. We create individually, but we are also part of the collective consciousness. The attitudes and belief systems of the collective mind predominate. It is much easier to manipulate circumstances that apply only to oneself than it is with circumstances that apply to everyone.

At the next level of reality, the ability to manipulate, control or create one's circumstances is greatly enhanced. To be ready for the next level one must have achieved the awarenesss that individuality is an illusion. We are not just individuals, we are a part of the greater system. Thus, 'individuals' existing at the next level would be reacting to circumstances—creating reality—in conjunction with the rest of the greater system. This is the nature of unity consciousness. We would be acting in unison. The creative power of this greater system is enormous.

The Law of the next level of consciousness, the fourth realm, is such that any thought would immediately manifest into reality. Much like an astral traveler, a sleeper who is dreaming or someone in a deep state of meditation, a non-physical entity can travel to wherever, do whatever, merely by thinking it. Such an entity must have complete control over all thoughts and feelings. Anyone who has experienced a dream knows that such control is not easy. If one were completely lucid and in control while dreaming, one could make their 'dream body' do anything just by thinking or imagining it. Within the dream, one's will thus determines one's reality in an immediate way. Dreamers, astral travelers and the like can only visit these non-physical realms, but to remain there indefinitely, one must be in complete control always. Thus, only a being of pure love, totally free of all fears and anxieties, could exist there because any fearful thought would quickly become real. One would be 'devoured' by one's own mental monsters. A being of the fourth realm is capable of many incredible feats because all it needs to do is 'think' it and it happens. Will is not thwarted by doubt, nor is it subject to the same laws, the same density as in the third dimension.

Fourth level beings are knowledgeable. Being free of all fears goes hand in hand with knowledge or awareness. To be aware of the illusory nature of death, illness, ego and the many things that feed our fear, is to be free of such fears. To be aware of one's divine nature, and thus one's invulnerability and creative potential, is to be free of fear and doubt. The greater one's awareness of internal power, the greater the power becomes. The greater the degree of doubt, the weaker the power, or more specifically, the less that power can be willfully controlled. This type of knowledge is more integral, much deeper than the superficial, cerebral type of knowledge that may come from reading this book or an equivalent pursuit. It is an inner knowledge born of experience. It is a knowledge sustained by balance. For many however, a cerebral knowledge is a good place to start in the process of overcoming fears. Eventually a profound knowledge will succeed in banishing fear for each of us. In the absence of fear, love and joy are all that's left. Love is the underlying constant, the ground state. Love is home.

QUESTION # 4: It is very difficult to conceive of time as being illusory—to grasp the idea that a soul can exist in all time frames simultaneously. *Can you shed some light on the concept of time?*

Time is a very difficult concept to define. Most dictionary definitions almost invariably end up containing the word 'time' itself, or words that are derivative of it, such as 'chronological', or 'past, present and future'. An anonymous definition reads; "Time is nature's way of keeping everything from happening all at once". Here's my stab at a definition; Time is a construct that enables us to perceive reality in terms of a measurable, sequential flow of events. In any case, most of us don't need a definition to have a good idea about what the word means in terms of our perception of it at this level.

A little harder to grasp is the idea that events don't actually flow sequentially; that time is also an illusion, a construct of the Game. A deeper understanding of time goes beyond any three-dimensional definition. The mystical definition, as well as the view that is emerging from modern physics, depicts time in a different way. According to mystics, all that ever was and ever will be actually exists at the same moment, so that all the 'levels' of evolution that a player goes through in the course of playing the Game are always present. It is this that allows a soul to exist in all realms simultaneously. It is only that fraction of the totality of soul, that part that we have called the personality or the Player, that has a limited awareness of only this realm. Likewise, the Player at this level is only aware of time as a sequential unfolding of events. One could say that it's the Player's awareness that is unfolding sequentially. Thus changes seem to happen over the course of eons, and yet they are always present. This is a good example of a paradox, something that makes very little sense to our normal consciousness at this level. This is due to the linear way in which our minds work in the three-dimensional, physical plane, or more specifically, in a physical reality that is so dominated by a more cerebral, logical, left-brained consciousness. (More on left-brain versus right-brain later.) As difficult as this is for us to accept, there really is no way to completely explain it verbally. Our perceptions of reality, based on our experience of the world through our five senses, are deeply ingrained. Experience of the world as enhanced by the tools of modern science or by the altered states of the mystics, however, show us a different reality; a supersensory view of reality. That view is telling us that our five senses have been deceiving us.

In the preceding paragraph the word *'**dimension**'* was used for the second time in this book. It is a word that is also commonly used in the same context as 'realm 'or 'level of reality'. I have been deliberately avoiding it until now because I feel it can be a confusing word to use in such a context. However, in discussing why it can be confusing, we can possibly get a little closer to a better understanding of the nature of time.

Dictionary definitions refer to a dimension as some sort of measurable quality of space, such as length, width and depth. There is no mention of anything to do with layers of perceived reality. Herein lies the confusion. So how did the word 'dimension' begin to be used in this context, as representing a level of reality? By offering an answer to this question we can take a new look at the concept of time.

In the world of modern science, which will be discussed in more detail in an upcoming section, the concept of time has undergone an evolution. In the old, classical, Newtonian physics, time was perceived in much the same 'common sense', linear way that we all tend to experience it. Since the revolution brought about by Einstein and his cohorts, time is now viewed in a totally different way. It is now seen as something that is intrinsically linked to space.

Our three-dimensional reality was seen by science as referring to the three measurable dimensions of space. A line, for example, has one dimension; a square or any shape that can be drawn on one plane has two dimensions; and a cube or any shape with depth has three dimensions. Space then has three dimensions, length, width and depth. Science now acknowledges time to be the fourth dimension. To try to understand this, let's consider the following scenario. To make an appointment to meet with someone in a city skyscraper, it would be necessary to establish the exact location of the event by defining the three dimensions of space, i.e. the latitude, the longitude and the floor of the building. Here we are using the analogy of a skyscraper to accommodate the notion of depth. We may know the exact location of the event, but in order to arrange a successful meeting, one more dimension must be established; the time. All four dimensions are needed. Time is the fourth dimension.

In the Newtonian view, three-dimensional objects, existing in three-dimensional space were seen as moving through time, which flowed evenly and uniformly throughout the universe. Time was thought of as something completely separate from space. It was thought that an object could be observed and measured without reference to time. Scientific observations at the sub-atomic level have shown that this is not the case. Modern science has now acknowledged that time is inseparable from space and it is said that objects or events exist within the fabric of space/time. A more accurate interpretation of reality, then, would be to describe it as four-dimensional.

Let's go back to the question of why the word 'dimension' was used to refer to a realm. In our current reality, the third realm, we have control over three dimensions. We can willfully maneuver in three-dimensional space, that is, decide where we want to be and then go about getting there. It may be difficult, but 'getting there' is within the realm of possibility. However, we can't decide where we want to be in time. In other words, we can travel in space, but travel in time seems not to be possible. In the next realm, the fourth, we ARE able to travel in time. Just as time travel is conceivable and achievable to someone dreaming or astral-travelling in deep trance, it is available to beings of the fourth realm. In the third realm we have willful control over three dimensions. In the fourth realm this expands to include control over the fourth dimension. Thus the word 'dimension' has come to represent a level of reality. From now on, in this book, I will use the words 'realm' and 'dimension' interchangeably, to mean the same thing.

Here is something else to ponder that may help to understand the concept of time. In the third realm, the fastest possible speed is said to be the speed of light, 186,000 miles per second. (Throughout this book, for the most part, I will be using the American system rather than the systeme internationale). Even a thought, which like light is an electro-magnetic wave, travels at this speed. The energy emitted by a thought moves through the universe at light speed. In the realm of our imagination, however, things can move at any desired speed. In our imagination we can instantly visualize ourselves basking on a distant beach. We can choose to transport ourselves to a distant galaxy instantaneously. In our imagination, we can also transport ourselves to the bed of Cleopatra, or to any point in time. The speed of imagination is instantaneous. The fourth realm is very much like, if not exactly the same as, the realm of the imagination. In that realm, if you think it, you're there; if you think it, it exists.

Consider that the measurement of speed is the measurement of how much space can be covered in a given amount of time. It is a space/time measurement. At the speed of light, one can 'experience' 186,000 miles of space in one second. The faster one could travel, the more space one could experience at one instant. Travelling at the speed of thought in the next realm, much faster than the speed of light, is almost the same as being in all places at the same time. Such a state is called omnipresence. Having knowledge of all things is called omniscience. Omnipresence and omniscience are two qualities attributed to the divine. A being of the fourth realm, having greatly expanded in knowledge by the ability to see through the illusion, and by being able to travel in time, is that much closer to omnipresence and omniscience; that much closer to divinity.

QUESTION # 5: It is said that energy is busy evolving in every corner of the universe. Does the entire observable universe, the one that astronomers talk about, belong to the physical plane, the third realm? *Is there a different* *universe for each realm, or do all the realms exist within the one observable universe?*

This is a question to which there is no easy answer, although it seems like a semantic issue that hinges on the definition of the word, 'universe'. I believe a key to this question lies in the adjective, 'observable'. Our perception of the universe has expanded greatly with the invention of ever more powerful telescopes, microscopes and other technology. In other words, our ability to observe has been enhanced technologically. Perhaps our ability to observe the other realms depends upon our ability to enhance our powers of observation. This means more than enhancing our five senses with external technology. It would probably be more accurate to say that such an enhancement involves developing new senses, possibly by applying what might be called 'internal technology'.

The perception of a realm, therefore, has to do with a state of consciousness, a level of awareness, rather than a place. Having said that, there are many bodies of information that do refer to realms as places. Earth, it is said, is a place where life exists at the third level. It is designed to be a place where evolutionary experiences of the third level can be gathered. There are other places in the universe designed to support life at other levels and those life forms are imperceptible to our five common senses. It's all very difficult for our logical minds to picture. It is somewhat paradoxical and the ability to provide a perfect explanation is probably beyond words. Suffice it to say that realms are both states of consciousness and places. To make things easier in this section, I will refer to the third realm as a place. It is said that there are many third level planets in the universe, but for the moment we'll just talk about our own.

QUESTION # 6: *How does a Player prepare for existence in the next realm?*

Life here on Earthschool is designed to prepare us. Through the workings of **karma**, we are continually being presented with opportunities to conquer fears. Every time something 'happens' to us, we have the free will to choose a way of reacting. We can react with a negative, ego-based, fearful response, or, having accumulated a certain wisdom, we can react in a positive, compassionate way, knowing that we are all part of the same unity and that beyond the illusory nature of any circumstance, there is absolutely nothing to fear. Most responses are neither totally fear based nor love based. Between these two poles or extremities there are countless possible responses based on varying degrees of compassion or fear.

Let's take a look at a possible example. If a homeless person were to steal money from me, I could choose to be angry or even to hate the offender. An angry person usually feels quite justified in his anger. To someone who is used to reacting with anger it often seems like the anger is overwhelming any ability to think clearly, to choose a different reaction. Although, to an angry person it may not feel as if there is a choice, ultimately all actions involve a decision. The anger or hatred is actually the by-product of an underlying fear. In this case, possibly it is the fear of feeling vulnerable to the criminal whims of other individuals, or maybe its a fear that there is not enough abundance in the universe to replace the lost money.

Whatever the fear, it is very likely to be the result of an inability to see the bigger picture. If I were a relatively wise person I could choose to react with compassion, understanding the unfortunate circumstances of the homeless person, realizing that this person is a player of the Game at his/her own level. I could thus see fit to withhold any hatred and to feel only anger at the misfortune of being subjected to this incident. If I were wiser still, I could use this as an opportunity to realize that this person is integrally connected to me, cut from the same cloth; that there is ample abundance in the universe; that life has its risks and that safety and security are not guaranteed. I might even realize that, somehow, I had arranged for this karma. I might thus choose to feel no anger. If I were very wise, I might even feel gratitude for this opportunity to learn; to exercise my compassion and my understanding that there is really nothing to fear.

This example, like any example, probably seems somewhat oversimplified. Most interactions, most opportunities, are more complex. Underneath all the complexity, however, the same basic lessons are being faced. One can choose to learn and grow, or one can continue to react in the usual way. If one chooses the latter, then the universe will keep sending similar circumstances until one decides to learn. If one has a tendency to react to certain situations with anger, then 'angry situations' will keep happening until that individual changes his/her behavior pattern. If this lesson is finally learned, then opportunities to learn some new lesson will present. Over the course of many lifetimes, the individual will eventually learn that no circumstance is worth the loss of joy that comes with a negative reaction.

Anger is always an easy example of a negative reaction. However, there are countless variations of possible negative actions. In many cases even seemingly benign or passive responses are the result of some underlying fear. For example, people who are unassertive are continually faced with situations whereby others are taking advantage of their passivity. Underlying this timidity is some fear, possibly the fear of rejection or of confrontation. Lack of self-confidence, low self-esteem, self-doubt; all of these types of feelings are based on fears. Such situations are actually opportunities to heal. Until an unassertive person learns to assert himself, these opportunities will keep recurring. Let's continue this example and say that this person goes to the other extreme and starts to stand up for himself by reacting harshly or cruelly to anyone that tries to take advantage of him. Consequences or situations will then begin to arrive until he learns to correct this new negativity. Eventually he will learn to assert himself properly; strongly and firmly, yet with compassion and understanding.

Lessons of this type keep happening, addressing one's issues until they have all been healed. This is all easier said than done, however, and most people need to find ways to deal with their fears and issues—concrete methods by which to heal and grow. There are countless methods available and one can choose the ones that seem most attractive. A guide to choosing healing methods is to find those that, although they may involve a certain amount of pain, are actually fun and enjoyable. Methods that amount to some sort of self-abuse, in the form of self-denial or rigid asceticism, are not often successful. In some cases, a healing method can start to become an 'end' rather than a 'means'. For example, a meditator or a yogi may become so involved in becoming accomplished, in becoming a master at the various positions, etc, that they lose site of the true function of such practices. If daily meditation is not resulting in an increased ability to greet life's situations with love and compassion, then one should question its usefulness. Ultimately, what is important is the quality of our actions in the classrooms of Earthschool; the various situations and circumstances that are continually being sent to us.

Although all of this sounds as if there are some incredibly busy entities in the higher realms who are keeping track of all these actions and reactions and then arranging for the appropriate circumstances to present themselves, it is not quite like that. No one is keeping score. These 'laws of karma' are built into the Game. They are energy interactions. Every action is an emission of energy with its own signature vibration, which attracts a corresponding energy pattern. This dynamic will keep recurring until a different emission causes the arrival of a different pattern. In this way, the energy in a system seeks equilibrium or balance. When all actions are free of all fears and are thus vibrating with the higher frequencies of love, then they will attract the corresponding frequencies or circumstances. (For a thorough, down-to-earth exploration of the workings of karma I recommend *The Seat of the Soul* by Gary Zukav.)

QUESTION # 7: *Could you please elaborate on the concept of free will?*

The third realm is a 'free-will zone', in which Players must decide for themselves how they wish to behave, think, feel, etc. A lesson cannot be forced upon another Player without his/her permission. One must be ready and willing to learn a lesson. It won't sink in simply because someone else wishes it to be so. It may be possible for one player to impose his will on another player's circumstances, but no life-lesson will be learned without the cooperation of the 'learnee'. (As well as individual will, there is also the collective will, the united will of all of humanity, which also makes decisions. In higher realms, where there is far less emphasis on individualism as we know it, a greater degree of the decision-making is done collectively. There is still free will, but it applies to a much larger system.)

By the same token, it is impossible to heal anyone who does not want to be healed. No method of healing will be effective on someone who, at a deeper level, does not want to be healed. It may seem that anyone who is complaining of an illness, at the most superficial levels of consciousness, genuinely wants to be healed. At deeper levels, however, this is often not the case. Some use their illnesses in subtle ways to avoid certain things, to get attention, or any number of motives. At a deeper level, the higher self may know that a particular illness is still useful in the learning process and thus decide to retain it. To heal oneself involves a willful choice. It is probably safe to say that all healing involves the learning of some lesson; a new awareness that leads to a willful shift in attitude, behavior, lifestyle, etc. All healing methods are merely ways to help one to heal oneself.

Free will dictates that entities from higher realms are not normally allowed to interfere in the progress of lower dimensional beings. Whenever help is offered, it is usually in the form of teachings, which can then be accepted or rejected. Again, circumstances may be affected, but assistance occurs only indirectly. People often wonder why God or entities from the higher realms would allow catastrophe and widespread suffering to occur on our planet. No matter how dire a situation appears to us here on Earth, the higher entities have a much better grasp of the Game and they understand that such a situation is a necessary illusion designed to help us grow. They do not wish to interfere in that process. They could possibly help if we asked them to, in which case they would be responding to our collective will. The higher entities could also help an individual who is asking or praying for help. It is good to bear in mind, however, that their version of help may not be the same as what is imagined by the individual. Due to their superior perspective, they would likely send assistance designed to facilitate the ultimate growth of the individual, rather than the solution that the individual had in mind.

In many spiritual teachings we are advised to surrender to the Divine Will. This has caused some confusion in the past. How can we have free will if we surrender to the divine will? All souls/entities/parcels of energy must play the Game. In this there is no choice. How one goes about playing the game, how long one chooses to take to learn lessons, these things are ours to decide. We can choose to play hooky, but we can't drop out of school. In a given incarnation, one may despair and decide to commit suicide, but in the next incarnation, the same lessons will present themselves. As previously mentioned, every soul will eventually graduate from Earthschool and go on to learn further lessons elsewhere, ultimately making it back to the whole. It is the Divine

Will. It may feel more comfortable being encouraged to 'align' one's will with the divine, rather than to 'surrender'. If there's no way to change the course of the river, then it might make sense to swim with, rather than against, the current. This is often done by following one's joy. Doing what makes the heart sing usually leads to joy. Joy is not the same as happiness or pleasure. Happiness, the opposite of sadness, is more of a fleeting feeling. Joy is a deeper, longer lasting contentment that includes both happiness and sadness. To exist in the fourth realm, one must be able to maintain a constant state of joy.

QUESTION # 8: *Why does life at this level involve so much suffering?*

Before we can answer this question we must address the idea of ***remembering***. Before coming to Earthschool, each Player agrees to temporarily forget that s/he is an all-powerful, all-knowing, divine entity. We have been using the analogy of Earthschool, but let me say that to refer to Earth as a school is not quite accurate. A school is a place where one learns new things and we have been using the analogy of 'learning lessons'. It would be safer to say, however, that all souls coming to Earth already know all there is to know. Before we came here we chose to forget. We are actually here to remember. This may sound a little befuddling, but let me attempt to explain.

Every soul is a perfect parcel of divinity. By definition, to be divine is to be all-knowing or omniscient, among other things. How is it possible for an omniscient entity to experience anything if they already know it all? It's a paradox. In order to fulfill the mysterious mandate of seeking to experience all there is to experience, the Source had to get its component parts, the souls, to agree to 'forget' their innate divinity. We have all chosen to forget that we are part of a greater whole.

The word 'remember' means 'to become whole'; it is the opposite of the word 'dismember', which means 'to come apart'. To 'remember' and to 'recall' are often mistaken to mean the same thing. Actually, recalling is largely a function of the intellect and is only a part of the total process of remembering. A soul's evolution, therefore, is a process of gathering experiences which results in a gradual coming together into wholeness—a remembering of its innate divinity.

In other words, the totality of consciousness that makes up a soul exists and perceives at all levels at once, yet at the same time, it is somehow divided into higher and lower levels. The portion of the soul that perceives at the third realm, the Player which is also sometimes called the 'personality' or 'ordinary consciousness', is not normally in contact with the higher selves or 'meta-consciousness' while in an ordinary five-sensory state of mind. Some personalities have developed the ability, possibly through the practice of meditation or some other method, to enter altered states of consciousness in which the barriers between realms break down. Some have just inherited an innate psychic ability to do so.

There are countless ways to enter such states, to make contact. Access to higher selves is thus possible for the personality and it can receive guidance and knowledge, which is beyond the limits of the five-sensory perceptions. Such access can lead to a remembering of divinity, a coming together of lower and higher selves. Until this happens, the lower self, in its unawareness, experiences suffering.

Here on Earthschool there are specific types of things to be experienced. If one's goal is to experience everything, then at some point that would include things that could be considered 'unpleasant'. Part of the Earthschool experience includes suffering. It is very likely that illness, death and many forms of tragedy have been experienced by all souls at some point during the many incarnations here in the third realm. Being temporarily unaware of one's divine nature facilitates such experiences. No experience could cause suffering in individuals who are aware of their own divinity because they would quickly see through these illusions. For example, how could someone be horrified by their pending death if they knew that death was not some kind of ending, but rather, a transition to a new beginning. One could not experience the fear of death if one knew that it was an illusion. One could not experience suffering if one knew that it was an illusion. In order to experience these things and thus fulfill the mandate, we had to agree to forget.

To someone who has suffered greatly by watching a loved one die or has been subjected to torture or other horrors, it may seem trite and heartless to suggest that such suffering is an illusion. Many people would balk at the notion that somehow their thoughts brought about the circumstances that caused suffering to themselves or their loved ones. Of course it is not nearly that simple. Inaccurate and simplistic understandings of the nature of karma have brought about a good deal of unnecessary grief, confusion and guilt.

Karma is not a cosmic slap on the wrist. Karma is energy seeking balance. To say that karmic circumstances are the direct result of someone's actions is to over-simplify the matter. It is folly to try to 'figure out' one's karma, to attempt to determine how one's actions could have brought about a particular set of circumstances. It is folly to look for something or someone to blame. The causal factors that bring about a given set of circumstances are complex. It only makes sense to try to greet such situations with positivity.

There are many forces at work bringing about the circumstances of life. There is karma from past incarnations. There is collective karma—consequences or situations brought about by the actions of all of humanity. Whether we like it or not, we are a part of this greater system of collective humanity which is going about learning its own lessons. Much of our life-circumstance comes from our higher selves. In its greater awareness, the higher self will bring about a circumstance that it knows will afford the personality the opportunity to learn a particular lesson. In other words, the arrival of a set of circumstances may make no sense to the personality, but the higher self may understand what lessons are at hand. It is more aware of the objective of experiencing all there is to experience and it is aware that some of those experiences may involve suffering.

As difficult as it is to accept for someone who is in a state of deep suffering, these 'tragic' circumstances are sent to us so that we can learn to feel love and compassion under **all** circumstances. It is relatively easy to feel joyful in an idyllic setting; much more difficult when one is the 'victim' of tragic circumstances. A 'young', inexperienced soul requires one extreme of any particular duality in order to know the other extreme. To know hot, one must know cold; to know right one must know wrong; to know up, one must know down, etc. To know joy, one must at first know suffering. For an 'old', experienced soul, these dualities begin to dissolve and suffering diminishes with the growing awareness that all is an illusion designed to awaken our forgotten divinity. As we become more aware, as we awaken, we begin to see suffering for what it is, a brief moment of discomfort in a long and glorious journey. Such a state of awareness is called grace or *gratitude.*

The eventual and inevitable consequence of suffering is *healing.* To 'heal' also means to 'become whole'. A great mystic and teacher, Brother David Steindl-Rast says that all healing, or remembering, involves a three step process; recalling, owning and celebrating. For example, in order to find healing after the ordeal of a tragic circumstance, one must first recall to the mind all aspects of the event. One must then 'own' the event, rather than feel like the hapless victim of a meaningless tragedy. This is a function of the will. Finally, one must 'celebrate' the event in a non-judgemental and grateful way. When grief is processed in this manner, the hidden lesson will somehow make its way into one's consciousness.

This applies not only to specific events, but to healing in general, as it takes place over countless incarnations. In one way or another, we must take responsibility for our lives in a guilt-free, blameless way, understanding that there is a greater purpose for all circumstances. With this understanding comes gratitude and a celebration of life with all its ups and downs.

QUESTION # 9: *What is the difference between coming to the point of 'awakening' and coming to the point of 'enlightenment'?*

As mentioned previously, achieving 'enlightenment' means coming to a state of mind, a level of awareness. One who is fully enlightened is capable of greeting any and all circumstances with love, compassion and gratitude. All illusions have been recognized, all fears have been faced and conquered. Such a Player is in complete control of all thoughts and feelings and is ready to continue the Game at the next level.

Coming to the point of 'awakening' also involves achieving a state of mind, a level of awareness. A Player reaching this level of awareness awakens to the realization that the purpose for being here in the third realm is to achieve enlightenment. Usually this is accompanied by a sense of inevitability and the Player begins to **consciously** work at the process of confronting and overcoming fears, the process of healing. This does not mean that one must retreat from life to meditate twenty-four hours a day, although that may be the ticket for some. It does not mean that one must start behaving like a saint. It does not mean that one must adopt some sense of urgency. It only means that one becomes aware of the healing process and strives to facilitate this process using whatever methods one finds useful. It is a conscious and consistent movement toward the light.

Some people believe that this awareness of the quest for enlightenment was much more widely acknowledged at other points in our ancient history, that mankind was more 'awake' back then. More recently, over the past two millenia, most of humanity has been in a deep sleep. Many of the ancient works of mankind are not understood by modern academia because the concept of a 'quest for enlightenment' is not understood and thus never considered as a motive. The Great Pyramid, for example, is usually explained as being a tomb. On the other hand, some believe, with very plausible justification, that it is a sophisticated, multi-functional instrument, and that one of its functions was to facilitate the process of enlightenment for those who had consciously chosen such a path. In the second part of this book we will talk about the Great Pyramid and some of the other mysteries and enigmas that have baffled us over the years. Hopefully they will make more sense when viewed from the perspective of the 'quest for enlightenment'.

QUESTION # 10: *How does the idea of 'evil' fit into the Game?*

Evil is part of the good/bad duality, which is an illusion. There is no such thing as evil. It is only a construct of the Game. Just as cold is an absence of warmth and darkness is an absence of light, evil is an absence of love. It is not an entity unto itself. Evil is a form of ignorance or imbalance. People who are thought of as perpetrators of evil are Players who have an imbalanced view of things; people who are not aware of the true nature of things. They do not sit in back rooms wringing their hands and wondering what new and fiendish things they can do to wreak havoc upon the Earth. They always feel they are the ones who know. Hitler, in his twisted logic, thought he was doing the right thing, that he was benefiting mankind by returning things to what he believed was the right order. This was due to an imbalance in his mental processes or, more specifically, he was lacking in a right-brained, more heart-centered intelligence.

harder to love everyone on the planet. Ironically, it is often even more difficult to love the being at the center of these concentric circles. Many people
have great difficulty loving themselves.

It is much easier to love someone with familiar values, attitudes and cultural characteristics than it is to love someone whose behavior is totally
unfathomable. It is easy to love Jesus and all the beautiful things he stood for.
It is much harder to love Hitler and all the deplorable things he stood for.
However, in order to graduate from Earthschool, one must eventually learn to
love everyone and everything.

I'm sure there are many more questions that could be addressed, but for now,
hopefully, we have arrived at a better understanding of the workings of the
Game. There's one more point to make before leaving this section. If desired,
third-dimensional graduates, beings from the higher realms, can choose to
take on bodies and return to the third level. They can 'volunteer' to return to
this level. Often this would mean that they would once again become subject
to the density and Law of this realm, forgetting much of what they knew in
the higher realm. Such a being would usually make such a choice for the purpose of 'helping', not because there were further third-dimensional lessons for
them to learn. Some more highly advanced 'ascended masters', such as Jesus
the Nazorene, have come to Earth and, at a very young age, remembered their
knowledge and powers. Some of our greatest teachers have spent the better
part of their lives remembering their own divinity before they got around to
teaching. There have been many such beings, some working in high profile,
some working quietly behind the scenes. Many modern opinions contend that
there are an extraordinary number of such helpers on the planet at present,
some in the form of great teachers, some in other roles. These helpers are
sometimes called 'lightworkers'. *Maybe you are a lightworker.* **Maybe you
just need to remember.**

In pondering this, consider what Nelson Mandella had to say during his
inaugural speech to the South African Parliament in 1994:

"Our deepest fear is not that we are inadequate. Our deepest fear is that we are powerful
beyond measure. It is our light, not our darkness that frightens us. We ask ourselves, 'Who
am I to be brilliant, gorgeous, talented, and fabulous?' Actually, who are you NOT to be?
You are a child of God. Your playing small does not serve the world. There's nothing enlightened about shrinking so that other people won't feel insecure around you. We were born
to make manifest the glory of God that is within us. It is not just in some of us; it is in everyone. And as we let our own light shine, we unconsciously give other people permission to
do the same. As we are liberated from our own fear, our presence automatically liberates
others."[1]

Chapter 2

ANOTHER MODEL

Now that we have explored the basics of the Game, let's take a look at the process again, using some different terminology. This can also serve as a summary.

In the beginning, the Creator made itself into an enormous sound. Within this sound were all the many variations of sound, each vibrating at its own frequency, each manifesting into a different form. All of these forms went about experiencing all there was to experience. Some of these forms became material physical entities. Although all of these forms were created at once, they also took eons to evolve. They arranged themselves into many different versions of reality; many different realms or dimensions; many different time-lines. (See BOX 3—TIME LINES)

Sound is equivalent to energy or information or light. At some point, some of the energy was and is the humble hydrogen atom, until it evolved into the other elements and then into molecules and combinations of elements of ever increasing complexity. After this 'mineral' state, it needed a very special component to experience further. This component we have called 'life'. It experienced what it was like to be vegetable, then animal, then (with the addition of free will) human, and then 'beyond' the physical into the 'ethereal' realms.

All of these 'states' of energy have a particular type of corresponding consciousness. A rock, for example, has its own brand of consciousness. A planet has another type of consciousness. *Gaia* is one of the names we've given to the consciousness of this planet. Gaia's purpose is to provide circumstances whereby the energy parcels choosing to come to Earth are afforded the opportunities to learn lessons, to incrementally move towards the full remembrance of divinity, to 'enlighten'. These circumstances can also be called 'life'. Gaia's purpose is to provide life.

The brilliant scientist/spiritualist, Gary Zukav, in his book, 'The Seat of the Soul', talks about the human condition as a state where energy is in the process of evolving *from a five-sensory personality to a multi-sensory personality*. The personality is defined as that portion of the total soul that is involved in evolution. The personality's capacity for understanding the true nature of its totality is evolving; that awareness, once confined by the five senses of physicality, is now evolving to a more complete knowledge by using 'senses' beyond the five senses.[3]

BOX 3—TIME-LINES; It is said that there are many realities in the form of different time-lines. When a certain key decision is made in response to a circumstance, the ensuing sequence of events is called a time-line. It is said that a time-line exists for each of the other possible decisions that apply to the same circumstance. For example, there is another time-line based on the consequences of John F. Kennedy deciding not to ride in the cavalcade on that fateful day in Dallas. There are billions of time-lines. This may be easier to comprehend if one thinks of each of these realities as a type of fiction existing in the consciousness of the souls involved. All of these realities eventually come together into one reality. A soul exists in many time-lines at once. When a young soul encounters a set of circumstances to which it must react (a point which we shall call 'A'), decisions can be made based on love, on fear or on any of the innumerable possibilities in between. Each of these possibilities becomes a time-line. Theoretically, each of these time-lines/choices can co-exist. From point 'A' then, many branches extend, each representing a choice/course of action. Each branch would then arrive at a subsequent set of circumstances from which many further branches could extend. As the soul becomes older, having learned from past mistakes, it would make better choices, resulting in fewer branches/time-lines. In other words, many possible decisions would no longer be considered. Eventually, the soul would come to realize that the only sensible choice in reaction to any particular circumstance, is one based in love. All other choices are no longer considered. Thus the time-lines eventually come together again to a single point (which we shall call point 'B'). This same model can be applied to the greater system, the collective, which also makes decisions. It can also be applied to the universe. If point 'A' represents the 'big bang', the start of creation, then energy exploding outward forms innumerable time-lines. Eventually, balance/homeostasis is reached and the time-lines resolve into point 'B'. The stage is then set for the process to repeat. The concept of time-lines can be found in the traditional mystical philosophies, and it made an appearance in the new physics midway through the twentieth century. The mathematics of quantum mechanics predicts many possible outcomes for a sub-atomic event and the 'Many Worlds Interpretation of Quantum Mechanics' presented by Everett, Wheeler and Graham suggests that each of these possible outcomes actually manifest into parallel realities.[2]

A five-sensory personality seeks *external power*, which is power to control others, including the environment. Someone with great external power is usually someone who has a position high up in the social pecking order, usually someone with great financial and military resources. This is because a five-sensory personality is concerned with survival and is not yet aware that there are no limits to the abundance that is available to everyone. Thus there is great emphasis on ownership of property and the accumulation of wealth. Survival mentality is based on fear, i.e. fear of the death of self. This often includes the death of progeny or procreative lineage, which is an aspect of self. The quest to dominate others is a fear-based way to avoid being dominated by others.

A multi-sensory personality seeks an internal or *authentic power*, which is the power to control self. It is power that is based on a deeper knowledge of the way that the universe works. A multi-sensory personality is fearless, aware that it can manifest whatever it needs. This deeper knowledge includes the awareness that we are all one, consisting of the same essence, and that any action affects the interconnected, integrated web that is the universe. This leads to compassion. Love becomes the basis of all actions. There is no need for a multi-sensory personality to dominate anyone or anything because it is obvious that cooperation and harmony get much better results for all.

The personality that is solely five-sensory represents an extreme, usually associated with a fresh soul newly arrived at Earthschool. The personality that is solely multi-sensory represents another extreme, usually associated with a soul that is ready to graduate with top marks. Most of us are somewhere between these two extremes.

In other words, the human condition is such that we have one foot in the physical and one foot in the ethereal, the next level 'beyond'. Those of us that put more weight on the foot that is in the physical are more concerned with matters of survival, i.e. eating, breathing, procreating, etc. For example, we tend to hoard food and wealth, oblivious to the plight of others, or to the effect this has on the environment. We often resort to violence against anyone whom we perceive to be an obstacle; lie, cheat, steal, enslave and oppress in order to further our position in society. We fear death, failure, poverty and many other things.

Those of us that have more weight on the foot that is 'beyond', tend to be more concerned with compassion, kindness and love. We know that survival is not an issue and that we do not need to cheat, plunder or otherwise hoard material goods because there is plenty for everyone. We know that we are all particles of the same vast entity, so that to hurt another being is to hurt oneself. We fear nothing.

Through the karmic process we learn to shift more and more weight from the foot that is in the five-sensory, physical realm to the foot that is in the multi-sensory, ethereal realm. When the energy that is us has all its weight on the foot that is 'beyond', then the entire entity evolves into the next level or dimension. Of course most of us have a great many lessons to learn, over a great many incarnations here on Earthschool, before that happens. Energy then continues to evolve until it inevitably arrives at the place from whence it started. I say 'inevitably' because sooner or later every soul completes the journey. There is no other way. At that point, having experienced all there is to experience of all the states of energy it is fully aware of its own perfection or 'godliness' and unites once again with the whole.

We are all here to remember that love is the prime ingredient in the endeavor to continue our evolution. We are here to conquer our fears, to see through the illusion, the 'maya'. We are here to remember that we create our own reality. We literally send energy in the form of thoughts, words and deeds out into the morphogenetic grid that surrounds our planet and links us to the universe. This ever-changing matrix generates matter and the other components of what we refer to as reality.

Chapter 3

REALITY ACCORDING TO ANCIENT MYSTICISM

What is a mystic? A mystic may or may not belong to an organized religion. In either case, a true mystic is not interested in dogma, but is concerned with developing an inner knowledge rather than a dependence on the interpretations of others. A mystic is someone who acquires insight into the mysteries of existence by direct access to the divine pool of energy/information. This access is usually achieved by entering some altered state of consciousness, which transcends normal methods of perception. It largely bypasses rational thought and information is gained by using the more intuitive parts of the mind. In this sense, it is almost the opposite of science. Although intuition may play a part in the scientific process, all information must then be tested in a rational way before it is taken seriously. Mystical information, on the other hand, is taken seriously by mystics because they are usually in a state of bliss, a state whereby something at the very core of their being is telling them that what they are witnessing is closer to the truth than what is witnessed in normal consciousness.

This sense of certainty gets reinforced when such information turns out to be very similar to the information of other mystics. Eventually a large body of mystical information accumulates in any given culture, which can then be compared to the accumulations of other cultures with whom there may have been no contact. When such comparisons are made, it is found that a great deal of the observations made by mystics all over the world, at different points in history, are very similar. In this way even non-mystics begin to take this body of information seriously, especially if it resonates with their own intuitive sense. Nowadays even more scientifically minded people are tending to lend more credence to mysticism because science, with its rigorous methodology, is beginning to agree with the observations of mystics dating back to antiquity. Before discussing these similarities with modern science, this chapter will take a brief look at some of this mystical information as it pertains to this book.

Most of the mystical information we'll be looking at comes from the eastern philosophies. Although the west has had its share of mystics, the east has produced huge volumes of such information that goes much further back in time. This is probably because the eastern cultures were developing these philosophies back in a time when the intuitive, right-brained type of mentality was much more valued. The west has come of age during a time when the more rational, left-brained logic predominated. Having said this, it is important to emphasize that all religions have a mystical core from which most of them have deviated. Most of the organizations built around the world's religions have motives that are largely political and one is just as likely to find eastern religions deeply encumbered by dogma and mindless ritual. Although we'll be focussing on eastern philosophy, we'll also take a look at the mystical traditions of Judaism (the Qabala), Islam (Sufism), Christianity, the mystery schools of Egypt and Greece as well as various indigenous, shamanic traditions throughout the world.

Hinduism is one of the oldest religious philosophies, consisting of countless sects, embracing many deities and concerned with practices ranging from facile rituals to deep, complex concepts. It is said to have been brought to the ancient civilization living in the Indus valley by Aryan invaders. It is the main religion of India, embraced by 85% of India's 800 million people. Hinduism is based on four texts known as the Vedas, the oldest of which is the 'Rig Veda', written some 3500 years ago by a number of anonymous sages. Although the essence of Hindu philosophy is contained in the part called the 'Upanishads', the more popular texts contain epic sagas such as the 'Mahabarata', which contains the famous 'Bhagavad Gita'.[4]

One of the key concepts of Hinduism is that all aspects of creation are manifestations of the same ultimate reality—a universal soul that they call 'Brahman'. All Hindu deities are aspects of this universal godness. Each human soul is a portion of Brahman called 'Atman', which is involved in a long process that will eventually culminate in reunion with Brahman.

The cycle of creation, which moves from the divine starting point, through the unfolding of the universe, then returning to a divine end point, is known as 'lila'. This grand cycle contains countless sub-cycles of destruction and creation.

The unfolding universe is created with a magical power known as 'maya', which originates in our own consciousness. Our consciousness uses maya to create the complex web of illusion, which constitutes our normal, physical reality. To be under the spell of maya is to be unable to see the true reality underlying this constructed illusion. Such a person is said to be bound by 'karma', the interconnectedness of all things. Karma is the cause and effect process of events and actions.

Someone can become free of karma and maya by 'glimpsing' or 'experiencing' Brahman. This experience is called 'moksha'. One of the ways this can be achieved is by using a practice called 'yoga', which means 'to yoke, to join or to unite'. Although nowadays most people think of yoga as a series of physical exercises or postures called 'asanas', they are only a small part of the whole practice which is designed to help with moksha. Yoga also includes techniques of breathing, chanting, meditating, etc. With repeated exposure to these glimpses of divinity comes liberation or enlightenment, known as 'nirvana'.

Of the many Hindu deities, the most important ones are Shiva, Shakti and Vishnu. Most of the other gods and goddesses are aspects of these three. Shiva embodies many aspects of Brahman, including its entirety as well as its various factions. The most popular depiction of Shiva is 'Nataraja', the cosmic dancer. Here Shiva represents the ongoing cycle of creation and destruction, the endless dance.

Shakti is often depicted as Shiva's sex partner and his equal. She also has several aspects, such as Kali the destroyer, Parvati the lover, Sarasvati the goddess of knowledge and Lakshmi the goddess of prosperity.

Vishnu, who also comes in many forms and guises, is the preserver. A very popular aspect of Vishnu is Krishna, the hero of the Bhagavad Gita and the Hindu deity bearing the closest resemblance to Christ, the 'god-made-man.'

One body of knowledge associated with Hinduism that is very relevant to our discussion of reality is known as the *Tantra*. Best known for its views that the sex act can be a powerful enlightening tool, Tantra is actually much more than that. (see Part Seven, 'Sexuality and the Return of the Goddess') It is a fusion of many disciplines including; astronomy, astrology, cosmogenesis, cosmic evolution, mathematics, geometry, chemistry and physics, even at subatomic levels. As we'll see, much of what Tantric science says is very similar to what modern physics has to say. The main difference is that Tantric knowledge was based on a metaphysical understanding of the nature of reality, rather than one that was gained using the empirical method. The word 'tantra' derives from a Sanskrit term with no direct English equivalent, but which approximates 'web', 'weave' or 'continuum'. It is now thought to mean 'method of going beyond'.

The *history of Tantra* goes back several millenia and the oldest texts are thought to be Indo-Aryan, dating back to the Indus valley of 3000 BC. There are 108 anonymous texts, the most recent being only a few hundred years old, which are most often associated with the Hindu god, Shiva. Within this vast body of information are 112 different methods of meditation, some of which include the sex act. The oldest forms of Tantra were non-religious, non-dogmatic, based on experiential knowledge. Often throughout history, it was considered to be heretical by the religious establishment.

Tantra suggests that all manifestations in the universe are the result of *male/female dualism*, giving rise to all the illusions of duality or polarity, ie, good/bad, light/dark, yin/yang, right/wrong, etc. The two components of the dualism are distinct yet inseparable aspects of the totality of truth.

The nature of the male aspect, called Purusha, is said to embody cosmic consciousness and is more static. It is associated with the god, Shiva. The nature of the female aspect called Prakriti, on the other hand, is said to be kinetic, corresponding to nature and the endless cycles of creation and dissolution. It is associated with the goddess, Shakti.

Prakriti consists of three forces, called gunas, which are responsible for the existence of everything in the universe. Two of these three forces are also seen as male (Rajas) and female (Tamas), with the remaining one a neutral, catalytic, balancing force (Sattva). The male Rajas force is positive, kinetic, creative and electric. The female Tamas force is negative, resistant, destructive and magnetic. These three forces are also distinct yet inseparable.

Tantra's version of **cosmogenesis**, the creation of the universe, is relevant to our discussion here. When the three gunas are in a state of complete balance or equilibrium, it is called the 'Mahabindu', or 'the great point'. Evolution begins when this balance is disturbed by Purusha, the universal consciousness, causing the point to explode. The three forces then go through a constant process of uniting and separating in an effort to restore equilibrium.

In all manifestations of energy, the three forces are present to varying degrees,with one force dominating. In gross matter, for example, it is said that the dominant force is Tamas. Energy cannot be lost or destroyed, but can only change form or transmute. All of these changes occur within a whole that remains unchanged. Thus the sum of all effects equals the sum of all causes, a concept that is very similar to modern physics' principal of 'superposition'. When all of these manifestations reach equilibrium, at maximum expansion, they begin to implode back to Mahabindu, the great point. Then the process starts again.[5]

We can see that this line of thinking is very similar to the idea of a 'Big Bang' which science has embraced. Measurements of the distances between cosmic bodies have shown modern scientists that the universe is expanding. Many of these scientists, including Einstein, speculate that it will eventually reach a state of balance or equilibrium, at which point there will be no further transmutation of energy and, thus, no time, no motion, no heat, no light, etc. The universe will then contract in a process that science has named the 'Big Crunch'.

As well as dealing with the macro-world, Tantra has a school of thought known as the 'Nyaya Vaiseshika', which deals with the micro-world. While acknowledging that the smallest material particles have no real form and are only points of energy, Tantra identifies four types of atoms corresponding to four types of matter; earth, water, air and fire.[6] It also recognizes an etheric, non-material/non-atomic substance, which permeates the entire universe and serves as a conduit for sound or energy waves. Thus, there is no such thing as a true vacuum. Again we can see dramatic parallels to the postulations of modern physics.

Tantra places a great deal of importance on **the power of sound**, (as do other mystical schools of thought such as the Qabala). According to Tantra, all objects including non-material objects, have their own innate sound, some of which are audible and some of which are beyond human sensory capacity. In other words, all things in the universe are manifestations of energy, each with their own vibratory frequency. The manifestation of matter is considered to be the third step in the process of creation, preceded by sound. The following quote can be found in the Hindu Vedas, "In the beginning was Brahman with whom was the Word. And the Word is Brahman."[7] This passage is clearly referring to the idea that sound, here represented by 'Word' or 'vaikhari'(Sanskrit), is a major component of creation. How similar this quote is to the opening lines of the Gospel of John, "In the beginning was the Word, and the Word was with God, and the word was God."

Science has also shown the relationship between sound and matter. Back in the 1800s a man named Ernst Chladni, and more recently a man named Hans Jenny performed experiments with sand on a thin sheet of metal. When the vibration of sound was applied to the sheet, the grains of sand arranged themselves into a pattern. The same note always produces the same pattern—the higher the note, the more complex the pattern. Jenny's branch of science, known as cymatics, has demonstrated the relationship between form and vibration in many ways.[8] If one takes a box filled with water in which dust particles are floating in suspension, and then introduces a vibration throughout the box, the particles will collect into symmetrical patterns with a crystalline effect. Recent experiments have shown that when sound is introduced to quantities of water, oil, dust or other things, it produces shapes and patterns that are often found in nature. In other words, vibration introduces order to a random collection of particles.[9]

Tantra recognizes that sound has great power, including the power to heal the human body. It has given us a wealth of knowledge about the relationship between the human body and the energy of life that is called 'prana'. We access this prana through vortices or points of contact called 'chakras'. This pranic life force then flows through the body along invisible channels, meridians or conduits called 'nadi'. These concepts will be discussed in Chapter Seven.

Hinduism is a religion that embraces many different factions and bodies of knowledge. One of the world's most important mystical religions is **Buddhism**, which grew out of Hinduism. It is the philosophy left to us by Siddhartha Gautama, a great spiritual leader who was disinclined to worship the Hindu deities and was opposed to the caste system that still prevails in India today. The Buddha was living in India in the sixth century BC. It is interesting to note that many other great leaders were on the planet at the same time, including Confucius, Lao Tse, Zarathustra, Varhamana, Pythagorus and Heraclitus.

Another key figure in the history of this religion was King Asoka, who brought Buddhism to the wider world. While it spread to many other eastern countries, such as Ceylon, Burma, Thailand, Tibet, Nepal, China and Japan, in India Buddhism was assimilated into the all-encompassing embrace of Hinduism, where Gautama Buddha is thought of as an incarnation of Vishnu. Like many great spiritual leaders, including Jesus, who consider themselves to

be messengers and not 'gods', Gautama eventually became deified by the popular religious movement that he spawned.

Buddhism is somewhat less concerned with metaphysics and is more of a
practical 'how to' guide with a distinct psychological flavor. At the heart of
Buddhism are the Four Noble Truths: 1) Suffering or frustration, called
'duhkha', is the main aspect of the human condition. 2) Suffering is the result
of resisting the natural flow and clinging to illusion and ego, unable to see
one's own divinity. Such clinging is called 'trishna'. The wrong view of life,
called 'avidya', leads to a futile vicious circle of karma known as 'samsara'. 3)
It is possible to break free from samsara and to move toward moksha and nirvana. 4) The best way to achieve nirvana was via the Eightfold Path of self-
development. The first two paths involve 'right-seeing', paths three through
six involve 'right-acting', paths seven and eight involve 'right-awareness', the
direct experience of mystical reality.

The two pillars of Buddhism are 'prajna'—transcendental wisdom, and
'karuna'—love and compassion extended to all things. One Buddhist meditation involves sending love to the visualization of someone who is easy to love.
Next, one would send love to someone a little harder to love until, eventually,
love would be sent to the visualization of someone that one might find totally distasteful. Love is said to be the true nature of consciousness, leading to the
loss of ego and the gaining of the awareness of unity, the knowledge that
everything including self is a part of the whole. The Buddhist concept of
'Dharmakaya' is much the same as Brahman and 'Bodhi' is like Atman. One of
the key Buddhist texts, the Avatamsaka Sutra, speaks of the unity and interre-
lationship of all things and events. Like other mystical traditions, Buddhism
stresses that the ultimate understanding of reality is available not through
rational thought and the perceptions of the five senses, but through direct
mystical experience.[10]

The culmination of **Chinese philosophy** happened between 500 and 200
BC. It is largely characterized by its recognition of two sides of human nature,
the intuitive wisdom of the sage and the practical knowledge of the king. Fully
realized beings that have acquired their knowledge through stillness develop
into sages, while those who self-realize by means of their actions are said to
develop into kings or rulers. This more practical way of being is embodied by
Confucianism, developed by a great teacher named K'ung Fu Tse, better
known by the Anglicized name, Confucius. It advocates an efficiency of living
which results from fairness and compassion.

The more mystical of the two philosophies is embodied in **Taoism**, which
developed from ancient shamanic practices based on the observation of nature
and the discovery of 'the way', known as the Tao. This refers both to the way
things are and the way one should conduct oneself in order to find joy.

According to the Tao, joy can be found by trusting intuition and joining the natural flow of things. Taoism is often symbolized by water, which takes the easiest path to the sea, flowing around obstacles rather than trying to overcome. Water is seen as softness, which in its perseverance, can wear away hardness. The first book of Taoism is the beautifully poetic 'Tao Te Ching', (roughly translated as the Way and Its Power), written by Lao Tse, the Old Master, around 500 BC. The second, much larger book of Taoism is the 'Chuang Tse', written by a sage of the same name about 200 years later. A famous passage has Chuang Tse waking from a dream in which he was a butterfly. He then asks, "Am I really a man dreaming that I am a butterfly, or a butterfly dreaming that I am a man?" A butterfly is an ancient symbol for the soul, which having been confined to life as a caterpillar, becomes transformed and is able to fly. (Modern scholars now believe that these two books were actually authored by several sages.)[11]

The concept of the Tao is very similar to that of Brahman/Dharmakaya—that all things are interrelated, different manifestations of the same thing, part of a perpetual flow within which are constantly repeating cycles or patterns. A true sage lives according to these patterns which manifest as an interplay of dualities called yin and yang. Those aspects of the duality that have yin qualities include dark, attractive, in-going, female, earthly, yielding, resting, intuitive, sage-knowledge. Those that have yang qualities include light, repulsive, outgoing, male, heavenly, unyielding, moving, rational, king-knowledge. This interplay of opposites is studied in depth in the 'I Ching', or the 'Book of Changes'. This is a book of no particular author that is thought to have developed over thousands of years. Its system of 64 hexagrams is used as an oracle, providing clues to the right way to live. The essential message of the I Ching is that nothing is static, everything is constantly changing.

Of all of the eastern philosophies, Taoism has the greatest mistrust of the intellectual, reasoning process. According to Taoism, change results not from outside forces, but from innate, preprogrammed codes or blueprints and thus, all actions arise spontaneously. The choices or actions of a wise person are also spontaneous, based on intuition. This type of wisdom, the following of nature's way, is known as 'wu-wei', which means 'non-action' or 'effortless effort'. This concept has often been misunderstood to mean that one should do nothing, withdrawing from the bustle of everyday life. On the contrary, life is seen as the vehicle or the means by which one can practice wu-wei, living mindfully and willfully yet effortlessly, as in the analogy of water moving toward the sea.[12]

Around 100 AD, Chinese thought merged with Buddhist thought to eventually form a pragmatic form of Buddhist discipline called Ch'an. This school of thought migrated to Japan circa 1200 AD to become ***Zen Buddhism***. The ultimate goal of Zen is the attainment of enlightenment, which they call 'satori'. The two main schools of Zen, 'Rinzai' and 'Soto', advocate two different ways of reaching satori. The methodology of the Rinzai school involves 'sanzen', interviews with Zen masters who often use a 'koan' to spark a sudden insight in the student, leading to satori. A koan is a puzzling quip which makes little sense to the reasoning mind, but when meditated upon, can bring a deeper awareness. The most famous koan is, "What is the sound of one hand clapping?" Another is, "What is your original face?"

The Soto School of Zen, on the other hand, advocates a slow, gradual gaining of awareness leading to satori. Both schools value daily meditation as a learning tool. Zen masters love to shock their students with bizarre and outrageous behavior in an effort to jar them out of their habitual patterns of thought. Beyond such patterns the student will hopefully be able to glimpse a purer form of the truth.[13]

The most ancient form of mysticism, which is still alive and well in many forms amongst various indigenous cultures, is **Shamanic mysticism**. Evidence of such practices have been found dating back to Neolithic times. The Aboriginal people of Australia have been partaking in mystical activities and rituals for 35,000 years. Taoism and Hinduism are thought to have derived from earlier shamanic knowledge and practices. Some branches of Buddhism incorporated shamanic ways, notably in Tibet where the shamanic religion of Bon was assimilated by Buddhism.

Most shamanic cultures are tribal and, in most cases, the entire tribe is involved in various mystical practices, led by one person in the tribe who has particularly highly developed skills. These leaders have a number of different names in the different cultures. In the case of native Australians, for example, they are called Karadji. The word 'shaman', now used to refer to any of these leaders, actually comes from Mongolian Siberia, where it was used to refer to someone who could easily access altered states of consciousness. Many of the mystical practices in the various cultures are for the purpose of achieving such altered states, usually the result of trances induced in a variety of ways. Dancing, chanting, drumming, exhaustion, star gazing, sky gazing, dreaming, sexual practices, ingesting psychotropic plants and other methods have been used to enter various levels or degrees of trance. Sometimes the entire tribe would enter deep trance together. During this time all the members of the tribe would clearly be able to see which one of them had the best control of their faculties while in an altered state. That person would become a chief or a shaman, guiding the actions of the tribe according to the higher wisdom gained in altered states.

Shamanic cultures highly value the knowledge gained from such mystical pursuits and usually, all tribal members are exposed to it in a wide variety of initiation ceremonies. These rituals often involve fear or suffering which the initiate must overcome. They were aware that access to higher wisdom was seriously hampered by fear. Reported descriptions of mystical experiences such as astral travelling, the entering of various underworlds, communication with spirits, etcetera, are very similar, whether they come from religious or shamanic traditions ranging all over the world. Most of them report fearsome entities or circumstances which bar the way to those who are afraid. It is considered very dangerous to enter certain mystical realms without being in control of ones fears. Tibetan Buddhists, for example, claim that these entities are the product of the initiates' own fearful thoughts, which must be overcome before further progress can be made.

Ultimately, initiates sought some form of unity with a 'great spirit', or universal entity. These forms of unity have many names. To many native Americans it is 'Wakan Tanka'; to native Australians it is 'Baime'. Belief in the concept of reincarnation is widespread amongst mystical traditions. Another common characteristic among shamanic cultures is a deep respect for ancestral spirits, from whom guidance is often sought. Communication with the creatures of the Devic realms, such as faeries and elves is also sought, as well as with spirits of animals and plants. It has been said that a good shaman had the ability to 'make a deal' with the spirit of a tribe's prey animals, thus ensuring the tribe's prosperity. At a spiritual level, both prey and predator are aware of the illusory nature of reality and of the role they play in the balance of nature. When prey was killed during the hunt it was common practice to apologize and thank the spirit of the animal. A good shaman also contributed to the prosperity of the tribe by being able to transcend time, and thus foretell the future.

Shamans from all traditions use herbs and other plants for many things, including healing, symbolic ceremonies, and the entering of altered states of consciousness. ***Psychedelic plants***, including peyote cactus, hashish, various mushrooms, etc, have been used by mystics for thousands of years as a way of breaking down the barriers to altered states of reality. Such plants are considered to be sacred gifts from God. A drug known as 'fly agaric', which comes from the Amanita muscaria mushroom, has played a big part in the early Greek Mystery Schools, where it was often called 'nectar' or 'ambrosia'. Mycenae, which predates Greece, means 'city of the mushroom'. Indian mystics used fly agaric to make a hallucinogenic drink called 'soma'. In the hymns found in the Hindu Vedas, there are over 900 references to soma.[14]

John Allegro, a well respected scholar and one of the few selected to work on the Dead Sea Scrolls, is a Bible expert and an adept in the deciphering and translating of ancient writing. He surprised the academic world by releasing a book in 1970 entitled, 'The Sacred Mushroom and the Cross'. He contends that the Amanita muscaria mushroom played a large role in the early cultures of the middle east going as far back as the Sumerian civilization of 4000 BC.

More controversial than this, he claims that many Biblical stories allude to it and that Jesus and the early Christian movement were part of a mushroom cult. There are many depictions of this mushroom in ancient art and many references to it in ancient writings.[15]

It seems to me that Allegro overstates his case, seeing allusions to the sacred mushroom everywhere. However, there's no doubt in my mind that psychotropic plants have been used extensively by shamanic and mystical traditions in a sincere effort to find enlightenment. I feel compelled to say a few words about this, considering the sorry state of drug abuse in the world today. The mystical use of drugs was always done with the deepest respect and with the highest of motives. It was not intended for recreational use, for 'partying' or forms of escapism. These rituals were taken very seriously. They were often considered dangerous and were supervised by a learned shaman. As Don Juan points out in the Carlos Castaneda books, the 'power plants' were useful mainly as a way of glimpsing other realities and thus opening the mind to such possibilities. Continued use of them could be harmful, addictive and not conducive to the spiritual path. The ongoing pursuit of knowledge in Castaneda's apprenticeship had little to do with drugs.

The oldest cultures from which most of civilization has descended, were the Sumerian and the Egyptian, dating back almost 6000 years, according to conventional academia. Alternative information suggests that these cultures go even further back. One of the earliest mystical institutions that we know about are the **Egyptian Mystery Schools**. Based largely on the teachings of the god Tahuti or Thoth (Hermes to the Greeks), they were set up in two parts; the greater and the lesser mysteries. The lesser mysteries were the teachings and rituals that applied to the population at large. Egypt, like most early civilizations, was a theocracy, where almost every aspect of life, every human endeavor, had a mystical or religious motive. This was especially true of the earliest Egyptians.

The greater mysteries, requiring much more commitment, involved initiation into a long process of learning. Whether this was reserved for the elite or offered to anyone who chose it, is not known. According to some sources, this process involved two phases, each of which took twelve years. The school of the Left Eye of Horus focussed on lessons involving the right brain/female aspect of consciousness, and the school of the Right Eye of Horus involved the left brain/male aspect of consciousness. These lessons used various means to acquire knowledge of innate divinity and to systematically face and overcome a series of fears. Some of the chambers in The Great Pyramid and other temples were used in this process. (More on this in subsequent chapters.)

There is very little information about the Egyptian schools, but we know that they heavily influenced the **Greek Mystery Schools**, about which we know a bit more. The roots of many aspects of western culture that we now think of as secular come from these mystical traditions, including mathematics, science, philosophy, art and even the Olympic Games. Born in 581 BC, Pythagorus spent at least twenty years as an initiate in the Egyptian Mystery Schools before he brought this knowledge back to Greece. He and Heraclitus are the most famous of the early Greek mystic philosophers. A hundred years later came Socrates, then Plato and Aristotle.

One of the rituals of the Mystery School was a drama during which the participants wore masks called 'persona', from whence derives the word 'personality'. The idea was to discover the essence of the soul beneath the mask. They placed great emphasis on the idea of a higher self and the many references to 'descending to the underworld' were meant to represent a part of the higher self that incarnated into the physical plane. In the words of Heraclitus, "Men are immortal gods—gods mortal men." Emphasis was also placed on the idea of liberation from the endless cycle of birth and death, which Pythagorus calls the Grievous Wheel. The Twelve Trials of the Hero was a method to break this cycle; to guide one towards enlightenment, usually by overcoming fears and obstacles. The most famous example of this is the Twelve Trials of Heracles(Hercules), which involved not only feats of strength, but also the discovery of his feminine side and the mastery of time.[16]

Initiates who entered the greater mysteries did so only if they felt a deep calling. This greater knowledge was kept secret and was not written down; to speak of it to the uninitiated was considered a crime. The learning of mathematics and geometry was also a sacred endeavor and Pythagorus referred to numbers as 'immortal gods'. They viewed science and mysticism as equals, as ways to discover the secrets of reality. Hundreds of volumes of scientific information were written, much of it gathered in a mystical way. Although many of these books were subsequently destroyed by the Christian Church, we know that they had a wealth of knowledge of geometry, physics, astronomy, etc. They were well aware, for example, that the Earth was a round planet that circled the sun.

In this next section I'll talk about the mystical traditions that belong to the western religions of Judaism, Christianity and Islam. In the east, mysticism forms the very basis of the bigger religious movements. In many cases, and to varying degrees, these major eastern religions have gone on to deviate from these mystical principles. In the west, on the other hand, mysticism has been something that the religious administration has had a hard time tolerating right from the beginning, even though both Jesus and Muhammad were mystics. In fact, many of the key western mystics have been put to death by the ruling establishment of their day. Nonetheless, there have been some significant mystical movements such as Sufism and the Qabala, as well as some fascinating individuals. A much more in depth discussion of Christianity and Judaism can be found in Part Six of this book.

The Judaic religion, with its ancient Hebrew roots, has had several mystical traditions. The most important of these is probably the **Qabala**, with its philosophies surrounding the Tree of Life. It is a set of knowledge and methodology, which includes metaphors regarding creation and the workings of the universe. It has much in common with aspects of the Tantra, including the seven levels of human consciousness, and will be discussed at greater length in a subsequent chapter.

There are several spellings, ie Kabballa, Cabala and Qaballah. There is also controversy regarding the history and origins of the Qabala. Some say that it started in medieval times, heavily influenced by Gnosticism and later by the Neo-Platonism of the Renaissance era. It contains a strong element of 'magical knowledge' or alchemy in its methodology, which includes the Tarot system of divining. Although the Qabala became increasingly ignored by the Judaic establishment and condemned by Jewish orthodoxy, it enjoyed a great surge of renewed interest by both Jews and Christians during the occult revival of the 19th century. It was a big influence on occult organizations such as the Hermetic Order of the Golden Dawn, founded by influential citizens such as Eliphas Levi. This led to other groups and such controversial figures as the magician/occultist, Aleister Crowley.

Others say that, according to tradition, the Qabala was given by God to Adam. In his book, 'Genesis of the Grail Kings', Laurence Gardner claims that the Kabballa of the middle ages was derivative of the original Qabala, but that much of the original meaning had been lost. He says that it was originally called the 'Ha Qabala', deriving from the Sumerian text, 'the Table of Destiny', also known to the ancient Hebrews as 'the Book of Raziel'. Anyone who possessed the Qabala knew the secrets of 'Ram', 'the highest expression of cosmic knowingness'. The original name of Abraham was 'Abram', which means 'he who has Ram'. This root can be seen in several names for divinity, such as Rama(India/Tibet), Ra and Ramtha(Egypt), and Aram(Celtic).[17]

Another mystical sect within the Jewish tradition was known as the Essenes, living in desert communities in Palestine and Egypt around the time of Christ. A sub-sect of the Essenes were the Nazorenes or Nazirites, who probably go back even further in time. These two groups are discussed at greater length in Part Six. There is much controversy surrounding the Essenes. It is thought that they were associated with and heavily influenced by the Mystery Schools of Pythagorus and Orpheus, with whom they shared many traditions and customs; they wore white robes, lived in isolation, were vegetarian, believed in reincarnation and practiced anointing with water (baptism) and oils.

Like the Mystery Schools, the Essenes had a system of initiation which was called 'Hekhalot'. This involved the initiate passing through a series of seven inner chambers, which were guarded by 'angelic forces'. Like other mystical systems, this involved the incremental accumulation of knowledge and disso-lution of fears. The idea of a seven-fold path can be found in many mystical traditions; the seven Shining Ones—Persia; the seven chanted vowel sounds—Egypt; the seven valleys to Allah—Islam; the seven gates and golden keys—Tibetan Buddhism; the seven sacraments—Christianity; and the seven heavens of Jacob's Ladder (Tree of Life)—Judaism, from whence the idea of 'seventh heaven'.[18]

Of all of the major religious establishments, the Christian Church based in Rome has been the least tolerant of mystics and mysticism. There are no well-defined examples of **Christian Mysticism** within this religion, and many of the greatest individual Christian mystics are virtually unknown. Many of these individuals were put to death by the Church. Some groups tried to break away from the extreme authoritarianism of the Roman Church, but were heavily persecuted. One such group was the Cathars, a mystically oriented communi-ty of about 100,000, living in the south of France circa 1200 AD. This entire community was slaughtered by the Church. Mystics advocate a direct contact with divinity, with no need for a 'middle man'. The Church felt that they were the intermediaries, the representatives of God on Earth and that all contact had to go through them. The power of the Church hierarchy felt threatened by the free-thinking mystics. Despite the persecution, mystical groups persist-ed in secret.

Outside of the jurisdiction of Roman authorities, especially in the first few centuries after Christ, there were several mystical groups such as the Manicheans and the Arians. Probably the most important of these groups were the Gnostics. Centered in the Egyptian city of Alexandria, the Gnostics claimed to follow more closely the true teachings of Jesus. Again, this involved a direct 'knowing' of divinity, which they called 'gnosis'. Their methods of achieving gnosis were much the same as those of other traditions, and they had their own forms of mystery school. They were openly opposed to any form of Christian establishment. A Gnostic text called 'the Apocalypse of Peter' quotes Jesus as having said, "Those who name themselves bishop and deacon, as if they had received their authority from God, are in reality waterless canals who do not understand the Mystery; although they boast that the Truth belongs to them alone." Jesus warns that a false Church will lead many astray.

In a Gnostic text called 'On the Origins of the World', the Old Testament God, Yahweh/Jehovah, is portrayed as a false god, obscuring the true nature of divinity from the people. Another text called 'The Testimony of Truth' tells the story of Creation from the serpent's point of view. The serpent is portrayed as the representative of true divinity, guiding Adam and Eve away from the tyran-ny of Yahweh and leading them to the Tree of Knowledge and the Tree of Life. It is interesting that in all cultures other than the Judeo-Christian, the serpent/dragon is a revered symbol that appears again and again in various art forms, insignia, legends, etc.

The Gnostics believed that Jesus was a man, and was the son of God in the same way that we are all children of God. They believed that he came to teach us how to become 'christened', how to become a Christ, how to become enlightened. In the Gnostic 'Gospel of Philip', Jesus says, "You saw the spirit, you became spirit. You saw Christ, you became Christ. You saw the Father, you shall become the father. You see your Self, and what you see you shall become." In the 'Testimony of Truth', Jesus urges his followers to listen to their own hearts and minds; "The Kingdom of Heaven is within you".[19]

It is easy to see how mystical groups like the Gnostics represented a big threat to the growing authority of the Christian Church of Rome. Over the centuries, they were ruthlessly persecuted into oblivion, their books were burned, their philosophies obliterated. Fortunately, many of these writings have recently become available to us once again. Back at the time of the book burnings, someone had the good sense to bury a collection of Gnostic scrolls. In 1945 in a small village in upper Egypt called Nag Hamadi, large clay jars containing these scrolls were uncovered. This collection has come to be known as the Nag Hamadi Library. Much of what these scrolls have to say about the life of Jesus differs greatly from what the Church has been saying. This information is covered in more depth in Part Six.

The Islamic religion started with the prophet Mohammed, who was born in 570 AD. Like Judaism and Chritianity, it is a monotheistic religion, advocating the worship of one God called Allah. The word 'Islam' means 'surrender', referring to the idea of surrendering to the divine will, which is a mystical concept common to many traditions. Like most organized religions, however, much of Islam has come to have very little to do with the mystical path and seems more concerned with rules and regulations. Despite this, mystical traditions have persisted. Let's now take a look at the mystical branch of Islam known as **Sufism**. It originated with ecstatic poets such as Rabi'a and Bayazid of Bastami, circa 874 AD. Some of these poets were also great scientists, such as Omar Khayyam. They wore plain wool garments called 'suf', from whence the name 'Sufi'.They soon came to be seen as a heretical threat and some, such as al-Hallaj, Suhrawardi and Ayn Hamadani, were put to death by Muslim authorities. Despite persecution the sect continued, culminating in the 13th century with the great poet and mystic, Rumi. The movement declined after that, but like many mystical schools, it is making a comeback in modern times.

Sufis believe that the purpose of life is to discover one's true divine nature, to unite with the whole. Like the Gnostics and other mystics, the Sufis believe that the best way to achieve such union is through direct experience of the divine, placing little value on religious ritual and dogma. To Islam the concept of 'Jihad' has come to mean 'holy war'- going to battle for some 'just and holy' cause. To Sufis, however, Jihad refers to the notion of battling one's own sense of ego and surrendering to the divine will. Suhrawardi taught that the roots of Sufism and of all mystical traditions was the wisdom that was handed down by Hermes/Thoth, the great god/magician of ancient Egypt.[20]

In practice, the Sufis seek divine union by means of meditation, breathing techniques and various methods of entering trance. Music, drumming, chanting and dancing are important methods. Perhaps the most famous of the Sufi dancers are the Whirling Dervishes, a group of monks established by Rumi. They seek to achieve a state of ecstasy by twirling continually to the point of exhaustion.

The purpose of this section was not to teach an in-depth understanding of the various mystical traditions and religions. There are many excellent books available to anyone seeking a deeper explanation. (For a good overview of many different traditions, I recommend 'The Complete Guide to World Mysticism', by T. Freke and P. Gandy. It is the source of some of the information in this section.) Rather, this section was meant to show the many significant similarities among the different mystical traditions. I believe that the philosophies and insights that they provide regarding the nature of reality are profound and important. If we are to make sense of our existence, our purpose, then we need a better grasp of this thing called reality. One of the reasons compelling me to write this book was that, the more information I gathered, the more I could see the links and connections among so many bodies of knowledge. Things just began to make more and more sense. One of the more convincing examples of this are the many parallels that can be drawn between mystically derived knowledge and the explorations of modern science. We'll take a look at some of these parallels in the upcoming chapters.

Chapter 4

THE ATHEIST AND THE BEAR

Once upon a time there lived an atheist. Even though he had been born into a Christian family, he began to feel awkward and embarrassed at the idea of God, after a long and thorough education in the sciences. The notion of a supreme being just seemed downright unscientific. Whenever the atheist had the opportunity, he would voice these opinions. He would point out that the universe came about, not through some all-powerful 'God' entity, but as a result of the 'Big Bang'. Matter, which had formerly been compressed to the

In the television series, 'The Simpsons', the wealthy tycoon, personified by Mr. Burns, is portrayed as a short-sighted, simplistic buffoon without any capacity for love, who believes he is entitled to accumulate huge amounts of wealth doing things that are harmful to everyone else. In his own way he is an 'innocent fool'.

Wrath, dishonesty or any form of wrongdoing including murder, is just a soul making poor decisions in the process of learning a particular lesson. Poor decisions are being made continually in reaction to life's circumstances, and these decisions vary in terms of their magnitude. There are little mistakes and there are huge mistakes. Someone who is able to see past the illusion of the dualities recognizes that all Players are at different stages of their evolutionary unfolding and that part of learning means making mistakes. That doesn't mean that we shouldn't take dangerous criminals off the street, it just means that it is futile to think of them as lower life forms. Our attitudes toward many things in life are shaped by such uninformed beliefs and prejudices. A more evolved Player realizes that it is folly to judge anyone as being some lower form of life. As players in the same Game, we are all equal. That is because, in this game, there are no losers. We are all winners. Before the Game is finally won, however, most of us do make some poor choices along the way.

A truly evolved person would actually feel grateful for the negative actions; the mistakes of others. The poor decisions of others and the consequences that they bring afford us opportunities to learn. While observing the horrors of street violence in the world's ghettos, for example, we are invited to look in the mirror. We have the opportunity to assess our own behavior. We have the opportunity to recognize the many factors, the socio-economic conditions that have brought about this criminal behavior and to determine if we, as part of society, have contributed to those factors. Again, we can choose to point the finger and hate, or we can choose a more compassionate attitude. We can feel grateful that we have the opportunity to learn a lesson without having to go through the horror that is the daily life of a ghetto criminal. It is easy to feel gratitude for the soul of the Christ for showing us the heights that can be achieved by a human being. It is more difficult to feel gratitude for the soul of Hitler, who showed us the depths of depravity to which humanity could sink. Jesus came to teach humanity a lesson, and so did Hitler.

We are continually being presented with circumstances which afford us an opportunity to learn a lesson of love, whether it be love of self, love of nature or love of the guy who just cut you off on the highway. Generally speaking, it is more difficult to feel compassion for someone who is far away, both physically or ideologically. It is easy to love one's immediate family, a little harder to love the members of one's extended family, a little harder to love the citizens of one's own city, harder still to love everyone in the nation and even size of a pin-prick with unimaginable density and enormous gravity, had simply exploded and has been expanding ever since. He explained that the cosmic dust which resulted from this event started to gather into vast clouds which, due to their increasing gravity, collapsed in on themselves and began to burn. As a result, many different elements began to form, which combined with each other to become more complex molecules.

Eventually material from these stars would form planets. It just so happened that, on one of these planets in an otherwise insignificant corner of the universe, some molecules came together in a very special way and suddenly became alive. This is how life came to be. It was a spontaneous occurrence, a cosmic accident. These primitive life forms began to evolve, becoming more and more complex. This evolution had nothing to do with any divine plan, creative design or any such nonsense. It was all based on the logical need for these life forms to survive. It was survival of the fittest and yadda, yadda, yadda. The idea of a supreme, divine intelligence just didn't make sense.

Some of the atheist's friends would disagree with him. Some would point out that the idea of 'God' actually made more sense than the 'cosmic accident' idea. One friend said that some computer whiz had devised a program that could figure out the odds of such a cosmic accident, and that it turned out to be about one chance in a gazillion. A different friend pointed out that there was actually a lot of evidence to suggest the existence of a supreme intelligence, including out of body experiences, near death experiences and yadda, yadda, yadda. Just look at the order that exists everywhere. Even what appears to be random chaos has been shown to have an underlying order. According to the atheist, however, this type of evidence was not scientifically sound.

Some of the atheist's fellow science students also disagreed with him. They pointed out that some of the world's leading scientists, such as Max Planck and Albert Einstein, had publicly proclaimed their conviction that there existed some form of cosmic intelligence; a great mind that had designed the universe. They pointed out that modern physics was coming to conclusions that were very similar to those of the ancient mystics. By this time, however, the atheist's total identity was tied up in his beliefs. No arguments could sway him, even if they had a scientific basis.

One day, after many years of adamantly proclaiming his views, the atheist was walking in the woods. He was admiring all the wonders that had resulted from this cosmic accident. "What majestic trees! What powerful rivers! What beautiful animals!" he said to himself. As he was walking alongside the river he heard a rustling in the bushes behind him. He turned to look. He saw a seven-foot grizzly bear charging towards him! He ran as fast as he could up the path. He looked over his shoulder and saw that the bear was closing. He ran even faster, so scared that tears were coming to his eyes. He looked over his shoulder again, and the bear was even closer. His heart was pumping frantically and he tried to run even faster. He tripped and fell to the ground. He rolled over to pick himself up but saw the bear, right on top of him, reaching for him with his left paw and raising his right paw to strike him.

At that instant the atheist cried out "Oh my God!....please, help me, please!" Suddenly, time stood still. The bear froze. The forest became silent. Even the river stopped moving. As a bright light shone upon the man, a huge voice came out of the sky: "You deny my existence for all of these years; teach others I don't exist; and, even credit creation to a cosmic accident. Now that you're faced with your own death, do you expect me to help you out of this predicament? Am I to count you as a believer?"

The atheist looked directly into the light: "I'm sorry. I was wrong. I guess the fear of death has made me change my mind", he said, sheepishly.

"I get a lot of that", said God.

"I guess it would be hypocritical of me to suddenly ask You to rescue me. Even though I was born a Christian, I guess I couldn't expect you to save me now, as though I were a devout Christian. Hey, here's an idea. Perhaps could you make the bear a Christian?"

"Hmm," Pondered God. "Very, well, then. So be it!"

At that very second the light went out. The river ran again, the sounds of the forest resumed. To the atheist's relief, the bear dropped its right paw. Suddenly it dropped to its knees, brought both paws together, bowed its head and spoke: "Dear Lord, for this food which I am about to receive, I am truly thankful."

Chapter 5

REALITY ACCORDING TO MODERN SCIENCE

"I know that I know nothing."
—*Socrates*

"Not knowing that one knows, is best."
—*Lao Tse*

"Every word or concept, clear as it may seem to be, has only a limited range of applicability."—"What we observe is not nature itself, but nature exposed to our method of questioning."
—*Quantum physicist, Werner Heisenberg*

I hope you enjoyed the goofy little story about the atheist. I thought it might be a good idea to throw in a little comic relief. You might need such a breather before entering this next section, which by its very nature, can be a challenge to understand. Some of the concepts that follow can be quite abstract and hard to visualize. Don't be discouraged if you don't emerge with a clear picture of these concepts in your mind. It could still be very useful to have even a rough idea about what modern science is saying, without necessarily gaining a complete understanding. Our mental images are largely a product of our common, everyday experience as it is interpreted by our 'linear' method of reasoning. Science is presenting a picture of reality that goes beyond our sensory experience, the thorough comprehension of which demands more of a 'lateral' mode of reasoning. If you choose to skip this section, it will not significantly diminish your experience of the rest of the book. Anyway, here goes.

In 1927, the world's leading physicists came together in the Danish capital of Copenhagen. The most famous gathering of scientists in history came up with a document called 'The Copenhagen Interpretation of Quantum Mechanics'. They came to several conclusions, one of which was the acknowledgement that quantum mechanics does not define reality, and that rational thought could not lead to a complete understanding of reality. In the 1970s a group of eminent physicists known as the 'Fundamental Physics Group' met at the Lawrence Berkeley Laboratory in California. They came to similar conclusions—that knowledge is limited and that it is impossible to construct a single scientific model capable of explaining reality. Where have we heard that before? Virtually all of the mystical traditions have made the same point.

Although this is only one example of the many parallels between mysticism and science, it is an important one and a good place to begin. Both scientists and mystics seem to be saying that the everyday, ordinary reality that we perceive with our five senses is an illusion. We simply can't rely on our five-sensory perceptions to give us the truth about the nature of reality. All of our common sense notions of the way the universe works are based on observations of that small part of the universe that our senses are capable of perceiving. A little over a hundred years ago, all of the laws of physics, brilliantly laid out by scientists like Sir Isaac Newton, were based on precise measurements of these common-sensory observations. The way that the observable universe behaved was predictable using these laws, which at the time were considered to be written in stone. Countless experiments proved over and over that certain causes always produced certain effects. The outcome of an experiment was predictable if one knew the causal factors. Newton's laws were very successful and were used to build the modern world.

Over the past hundred years, however, this has changed dramatically. The

Newtonian laws can no longer account for all that we observe. That is because we are now capable of observing far beyond the limits of the five senses. Normally, we cannot observe the workings of the distant macro-universe—that which is far beyond the Earth. We can't observe the workings of the micro-universe—that which is too small to observe. We can't observe things that move at very high speeds; motion that approaches the speed of light. Without enhancement, there is much that our five senses cannot witness. However, in the modern technological era, we have sophisticated tools which effectively enhance our senses, our ability to observe. We have great telescopes allowing us access to the macro-universe, and great microscopes with which we can peer into the micro-universe. Low and behold, the observations we can now make with our enhanced senses do not conform to the old Newtonian laws. At a sub-atomic level and at a galactic level, things do not happen in a way that is predictable, using the old laws. Our perceptions, as enhanced by modern technology, are showing us a different reality. It is interesting to note that our perceptions, as enhanced by the mystical methods such as meditation or shamanic trance, have also shown us a different reality. Both disciplines are saying that, even though we have an enhanced view—an expanded understanding of this different reality, it is unlikely that we will ever totally grasp the true nature of reality using only our rational minds.

Although some may feel that it is a waste of time to attempt to scientifically seek an understanding of reality, I believe it is useful to examine what science has to say and this section will attempt to do so. As well as coming to a renewed understanding of the workings of the universe, such an examination could also be useful as a means of cleaning the slate, liquefying old belief patterns and opening the mind to new possibilities. The observations of science over the past century have literally pulled the rug out from under our old ideas. Even though a hundred years have passed since the old views were shown to be inadequate, 99.9% of the population is totally unaware of the profoundly different view of reality that science is showing us. We continue to go about our business as though nothing has changed. Perhaps an examination of the new scientific paradigms would lead to more humility, to an awareness that we don't have it all figured out. Perhaps we would then think twice about the way we behave, about the reason we are all here.

The information in this chapter will be presented as simply as possible. I will try to present the essence of ideas, without getting bogged down with supportive detail. For example, I will not necessarily describe the series of experiments or means by which science may have arrived at a certain conclusion. If one desires a more detailed understanding, there are many good books available, and I would like to recommend some. The following books are translations of the mathematics of physicians into the plain English of the lay person. Even though the concepts are sometimes hard to grasp, usually because they are so defiant of our common sense perceptions and mental images, these books succeed in explaining them in a way that is comprehensible to the average reader. 'The Tao of Physics', by Fritjof Capra, offers a good explanation of the new physics (the theories of relativity and quantum mechanics), and extensive comparisons with mystical thought. 'The Dancing Wu Li Masters', by Gary Zukav, is an easy, entertaining description of the new physics with some allusion to the mystical connections. Brian Greene, in his book 'The Elegant Universe', discusses the latest development in scientific thought known as 'string theory'. It also includes a lucid and entertaining explanation of relativity and quantum physics, but does not mention any connections to mysticism. Another delightful book which I found helpful in understanding the workings of energy and the mechanics of consciousness is 'Stalking the Wild Pendulum' by Itzhak Bentov. Yet another book is 'Mysticism and the New Physics' by Michael Talbot. The information that I present in this section owes much to these sources.

A good way to begin to get a grasp of the new paradigms of modern science is to take a look at the *history of physics*. It goes back more than 2500 years to the early Greeks. The word 'physics' derives from a Greek word, 'physis', which means 'the essential nature of things'. In those days, schools of science, philosophy and mysticism were not separate disciplines, but rather a unified endeavor to discover physis. The disciples of the Milesian school in Ionia were called 'hylozoists', which means 'those who think matter is alive'. They saw no difference between matter and spirit. Thales saw all things as god-like manifestations; Anaximander saw the universe as an enormous organism supported by 'pneuma' or 'divine breath'. Heraclitus of Ephesus saw the universe as a constantly changing interplay of opposites, with each pair of opposites combining to form a whole, which he called the 'logos'. We can easily see the similarity of such views with those of the mystics.

This similarity to the mystical outlook slowly began to change. The Eleatic school began to embrace the view of a universe made up of various combinations of a basic, irreducible unit of matter. This universe was ruled by an unchanging, all-powerful supreme being. Around the time of Democritus and Leucippus, matter and spirit were seen as two separate things. Matter was made up of basic, lifeless building blocks that they called 'atoms'. This matter was subject to external forces or spirit. This notion of duality—the distinction between matter and spirit—was further established with Aristotle, and was reinforced by the Christian Church. By the Renaissance, science was beginning to be thought of as the kind of knowledge that could be tested, knowledge that was based on experimental research. Galileo, considered to be the father of modern science, combined this empirical knowledge with mathematics. The thing that science and mysticism still had in common was that they both relied on observation as the means of coming to understand reality. The big difference was that information that was not 'provable' to the five senses, via the empirical method, was no longer considered to be true science. Eventually, such non-testable information was dismissed as conjecture.

The Age of Reason had arrived. Rene Descartes stressed that mind and matter were two separate things, an idea that came to be called the 'Cartesian division'. The universe was seen as a huge complicated machine whose workings could be understood. This was known as the ***mechanistic view*** of the universe. Scientists, culminating with Newton circa 1700, began to define these workings—the laws by which this great machine operated. These laws were seen as the fundamental, unchanging dictums of a supreme, all-powerful God. In our everyday reality, these laws were very useful and they passed every test. Calculations based on these laws were (and are still) used by engineers as they constructed the technological wonders of the modern world.

At the end of the 19th century, the western definition of reality had become greatly different from the mystical eastern definition. According to the mystical interpretation, the universe was alive; an ever-changing, interconnected web. Spirit and matter were different aspects of the same thing. The forces that govern the universe, that affect all change and motion, were not external to matter. They were intrinsic aspects of matter. 'God' was not seen as a 'ruler', but as a principle. Western thought had evolved to become almost diametrically opposed to such views.[21]

By the beginning of the 20th century, however, this mechanistic view began to change dramatically. Max Planck, often called the father of quantum physics, showed that energy was not emitted or absorbed in a constant stream, but as a series of 'energy packets'. In 1905, Albert Einstein rocked the scientific world with the release of his Theory of Special Relativity. Space and time were no longer seen as separate entities. They were intimately connected in a 'time-space continuum'. Our three-dimensional reality was now four-dimensional, with time as the fourth dimension. With his famous equation, $E=mc^2$, Einstein declared that matter and energy were different aspects of the same thing; that any piece of matter was a storehouse of vast potential energy. In 1915 Einstein released his Theory of General Relativity. Gravity was now seen in a new way, as a force that 'curves' the fabric of space-time. The bodies of matter in the universe bent space-time itself, so that it could no longer be assumed that light or anything else traveled in a straight line, or that clocks everywhere kept the same time. Cosmic bodies and the space in which they existed were no longer seen as separate entities, but as part of an interconnected web or network. There was no such thing as empty space; every nook and cranny now seen as part of an enormous force field.

As the century unfolded and exploration of the quantum, sub-atomic world proceeded, a startling new picture began to emerge. In the quest to discover the basic building blocks of matter, it became evident that the nature of reality at the sub-atomic level was far different than anyone had previously imagined. Around 1930 Ernest Rutherford introduced the 'planetary model' of the atom, with planet-like particles called electrons revolving around a sun-like body consisting of a cluster of particles called neutrons and protons. This cluster was called the nucleus. Closer examination of these nuclear particles began to yield ever more astonishing observations; they consisted of many sub-particles that behaved in very strange ways. By 1935, a total of six particles had been discovered. By 1955 this number grew to eighteen. Currently science is aware of over 200 such particles and many scientists are still trying to find a 'basic building block', a sub-particle that is common to all particles and thus all matter. Before we take a look at these particles and their strange behaviour, and the subsequent implications about the nature of their reality, lets paint a picture of *matter as it appears at the sub-atomic level.*

If we magnify any blob of matter, we will start to see an emerging order. Combinations of atoms called molecules can be seen in orderly, repeating 'crystalline' patterns. Further magnification will isolate what seems to be solid atoms which, for the sake of clarity, we'll envision as ping-pong ball-like spheres. Let's demonstrate the size of an atom. It would take 100 million atoms laid side by side in a straight line to measure a centimetre in length. If a plum were the size of the planet, its atoms would be the size of ping-pong balls. In other words, the number of ping-pong balls packed together into a ball the size of Earth, would be the same as the number of atoms in a plum.

The solidity of the surface of the atom, the shell of the ping-pong ball, is an illusion. We know that a propeller, spinning at high speeds, effectively becomes a solid disc. Similarly, the shell of the ping-pong ball consists of several electrons whipping around the nucleus at the astounding speed of 600 miles per second. Thus, the shell seems solid. What is almost entirely empty space effectively becomes a sphere. To appreciate how much of an atom is empty space, visualize the atom magnified to the size of a football field. The nucleus would be the size of a tomato seed and the electrons orbiting at the perimeter of the football field would be the size of grains of salt. Because these electrons are orbiting at such speeds, the illusion of a solid shell is possible. The nucleus is very dense; its mass being almost 99% of the mass of the entire atom. The size of the nucleus, however, is only 1/100,000th the size of the entire atom.

However unimaginably small the nucleus may seem, it too is mostly space. The particles that make up the nucleus are moving even faster than the electrons, at a speed of 40,000 miles per second. It seems that, in the micro-universe, the smaller the space to which a particle is confined, the faster they are compelled to move. Other than the tiny particles, matter is almost entirely empty space. The thing is, further experimentation showed that even the particles are not solid. **There is no such thing as solid matter, in the way we typically think of it!**

By mid-century physicists were saying some things that were very different to the old physics and to the common sense way we tend to view reality. Some of these startling statements were:

- that sub-atomic particles were not small points of matter as we tend to visualize, but points of interacting energy fields
- these particles did not behave in a logical, predictable way, but seemed to be 'making decisions' on their own
- the role of the observer could no longer be thought of as arbitrary or objective—the presence of the observer affected the outcome of the experiment
- some particles traveled backward in time
- some particles seemed to appear out of nowhere, some disappeared
- two particles separated by a large distance are somehow connected, so that the behavior of one affects the other, etc.

The implications of such statements seem unimaginable. There's no such thing as matter! There's no such thing as an objective experiment! We can't really know anything! What appears to be matter seems to have its own consciousness! Our standard understanding of cause and effect is meaningless! These implications defy our common sense and are very hard to understand. We'll try to explain some of these phenomena later.

It could be said that, by the latter part of the century, theoretic physics was splitting into two directions; the larger faction, those that think more like the 'old way' are still pursuing the particle that is the basic building block of all matter. The best contender for this title is a group of particles called quarks. The other branch, those that think more in the 'new way', were examining all kinds of possibilities, including the notion that mind affects matter, that consciousness itself is a force—maybe the ultimate force. One of the latest branches of physics has put forth an explanatory model known as 'String Theory'. It contends that particles are not 'points' of matter, but consist of vibrating loops of energy called 'strings'. It claims that, as well as the four dimensions currently acknowledged, there are seven more,—that our universe consists of a total of eleven dimensions.

Now that we have looked at the chronological history of physics, we may have a vague idea of the magnitude of the change in scientific thought that has evolved. Hopefully we have gained an overview, a general knowledge of the scientific revolution of the 20th century. As this section progresses, we'll discuss in greater detail some of the specific components of the new physics in four sections; special relativity, general relativity, quantum mechanics and string theory. We'll try to get a better understanding of some of the key concepts of the new physics and the ways in which they accord with mystical thought.

THE SPECIAL THEORY OF RELATIVITY

One of the first developments in physics to challenge Newton's laws and the mechanistic view happened in the mid-1800s with the work of Michael Faraday and Clerk Maxwell. They studied force fields, regions that have a 'charged condition' which exerts an effect on objects. Whereas classical physics saw force fields as being connected to or generated by a body of matter, new studies showed that they were entities unto themselves. A field has a reality of its own, independent of any body. This led to the theory of electrodynamics which showed that x-rays, radio waves, gamma rays, infra-red, ultraviolet and visible light are aspects of electro-magnetic radiation—parts of the electro-magnetic spectrum, a field that moves through the universe at the speed of light. Different aspects of this vast field are actually bands of wave frequencies. Visible light is that narrow portion of this spectrum of frequencies that are perceivable by our sense of sight.

Along came a humble patent clerk named *Albert Einstein* who was about to stand the scientific world on its ear. He was concerned with the incongruities and conflicts between the physics of Newton and that of electrodynamics. According to the inadvertent results of groundbreaking experiments by Albert Michelson and Edward Morley, light (or any part of the electro-magnetic spectrum) always moved at the speed of 186,000 miles per second, no matter what the relative speed of the observer. No matter how fast one is moving, one cannot catch up to a light beam. Picture this: a spaceship and a light beam leave the same spot at the same time. The Spaceship is travelling at 180,000 miles per second. It stands to reason that the light from that source should be moving away from the spaceship at 6,000 miles per second. 186,000 – 180,000 = 6,000. But this is not the case. If you were following the light beam at 180,000 miles per second, it would still be moving away from you at the speed of light, 186,000 miles per second!

This result, which has been subsequently tested many times in many ways, completely defies common sense. Galileo's 'principle of relativity' and all of classical physics up to that point in time stated that the speed of light, like the speed of anything else, should be relative to the speed of the observer. The Michelson-Morley experiments showed that this was not the case. As difficult as this is for us to accept with our common sense, it was equally difficult for science to accept. However, it was only the beginning of many more developments that would seriously challenge our way of perceiving reality.

It was this quandary regarding the speed of light that Einstein set out to solve. In 1905 he published his Special Theory of Relativity. It claimed that our notions about *space and time* were inaccurate; that space was not three-dimensional and that time was not something that was separate from space. Time did not flow in a uniform, absolute way, unaffected by circumstances such as velocity. A clock on a speeding spaceship will not measure time in the same way as a clock at rest. Space and time can actually differ according to different observers. This is because time and space are intrinsically connected and can no longer be thought of as separate things. Time was the fourth dimension, part of the *space-time continuum*.

A clock, or any type of time-measuring device, counts time more slowly the faster it is moving. This is only the case as it appears to someone at rest. Someone travelling at the same speed as the clock will notice no discrepancy. An observer at point A, reading a clock that is aboard a fast moving spaceship, point B, will yield different results than from a clock that is with him at point A. The clock at point B will show the observer at point A that time has elapsed more slowly at point B than at point A. For an observer at point B, however, his clock will seem to be running fine, and the clock at point A will seem to be running slower. Time is relative to one's motion through the fabric of space-time.

Similarly, a ruler being used to measure a distance in space will become shorter, the faster it moves through space. This will only be the case as it appears to someone at rest. Someone travelling at the same speed as the ruler will notice no difference. To an observer at point A, the twelve-inch ruler moving at point B will appear shorter than the twelve-inch ruler in his hands. To the observer at point B, his ruler seems fine, but the ruler at point A seems shorter to him.

This may make a bit more sense if it is understood that no one can say for sure whether it is point A or point B that is in motion. This is the principle of relativity. To make this clear, let us imagine that point A and point B are floating out in space with no gravity or atmosphere to confuse us. Point A feels stationary, while point B is hurtling away. From point B's perspective, however, it is the one at rest and it is point A that is hurtling away. Our perceptions of space and time are relative to our perspective. Traditionally, both the passage of time and a distance in space were thought to be constant and universal. Special relativity has changed that.

One might ask, 'How does this explain that the speed of light remains constant no matter what the relative speed of the observer?' It is the velocity at which the measuring tools are moving that distorts them, thus distorting the measurement. To an observer at rest, the clock and ruler in motion are distorted and thus their measurement of the speed of light will be distorted. To the observer moving with the clock and ruler, there is no distortion. To both observers, their measurement of the speed of light will be the same. The ruler moving toward the light source will be shorter, and so the shortened distance to the light source will still measure the same number of ruler lengths. Thus the stationary perspective and the moving perspective will both yield the same number of ruler lengths—the same measurement.

The amount of distortion, which depends on the speed of the moving tools, is very closely related to the speed of light. The higher the speed, the shorter the ruler. This happens in a specific way; no matter the speed, the ruler will always be shortened so that the same number of ruler lengths will be required to measure the distance to the light source. At the speeds that are familiar to our normal, daily experience, the ruler would be shortened to a very small degree. At such earthly speeds, the length of the moving ruler is so close to the length of the stationary ruler that the difference is virtually unnoticeable. As speeds approach 186,000 miles per second, however, the differences become much greater. To a stationary observer, a ruler moving at 87% of the speed of light will be shortened along its direction of motion, and will appear half-length. At 98% of light speed it will have only 20% of its original length. At 186,000 miles per second the ruler, from the perspective of the stationary observer, will disappear. The amount of distortion increases dramatically as light speed is approached.

The same is true of time, which slows down to an increasing degree as light speed is approached. A clock moving at 186,000 miles per second, from the perspective of the stationary observer, seems to be recording no time at all. Time seems to be standing still. A third observation made by relativity theory is that the mass of a moving object increases as it approaches light speed. At the speed of light its mass becomes infinite. This is why it is impossible for an object to move faster than light.

In order to truly make sense of this, we must suspend our common-sense view of the universe and try to understand that time and space are actually inseparable; part of the same thing; something that has been named space-time. So the fabric that makes up our physical reality is space-time. One cannot speak of the precise location of an event without including time. The event occurs at a certain place in three-dimensional space, as well as at a certain place in time. Everything that happens involves all four dimensions. The measurement of speed involves both space (distance) and time. Miles per hour equals distance per time. The speed at which we are moving is 'shared' by all four dimensions. According to relativity theory, and this is very hard to grasp, we are always moving at the speed of light. When we are stationary, i.e., not moving through space, we are moving through time at the speed of light—all of our motion involves the dimension of time. The faster we move through space, the slower we move through time, so that the combination always adds up to the speed of light. Said another way, time is equal to the speed of light minus the speed at which we are moving through space. Thus, to be travelling through space at the speed of light, time would be at a standstill. To be stationary means that all of one's motion is being taken up by the time dimension. The speed at which we exist is always the same, shared by all four dimensions. Time and space are inseparable aspects of the same thing.

Still confused are we? Have no fear. It took me ages to figure this out. If you think this kind of stuff is difficult to read, you should see what it's like to try to articulate and explain it. Although it is fun and useful to truly understand this new science, for the purpose of this book, it is not necessary. It is more important to see this development in science as a lesson to mankind; an invitation to let go of preconceived convictions, even if they are deeply ingrained, and to open our minds to new possibilities. It is more important to realize that our ability to understand the nature of reality is limited by our five-sensory experience of life. Much of the new science is showing us that our everyday sensory reality does not represent the greater reality. At the speeds to which we have become accustomed in our everyday experience, the distortions of time and space revealed by special relativity are not noticeable. This is why the calculations based on Newton's laws fit so well with those of relativity. At speeds that approach that of light, however, the two approaches don't agree at all. In other words, our five-sensory experience does not give us an accurate picture of the nature of reality. It gives us an illusion.

Speaking of illusion, let's now take a look at another aspect of relativity, Einstein's famous equation, $E=mc^2$. This is the translation: if you take a chunk of matter, multiply the mass of that matter (m) by the speed of light (c) squared, you get the amount of potential energy in the piece of matter. In other words, to use Einstein's own words, "Mass and energy are both different manifestations of the same thing"[2]. There is an enormous amount of energy in a small piece of matter and we'll be looking at the nuclear forces involved in holding an atom together in the section on quantum mechanics.

Let's quickly review the main philosophical lessons of special relativity:
- time does not flow in an absolute, universal, equable way
- time and space are inseparable aspects of the same thing
- matter and energy are aspects of the same thing
- everything in the universe is in motion, relative to something else
- no physical entity can move faster than the speed of light
- we cannot trust our common-sense experience for a clear picture of reality.

As difficult as it is to thoroughly understand these things, it is important to realize that they come from strong theories that have been subjected to rigorous testing. The mathematics of special relativity have proven to be very effective at predicting phenomena.

THE GENERAL THEORY OF RELATIVITY;

With special relativity, Einstein resolved the problem of the consistency of the speed of light regardless of relative perspective. In its wake, however, was another quandary. According to Newton, all bodies exerted a force of gravity, the larger the body, the greater the force; the smaller the distance between two bodies, the greater the force. This force acted like a tether on other bodies within its range. Newton's laws of gravity can be used to accurately predict the motion of cosmic bodies, as well as earthbound bodies. According to Newton, the effects of gravity were instantaneous—if the sun ceased to exist, its gravitational influence would cease instantly. According to special relativity, nothing can move faster than light, and since the light from the sun takes nine seconds to reach us, the force of its gravity should also take this long. Or, to make a long story short, the quandary was that special relativity did not explain *gravity*.

Einstein tackled this problem by acknowledging that accelerated motion could approximate gravity. Accelerated motion is defined as motion whose speed is increasing or decreasing, or the direction of motion is changing. As your car is accelerating, for example, your back feels a pressure against the seat back which is much like the effects of gravity. Centrifugal force is a type of accelerated motion whereby the direction of motion is changing. If you are on a midway ride that spins, you will be pushed against the outer wall in a way that is similar to gravity. A space station is built like a spinning wheel (like the one in the movie '2001, A Space Odyssey') so that it can simulate gravity.

By studying accelerated motion, Einstein came up with his general theory of relativity, which was released in 1915. He proclaimed that gravity existed because massive objects were causing the fabric of space-time to bend or warp. Again, this is very difficult to visualize, and requires that we let go of our common sense views. Try to imagine that empty space and the massive objects that it contains are not separate, but part of the same thing. There is no such thing as empty space. The entire universe is composed of a 'fabric' that includes stuff that we call space, and stuff that we call matter. The space and the matter are intrinsically connected. They are connected in such a way that, when a body of matter is present, it causes the space around it to warp.

The best way to visualize this is to imagine that space is represented by a latex rubber membrane on which straight grid lines, similar to lines of latitude and longitude, are drawn. If we were to sit a bowling ball in the middle of this latex membrane, it would sink somewhat, because of the ball's weight. The grid lines would bend. The lines closest to the ball would be bent to a greater degree than the lines further from the ball. If we were to roll a marble towards the bowling ball, it would be drawn into the ball by the downward bend of the latex membrane. (See **DIAGRAM 2—THE FABRIC OF SPACE-TIME**)

DIAGRAM 2—THE FABRIC OF SPACE-TIME

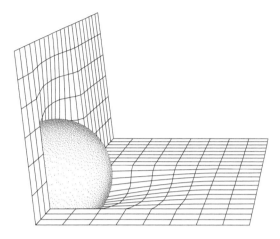

The gravity of a large object warps the fabric of space-time.

This is just an analogy to help one imagine the way that space is bent by a massive object. However, it is actually impossible to truly visualize the bending of space. There are several reasons for this. Firstly, the membrane in the analogy represents only one thin, two-dimensional plane of space. But, of course, the surrounding space is three dimensional, completely engulfing the massive object. All of the space around the ball is warped. Secondly, as we have established with special relativity, space and time are inseparable. Therefore, it is the fabric of space-time that is warped by the presence of the massive object. Time is also affected by the presence of massive objects. There is no tether between cosmic bodies. There is no empty space. It may be difficult for our three-dimensional minds to picture four-dimensional space-time, but deductions based on this premise have proven to be accurate.

Picture the universe, then as a hilly, curvy 'terrain' or 'topography'. Woven into this lumpy fabric are the various chunks of matter. This picture implies a static universe, but of course, everything is in constant motion. One could say that matter causes a warping of the space-time continuum, although it would be more accurate to say that matter **is** the warping of the space-time continuum. No object could truly travel in a straight line through such a terrain. Neither could time travel uniformly through such a terrain. They would be affected by the gravitational force of the massive cosmic bodies. Objects move through space-time along paths of least resistance, so that if the space is warped, the paths will be curved. In the words of physicist, John Wheeler, "Mass grips space by telling it how to curve, and space grips mass by telling it how to move".[22]

Einstein predicted that the path of a beam of light would be bent by passing near a large body. This was put to the test on May 29, 1919, during a solar eclipse. The position of the stars relative to each other has been mapped to a high degree of accuracy. This mapping has taken place at night because, during daylight, we cannot see the stars. At night the Earth is between the stars and the sun, so the light from a star at night does not pass by the sun on its way to the eye of an observer on Earth. The path of this light would not be affected by the sun's gravity. The key question was—does the sun's gravity affect the path of light from a star if that path passes close to the sun during daylight? The eclipse gave us the opportunity to test this. Pictures of the stars taken during the darkness of the eclipse were compared to the familiar map of that same section of sky. They showed that the positions of the stars that were closest to the sun were different than their typical positions. The paths of the light coming from them had bent slightly as they passed the sun. The world was very excited by this verification of Einstein's very precise prediction. It has been subsequently verified many more times, in many more ways, as technology has become more sophisticated.

General relativity has had some very interesting by-products. Matter is affected in many ways by gravity. It has been shown that matter vibrates at a slower frequency when in the presence of greater gravity. Sodium atoms from the sun have longer wave-lengths than sodium from Earth. Time is also affected by gravity; the greater the gravitational force, the slower the flow of time.

Based on Einstein's theory, German astronomer, Karl Schwartzschild predicted the existence of **black holes**. These are regions in space-time of incredibly strong gravitational force; so strong that matter is crushed out of existence. This implosion is so strong that even light that is within a certain distance cannot escape; hence the name 'black hole'. The distance around a black hole at which the gravitational force exerts its iron grip, the point of no return, is called the 'event horizon'. A clock dangling within the event horizon would be slowed down greatly. Matter would be pulled apart—it would disintegrate. At the center of the black hole matter would be compressed to densities that are beyond imagining. If our entire planet was condensed to such a degree, it would be reduced to the size of a cherry, while retaining all of its mass. Many years after Schwartzschild's prediction, there is a growing body of very convincing evidence that black holes do in fact exist. Astronomers now believe that, at the center of our galaxy—the Milky Way, there is a black hole that is 2 million times as massive as our sun.

Using his equations of general relativity, Einstein claimed that the universe is constantly expanding. Years later, precise observations of the relative positions of distant galaxies and detailed measurements by astronomer, Edwin

Hubble, have verified Einstein's contention. From these observations came the theory of **the Big Bang**. It has been deduced that, about 15 billion years ago, the entire universe was compressed to the size of a tiny pin-prick. More accurately, it was said to have been compressed into nothingness, compressed out of existence. For some unknown reason, the point began to rapidly expand. Although many refer to the big bang as an explosion, it was probably more like an unfolding of the space-time continuum. An explosion implies that space already existed.

An interesting point about the Big Bang is that, according to calculations, it should have produced an equal amount of matter and anti-matter. (Anti-matter has an elecrical charge and nuclear charges that are opposite to matter.) This should have resulted in the two amounts canceling each other out. Some mysterious mechanism produced an excess of matter, which led to the formation of galaxies, stars, planets, etc.

Based on Einstein's equations, scientists have been able to calculate the quantity of matter in the universe—and thus the amount of gravity required to hold the universe together. This sum turns out to be much larger than the amount of matter that science has detected in the universe. All the matter that scientists can find adds up to only 4% of what is required to hold it all together. The work of scientists such as Vera Rubin, Chris Stubbs and Stephen Hawking suggests that dark matter accounts for the remaining mass. Dark matter is a type of substance which we are not able to see and scientists have several theories attempting to define it. Stubbs suggests massive, condensed, invisible stars. Others say it is comprised of chargeless particles such as neutrinos, neutralinos and axions. According to Hawking, this dark matter will eventually cause the universe to start contracting back to a 'Big Crunch'.

In Hawking's words, "The evidence suggests that much of the universe is made up of something no-one has ever seen." It has been proven that some form of dark matter[23] exists, but the nature of it is still unknown. Whatever it is, it's not like the stuff we're made of. Although our knowledge of the universe has grown in leaps and bounds, there are still many calculations and observations that don't add up.

Let's take a moment to review the main philosophical lessons of general relativity:

• there is no such thing as empty space
• gravity is a result of the warping of the space-time fabric
• it cannot be assumed that light travels through space in a straight line
• time does not unfold uniformly
• time, space and matter are all interwoven aspects of the same thing
• everything in the universe may once have existed as a tiny point

- we cannot trust our common-sense experience for a clear picture of reality.

As difficult as it is to thoroughly understand these things, it is important to realize that they come from strong theories that have been subjected to rigorous testing. The mathematics of general relativity has proven to be very effective at predicting phenomena.

QUANTUM MECHANICS;

Before the year 1900, scientists thought that energy moved in a smooth, continuous flow. German physicist, Max Planck ushered in the new century with the discovery that this was not the case, that energy was absorbed and emitted in tiny 'packets'. Einstein named these packets 'quanta', which means a quantity of something. Over the next few decades, thanks to the efforts of physicists such as Niels Bohr, Louis De Broglie, Erwin Schroedinger, Werner Heisenberg, Max Born, Paul Dirac and others, quantum mechanics came of age.

Basically, quantum physics or mechanics is the study of the way things work at a microscopic, sub-atomic level. Over the past hundred years, investigation at that level has yielded some radically bizarre observations. Things happen at a quantum level that are completely foreign to our everyday perceptions of reality. In this realm, Newton's laws just don't work. However, the formulas and equations of quantum mechanics have proven to be very precise and accurate in predicting the strange workings of the sub-atomic realm. As difficult as it is to accept these bizarre phenomena, thousands and thousands of observations and experiments have reinforced these findings. And yet, physicists have no idea as to **why** things are the way they are in the micro-universe.

Underlying the birth of quantum physics was the quest for the true nature of light. Is it a stream of particles, or is it energy carried by wave patterns? In 1887, German physicist Heinrich Hertz discovered that light could displace electrons on certain metals. This phenomenon, known as the ***photo-electric effect***, strongly suggested that light was a stream of particles that, upon striking the surface of the metal plate, could knock some of the metal's electrons loose. The more intense (bright) the light beam, the more electrons were displaced.

The problem was that, back in 1800, some famous experiments conducted by Thomas Young showed that light behaved like waves of energy. Throughout most of my abbreviated presentation of modern physics, I have avoided describing the complicated experiments and means by which science has drawn its conclusions. In this case, however, our understanding of quantum mechanics will be greatly facilitated by discussing the ***double slit experiments***, as they have been used throughout the history of quantum science.

Picture parallel waves of water (with wavelengths that are equal) coming in to shore. Before they reach the shore they meet an obstacle, a wall with a slit in it that is narrower than the wavelengths of the water. As the water goes through this slit, it will no longer move in straight parallel lines, but will fan out and move in a semicircular fashion as if a stone had been dropped in still water at the location of the slit. (See **DIAGRAM 3—DOUBLE SLIT EXPERIMENT**) This is behavior that is characteristic of wave motion, known as 'diffraction'. All waves behave in this way. It stands to reason that, if light was a wave phenomenon, the same thing should happen. What would happen if a beam of light is shone onto a surface into which a fine slit has been cut? This slit is narrower than the light's wavelength. The same thing happens. Light behaves like a wave. What if we had two slits, side by side and parallel to each other? In the case of every other type of wave, the semicircular motion of the waves beyond the slit run into each other and 'interfere' with each other. This is called an 'interference pattern'. Does light also behave in this way? Yes it does.

We can now see the problem. The photo-electric effect suggests that light is a stream of particles. However, according to Young and his double slit experiments, light is a wave. How can it be both? How can light be both particles of matter and waves of energy? This is probably science's most famous paradox, which has been called the **wave-particle duality**. As weird as it may seem that light is both matter and energy, hang on, it gets even weirder.

DIAGRAM 3—DOUBLE SLIT EXPERIMENT

DIAGRAM 3—A

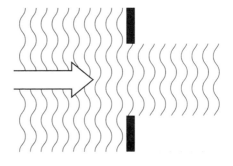

DIAGRAM 3—B

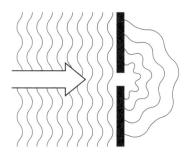

In Diagram 3—A we see waves moving through a slit that is wider than the wave-length. In Diagram 3-B the slit is narrower than the wave-length, causing the waves to fan out in a semi-circular pattern. If there were two slits, the two semi-circular patterns would interfere with each other.

During the early 1900s, countless double slit experiments were undertaken as scientists tried to solve the mystery of the wave-particle duality. When light is shone through the slits, it records its pattern by striking a photographic plate, which is set up beyond the slits. When only one slit is open, the light shining through it makes the shape of a narrow band or line on the photographic plate. This bright, narrow band of light is the same shape as the slit that it has just passed through. When both slits are open, the marks on the plate should look like two bands, the same shapes as the two slits. Instead, they form a group of parallel bands, some bright, some not so bright and some dark. The two paths of light emerging from the two slits interfere with each other in the typical way that energy behaves. This typical interference pattern is already a strange phenomenon, because light is behaving like energy and not a stream of particles. What comes next is even stranger.

Individual particles of light are called photons. When experimenters fire them at the plate one at a time, while only one slit is open, they take the expected straight trajectory and land at the predictable spot on the plate. One photon, if it makes it through the slit, leaves a tiny mark on the photographic plate. When enough of them are fired, the tiny marks on the plate take on the shape of the slit. They look like a narrow band of light in the same way as the beam of light described above. What happens when both slits are open, with single photons being fired through only one of the slits? The trajectory of the single photon is changed. It no longer lands where expected, but lands in accordance with the interference pattern! If enough individual photons are fired, we eventually get the same interference pattern mentioned above. How does each individual photon know where to go? How does the photon know whether only one slit is open or that both are open? We don't know the answer to these questions, the 'hows' and the 'whys'. We just know, from the results of countless experiments, that this is what happens! It's as if the particles are making decisions, have their own consciousness, or are somehow being informed by some force as to where to go.

In 1924, Louis De Broglie took this to the next step. He showed that electrons and all particles also behave in this wave-like way. They all seem to be making these decisions about what path to take beyond the slits. In other words, at a sub-atomic level, all matter behaves the same way as light. These experiments have shown that we can never be sure where an electron will land. We can, however, predict where, within the interference pattern, an electron is likely to land. In other words, we can make certain predictions based on 'probability'. In fact such predictions of probability can be made with astonishing precision, using mathematical formulas like those developed by Physicist, Erwin Schrodinger, called the *equation of wave function*.

Whereas, with the Newtonian mechanistic view, it was felt that future outcomes could be predicted with certainty, now it seemed that only probable futures could be predicted. Particles seemed to be choosing their paths, choosing their futures. Why should a particle care whether both slits are open? One attempt to explain this mystery was offered in the late 1940s by Richard Feynman, who suggested that each electron actually takes countless paths before striking the plate. Each of these paths represents its own future, its own time-line. In other words, one electron can have many possible futures. When these ideas were tested with a mathematical formalism, with each path being assigned a numerical value and then averaged out, they yielded the same results as the wave function equation. Both approaches, although completely different conceptually, are equivalent and yield identical results. A quote from Feynman may be appropriate at this point. "Quantum mechanics describes nature as absurd from the point of view of common sense. And it fully agrees with experiment. So I hope you can accept nature as she is—absurd."[24] Another theory having to do with time-lines was put forth by scientists Everett, Wheeler and Graham in 1957 called the Many Worlds Interpretation of Quantum Mechanics. It states that all the possible outcomes, as suggested by the wave function equation, actually happen. Each of these happenings represents a different time-line, a series of parallel universes that are unaware of each other.[25]

In 1927 Werner Heisenberg had put forth *the principle of uncertainty*. It showed that one could not know, with certainty, both the exact position and the velocity or momentum of a particle. The role of the experimenter could not be objective or incidental. The effort of the observer to 'shed light' on an experiment affected the outcome of the experiment. The light needed to observe an electron could change the velocity or position of the electron. The efforts to pinpoint the location of an electron cause it to move faster. At the quantum level, it is impossible to objectively observe. In his book, 'Physics and Philosophy', Heisenberg writes, "What we observe is not nature itself, but nature exposed to our method of questioning."[26] The whole idea of a causal universe, one where specific causes yield specific effects, is undermined by the uncertainty principle.

Various explorations throughout the century have yielded more and more quantum weirdness. At the sub-atomic level, matter is continually manifesting and de-manifesting. Particles are transforming into entirely different particles, usually as a result of a collision with another particle. Certain conditions result in particles materializing out of what appears to be nothing. Just as quickly, they disappear. When a particle of matter (such as an electron) meets a particle of anti-matter (such as a positron), they cancel each other out, transforming into two photons, which then split the scene at the speed of light. Even a chunk of what we call empty space, when magnified to such a degree, displays the same mad frenzy. All of the various forms of energy exchange and fluctuation cancel out to form the appearance of smooth tranquillity at the normal level of reality. This obscures the reality of the micro-universe—a roiling, turbulent place, with particles zipping around at wild speeds, bumping into each other, creating and annihilating each other—a land-scape that John Wheeler named **quantum foam**.

Scientists became painfully aware of a problem in modern physics; the turbulence of the quantum foam does not jibe with the tenets of relativity, especially general relativity. The equations of general relativity, when mingled with those from quantum mechanics, yield results that are nonsense. One theory serves well in describing the macro-universe, the other describes the micro-universe, yet the two are incompatible. The smooth model of space-time and the equations of general relativity do not yield a description that matches the quantum foam. Scientists began to search for a model to resolve this disagreement.

An effort was made to better understand the nature of these particles with their erratic behavior. What is a particle? In our mind's eye, we can't help but visualize a small, irreducible point of matter, similar to a tiny billiard ball. When particles collide, we see billiard balls bouncing off of each other. Even physicists tend to see particles this way, even though they are well aware that our language and the linear type of thinking that it represents is not capable of perceiving the true picture of a particle. A particle's true nature is much more abstract than a billiard ball. While attempting to merge quantum mechanics with general relativity, science came up with a theory that offers a different concept of a particle.

This theory is called **quantum field theory**. In short, it says that all of reality is composed of interacting force fields. Particles are tiny points of interaction between fields. The continual creation and annihilation of particles is the result of fluctuations in these interactions. This is hard to visualize because a field is spread out over a large area, like a gravitational field surrounding a planet, while a particle is an unimaginably tiny point. One must completely surrender one's preconceived notions of reality to envision this. It is yet another paradox. Fortunately for scientists, their understanding does not depend on their ability to envision. They rely less upon their mental pictures because this new and strange reality makes sense when described in the language of mathematics. In this way, the predictions made with quantum field theory agree spectacularly with experimental results.

According to field theory, there are four basic forces that hold the universe together. Actually, it would be more accurate to say that these forces are the universe. In any case, the four forces, in order of their strength, are: the strong nuclear force, the electromagnetic force, the weak nuclear force and the gravitational force. The strong force is the one that holds the nucleus of an atom together. It must be strong enough to overcome the electro-magnetic force that wants to push the positively charged particles apart. This is the enormous force that is released from a small amount of matter in a nuclear explosion. The next force, the electro-magnetic, is the one that holds the orbiting electron to the nucleus, and is thus the agent by which atoms bond with other atoms to form molecules, resulting in all the various forms of matter. There is another force, about which less is know and which has something to do with the radioactive decomposition of unstable elements such as uranium or cobalt; it is called the weak force. The mildest of all the forces is the gravitational force. This may seem strange because we picture it as an incredibly strong force, especially in the case of black holes. However, it is only strong when associated with cosmic bodies having enormous mass. Also, forces of gravity are solely attractive, while electro-magnetic forces are both attractive and repulsive, so they tend to cancel each other out. At the quantum level, with the tiny masses that exist there, the force of gravity is insignificant. The strong force is about 100 times as strong as the electro-magnetic force, 100,000 times as strong as the weak force, and billions of times stronger than the gravitational force. The range of the strong force, however, is very shallow.

At this point it might be interesting to pause and admire the delicate precision of balance that exists between these forces. The strengths of each force must be very specific for matter and the universe to exist. Just the right ratio of strength between the strong force and the electro-magnetic force maintains the integrity of the atom, the molecule and all matter. If the strength of gravitational forces were any different, it would mean a different relationship between cosmic bodies and the forces governing the functioning of stars. Stars would not form and thus matter would not form. The existence of the universe depends on the balance of forces.

Physicists have discovered over 200 different types of particles. Some of these, such as electrons, muons, neutrinos and quarks are 'matter' particles, which have been divided into three families. Others are 'force' particles, corresponding to each of the forces. There is a field theory for each force and its related particles. Again, the equations from these theories yield highly accurate results. Certain particles carry the 'message' of the force that they represent. The photon carries the message of electro-magnetic force, the gluon carries the message of the strong force, and the weak gauge bosons for the weak force. As of yet, there has been no discovery of a particle corresponding to the gravitational force, although one, called the graviton, has been hypothesized. The ongoing process of categorizing and characterizing these forces and particles, which has come about as a result of extremely accurate observation and documentation, is called the *standard model.*

Some of the most interesting and astonishing developments in particle physics are the ones that demonstrate the interconnectedness of things. This field of study gained more momentum in the 1980s, but it started in 1935 when Einstein, Boris Podolsky and Nathan Rosen conducted what came to be called the EPR experiments. A particle has three qualities; mass, charge and direction of spin. Without getting into too much detail, imagine that a particle can spin or rotate on its axis in either a clockwise or a counterclockwise direction. A two-particle system of zero spin is equal to two particles with opposite spin that cancel each other out. The two particles have a total of zero spin. In such a system, if one were to reverse the direction of spin on one particle, the direction of spin in its twin particle would also reverse. They would still have a total of zero spin. This raises an obvious question; how does particle B know that the spin of particle A has been reversed? What is even more remarkable, if particle A and particle B are separated by great distance, the same thing still happens! What's more, it seems to happen instantaneously, at a speed that is 'superluminal', faster than the speed of light. This is not supposed to be possible.

These results and the attempts to explain them, caused a good deal of controversy amongst physicists. One faction, which included Niels Bohr, contended that the two particles were part of an interconnected system, an indivisible whole,—no matter how far apart they were. The other faction, led by Einstein, could not accept that the signal passing from one particle to the other could be superluminal, or that a cause that happens a great distance away could produce such an effect. But Bohr claimed that the message between particles did not travel like a conventional signal and that we had to step out of our conventional views to try to understand this phenomenon.

A big step in the process of resolving this debate occurred in 1964, when physicist J. S. Bell published a mathematical proof called ***Bell's Theorum***. It showed mathematically that Bohr was right, the universe is interconnected; one can no longer think in terms of independent elements separated by space, or of classical notions of 'cause and effect'. Things happen as a result of causes that exist elsewhere. Bell's Theorem was a mathematical proof, a hypothetical construct. But in 1972, experiments by Clauser and Freedman, and then by Alain Aspect in 1982, confirmed the findings of Bell's equations. This represents a radical departure from our traditional ways of perceiving the universe. Many, including physicist Henry Stapp, believe this to be among the most important of all scientific developments.

A complicated mathematical framework, called 'S-matrix', was introduced by Werner Heisenberg in the forties and has been developed over the decades. The philosophical offshoots of S-matrix theory are very profound. It predicts that the universe cannot be observed objectively because the role of the observer is itself a causal factor. The setting up and measuring of an experiment, for example, become factors in the outcome of the experiment. This is most obvious in the experiments to determine the nature of light, as described earlier. If the observer sets up the 'photo-electric experiment', light reveals itself to be a stream of particles; if the 'double slit experiment' is set up, light reveals itself to be waves of energy. The very intent of the experimenter becomes a factor affecting the outcome of the experiment.

Physicist, Henry Stapp, writing in the 1970s says that the basic problem with sub-atomic observations is that, "the observed system is required to be isolated in order to be defined, yet interacting in order to be observed."[27] We cannot separate the observer from the observed. John Wheeler, in his book, 'The Physicist's Conception of Nature', says that the word 'observer' should be replaced by the word 'participator.'[28] This has many implications. Similar to the conclusions drawn by that famous gathering of physicians in the late 1920s called the Copenhagen Interpretation of Quantum Theory, it suggests that we can really know nothing with certainty. It implies that we are all part of a vast, cosmic web and that the actions of any part somehow affect the whole. It ultimately implies that the natural phenomena that we observe are products of our assessing, measuring minds—our consciousness.

In the latter part of the century some of the most profound thought in modern physics has grown out of S-matrix, with the work of Geoffrey Chew, chairman of the physics department at Berkeley, and David Bohm of the University of London. Their 'works in progress' suggest strongly that the universe cannot be thought of as separate parts, but must be seen as an interconnected, dynamic web of relationships. They also claim that, ultimately, no meaningful discussion of the nature of reality can occur without recognizing that *consciousness* itself is a key aspect. In fact, consciousness may be **the** key aspect.

Let's take a moment to review the main philosophical lessons of quantum mechanics:

- light behaves both like waves of energy and particles of matter
- not just photons, but all particles behave this way
- under certain circumstances, particles seem to be 'making their own decisions'
- we can know nothing with absolute certainty, but can only make predictions of probable outcomes
- the possibility exists that there are many time-lines or parallel universes
- objective observation is impossible—the role of the observer has the potential to affect the outcome of an experiment
- at any point within the time-space continuum, matter is continually manifesting and demanifesting
- a particle is not a tiny chunk of matter, but a point at which force-fields interact
- the universe exists because of a delicate balance of forces
- the universe is not a series of independent parts, but an interconnected system, an indivisible whole
- consciousness itself seems to be a key aspect of reality
- we cannot trust our common-sense experience for a clear picture of reality.

As difficult as it is to thoroughly understand these things, it is important to realize that they come from strong theories that have been subjected to rigorous testing. The mathematics of quantum mechanics has proven to be very effective at predicting phenomena.

STRING THEORY

"When these little strings vibrate, they create notes and we believe these notes are in fact the subatomic particles that we see around us. The melodies that these notes can play out is called 'matter' and when these melodies create symphonies, that's called the 'universe'."[29]

—*physicist, Michio Kaku*

It is the dream of most physicists to discover 'the unified theory of everything', a theory that explains every aspect of how the universe works. Physicists are divided into two main groups, those that feel that consciousness itself is a big part of any definition of reality, and those that are still looking for the basic, irreducible building blocks of the universe. This second group is the larger of the two. Many of the physicists in this group are now working enthusiastically on a new development, which they believe could well be the theory of everything (TOE). It's called string theory, short for superstring theory or supersymmetry string theory.

Pioneered by scientists like John Schwartz, Joel Scherk and Michael Green, string theory was largely ignored until the mid-1980s, when a renewed interest led to what has been called the 'first superstring revolution'. The movement gained momentum and by 1995 the 'second superstring revolution' was ushered in by physicist, Edward Witten. The international community of physicists was becoming excited by string theory's potential to solve the problem of incompatibility between quantum mechanics and general relativity, to explain the makeup of all matter and all forces, and to radically change our understanding of the space-time continuum.

String theory contends that the basic building blocks of the universe are not point particles, tiny lumps of matter analogous to quantum billiard balls. Instead they are tiny loops of thread-like filaments, called strings, which are vibrating or oscillating. These loops are truly fundamental to all matter and forces and are 'uncuttable' or irreducible. Each loop oscillates in a specific way, with a specific amount of energy. It is this pattern of vibration that distinguishes one loop from the other. In other words, every different type of particle, each of the particles in the standard model, is actually a string vibrating in a specific way. Every particle is made of the same 'stuff'. This is a radical departure from the previous standard model, which viewed each type of particle as uniquely different from the others. As it thus explains the makeup of all matter and all forces, string theory began to be hailed as a possible 'TOE'—*theory of everything*.

To qualify as a TOE, it is necessary to explain many aspects of reality, and the mathematical formalism built around string theory does so admirably. The elegant orderliness of the theory's potential to mathematically describe the universe made many physicists very excited. The problem is that, so far, the theory is un-testable. Strings exist at a micro-level so small that it is beyond the means of modern technology. A string is said to be approximately the size of one 'planck length', 10^{33} cm, or one millionth of a billionth of a billionth of a billionth of a centimeter. If a single atom were magnified to the size of the entire universe, one planck length would be about the size of an average tree.

Conventionally, the characteristics of a particle are explored by firing much smaller particles at it, and thus probing it. As string loops are the smallest possible objects, there is nothing smaller that can be used to probe them. Many feel that string theory will never be testable in this way and some physicists have difficulty taking it seriously. Others feel that the time has come when we must be willing to tackle concepts that are beyond our technical ability to test. Although other methods of testing are being explored, at this point, string theory remains an elegant set of complex mathematical equations. However, these equations yield results that make a great deal of sense, explaining puzzles that have eluded physicists for years. At this point, string theory bridges an impasse, as it is the only theory that successfully combines the physics of the macro-universe with that of the micro-universe. We will be taking a look at some of string theory's new ways of looking at reality, especially those that relate to our topic.

Firstly, how does string theory resolve the conflict between quantum mechanics and general relativity? Remember Einstein's picture of gravity as an integral part of the smooth curved landscape of space-time. This picture, and the mathematics that describe it, are not compatible with the turbulent, frantic, 'quantum foam' landscape that exists at a sub-Planck-length level. Simply stated, string theory resolves this quandary because it does not recognize that any kind of landscape could possibly exist at such a tiny level. In other words, the mathematics of string theory does not allow for anything to exist at a level below the planck length. In quantum mechanics, because we could postulate the existence of a point-like object with no volume—no extended shape, we could allow ourselves to postulate a quantum foam landscape. According to string theory, there is a limit to the smallness of the micro-universe. This conveniently solves the quandary. Furthermore, unlike quantum mechanics, string theory incorporates the notion of gravity and has mathematically verified the existence of the associated particle, the graviton.

One of the reasons that physicists are attracted to string theory is its potential to accommodate something called **supersymmetry.** In physics, symmetry refers to the idea that physical laws are the same—consistent—in any place in the universe and at any time in the past or future. According to modern science, all laws should be symmetrical. Any theory that has a high degree of symmetry, suggesting a high degree of order and elegance, is greatly valued by physicists. Although there are other aspects of symmetry, the one we are interested in here has to do with a particle's spin.

All particles, like planets, rotate on their axes, which is called spin. (Particles don't actually spin in a classical way, as in planets, but in a quantum way that is similar but different and hard to picture.) The idea of supersymmetry is that all particles have a partner particle that has a corresponding spin. This correspondence is such that the partner particle would have a much greater mass, and thus be more difficult to discover within our current technological limits. With the point-particle view, supersymmetry is not practical and all of these partner particles remain undiscovered. According to the equations of string theory, however, supersymmetry becomes mathematically possible. Although string theory provides only circumstantial evidence for the existence of supersymmetry, it has the potential to solve many of the problems in modern physics. If experimentation ever proves supersymmetry, it would be hailed as a huge breakthrough in the process of acknowledging string theory as the TOE.

Central to string theory is the notion that reality consists *of more than three spatial dimensions*. This idea was first introduced back in 1919 when

Theodor Kaluza attempted to unite Einstein's theory of general relativity with Maxwell's theory of electro-magnetics. When an extra dimension was added to Einstein's equations, Kaluza found that they perfectly matched Maxwell's equations for electro-magnetic force. After raising a few eyebrows, Kaluza's ideas were dismissed when they did not accord with experimental findings.

String theory suggests that, as well as the three 'extended' spatial dimensions of length, width and depth, there are seven further dimensions that exist at a planck length level. (Some have also speculated on the existence of extra time dimensions as well.) It is almost impossible to visualize these dimensions and any attempt to explain them would be quite involved and lengthy. Suffice it to say that these extra dimensions remain 'curled up' and are imperceptible to us. The geometrical form of these curled up dimensions plays a critical role in the resonant pattern of vibration of strings. Not only does string theory suggest this, its mathematics are completely dependent on this idea. Any verification of string theory would strongly imply that these extra dimensions actually exist.

One of the most fascinating concepts in cosmology is that of black holes, about which string theory has some interesting things to say. All elementary particles can be characterized by different values of mass, spin and force charges. It is these characteristics that distinguish one particle from another. Black holes also have mass, spin and force charges, which has led to the speculation that black holes are actually enormous particles. This may be easier to understand if we imagine that a small chunk of matter, condensed to the same degree as a larger chunk of matter in a black hole, would become a mini black hole. Such a mini black hole would be very similar to a particle. The equations of string theory are the first to offer a sound connection between particles and black holes. It suggests that, like ice and water, they are different 'phases' of the same substance.

According to the standard model of cosmology, the universe started with a big bang and has been expanding ever since. Before the bang, all of the matter that is now the universe, was condensed to such an incredible degree that it was virtually non-existent. String theory modifies this standard model by suggesting that it is not possible for the universe to condense to a point smaller than the planck length. Although it is still mind boggling to envision the universe squashed down to such a size, it is somewhat easier to fathom than being squashed into nothingness.

There have been many interesting musings and offerings recently by some string theorists. Although I would refer to such musings as 'educated speculation' (a relative of the 'educated guess'), they are worth mentioning, as some of them bear a resemblance to the views of mystics and are thus relevant to this chapter.

It has been postulated that the big bang is not a one-time event, but that there have been many such events. Each of these results in a distinct universe with differing physical laws. This idea has led to the coining of the term, 'multiverse', a larger reality of which our universe is only a part. A variation of this idea claims that every black hole may be the 'seed' of a new universe. Matter is sucked into the black hole by its huge gravity, to emerge on the other side in big bang fashion, expanding into a new universe. The event horizon of any black hole prevents us from perceiving any of this. Yet another variation suggests that there are other universes that exist at a sub-planck length level, where there is no time and no space! (Possibly, in such a minute universe, our particles are their black holes.)

String theory also questions our notions of distance, showing mathematically that two different distances can be deduced from the same set of data. Another strange result of string theory equations suggests that the fabric of space-time can actually tear. Although this is said to occur continually in the other folded spatial dimensions, it can also occur in our familiar unfolded dimensions of space-time.

Let's take a moment to review the main philosophical lessons of string theory:
- the basic constituent of everything is a vibrating loop of energy
- the different patterns of vibration account for all the variety of matter and forces in the universe
- there are more dimensions than meet the eye
- a black hole could be a type of particle
- we may be part of a bigger 'multiverse'
- we cannot trust our common-sense experience for a clear picture of reality.

As difficult as it is to thoroughly understand these things, it is important to realize that they come from theories that have not been scientifically tested. The mathematics of string theory, however, come together with great elegance and are capable of explanations that make it very compelling and worthy of further investigation.

Chapter 6

THE PARALLELS BETWEEN MYSTICISM AND PHYSICS

"Death signifies nothing. For us believing physicists, the distinction between past, present and future is only an illusion, even if a stubborn one."
Albert Einstein[30]

We can clearly see that there are some interesting parallels between what ancient mysticism and modern physics have to say regarding the nature of reality. Some of these are easy to see. Both the scientific and the mystical perspectives allude to the idea that much of what we think of as reality is an illusion. There is no matter as we know it. There is no time, flowing in a constant, linear way. There is no such thing as empty space. For a body floating in space there is no up, no down. We can't determine what is moving and what is at rest. Relative to something else, everything is in motion. What appears to be a static object, when sufficiently magnified, reveals a frenzy of activity, with energy continually changing form. Empty space, when magnified sufficiently, reveals the same thing. It must be clear by now that we can't rely on our five-sensory experience to see through the illusion. In this section we'll discuss the parallels between science and mysticism, looking at them in the same order as presented in 'The Tao of Physics', chapters 10 through 18.

There is an old African word, 'ubuuntu', which means 'all is connected'. One of the most clearly stated tenets of mysticism and the very essence of eastern philosophy is the idea of the ***unity of all things***. We are all part of a greater whole that some people like to call 'God'. This is alluded to in the Christian tradition as the concept of the Corpus Christi, the idea that we are all 'cells' in the body of Christ. In one form or another, many mystical traditions embrace the idea that the universe is a vast, interconnected web. Everything within the web is cut from the same fabric, different aspects of the same thing. Every part of the universe contains the whole; the universe is a system of systems, a hierarchy of wholes, which make up the ultimate whole. This holographic image of reality is represented by the 'flower of life' in sacred geometry and by the granddaddy of all mystics, Hermes Trismegistus who said, "As above, so below." (More on this in a subsequent section.)

Science has arrived at much the same conclusion. In particle physics, each particle 'contains' other particles. The forces holding particles together are themselves particles. Although these things can be very difficult to envision, they can be expressed mathematically. At the sub-atomic level, solid matter becomes a 'probability' of interconnected patterns of energy. All matter, all forces, are interdependent and composed of the same substance. What that substance actually is, we don't know. We do know that it can exist as both matter and energy.

According to eastern mysticism, the observer's consciousness is an integral part of the perceived reality. No reality can exist separate from the self. The reality we perceive is continually created and shaped by the collective mind, of which we are all a part. Scientific thought is headed in this direction, acknowledging that no observation is totally objective. The presence of the experimenter affects the outcome of the experiment. Science is in accord with mysticism when it admits that we can know nothing with true certainty, largely because we cannot separate ourselves from whatever it is we are trying to observe. While trying to make other sub-points in the rest of this chapter, this notion of the underlying unity of all things keeps recurring.

The mystical traditions recognize that our perceived reality is made up of a series of *dualities* which obscure a 'truer' perception of the way things work. Again, all polar opposites are aspects of the same phenomenon. We can't see beyond these dualities using only our five senses and our left brain logic. Modern physics seems to be in agreement. There are many paradoxes in physics, such as the wave-particle duality. Force and matter are different aspects of the same phenomenon. At the sub-atomic level, matter is both continuous and discontinuous, both destructible and indestructible. Niels Bohr recognized the similarity between the uncertainty principle and the Taoist principle of yin-yang. When he was knighted in 1947 for his contributions to science, he incorporated the yin-yang symbol into his family coat of arms.

The two perspectives of science and mysticism have much in common with their thoughts on the concepts of *space and time.* According to the old mechanistic view, space was an empty region that existed independently of any objects contained within it. Time was thought of as a separate dimension, flowing evenly and consistently, completely detached from matter. Relativity theory has suggested otherwise. At speeds approaching the speed of light, the elasticity of time has been proven on countless occasions. Time has been shown to be integrally connected to space and to matter. This view is also held by the eastern mystics, who consider perceptions of time and space to be relative to different levels of consciousness. D. T. Suzuki, speaking on the Avatam-saka philosophy of Buddhism, says, "There is no space without time, no time without space."[31]

The elasticity of space at high velocities has also been demon-strated many times. At low speeds, a particle has a shape that is spherical. At very high speeds it shortens along the length of the direction in which it is moving. This flattens the spherical particle into a pancake shape. Which of these two shapes is the true reality? Capra points out that this is like asking which length of a shadow, which changes with the angle of the sun, is the real one. A shadow is the projection of three-dimensional points onto a two-dimensional plane, and so the length changes with the angle of projection. Similarly, the length or shape of a moving object is a projection of points in four-dimensional space-time onto a three-dimensional space. It changes according to the speed with which it is moving.

General relativity suggests that gravity is the bending or warping of the fabric of space-time. The structure of this fabric correlates to the distribution of matter within the fabric. Space is warped to accommodate large bodies, and so is time. Time flows at different rates at different locations in the universe. The reports of countless mystics also allude to the inconsistent elasticity of time and space. Their experience of it while in altered states of consciousness is very different, allowing mystics to 'travel' in space and time. While such travels are often dismissed as 'imaginary', there are many reports of the effects of such travels manifesting in our physical reality. Information has been brought back from different time travels, for example, which later prove to be true. Events that have occurred in our physical reality have been witnessed 'elsewhere'.

All events are somehow interconnected, yet without the defin-ition of time as being a consistently linear unfolding of events, our notions of cause and effect become increasingly meaningless. On the other side of the time illusion, there is no before and after, no cause and effect. These philosophical conse-quences of the experiments of modern physics are in agreement with mystical experience.

Another concept common to both perspectives is the idea that everything in the universe is in **constant motion**. The mystic writings of ancient Greece and the teachings of shamans make frequent reference to the liquid, ever-changing nature of reality. In the Hindu 'Rig Veda', this idea of continual motion is called 'Rita'. In Buddhism it is called 'samsara'. At the sub-atomic level, as witnessed by science, everything is in constant motion. This is also true of the macro-universe. Every cosmic body is in motion, relative to other bodies. Countless calculations and observations testify that the universe is continually expanding. The further a body is from us, the faster it is moving away. No matter how powerful some future telescope may be, it will never tell us the true size of the universe. The galaxies furthest away from us are moving away at the speed of light, so that the light that would indicate their presence never reaches us.

The entire concept of a big bang and subsequent big crunch is nothing new to the ancient Tantric writings. This concept is called 'lila' and the amount of time required for one cosmic 'breath', one complete cycle of expansion/con-traction, is called a 'kalpa' by the Hindus. When the entire universe is com-pressed to the size of a pinprick, this point is called the 'mahabindu' or 'great point' in the Tantras.

One of the most fundamental laws of physics is the conservation of ener-gy. It states that the many manifestations of energy continually change form, but that the total energy in the universe never changes. No violation of this law has ever been witnessed by science. When particles collide in the micro-world, the energy of collision forms new particles of matter, which then become energy once again. A particle can be described as both an event and a chunk of matter—'processes' rather than 'solid objects'. Matter and the activi-ty of matter are one and the same thing. This is also in line with mystical thought and in the ancient language of Sanskrit, the word 'samskara' means both an object and an event.

Several of the mystical traditions refer to the idea of a 'cosmic dance' as an analogy to describe one characteristic of reality. It is the idea that the universe is in a constant state of creation and destruction—endless cycles of life and death, coming and going, inhaling and exhaling. In the Hindu tradition, this is the 'dance of Shiva'. The observations of modern physics are very reminiscent of these ideas. We are continually being bombarded with cosmic radiation, streams of particles that collide with each other and with our earthbound particles. These collisions result in endless transmutations, with particles being annihilated while others are being born. At the sub-atomic level, particles are coming and going continually. This constant motion, this 'dance' of microscopic matter, is very much like the dance of Shiva.

Let's now take a look at the concepts of **emptiness and form**. In the classical, mechanistic view, indestructible particles moved about in an emptiness or void. In the new view, this is not the case. Both the void and the particle are part of the same thing. Quantum field theory has shown us that the void is an important, dynamic quantity that is inseparable from the particles that it contains. A force field is a region characterized by a 'condition', which has the ability to affect matter or energy within the range of the region. A field is the means by which a force communicates its influence. Electro-magnetic fields— of which radio waves, light, x-rays, etc. are a part—travel through space at the speed of light. A gravitational field is a condition that affects the very structure of space, in fact it actually is space. In other words, matter affects space which in turn affects matter. Matter is inseparable from its environment.

According to quantum field theory, every type of particle corresponds to a particular force field. They are actually points of interaction between fields. A particle can be thought of as a transient 'concentration' of force field. In Einstein's words, "We may therefore regard matter as being constituted by the regions of space in which the field is extremely intense...there is no place in this new kind of physics both for the field and matter, for the field is the only reality."[32] Modern science recognizes no emptiness, no true vacuum. The void is a 'living', ever changing thing where matter spontaneously manifests and de-manifests.

This is another similarity with mystical thought, which has always viewed the ultimate reality as a void that gives birth to all things. In one way or another, all eastern philosophies refer to this void. In their view of how the universe works, forces are not seen as the external causes of effects on objects. Energy behaves as it does because of intrinsic qualities that are integral to everything. In his translation of the I Ching, Richard Wilhelm says, "Laws are not forces external to things, but represent the harmony of movement immanent in them."[33] According to the Tao, the laws of nature do not come from some external being; they were not 'handed down by God'. They are the internal dictates of nature itself. The many manifestations of reality are 'coded' in the 'blueprint' that is the essential aspect of the void. All of reality springs forth from the living void.

As mentioned previously, physics seems to have seperated into two branches. One branch of physics that includes Geoffrey Chew and David Bohm feels that it is somewhat futile to try to know reality by looking for the basic, irreducible elements of the universe. For them, no aspect of reality is fundamental to the whole. None of the characteristics of any particular part of the web can speak for the entire web. All the parts are interrelated and mutually dependent. The web of reality consists of a collection of relationships. There are no fundamental laws.

There is a strong implication that reality is dependent upon our **collective consciousness**. Physicist Eugene Wigner says,

"It is not possible to formulate the laws of quantum theory in a fully consistent way without reference to consciousness."[34]

Capra says,

"Physicists have come to see that all their theories of natural phenomena, including the 'laws' they describe, are creations of the human mind"[35]

Zucav says,

" 'Reality' is what we take to be true. What we take to be true is what we believe. What we believe is based upon our perceptions. What we perceive depends upon what we look for. What we look for depends upon what we think. What we think depends upon what we perceive. What we perceive determines what we believe. What we believe determines what we take to be true. What we take to be true is our reality."[36]

Statements like these bear an unmistakable resemblance to mystical thought, which contends that consciousness actually is reality. As Capra points out, if we have individual consciousness or intelligence and we are part of the whole, then the whole must also have intelligence. If this is so, then like consciousness, reality is subject to change, to growth. Science has always assumed a 'symmetry' of nature—that the laws of nature, whatever they are, have always been the same and will always be the same. Perhaps we can't make that assumption. Perhaps reality evolves as the collective intelligence evolves.

The other branch of physics has decided to set these concerns aside and to continue to search for the basic, irreducible building blocks of the universe. This branch has given birth to string theory. It is interesting to note that many of the concepts of string theory also bear a strong resemblance to things that are said by mystics. Fundamental vibrating loops of energy; the idea that everything, every aspect of reality is a manifestation of a certain pattern of vibration; the idea of multiple dimensions; the concept of a 'multiverse'; these notions would all have a familiar ring to a mystic.

It is also interesting to note that both branches of physics seem to have arrived at a type of impasse regarding the continued *usefulness of the scientific method*. String theory has yet to find a way to experimentally test its mathematically elegant contentions. Although some of this is due to inadequate technology, many feel that much of it is virtually un-testable. Some physicists feel that string theory is outside the world of science, belonging to the world of philosophy. Those that are more interested in exploring consciousness will also find that scientific experimentation, in the traditional sense, will be of limited use. Is science on the verge of admitting that empirical observation is incapable of showing us reality? If so, then we are definitely agreeing with the mystics.

Many scientists are content with seeking a partial knowledge of reality, of seeking to understand nature one piece at a time. This could be a valid approach, as long as we don't allow ourselves to be fooled into thinking that any particular piece could define the whole. Partial knowledge will always be partial knowledge. Many scientists acknowledge that they will never have the total, irrefutable answer to the mystery. Brian Greene says, "Sometimes attaining the deepest familiarity with a question is our best substitute for actually having the answer."[37] Most mystics say that it is futile to try to understand the whole by examining the parts. For them, the only process that has meaning is to attempt to experience, to glimpse the entirety of reality. Despite this, I believe that most of them would agree with Greene. At the human level, a more thorough understanding of the question may be the best we can do.

I personally believe that, even if it will never give us the complete answer to the question, 'What is the nature of reality?', the pursuit of science will always be useful to us. However, I also believe that we need to move away from the idea that science is the sole and ultimate authority. It is one of my deepest wishes that science begin to seriously consider the things that mysticism has to say. In fact there is a growing movement, thanks to Fritjof Capra and others, which seeks to marry the two schools of thought. Hopefully this will better inform the masses, who have been taught over the last few centuries to lend a greater degree of credence to science than to mysticism. Maybe it will also fuel the increasing interest in the wisdom of our mystical heritage. In the meantime, most of the world, including scientists, goes about its daily business firmly entrenched in the old mechanistic mind-set.

"When science begins the study of non-physical phenomena, it will make more progress in one decade than in all the previous centuries of its existence."
—*Nikola Tesla*[38]

Chapter 7

CHAKRAS AND THE TREE OF LIFE

In our quest for a better understanding of the nature of reality, it is important to try to see how humanity fits into the picture. How do we relate to this universe of energy? How does the human condition interface with the rest of reality? In this section we'll attempt to answer these questions by looking at two different yet related ancient schools of thought, the Tantra and the Qabala. Both of these schools of thought have things to say about how each human individual is connected to the rest of the universe, and how consciousness manifests into reality. They also speak, in their own ways, about the process of enlightenment, or the process of healing.

Many cultural traditions view the human body as consisting of both gross and subtle manifestations of energy; many cultures, including the Hopi and the Chinese, see the body in terms of a hierarchy of 'levels' of energy. In the Tantric philosophy these levels are known as **the chakra system**.

As part of the yogic philosophy, which is based on the ancient Vedas and Tantras, the chakra system is enjoying renewed interest in today's modern era. Many of the recent alternative healing methodologies that are emerging are based on a good understanding of this ancient knowledge. Healers are increasingly recognizing that no pathology or diagnosis can be complete without an understanding of the ways in which the human body interacts with the energies in the cosmos, and with consciousness. Studying the workings of the chakra system can provide such an understanding. There are many useful books, understandable to the lay person, about the science of chakras: 'Anatomy of the Spirit', by Caroline Myss, 'The Book of Chakra Healing', by Liz Simpson and 'Way of Chakras', by Caroline Shola Arewa. Although I recommend any of these books, my favourite is 'Wheels of Life' by Anodea Judith.

Although there are several takes on this type of information, with some minor conflicting points, the model that I will present here seems to be emerging as the dominant. Before we get into this model, lets take some time to try to formulate a **definition of a chakra** and to get a rough idea as to how they work. As with most of the information in this chapter, that is not the easiest thing to do, as we are dealing with a non-physical phenomenon that is difficult to explain and to envision. The idea that they do in fact exist, however, is becoming more and more accepted. Modern technology has been able to detect them and to accord with descriptions given by those who have encountered them psychically. Developed in the 1980s by Robert Dratch, a 'holographic spectrum analyzer' is a machine that can detect and read a body's radiant frequencies with precision.[39]

The word 'chakra' is Sanskrit, meaning 'wheel'. In this context it has come to represent a spinning wheel or vortex, a point on the human body which interfaces with different frequencies of cosmic energy. As previously mentioned, the universe consists of an enormous range of frequencies of energy vibration (Energy is the same as information). Each of us humans can interact with only a limited number of these frequencies, with a more enlightened individual being able to access more frequencies than one who is less enlightened. Chakras are points on the body at which these interactions can take place. They 'step down' or 'filter' the totality of information, allowing only that which our awareness can handle at this level of experience. If a typical human, a Player in the third realm, was exposed to the total information of reality, it would be completely overwhelming and would cause a type of 'circuit meltdown'. The process of enlightenment involves an incremental opening, so that more and more information can be accessed.

Although I've said that chakras are points along the body, it is more accurate to say that they are points along **the non-physical bodies**. Many traditions around the world suggest that the human form consists of a series of subtle, non-physical bodies as well as a physical, material body. Again, there are many varying viewpoints as to the number and shape of bodies and different names for them, but essentially all the varying definitions are quite similar. In the Tantric view, there are at least three non-physical 'bodies' or 'cloaks' which surround and interpenetrate the physical body. Clairvoyants, or those who are gifted with the ability to see auras, have been able to observe and describe them.

Associated with intellectual thinking, **the causal body** (some-times called the mental body) appears to a clairvoyant as an egg-shaped field surrounding the physical body. Its size and the quality of its shape depends on the individual's mental capacities. Within this field, thoughts manifest as colorful geometric patterns. One who is clear-minded and focussed emits forms of greater geometric crispness with vivid colors. One whose thinking is more muddled and scattered produces forms that are less defined and less colorful. The combination of the astral and causal bodies forms what has come to be called the aura. It is largely these energy fields that are manipulated, in a variety of ways, by energy healers.

Consisting of a slightly coarser substance, **the astral body** corresponds to the emotional activity of an individual. It is also ovoid, looking much like a torus-shaped electro-magnetic field. A more enlightened individual has an astral body that is clearer, more vibrant, well-defined and filled with colors that are more luminous and radiant. The astral body is very intuitive and sensitive to the feelings of others. As one becomes increasingly aware of one's astral self, one becomes more psychic, more in touch with the subtle energies and information coming from higher realms.

The etheric body conforms more closely with the shape of the physical body, like a glove that extends an inch or two out from the skin. It consists of a web or network of luminous fibers of energy that extend in all directions. These fibers connect to the outside world. They are also related to the nervous system, including the senses. The etheric body brings life to the physical body and separation from it becomes instant death. It forms the link between the physical and the other bodies.

It is not the physical body that gives rise to these subtle bodies. The opposite is closer to the truth. It is the subtle bodies that contain the blueprint, giving rise to the physical. They are encoded with information that produces and continues to affect the material body. This is another way of saying that both mental and emotional activity produces effects that manifest in the physical body. To profoundly address one's health, it is important to take into account the kind of activity that is taking place on a mental, spiritual and emotional level.

There are many chakras in the body, in fact every cell can be thought of in this way. There is a minor chakra in the center of each hand and foot. There is said to be twelve major chakras, seven running along the spinal column (or more accurately, along the spine of the etheric body) within the body and five beyond the body. The lower the chakra's position along the spine, the lower the range of frequencies it can access. The five 'external' chakras access frequencies that are the very highest, representing the greater systems of which we are a part, the totality of information. The eighth chakra is said to be about twelve inches above the head. The ninth is said to be several feet above the head and connects us to the morphogenetic grid of Earth. The tenth connects us to the solar system, the eleventh to the galaxy and the twelfth to the entire universe. Although there are twelve major chakras, we are mainly concerned with seven of these energy vortices.

The lowest of the seven 'internal' chakras is at the very base of the spine, the next is at the sacrum, then the solar plexus, the heart, the throat, the brow and the highest one is at the crown of the head. The seven chakras represent a 'spectrum' of frequencies, much the same as those of the color spectrum or the notes of a musical scale. A clairvoyant would describe them as spinning, funnel-shaped wheels containing mental, astral and etheric 'substance'. Thus, the body interacts with cosmic vibrations through these chakras, taking in vital energy from the infinite universal source. This vital energy has been given many names by various cultures, for example; prana, orgone, manna, sexual magis, Chi, Kia, Vril and Od.

An invisible, non-material channel, pathway or conduit within the body that distributes this vital energy is called a *nadi*. The subtle energy from the chakras animates the nerve ganglia as well as this matrix of nadis. Other cultures have also referred to these pathways. In ancient Egypt they were called 'metu' and are the same pathways or meridians used in the Chinese practice of acupuncture. The nadis are connected with the fibres of the etheric body. The chakras take cosmic prana into the etheric body, which is then distributed via the nadis. There are some 72,000 nadis, with fourteen being identified as major. Within this fourteen, the three most important are the lunar/female/right nadi, called 'Ida', the solar/male/left nadi, called 'Pingala', and the central channel called the 'Sushumna'.[40] These energy conduits criss-cross or intersect along the spinal column, meeting at the chakras. This arrangement is also called the Tree of Life, and is represented in the ancient symbol of the caduceus, which has been adopted as the symbol of modern medicine. The caduceus was the winged staff of Mercury/Hermes/Thoth. (See **DIAGRAM 4— THE CADUCEUS**)

According to the Tantra there is a power source, an energy called **kundalini** that lies dormant at the base of the spine. The process of enlightenment involves awakening this energy and causing it to rise up through the chakras along the Sushumna to the crown. When this connection is maintained, an individual experiences bliss, an awareness of unity with all things, leading to enlightenment. This kundalini energy is represented by a serpent which, while dormant, lies coiled at the base, but when awakened, rises in a criss-cross fashion up the Sushumna. The symbol of the caduceus depicts this process.

DIAGRAM 4—THE CADUCEUS

The Winged Staff of Hermes, also called the Caduceus, has been adopted as the symbol of modern medicine.

Yoga is a methodology that facilitates this process. The kundalini can be awakened in many ways, i.e., meditating, having sex, taking drugs, etc. One can choose to do this reverently and carefully, or with reckless abandon, according to one's level of wisdom. There are slower methods which clear 'blockages' from the chakra centers before awakening the kundalini, as well as faster methods which awaken the kundalini which then 'burns' its way through any blockages. This latter method, if done incorrectly, can lead to damage in the nervous system. This uniting of the lower energies with the higher is a key to achieving enlightenment, which is another way of saying that it brings immortality. This process is also a part of the concept of the Tree of Life (Etz Chaim) in the Qabalic traditions of the ancient Hebrews, and is referred to in the Biblical story of Adam and Eve (Genesis 3, 22–24). If one eats from the Tree of Life, one lives forever.

Each of the chakras is like a power station that corresponds to a certain range of frequencies, the root chakra at the base of the spine being the lowest, and the crown chakra on the top of the head being the highest. Thus the entire spectrum of frequencies accessible to all of the seven chakras represents the total reality of the individual (the other five 'external' chakras represent realities larger than the individual). This spectrum corresponds to others, such as the color spectrum or the major scale in music. Thus each chakra has a related color and note, as well as many other relationships, ie; a gemstone, a seed sound, an element, a sense, and an endocrine gland. Chakras are traditionally symbolized as lotus flowers, each chakra having a specific number of open lotus petals which represent the number of nadis that radiate from them to the rest of the body.

The chakra system is like a description of the way that consciousness relates to the material world, of how creation happens. What I'm about to say can be a bit confusing, but just try to grasp the general idea without taking the words too literally. The lower chakras correspond to the lower frequencies, to the Earth, the manifestation of physical matter. The highest chakras correspond to the higher frequencies, to the cosmic consciousness, to energy that is not manifest as matter. The chakras between these two extremes correspond to varying degrees of interaction between these two aspects of reality. This interaction is represented by two 'streams' of manifestation, called the *liberating current,* and the *manifesting current.*

The liberating current moves upward from the base to the crown. It represents the denser consciousness of the material world as it moves upwards, accessing more and more of the higher frequencies until it unites with the cosmic consciousness, bringing liberation. The manifesting current moves downward from the crown to the base. It represents the process by which consciousness manifests into physical reality. Pure awareness at the crown chakra descends into the more visual thought processes of the brow chakra, and then into the denser verbal domain of language at the throat chakra. Each step down represents a denser, less subtle version of energy. At the bottom step, consciousness expresses as the material, physical world. Each chakra has a different ratio of the two extremes, a different balance of pure cosmic consciousness versus physical matter. Each of these steps represents the movement of consciousness from a more abstract, less specific, less tangible expression, to a more solid, clearly defined expression. In the lower, denser consciousness resides our desires, our physical pleasures and our concern for survival in the material world. In the higher, more subtle consciousness resides our capacity for abstract thought, our higher concerns of love and compassion.

In Hinduism these two extremes of consciousness are represented by the deities, Shiva and Shakti. Shiva, representing the male aspect of cosmic consciousness, and Shakti, representing the female aspect of Earth consciousness, are often depicted in a loving, sexual embrace. This symbolizes the awareness of unity that can be achieved by bringing together these two aspects of consciousness. It is interesting, from an etymological point of view, that the root of 'paternal' is 'pater', which is also the root for 'pattern'. The root for 'maternal' is 'mater', which is also the root for 'matter'. Patterns of thought and matter are deeply related and combine to form our reality.

A body that is in perfect health has a chakra system that is completely open, with prana coursing through the body unobstructed. It is accessing all of the available frequencies in a balanced way. A more enlightened individual has access to a greater range of frequencies, and thus to a greater range of reality. If there is a blockage or malfunction in one of the power stations it can result in *sickness and disease* due to the unavailability of sufficient life energy. Illness is associated with a disturbance in the flow of energy through the chakras. This disturbance manifests as a physical ailment or 'disease'. By balancing and opening the chakras, thus improving the flow of energy, the body regains its 'ease' and functions harmoniously.

A blockage in the flow of prana is usually due to some fear-based 'issue', some 'lesson' that the individual has yet to work out. Certain issues are associated with certain chakras, and we will look at these relationships when we examine each specific chakra. In other words, the ancient Tantra recognizes that illness of the physical body is associated with some sort of illness of the spirit. Some fear based attitude or behavior pattern is inhibiting the healing power of love, which is the essential ingredient of prana. The life-force, prana, can be thought of as pure love.

For an individual who is awake, who is consciously facilitating her own process of enlightenment, knowledge of the chakra system can be a great tool. There are many ways to stimulate or open a chakra, allowing healing energy in. Such methods can include the use of vibration in sound, color or aroma, the assistance of a healer who can manipulate energy, the ingesting of homeopathic remedies that work on an energetic level, and the alignment of the spine via chiropractic adjustment or the practice of yoga positions. This increased energy flow can aid in the process of confronting deep-rooted fears, resolving issues and learning to be a better lover. These facilitating methods offer a period of respite, a temporary increase in pranic flow, which often brings with it a clearer mind, awakened memories, opportunities to confront fears and issues. However, many people become addicted to these temporary periods of respite, preferring the delusion of a 'magic wand' therapy, rather than the honest homework that true healing requires. No healing method can be effective without a sincere, willful effort to change the negative pattern or attitude that underlies the ailment.

In other words, the healing of the body is synonymous with the healing of the soul, which is synonymous with knowledge, the ability to see through illusion and to accept all circumstances with loving gratitude. Attending to the chakras can help this process greatly. Aches and pains can become little wake up calls, pointing to a specific chakra and the issue that resides there, waiting to be healed.

Caroline Myss identifies some *basic principles of healing*;

Biography Becomes Biology—Basically, our bodies contain our history, conveying our strengths, weaknesses, hopes and fears.

Personal Power is Necessary for Health—It is important to recognize and acknowledge the things in our lives that hold power over us (money, authority, title, beauty, security) and to learn to access a more authentic source of power.

You Alone Can Help Yourself Heal—Healing (versus cure) is an active, internal process, engaging the emotional, psychological and spiritual aspects of a person. To heal is to become whole.[41]

Healing is a process of awakening, of becoming conscious. Becoming a conscious individual means seeing through the illusions of one's life, seeing the universality or symbolic meaning of events in our lives. In this way, we wake up the energy inherent in each experience, which is ultimately meant to empower us. Each event, person, experience comes to us as an opportunity, benevolently designed to help us heal a fragment of ourselves. **It is important to realize that everything is as it should be and that everything is designed to awaken us to our higher purpose and meaning in life.**

Conventional medicine, with its emphasis on the surgical removal of body parts and its alliance with the pharmaceutical corporations, has little or no interest in such approaches. The use of a pharmaceutical drug may be effective in relieving or even curing a specific condition, but it almost always results in side effects, which according to energy healers, represents some other part of the physical system being thrown out of balance. Conventional medicine shows little concern with the notion of balance and pays no attention to the ancient wisdom regarding chakras. However, there are many effective alternative healing methodologies, many of which are interrelated, that deal with the chakras. This is a list of some of them; color therapy, crystal healing, the use of essential oils and flower essences, meditation, breathing exercises (pranayama), fasting, positive thinking, ritual, energy work (therapeutic touch, polarity, Shiatsu, Reiki), sound (chanting, mantras), visualization, homeopathy,

Acupuncture, Yoga, movement (Tai Chi, dance).

At this point, let's look at each chakra individually. Each has several symbols and things (colors, notes, gems, etc.) with which they are associated, and we'll look at a partial list of these. We'll see which health concerns correspond to which chakras, what physical conditions are associated with a state of balance or of blockage in a particular chakra. We'll discuss the life issues, the aspects of the human condition that reside at each chakra. Most individuals, as they move toward enlightenment, resolve these issues a step at a time, moving from lower chakra lessons up to the higher chakra lessons. In other words, each chakra tends to 'open' or 'become balanced', starting at the bottom with its concern for physical survival, and ending at the crown, with concerns based in 'cosmic awareness' and knowledge. (Although it is less common, some individuals open from the top down.)

It should be noted that the information below is merely scratching the surface. It is meant to assist with a general understanding of the chakra system and a recognition of its usefulness in the healing process. Many of the ideas here represent a simplified overview.

FIRST: BASE/ROOT CHAKRA (Sanskrit name—MULADHARA)
Meaning—root/support
Location—base of spine, from coccyx to pubic bone, perineum,
Systems Involved—circulatory, muscular
Gland—adrenal (survival-fight/flight)
Musical Keynote—C, *Gemstone*—ruby, *Element*—earth
Sense—smell, *Seed Sound*—Lam, *Verb*—I have/I am, *Color*—red
Main Function—Embodiment, survival, grounding

The entire chakra system is often compared to the lotus plant. The first chakra is like the root of the plant, anchored in the mud at the bottom of the pond. The middle chakras correspond to the stem and the upper chakras to the flower. The root brings nourishment from the earth and sends it upward to the rest of the plant. The flower absorbs nourishment from the sun and carries it down to the rest of the plant. The root chakra connects the individual to the Earth. One whose consciousness resides primarily at this root level is concerned with issues of survival, of belonging to family and community.

- *Emotional, Mental and Spiritual Aspects/Issues:* When we are in balance in this chakra, we are able to feel safe and secure within our family, group, society, universe, etc. We feel connected, we feel a sense of belonging, we feel 'at home' in our bodies and the world at large. We feel secure in our ability to provide for our survival needs, for food, shelter, warmth, etc. Our concern with security and connection also expresses itself in our need for logic, structure, and law and order. We express our bond to our family/tribe through the qualities of honor, loyalty and justice. In this chakra, our spirit needs to be anchored to our body and our bodies to the earth. Our ideas and intentions also need to be grounded or given physical expression.

An imbalance in this chakra manifests in fear of physical survival, (possibly resulting in theft, greed, aggression), fear of abandonment and non acceptance. It can result in 'money issues', fear of non-abundance. Emotional and psychological problems like depression, mental illness and obsessive-compulsive behaviors can manifest from these fears. Interestingly, psychological studies have shown that tension held in the anal sphincter has a direct correlation with depression. A tool in fighting depression is to learn to relax the anus, or to deal with the issues that cause the anus to tighten.

- *Physical Functions of the Root Chakra:* It is connected to the functioning of the muscular and skeletal systems, base of spine, feet, legs, bones, rectum/colon and the immune system. It also affects body heat and the quality of blood produced.
- *Physical Malfunctioning:* Energy blockages at this level manifest as spinal ailments, especially lower back problems, blood ailments, bone and rectal cancer, allergies, growth problems, low vitality and slow healing of wounds and broken bones.

SECOND: SACRAL CHAKRA (SVADHISTHANA)
Meaning—sweetness, sacred home of self
Location—lower abdomen, genitals, sacrum
Systems—sexual organs, intestines, kidneys, hip
Gland—gonads (ovaries and testes)
Musical Keynote—D, *Gemstone*—carnelian, *Element*—water
Sense—taste, *Seed Sound*—Vam, *Verb*—I feel, *Color*—orange
Main Function—desire, sexuality and pleasure

The sacral chakra is closely related to the root chakra, with concerns that are still very close to the Earth. It is our center of creativity, including procreation. Consciousness at this level is preoccupied with the need to be held, loved and nurtured, to be in relationships with others. This is our center of sexuality, of desire and physical pleasure. Concerns about money and abundance are also related to this chakra.

- *Emotional, Mental and Spiritual Aspects/Issues:* An individual who is balanced at this level has learned to interact consciously and form relationships with people who empower and support development, releasing relationships that suppress spirit and handicap growth. In order to be in healthy relationships, one must know, love and honor oneself, operating from a place of harmony in order to share with others. This, in turn, leads to an ability to know, love and honor others, to sexual confidence, positive self image and creative freedom. Such an individual would feel content and confident that the universe contains great abundance, which is always available. Balance at this chakra involves knowing and being comfortable with one's body, confronting inhibitions and fears and feeling free to explore ways to heighten one's pleasure. This leads to comfort with the bodies of others, with physical functions in general, and to better sexual relationships.

Imbalance at this level could manifest in a variety of disempowering emotions, such as fear of rape, betrayal, abandonment, isolation, sexual impotence, creative impotence, financial loss and poverty. These fears are often accompanied by feelings of resentment, anger, victimization and vengeance. Such an individual is often haunted by guilt and may have a tendency to blame oneself as well as others. Money and the management of money are central issues in this chakra. Money is often equated with power and sexual potency and therefore the lack of it may bring about financial stress and accompanying problems in the sexual organs. In the sacral power center, it is necessary to discover the external forces that control us and to develop a code of ethics whereby we can honor others and ourselves.

- *Physical Functions of the Sacral Chakra:* This center governs the whole pelvic region and fuels our reproductive organs and our desire to procreate. It also fuels our need for affection and for sexual pleasure. As its dominant element is water, water related body parts are associated with it, including bladder, kidneys, ovaries, and testes.
- *Physical Malfunctioning:* Energy blockages at the sacral chakra can manifest as sex related problems (infertility, impotence, fibroids, cysts, cancer), pelvic and lower back pain, urinary tract problems, and sciatica.

THIRD: SOLAR PLEXUS CHAKRA (MANIPURA)

Meaning—lustrous gem or inner sun
Location—navel to solar plexus
Systems involved—digestive organs, stomach, liver, gallbladder, spleen, middle spine
Gland—pancreas, adrenals
Musical Keynote—E, *Gemstone*—citrine, amber, *Element*—fire
Sense—sight, *Seed Sound*—Ram, *Verb*—I can, *Color*—yellow
Main Function—will, power, energy in the form of heat, enthusiasm

The solar plexus chakra is the seat of our will. It is the center of our self-esteem, ego and personality. The solar plexus provides the force behind our will, our ability to act consciously, make decisions and follow through with strength and endurance. Honoring oneself means loving and respecting oneself and thus having the power and courage to take risks, generate action, and handle stress.

- *Emotional, Mental and Spiritual Aspects/Issues:* When balanced in this power center, a person demonstrates great strength of character, strength of will, decisiveness, strong ethics and generosity. With a strong sense of self, one is also better able to follow one's inner guidance and thereby develop strong intuitive powers. Such an individual feels trustworthy and is also able to trust others. Balance at this level of consciousness results in a person who has great personal power and self-confidence.

    Imbalance in this power center can be associated with fears of rejection, failure, criticism and responsibility. This could lead to a weak-willed, insecure, indecisive person, someone who is oversensitive to criticism or someone who hides those feelings by trying too hard to be the opposite. Someone who is over-concerned with power, exercising inappropriate ways of achieving power, is often an individual with imbalance at this level of consciousness. One's challenge in this power center has to do with respecting oneself and others and not compromising one's spirit or honor code for money or to appease some fear. By developing a strong sense of integrity, power is not abused in this center. Instead, we are able to empower ourselves and others.

- *Physical Functions of the Solar Plexus:* This is the body's powerhouse of energy, the body's 'sun', symbolized by the color yellow. The solar plexus animates the body and keeps it alive. The main physical function in this area is that of digestion, including the stomach and small intestines. Organs such as the kidneys, spleen, gall-bladder and pancreas relate to this chakra. The liver, which filters toxins and stores nutrients, is the largest organ governed by the solar plexus. This organ is therefore affected by bad diet, pollution, drug and alcohol abuse.

- *Physical Malfunctioning:* Energy blockages in this chakra could manifests as problems with the digestive system (ulcers, gallstones), intestinal problems, food disorders (bulimia, anorexia), liver and adrenal dysfunction (hepatitis), diabetes and arthritis. Psychologically, the solar plexus is also responsible for digesting emotions. Trauma, anger, conflicting and stagnant emotions can be held here, bringing about many of the physical ailments mentioned above.

FOURTH: HEART CHAKRA (ANAHATA)

Meaning—unstruck
Location—center of the chest or thoracic cavity
Systems & Body Parts—heart and circulatory system, breasts, lungs,
    diaphragm, shoulders, arms and hands
Gland—thymus
Musical Keynote—F, *Gemstone*—emerald, *Element*—air
Sense—touch, *Seed Sound*—Lam, *Verb*—I Love, *Color*—green
Main Function—love, compassion, transformation

This chakra is the seat of love and compassion. Although it includes the
kind of 'partner love' of the second chakra, at this level it is a love that extends
to all things. The heart mediates between the lower three chakras of the body
and the higher three chakras of the spirit, symbolized by two interlaced triangles forming a six-pointed star. This star represents the movement of energy
upward from the earth and down from the heavens. From this center, which
is the gateway to the universal consciousness of the higher chakras, we develop emotional balance and harmony.

- *Emotional, Mental and Spiritual Aspects/Issues:* An individual who is balanced
  at the heart chakra is someone who cultivates qualities such as unconditional love, compassion, forgiveness and dedication, moving towards
  wholeness. The capacity to forgive family and friends, humanity at large
  and especially oneself, is the key that unlocks the heart. At this level, we are
  challenged to love and respect ourselves enough to become fully empowered. We are also challenged to release old patterns and habits that don't
  serve us. A balanced individual allows the expression of genuine feelings of
  grief, without overindulging; is sensitive to the needs and feelings of self as
  well as others.

  Imbalance in this chakra can result in a person who feels desperately
  lonely, bitter and self-centered. Holding on to negative emotions such as
  anger, jealousy, hatred and resentment stifles the diaphragm, causing much
  emotional pain and trauma. There can be a loss of energy in this power center due to the fear of loneliness, commitment, betrayal and the fear of following one's heart. Healing ourselves and others is possible through the
  balancing of emotions, recognizing the futility of self-pity, and acting out
  of love, compassion and forgiveness.

- *Physical Functions of the Heart Chakra:* This chakra powers the heart, the
  lungs, respiratory and immune systems, as well as the shoulders and arms.
  The breasts, both in their maternal and sexual roles, can be great reservoirs
  of love. Raising the quality of prana through the body is essential to the
  healthy functioning of this power center.

- *Physical Malfunctioning:* Blockage at this level can lead to several diseases such as heart disorders, breast cancers, asthmatic and immune disorders, fatigue, pneumonia and allergies, as well as upper back and shoulder problems.

FIFTH: THROAT CHAKRA (VISHUDDHA)

Meaning—purification
Location—throat
Systems or Body Parts—throat, ears, mouth, teeth
Gland—thyroid, parathyroid
Musical Keynote—G, *Gemstone*—turquoise, *Element*—sound/ether
Sense—hearing, *Seed Sound*—Ham, *Verb*—I speak, *Color*—bright blue
Main Function—communication, creativity

The throat chakra is the center of personal expression. It has to do with communication on a spiritual level as well as the physical level of words and creativity. It has to do with being honest with oneself and with others. This is the center of our beliefs, our faith that we are a part of a greater wisdom, a greater power. This is also the center most associated with sound, which is the product of vibration. It is sound that gives solid form to the higher energies, shaping our reality. The throat chakra has to do with our words, our expression and communication. What we say is very important because it becomes what we do. What we do shapes our world. Even in the form of words, sound manifests our reality, creates our future. If we are able to voice our truth individually, then we will be able to voice our truth collectively, thus creating a future world that embraces the things we feel are important, shaped by deeply held values.

- *Emotional, Mental and Spiritual Aspects/Issues:* Communication at any level necessitates speaking one's truth and living according to one's principles. One who is balanced in this chakra is at ease with this. Such a person seeks to align the individual will with the divine will, faithful and secure in the notion that this higher intelligence is benevolent and wise. Speaking one's truth also has to do with making powerful, conscious choices and accepting responsibility for those choices. Actions or choices that are guided by divine authority yield the best results. The challenge here is to open oneself up to divine guidance, courageously making choices that truly empower and assist in the process of becoming a fully conscious human being.

  When we don't speak our truth, we lose our spirit, our energy dissipates and we become alienated from our core. Imbalance at this level often has to do with the fear of showing one's true self and living according to one's true values. This fear is often based on underlying fears of rejection, of being alone and of failure. Such imbalance often leads to addictions to unhealthy substances as well as unhealthy habits and attitudes. One such attitude is the tendency to be close-minded and judgmental, which often results in the individual being blinded and weakened by negativity. Being honest with oneself and with the rest of the world, calling one's spirit back from bad habits and respecting the truths and ways of others can bring healing and can help restore one's personal power.

- *Physical Functions of the Throat Chakra:* Energy at this level governs the throat, the larynx, mouth parts, neck vertebrae, esophagus and thyroid gland. This gland is responsible for metabolism and the overall functioning of our bones, muscle tissues, and brain activity, including memory and sleep patterns. It supervises the overall vitality and well being of a person.
- *Physical Malfunctioning:* Blockage at this chakra can lead to sore throats, loss of voice, thyroid problems, mouth and gum problems, scoliosis, headaches, ear infections.

SIXTH: BROW CHAKRA (AJNA)

Meaning—To know, to perceive

Location—slightly above and between the eyebrows

Systems & Body Parts—left and right cerebral hemispheres, mind function, eyes, ears, nose, neurological system

Glands—pituitary & pineal

Musical Keynote—A, *Gemstone*—lapis lazuli, *Element*—light

Sense—intuition, *Seed Sound*—Om, *Verb*—I see, *Color*—indigo

Main Function—seat of wisdom, center of inner knowing

This chakra, slightly above and between the eyebrows, is often called the third eye. It is the center of psychic ability and intuition, which is used to see through illusion to the universal knowledge that lies beyond. It is the seat of our mental capacity, our ability to perceive, to evaluate, to think. The brow chakra powers our intellect, which includes rational, emotional and spiritual intelligence. This level is associated with light, which is produced by finer vibrations—higher frequencies than those that produce sound.

There is some controversy regarding whether the pineal and pituitary glands are associated with the brow or crown chakra. Some say the pituitary corresponds to the brow and the pineal to the crown. Others say it is the opposite. Some say that both glands correspond to the brow chakra. Both of these glands are of utmost importance to the functioning of the body. The pituitary is said to be the 'mother' of all glands, releasing hormones that inform all the other glands. The pineal gland has long been a mystery to modern science. Many mystics and some philosophers such as Rene Descartes have referred to it as the seat of the soul and many 'mind-expanding' methods involve some sort of stimulation of this gland. It is interesting that embryos are said to have something on the forehead that looks like a third eye. This 'growth' eventually becomes the pineal gland.

- *Emotional, Mental and Spiritual Aspects/Issues:* An individual who is balanced at this level is open-minded and levelheaded, with clear and focussed thought processes. Such a person recognizes that there is more to life than meets the eye and tends not to see things as either black or white. Such a person has a confident, objective way of dealing with information, including a strong faith in any perceptions that are gathered intuitively. From this powerful psychic center, one is able to discern a greater degree of the 'truth' and ascend towards spiritual liberation.

  The challenge in this center is to recognize the illusions that threaten one's sense of self worth. Imbalance at this level often involves a fear of truth, of becoming more conscious, of change, and of the discipline required for change. The challenge is to develop one's intuitive powers, to avoid clinging to belief systems, to be receptive to the new information that often accompanies change. Such efforts lead to clear insight into one's fears so that such fears will no longer have authority over one's actions and attitudes. When we are able to do this, we can visualize our direction in life and with confidence make manifest our aspirations. The wisdom that is gained from such clarity of mind is one of the divine powers of the sixth chakra.

- *Physical Functions of the Brow Chakra:* This center governs the functioning of the brain and nervous system, the eyes, ears and nose and the important pituitary and pineal glands.

- *Physical Malfunctioning:* Blockage at this level could lead to learning difficulties, brain tumours, stroke, blindness, deafness, insomnia, seizures, neurological disorders and spinal difficulties.

SEVENTH: CROWN CHAKRA (SAHASARA)

Meaning—thousandfold, infinity
Location—top of head, fontanelle
Systems & Body Parts—muscular system, skeletal system, skin, central nervous system
Glands—pituitary/pineal
Musical Keynote—B, *Gemstone*—amethyst, *Element*—thought
Seed Sound—none, *Verb*—I know, *Color*—violet
Main Function—understanding, liberation, union

This chakra is our link, our connection to the vast cosmic consciousness, that level of being that is beyond the human experience. As such, it is more abstract than the other chakras and less is known about it. Although it is said to be closely related to the brow chakra, there seems to be controversy as to its associations. It corresponds to vibrations of even higher frequency, and thus represents information that is even closer to the ultimate truth. Individuals who are more enlightened have a greater access to such information, while for most people, it is out of reach. It is possible that some less enlightened individuals, who may be blocked in lower chakras, can have an extraordinary grasp of such information. Such a person may experience turmoil or confusion until the lower chakras are opened. The crown chakra is the location where the purest, strongest currents of prana or cosmic energy stream into the body, with great healing potential. An open crown chakra allows this energy to stimulate the pineal gland, to charge and inform the body and the mind.

- *Emotional, Mental & Spiritual Aspects/Issues:* Balance at this level means that duality is transcended and one embraces universal consciousness. One experiences knowledge or understanding of divine truth and bliss, with little or no illusion to block the way. One lives in faith, trusting insight and inner guidance. Living in a fast paced, materialistic society can be a real challenge for such an individual. Witnessing the workings of a society that is lacking in compassion is difficult because, at this level, one becomes less concerned with the ego and feels a great responsibility to all of mankind. Increased humanitarian concern and selflessness is accompanied by an ability to see the bigger picture.

  At the same time, one often feels an alienation from the rest of society, an inability to relate to other individuals. One may feel very alone, depressed and in spiritual crisis. Previously held values, religious convictions and definitions of divinity may be suddenly called into question as new visions of reality come into focus. Such an awakening can be very distressing. One of the most effective ways of achieving balance at this level is to practice some form of daily devotion, such as meditating, praying, or anything that brings stillness and focus to the mind.

- *Physical Dysfunctions:* Blockage at this level can lead to depression, lack of spiritual direction and chronic exhaustion. Some schools of thought say that it can cause nervous disorders such as paralysis, multiple sclerosis and Alzheimer's disease. Other schools say that such disorders are associated with the brow chakra and the pituitary gland.

At this point I'd like to reiterate that there are many interpretations of the chakra system which vary in little ways. For example, some say that it is the throat chakra and not the solar plexus that is the seat of the will. Some say that it is the color white and not violet that corresponds to the crown chakra. It is important to note that many chakras have overlapping concerns or that sometimes more than one chakra will be the seat of certain issues. For example, just like in music where the second note of the scale and the fifth note are related, the second and fifth chakras are related, both corresponding to different aspects of creativity. The third and fifth notes, combined with the root note, make up the major chord. The third and fifth chakras are related, both having to do with will. There are many such interrelationships among the chakras.

Some chakras, particularly the even numbers, the second, fourth and sixth, seem to be stronger in females. They are typically more intuitive and have an easier time expressing feelings of love. Males tend to be stronger in chakras one, three and five, the odd numbers. They are usually more concerned with power issues and have an easier time expressing their views. (The seventh chakra is genderless.) Also, different chakras tend to want to open at different points in one's life. For example, at mid-life females tend to become more vocal, to feel the need to express themselves more truly and to be who they really are. Issues at the throat chakra begin to demand attention. Similarly, men at mid-life tend to soften, to allow themselves more expression of love and compassion. Issues at the heart chakra begin to beckon.

The sex act has great potential as a healing tool and we'll be discussing this idea more fully in Part Seven. One of the objectives of Tantric sex is to align the chakras during sexual union. This allows the male's root chakra to feed the woman's, the woman's sacral chakra to feed the man's, etc. In this way the energy coursing through the united couple becomes greatly amplified, with a powerfully increased capacity to heal. Thus every sexual union is an opportunity to see through the illusion of duality, to feel unity and to 'make love'. What better thing can one possibly make?

THE TREE OF LIFE

Several cultures throughout history have used the tree as a powerful metaphor to explain the mysteries of reality. In Norse mythology we have the concept of the 'Yggdrasil'. The body of knowledge known as the 'Tree of Life' or the 'Tree of Sephiroth' comes from the school of Jewish mysticism, the Qabala. Its basic text is the **Sepher Yetzirah**, or the Book of Formation. Tradition contends that the knowledge contained in this book was handed down to Adam and was preserved through the generations by strict oral ceremonies and ordained storytellers, until it was finally written down, eventually evolving into the Sepher Yetzirah. There is great controversy regarding the antiquity of this knowledge. Some contend that much of this information became distorted over the years. (Anyone wishing to learn about the Qabala in more depth is referred to the work of David Godwin, Carlos Suares and many others.)

Much of the information in the original texts, however, seems to make sense and corresponds to other ancient knowledge such as the Tantra. It covers a wide range of topics including the creation of the universe by means of **the ten Sephiroth**. (A sephirah is a divine emanation or sphere of light). The divine force which fills and contains the universe, the source of all things, is called 'En Soph', corresponding to the concepts of Brahman or Tao. From this primal force came a great emanation, which spawned another emanation, which in turn spawned another, etc. There are a total of ten such emanations, called sephiroth, which divide into seven levels that correspond to the seven chakras.

The first level, corresponding to the crown chakra, is a single sephirah called the 'Crown' (Kether). It represents the original intention to make manifest the universe, and it contains all the other nine 'intelligences'. It corresponds to the Hindu concept of Atman and is considered to be beyond gender, having no male and female aspects. The next level, corresponding to the brow chakra, consists of two sephiroth, the female/right-brained/yin/supernal mother called 'Wisdom' (Binah), and the male/left-brained/yang/supernal father called 'Knowledge' (Chokmah). These first two levels, consisting of three sephiroth, combine to form the 'supernal triad', representing intellectual qualities and the head of the human body.

The next level corresponds to the throat chakra and consists of two sephiroth, 'Mercy' (Chesed) on the left side, and 'Severity' (Geburah) on the right. These two qualities are like opposite sides of the same coin and together they spawn the fourth level—the sixth sephirah, 'Beauty' (Tiphareth) at the heart. One way of understanding this process is to think of it in the context of parenthood. The soft, forgiving quality of mercy, combined with the firm, principled discipline of severity produces a beautiful child. These three sephiroth form the triad that represents moral or ethical qualities and the upper torso and arms/hands of the human body.

Going down to the next level, corresponding to the solar plexus chakra, we have two sephiroth that again represent two extremes of the same aspect. On the creative, intuitive right side we have 'Victory' (Netzach), and on the analytical, linear left side we have 'Splendor' (Hod). These two aspects of manifestation, the inspirational, passive force on the right and the deductive, active force on the left, combine to spawn the next level—the ninth sephirah, 'Foundation' (Yesod). These three sephiroth form the triad that represents the physical qualities and the lower torso and legs/feet of the human body. At the base of all of this is the final level of manifestation, the tenth sephirah, 'Kingdom' (Malkuth) which corresponds to the root chakra. It is closely related to the ninth sephiroth and represents the material world, the physical plane.

In **Qabalistic cosmology**, the universe consists of four different yet inseparable worlds, similar to the four levels of 'substance' that interact with the mental, astral, etheric and physical bodies in the Tantric philosophy. Although the four worlds correspond to the four divisions of the Tree of Life, three triads and the Malkuth, it is equally accurate to say that the tree, in its entirety, exists in each of the worlds. The first world is the direct emanation from En Soph, the primordial void, inhabited by archangels Metatron, Raziel and Tzaphqiel. The second, called the 'Briatic' world is slightly less subtle and constitutes the world of pure spirit. It is inhabited by the archangels Tzadqiel, Kamael and Raphael. Less subtle yet is the 'Yetziratic' world, the residence of the angels. It is governed by archangels, Haniel, Michael and Gabriel. (Gabriel is said to be the same entity as Thoth, incarnating as many avatars throughout history, including Jesus.) The densest, least subtle realm is Malkuth, the world of action or matter, which contains the ten 'hells' and is the abode of mankind/the beast. The corresponding archangel is Sandalphon.

We can see the similarity with the chakra system in that the path from top to bottom, from Kether to Malkuth, represents the manifestation of reality from the universe of consciousness or divine intent, to the physical, material universe. Accordingly, the path from bottom to top represents the way to enlightenment, often called the ***path of the serpent***. There are actually three ascending pathways, corresponding to the three 'pillars' of the Tree of Life. Up the right side of victory/mercy/wisdom toward divinity is sometimes called the way of the saint. Up the left side of splendor/severity/knowledge toward the same divinity is sometimes called the way of the dark magician. The safest path, recommended to most people, is the one up the middle, through kingdom/foundation/beauty, sometimes called the pillar of mildness.

One of the mystical aspects of the Qabala involves a journey up Jacob's Ladder, through the seven heavens in a 'cosmic vehicle' called the 'merkaba'. This is a type of guided meditation that allows the initiate to travel 'astrally' through the seven levels, the sephiroth, to arrive at seventh heaven and glimpse the throne of God. Other Qabalic techniques are more similar to conventional meditation.

On the ascending journey toward enlightenment there is an ***abyss*** between the supernal triad and the rest of the tree. In other words, progress into the higher chakras and into an enlightened state of being is sometimes thwarted by a condition that has been referred to as the 'dark night of the soul'. This passage, often marked by confusion and spiritual crisis, is successful only if the individual overcomes all fears and sees through all illusions. This abyss is ruled by 'Choronzon', the demon of chaos, sometimes called the Guardian of the Threshold (an aspect of the entity known as Thoth/Hermes). One who passes through the abyss must confront this fearsome demon and recognize it as the manifestation of one's own fear, an illusion. Someone who seeks a faster path, such as that of the dark magician or by the ingesting of psychotropic drugs, risks the danger of an unsuccessful, and thus horrifying, encounter with Choronzon.

There are ***thirty-two paths of wisdom*** within the Tree of Life; ten sephiroth and twenty-two links between them. These links or paths relate to the twenty-two cards in the Tarot, and to the twenty-two letters of the Hebrew alphabet; three 'mother letters', seven 'double letters' and twelve 'single letters'. In the first chapter of Genesis, the part that tells of the seven days of creation, there are thirty-two references to God (in the original Hebrew text God is actually called the Elohim). Ten of these are occasions where God 'said' something, three where God 'made' something, seven God 'saw' and twelve God 'did'. Each of the Hebrew letters also has a number value, so that words have a 'numerical' as well as a 'textual' meaning. It is interesting that the Hebrew word for 'love' adds up to thirteen, the number of Christ consciousness. The path linking the heart to the crown is path number thirteen, again that enigmatic number.

One of the interesting mysteries of the Qabala, which has turned out to be a big factor in the shaping of our world, is the concept of the **Tetragrammaton**, which means 'name of four letters'. The one that represents the 'name of God' is YHWH, which became Yahweh and then Jehovah. Each of the Hebrew letters has a name, such as Aleph, Beth, Gimmel, Yod, Heh and Vav. Thus the original pronunciation of YHWH was closer to Yod Heh Vav Heh. This word is considered by the Qabala to be the most powerful of all mantras (although the Qabala does not use the word 'mantra'), and the possessor of its correct pronunciation is said to be capable of great feats of magic. This true pronunciation is thought to be lost or to be a closely guarded secret and it was traditionally forbidden to even attempt to say the name. Ancient Hebrews used the word 'Adonai' to refer to God. This led to the use of the name 'Jehovah', which according to the Old Testament, was the true and only God. *This insistence on the 'only true God' and the notion of the Jews as Jehovah's 'chosen people' has led to many problems throughout history, including the current problems in the Middle East. This issue will be examined in greater depth in Part Six.*

The four letters of the Tetragrammaton represent the four levels of the human being, the four worlds mentioned earlier, as well as the four elements— air, fire, water and earth. The first letter, Yod, represents the primal father, Heh represents the Primal mother, Vav is the son and the second Heh is the daughter. The numerical value of this four-letter word is 13 + 13 = 26.

This brings us to another Qabalic concept, that of the **Shekinah**. Related to the Mesapotamian goddess, Anath/Ashtoreth/Astarte/Ishtar, the Shekina is considered to be the bride or consort of YHWH. She is also an archetype, the female representative of God on Earth, the embodiment of wisdom and all things feminine. The concept of the Shekinah is actually quite elaborate, similar to the idea of Shakti in Hinduism. Tradition says that the Shekinah, the female aspect of divinity, vanished from the Earth circa 600 BC, leaving Jehovah, the male aspect, to rule alone. Some would say she was 'banished' or ignored by the emerging patriarchy. The mystics feel that Jehovah is incapable of ruling, of moving mankind forward, without this feminine presence. They long for the return of the wisdom of the Shekinah, the restoration of balance. This reunion has been named the 'tzaddig'.

The Qabala recognizes **four levels of meaning** or classifications; the practical, the dogmatic, the literal and the unwritten. The practical interprets the Qabala in terms of hidden meaning pertaining to magic, talismans, etc. The dogmatic or academic Qabala refers to the study of texts. The unwritten Qabala is concerned with the many correspondences of the Tree of Life and its paths, ranging from the Hebrew archangels to the hexagrams of the I Ching. The literal interpretation, called the 'gematria', is concerned with the meaning of the Qabala, not in terms of its text, but in terms of the numerological meaning as mentioned earlier. Many attempts have been made to explain strange passages in ancient texts using this method and there is a general agreement that many ancient texts were purposefully written with different levels of meaning. The Torah is said to have at least four such levels, the literal, the allegorical, the hermeneutical (relating to Hermetic magic), and the mystical.[42]

The Tantra and the Qabala are two huge bodies of information that attempt to make some sense of our mysterious reality. One could easily spend a lifetime in the study of either of them. For our purposes here, the inclusion of this information is offered as a way to gain a general understanding of what they're about and to recognize the value of such ancient knowledge. One can't help but marvel at the depth and complexity of these ancient schools of thought and at the degree of similarity between their concepts, even thought they come from different cultures. There is also a great degree of accord with other mystical knowledge, and with modern science.

Most of this material resonates deeply with me. It makes sense. I feel that it needs to be taken seriously and given the respect it deserves. I believe that we would do well to re-acquaint ourselves with this wisdom, to demystify it, to include it in school curricula and to use it as a guide to a more meaningful life.

Chapter 8

CONSCIOUSNESS

"We are what we think.
All that we are arises with our thoughts.
With our thoughts we make the world"
—*from the Buddhist Dharmapada*

Throughout this chapter we have been trying to get a better understanding of the nature of our reality. This is an important step in the process of addressing the issue, 'why is life?' Ancient bodies of knowledge such as the Tantra, the Qaballa, other mystical perspectives and modern physics have given us much insight into many aspects of reality. Of these aspects, one stands out as the most important. Currently, many eminent scientists and scholars such as John Hagelin, Michio Kaku, Don Beck, John DeMartini, Daniel Kinderlehrer, Peter Russell, William Tiller, Amit Goswami, Stanislof Grof, Arny Mindell and others have been working with mystic and shamanic perspectives to gain a better understanding of this important aspect of reality. They all seem to be arriving at a similar awareness—*reality is equivalent to consciousness.*

What do we mean by such a statement? Modern science seems to be agreeing with mystical thought which suggests that our physical reality is a product of our collective consciousness and that the totality of reality is the product of the totality of all consciousness which could be regarded as The Source or 'God'. One could say that reality has been and is being created, from moment to moment, by consciousness. The total collective of all types or factions of consciousness is the 'creator'.

What do we mean when we refer to 'different types of consciousness'? Maybe we can shed some light on this question by trying to think of the universe as a *system of systems.* This concept is represented by the famous Hermetic quip, "As above, so below", and by the sacred geometrical symbol known as the 'Flower of Life'. (See **DIAGRAM 5—THE FLOWER OF LIFE**. Also, See **BOX 4—SACRED GEOMETRY**)

The universe is a large system made up of smaller systems, which in turn contain smaller systems, and so on. These sub-systems are like holograms of the larger systems, that is, they are organized in a similar way and have similar characteristics. This 'system of systems' applies to all forms of energy, to both physical and non-physical manifestations.

DIAGRAM 5—THE FLOWER OF LIFE

Each of the spheres in this cluster represents a system. This cluster of interacting spheres can, in turn, be contained by a single larger sphere, which interacts with other large spheres. This pattern continues upward to macro-infinity and downward to micro-infinity.

In the physical, material realm we can think of a particle as a very small system. Several particles together form a larger system—the atom, and several atoms together form a molecule. Several molecules combined in just the right way form a larger system, the living cell, which combine in various ways to form organs, bones and other systems. The human body in its entirety is a system which, in combination with other bodies, make other systems such as communities, nations, races, etc. These sub-systems in turn come together to form the greater system that is all of humanity.

> **BOX 4—SACRED GEOMETRY:** In the process of trying to describe reality, we can use several different languages. The most obvious are those that are based on words. Visual imagery can be a language and it is often said that a picture is worth a thousand words. Physicists attempt to describe reality using the language of mathematics. Another ancient language that can help our understanding is geometry. This knowledge has been getting more attention lately, after having been preserved through the dark ages by the secret societies and the architecture of the Freemason traditions. 'Sacred' geometry illustrates the order that underlies every expression of energy in the universe. There is a geometric sequence that is a metaphor of the process of creation; the Tree of Life shows us the holographic nature of the universe; the five platonic solids represent the basic structure underlying all forms of matter; the 'golden ratio', also known as the 'phi' ratio (1:1.618) represents the archetypal interrelationships between many forms of matter—the pattern inherent in all movements of energy; etc. (For more info on sacred geometry check out the websites listed at the back of the book.)

In terms of cosmic bodies, we can see that a planet is a system and that several of them form a solar system. Many solar systems make up a galaxy and many galaxies make up the physical universe. These systems, and all systems, are designed to behave in certain ways that could be referred to as 'laws'. For example, it is the nature of these manifestations of energy to seek balance or equilibrium. (See **BOX 5—SYSTEMS SEEKING BALANCE**)

The non-physical universe also exists in this 'holographic' way. Consciousness exists as systems within systems. One could say that every living cell has a type of consciousness, as do each of the organs. They go about their business without needing conscious 'orders from headquarters'. The consciousness of each of these levels is separate, but it also is a part of the consciousness of the greater system, in this case, the entire individual human being. Our individual human consciousness is part of the collective human consciousness, which in turn is part of a still larger collective. The total of all expressions and manifestations of energy, the sum of all consciousness is the unity, the oneness that we could refer to as the Source or God.

The various levels, the many systems with their separate 'consciousnesses', exist as individuals but are completely interrelated and interdependent. It is part of the Game at this level that we choose to forget this interconnectedness. Over many incarnations, many experiences, we eventually remember this on our way to enlightenment. We remember that we are all one.

It is interesting to note that almost all cultures at one time worshipped the sun, the moon or other cosmic bodies. In the case of the sun it is clear that we highly value its ability to warm and nourish us, but further to this, there was a recognition that the sun corresponds to a consciousness. This consciousness, this 'god', presides over and contains our individual and collective consciousness. We are a part of it. Other cosmic bodies, other 'gods', have also interacted with us. We are a part of many levels of consciousness.

BOX 5—SYSTEMS SEEKING BALANCE; It is the nature of all energy systems, whether micro or macro, to seek balance. From the first point of creation; from the initial calamity of the 'big bang', energy forms are continually expanding, seeking relationships with each other that would result in a state of homeostasis, that is, a state in which energy no longer needs to dynamically transform into different manifestations of itself. Energy would thus be at a static state of equilibrium. Scientists speculate that it would then start to contract, imploding back to a micro-point in a process they have named the Big Crunch. At present, however, the universe is a swirling, churning sea of energy-forms that are constantly changing and affecting each other as they seek balance. One system seeking balance is often affected by another system seeking balance. For example, a planet could have its quest for balance seriously impaired if it were struck by an asteroid, which is in motion as part of a greater system seeking balance. Understanding this can lead to a better grasp of the concept of karma. Every action is an energy emission, a small system vibrating at a certain frequency which is seeking balance, and which is interacting and affecting other similar systems. More on this in Part Two.

Many cultures over the ages have referred in some way to the various levels of consciousness. This is true of native Americans, Africans, Polynesians and Australian aborigenese. Sometimes they are seen as *pantheons of gods* and demi-gods, as in Greek, Roman, Norse, Sumerian and Egyptian mythology. Judaic, Islamic and Christian traditions recognize *a hierarchy of angels*. These angelic realms are larger systems, greater levels of consciousness that contain the smaller levels. The sum total of all of these angelic realms is the Source, the Creator, God. Every level of consciousness, in its own way, is acting out a part of the divine plan. Some of the smaller systems may be less aware of this, but at the higher levels, those that could be called the angelic realms, they are well aware of this plan. They are playing the Game at their level, but their awareness of the divine plan is always foremost in their minds.

Because their wills are closely aligned to the divine will, the angels and archangels have a different kind of free will than we do at the human level. Although each of them has a different 'flavored' energy, they all exist as forms of pure love. (See **BOX 6—THE ANGELIC REALMS**.) These energies can be called upon by a human. In other words, we can use our free will to decide that we want help. An angel will help, but only if what we are requesting is in line with the divine will. They have free will, but because of their level of awareness, they can do nothing that does not accord with the divine will. They cannot make the same kind of 'mistakes' that we do in the process of exercising our free wills.

> **BOX 6—THE ANGELIC REALMS:** The energy that we refer to as 'angels' are larger systems of consciousness that 'contain' smaller systems, such as the system of humanity. According to some traditions, the hierarchy of systems breaks down in the following way: the ultimate system, God/source/unity, divides into two streams or rays—the spiritual ray and the materialization ray. The largest system of the spiritual ray is known as Metatron. Next is the Archangels, then the angels, then humanity. The largest system of the materialization ray is called Melchizedek, followed by 'earth angels', the devic entities and then humanity. (This order is from the human perspective.)
>
> There are several variations of the hierarchy of Archangels, using different names and different orders, but the one that follows is one of the better known interpretations. I will list them in ascending order, first stating the name and then the 'flavor' of energy that it represents. (Most angel names end with 'el', which means 'of God')
> • Uriel; most earthly of all archangels—money, survival
> • Haniel; insight, self-recognition, seeing through illusion
> • Chamuel; relationships, creativity
> • Gabriel; joy, letting go, rebirth
> • Raphael; soothing, healing, transformation
> • Michael; clarity, protection, willpower, courage, strength
> • Jophiel; integration, relaxation, bringer of light
> • Zadkiel; perfection, wisdom, completion
> • Metatron; different from the other archangels, all-encompassing love, supervisor of all creation

However, they do make their own brand of 'mistakes', all as part of the great Game, accumulating experiences on the way to unity with the god-head. Some feel that the current situation on Earth is the result of a mistake in the supervising of the human journey, an oversight in the ongoing 'humanity project'. They feel that the situation on Earth is similar to a 'bottleneck' in the processing, the evolution of energy towards enlightenment. In other words, certain circumstances such as the 'density' of our planet, the 'Fall of Lucifer' and certain events in our past have created a situation whereby it is more difficult than usual for us to accumulate the necessary experiences, to learn all the lessons of the third realm. However, some say that we are on the brink of a new circumstance, one that represents an opportunity to rectify this situation. This new circumstance has been given several names, but in this book we will refer to it as the 'Big Shift', and it is the subject of the next section.

Of course, the rectifying of our current situation must be done in accordance with the rules of the Game, involving a willful change in our collective consciousness. This brings me to the next point, maybe the most important point in our effort to understand the nature of reality. In order for us to take advantage of the coming opportunity, we must reclaim our power. We must become aware of the concept that ***consciousness creates reality.*** We must awaken to the realization that it is our thoughts, our emotions, our will, our intent that shapes everything about our world. We control the destiny of our planet, of humanity, of our consciousness, both individual and collective, as it moves toward enlightenment. We must remember the awesome power that we have at our command. We must awaken.

I have used the phrase 'we must' many times in that last paragraph. I feel compelled to point out that I wrote "in order for us to take advantage of the coming opportunity, we must…" I feel it is important to say that there is no need for any kind of anxiety. If we can accept the idea that this is a big Game, then this approaching opportunity, this Big Shift, is only part of the Game. If we fail to fully take advantage of this pending opportunity, we will simply continue to play the Game in some other way. If this sounds somewhat confusing at this point, hopefully the next section will help to clear it up.

The important point to drive home at this time is the idea that consciousness is equivalent to reality. Currently there is a growing awareness of this concept and of all the phenomena that it implies. An increasing number of respected scientists, as cited at the beginning of this chapter, are embracing, studying and teaching this awareness. Some are seeking scientific ways of 'proving' that we can consciously change reality. (See **BOX 7—SCIENTIFIC EVIDENCE OF A COLLECTIVE MIND**)

BOX 7—SCIENTIFIC EVIDENCE OF A COLLECTIVE MIND: Although there may be no concrete proof, there has been significant scientific evidence of the existence of a collective human consciousness. Some interesting results came from experiments conducted at Princeton University in recent years, from something called the 'Global Consciousness Project'. It is made up of a collective of international scientists led by Roger Nelson. They share an interest in this subject and have agreed to volunteer their time. Their work involves the use of a 'random events generator' (REG), a computer that produces a series of random events, such as flipping coins. These random events can then be recorded in a graph. Experiments have suggested that these outcomes can be influenced by human consciousness. A group of people have 'willed' a different, more ordered set of results from the REG. Also, global events such as the destruction of the trade towers on 9/11 have produced measurable effects on REGs. (For more info see **www.noosphere.princeton.edu**) (footnote—*Golden Thread Magazine*, Aug. 2002 edition.)

Seminars and conferences devoted to this new perspective are popping up with increasing regularity. There is the annual 'International Conference on Science and Consciousness', a weeklong event featuring presentations by the brightest minds in the field. Fritjof Capra is its founding director. (For more info on this conference see their web site at **www.bizspirit.com** or by phoning 505-474-0998.) Several times per year there are gatherings known as the 'Prophets' Conferences', organized and presented by Gregg Braden and his associates. These conferences feature scientists, spiritual leaders and teachers who contribute to the new awareness in a variety of ways. (See **www.greatmystery.org** for more info.) There are many other such events. They are very well attended and are testimony to the fact that more and more people are beginning to see reality in a new light and to have a better idea about why we are all here.

The following quote is an excerpt from a speech given by nuclear physicist, Max Planck, after he was awarded the Nobel Prize for his contributions to quantum physics.

> "All matter originates and exists only by virtue of a force...
> We must assume behind this force, the existence of a conscious
> and intelligent mind. This mind is the matrix of all matter." [43]

Albert Einstein had similar feelings;

> "That deeply emotional conviction of the presence of a superior
> reasoning power, which is revealed in the incomprehensible
> universe, forms my idea of God." [44]

Isaac Newton contributed so greatly to science that we overlook the fact that he spent an even greater amount of time and energy exploring and writing about things spiritual and metaphysical. One tenth of his personal library consisted of texts on alchemy and 'magic'.

I believe that these great scientists were on to something. They speak of a universal intelligence, a unified cosmic consciousness. I believe that, thanks to their efforts and those of a great many others, collective humanity is once again gaining a better understanding of the nature of reality. We are getting closer to the ever-elusive 'truth'.

In trying to establish new paradigms of reality—to figure out 'what's really going on', there is a great deal of information to consider, and the process of considering such information is, for me, a tool for my own personal healing. Finding all 'the answers', is not as important as the process, and is ultimately of no great concern. For me it is more important to remain open to all ideas, whether they come from research or from my own meditations. It is important to keep my beliefs liquid. However, the more information I gather and sort through, the more I agree with Isaac, Albert and Max. I confirm the fervent core belief that I've always held in my deeper awareness—no matter how the pieces of the puzzle come together, behind the illusion of chaos, underlying all phenomena, there is order—a divine plan—a benevolent creative entity of which we are all a part.

"In some sense man is a microcosm of the universe; there-
fore what man is, is a clue to the universe. We are
enfolded in the universe."
—physicist, David Bohm"

Man shall not live by bread alone, but by every 'word'
(sound/vibration/energy) that proceeds
from the mouth of God."
—the Holy Bible, John 4:4

" Matter is nothing but energy, energy is only thought and
thought is only a vibration on the surface of the calm
Ocean, the Supreme Spirit. The entire universe,
from its subtlest to its grossest
manifestations, exists as vibration."
—*Swami Kriyananda*

"Matter is fluid and flows like a stream, constantly changing
from one thing to another. The key to worlds within
thee is found only within, for man is the gateway of
mystery, and the key is that One is within
One. Look thee above, or look thee below,
the same shall ye find, for all is but a
part of the Oneness."
—*The Emerald Tablets of Thoth*

If the mind makes no discriminations, the ten thousand
things are as they are, of single essence. To come
directly into harmony with this reality just simply
say when doubt arises, 'not two'. In this 'not two'
nothing is separate, nothing is excluded.
There is neither self nor other-than-self.
To understand the mystery of this
One-essence is to be released
from all entanglements."
—*Sin Sin Ming*

"One love, one heart, lets get together and feel alright"
—*the Gospel of Bob Marley*

ENDNOTES—PART ONE

1. From the inaugural speech of Nelson Mandella to the South African Parliament in 1994: Originally a poem by Marianne Williamson in her book, 'A Return To Love', Harper Collins, 1992, chapter 7, section 3
2. Zukav, Gary—*The Dancing Wu Li Masters*, Bantam Books, 1979, New York, p. 83–87
3. Zukav, Gary—*Seat of the Soul*, Simon & Schuster, 1990, New York, p. 13–32
4. Capra, Fritzof—*The Tao of Physics*, Harper Collins, 1976, London, 98–99
5. Mookerjee, A. and Khanna, M.—*The Tantric Way*, New York Graphic Society, 1977, Boston, p. 9–21
6. ibid. p.107
7. Judith, Anodea—*Wheels of Life*, Llewellyn Publications, 1995, St. Paul MN, p. 270
8. Jenny, Hans—*Cymatics*, Basilius Press, Ag. Switzerland, 1974, as quoted by Braden, Gregg—*Awakening to Zero Point*, Radio Bookstore Press, 1993, Bellevue, WA, p. 71
9. Bentov, Itzhak—*Stalking the Wild Pendulum, On the Mechanics of Consciousness*, Destiny Books, 1977, Rochester VT, p. 16
10. Freke, Timothy and Gandy, Peter—*The Complete Guide to World Mysticism*, Judy Piatkus, Inc., 1997, London, p. 48–53
11. ibid. p. 61–62
12. Capra, Fritzof—*The Tao of Physics*, Harper Collins, 1976, London, p. 121–123
13. ibid. p. 57, 131, 135
14. Freke, Timothy and Gandy, Peter—*The Complete Guide to World Mysticism*, Judy Piatkus, Inc., 1997, London, p. 28–29
15. Allegro, John—*The Sacred Mushroom and the Cross,* Doubleday,1970, New York
16. Freke, Timothy and Gandy, Peter—*The Complete Guide to World Mysticism*, Judy Piatkus, Inc., 1997, London, p. 66–73
17. Gardner, Laurence—*Genesis of the Grail Kings,* Bantam Press, 1999, London, p. 137
18. Freke, Timothy and Gandy, Peter—*The Complete Guide to World Mysticism*, Judy Piatkus, Inc., 1997, London, p. 78–79
19. ibid. p. 101–106
20. ibid. p.108 –116
21. Capra, Fritzof—*The Tao of Physics*, Harper Collins, 1976, London, p. 24–29
22. Greene, Brian—*The Elegant Universe*, Vintage Books, 1999, New York, p. 72
23. **www.generationterrorists.com/quotes/abhotswh.html**
24. Greene, Brian—*The Elegant Universe*, Vintage Books, 1999, New York, p. 111
25. Zukav, Gary—*The Dancing Wu Li Masters*, Bantam Books, 1979, New York, p. 83–87
26. ibid. p. 114
27. Capra, Fritzof—*The Tao of Physics*, Harper Collins, 1976, London, p. 148
28. ibid. p. 153
29. From a profile of Michio Kaku on the website—**www.greatmystery.org**
30. From a film, *Einstein,* written and directed by Patrick Griffin for the television series, *Nova*
31. Capra, Fritzof—*The Tao of Physics*, Harper Collins, 1976, London, p. 189
32. ibid. p. 233
33. ibid. p. 245
34. ibid. p. 332
35. ibid. p. 317
36. Zukav, Gary—*The Dancing Wu Li Masters*, Bantam Books, 1979, New York, p. 310
37. Greene, Brian—*The Elegant Universe*, Vintage Books, 1999, New York, p. 365
38. Judith, Anodea—*Wheels of Life*, Llewellyn Publications, 1995, St. Paul MN, p. 191
39. Braden, Gregg—*Awakening to Zero Point*, Radio Bookstore Press, 1993, Bellevue, WA, p. 100
40. Camphausen, Rufus—*The Encyclopedia of Sacred Sexuality,* Inner Traditions International, 1999, Rochester, VT., p. 155
41. Myss, Caroline—*Anatomy of the Spirit*, Harmony Books, 1996, New York, p. 40–48
42. Goodwin, David—*The Truth About Cabala*, Llewellyn Publications, 1994, St. Paul MN. Much of the information regarding the Qabala comes from a summary of the work of Goodwin and other various writings.
43. Braden, Gregg—*Awakening to Zero Point*, Radio Bookstore Press, 1993, Bellevue, WA, p. 81
44. From a website of Einstein quotes—**www.sfheart.com/einstein**

Part Two

The Big Shift

High up in Wollumbin, the sacred mountain in the Australian rainforest, my friend Jayavinda taught me the art of overtone singing. One night a group of us got together and he led us as we chanted at the full moon. It was a magic night. I felt my inhibitions dissolve and my spirit soar. At that moment I felt more alive than ever. There was an overwhelming sense that I was—that we all were—on the verge of a great transformation.

What would the future bring? Would it find me basking in the tropical sun, dining on fresh mangoes, enjoying some sort of utopian existence without a care in the world? Would I be fighting for survival in some post-apocalyptic hell? Without really knowing the flavor of the new reality, I felt certain that it was just 'round the corner.

In the past few years, almost every time I have the misfortune of being exposed to 'the news', I hear a story about some weather anomaly occurring somewhere in the world. It could be a flood here, a drought there, unseasonably warm, a freak cold snap, hurricanes, tornadoes, earthquakes and volcanoes. Oh it's that darned old El Nino, the reporter usually says. No one pauses to explain that El Nino is an effect and not a cause. We rarely hear the reporters talking about global climatic change, even rarer to hear them talk about the many other factors affecting the behavior of this planet at this time. El Nino is a nice, temporary condition to cite; much more comfortable than talking about the **end of the world**.

So what is really going on? No one has the authority to answer that question with any degree of finality. However, if one is truly interested in taking a hard look at this question, then I might suggest that there is a great deal of relevant information that is not readily found in the mass media or the educational institutions. As I've previously mentioned, I like to call it 'alternative information' or alterinfo. It is my belief that we are, at least, actively discouraged from hunting down such information and, at most, actively denied access to much of it. This chapter represents an effort to offer the reader an overview of information which attempts to address the question, 'where, in the next few years, are Earth and its residents headed?'

Chapter 9
━━━━━━━
GLOBAL CHANGES

Some call it the 'End Times', some the 'Apocalypse' or 'Armageddon', while others refer to it as 'the Big Shift'. Whatever you call it, there is a good deal of evidence to suggest that this planet and its inhabitants are on the verge of enormous change. Some say that change will be brought about due to the activities of mankind. Others say that catastrophes, purges and global shifts are just a part of the planet's natural evolution and that changes, varying in intensity, have occurred approximately every 13,000 years. There are various explanations for such changes, ranging from the conventional to the not-so-conventional. Let's take a quick look at some of these possible causes, starting with more familiar views and moving into newer territory.

Many conventional perspectives paint a grim picture for Earth's immediate future. There are many serious threats such as disease, nuclear war, overpopulation, lack of food, water and oxygen, etc. Even the most conservative scientists would not attempt to disagree with the environmental warnings that have been expressed for decades. In 1992, over 1500 scientists from 69 countries issued the 'World Scientists' Warning to Humanity', which stated, "Human beings and the natural world are on a collision course....A great change is required if vast human misery is to be avoided and our global home on this planet is not to be irretrievably mutilated."[1] We simply cannot continue to pollute our air and water, deplete our ozone and treat our mother Earth with contempt if we hope to survive.

With *global warming*, rising water levels and climatic change represent a real threat. The ten warmest years of this century took place within the last fifteen. The year of 1998 is the warmest year on record, 2003 and 2002 the second and third warmest. The Intergovernmental Panel on Climate Change cited the Greenhouse Effect as the main factor, caused by a build up of carbon-dioxide and other gases due to the burning of fossil fuels and other by-products of the industrial age.[2] An increase in sub-oceanic volcanic eruptions has been cited as another factor in the rise in water temperatures. There are thought to be other causes as well, having to do with Earth's natural cycles.

During the past century, ocean levels have risen by about eight inches. Only a portion of the polar ice fields need melt in order to cause a global crisis. If ocean levels were to rise by several feet, major world ports would become useless. Much of the economy would collapse and, in an era when we are becoming increasingly dependent on global trade, mass starvation would ensue. Isaac Asimov 'did the math' and calculated that a complete meltdown would result in a 200-foot rise in sea levels—surely resulting in the death of billions and the end of civilization as we know it.[3] Well known psychic Gordon Michael Scallion, who gained much media attention after successfully predicting earthquakes, has released a 'future map' which came to him in a dream, showing what the world will look like after the water has risen and the plates shifted. (see Scallion's website—**www.matrixinstitute.com**) Many believe that, long before we feel the effects of rising ocean levels, the planet will be devastated by *climatic change* and its subsequent mega-storms. (Reems of information re: climate change and global warming is available on the Internet. One good site developed by the American Institute of Physics is **www.aip.org/history/climate/index**.)

The most violent weather in our 150 years of record keeping occurred in 1999. In that year, 30,000 people were killed by torrential rains in Venezuela; 12,000 died in a supercyclone in India; Europe saw wind speeds approaching 125 miles per hour and hailstones weighing eight pounds. The years 1998, 1997 and 1996 were also record breakers. Many say that storms will increase in number and severity as global warming increasingly affects climate. Since 1940, temperatures have risen by 8°F. in the Arctic, and by 6°F. in the Antarctic. According to the August, 1999 edition of *New Scientist* magazine, the Arctic is losing 26,000 square miles of ice per year. Antarctica is also experiencing huge meltings, affecting the crucial ocean currents which regulate Earth's weather patterns. Melting ice, which is freshwater, impacts the ocean's salinity levels, greatly affecting marine life and food chains. Greenhouse effects cause the lower atmosphere, the troposphere, to retain heat while the upper atmosphere, the stratosphere, becomes colder. The greater this difference in temperatures, the greater the potential for extreme weather, including ferocious winds, giant hailstones, torrential rains, tsunamis, etc. Some experts feel that these conditions will trigger a new ice-age.[4]

Perhaps the change will be in the form of a 'pole shift', with the north and south poles shifting to new locations on the globe, causing enormous destruction and virtually eliminating life from the face of the planet. There is evidence showing that such *pole shifts* have taken place often in the 4.5 billion year history of Earth, possibly as recently as 13,000 years ago. In a new branch of science called 'paleomagnetism', core samples are taken from the ocean floor and subjected to ionium and radiocarbon dating, showing the layers of change. Different strata show different magnetic alignments in the polarity of iron molecules, indicating a likelihood that the polarity of the planet has changed often. Scientist Alan Cox's work shows 171 different geomagnetic alignments in the strata of core samples which go back 76 million years.[5]

Many significant changes happened about 13,000 years ago. There was an extinction of such animals as woolly mammoths, mastodons, saber-tooth cats, etc. The Wisconsin ice age came to a rather abrupt end. During the ice age,

which lasted about 100,000 years, a greater amount of the planet's water existed in the form of ice-sheets gathered at the poles, covering most of the northern hemisphere, and thus the ocean levels were much lower than they are
today. The research of Dr. Bruce Heezen, an oceanographer working out of
Columbia University, shows that the oceans rose by about 300 feet after the
ice-sheets melted.[4] Some feel that this was the time of the Biblical flood. Some
feel that this was the time of the sinking of the lost continent of Atlantis.

Whether one believes in Atlantis or not, there is a good amount of evidence
suggesting that something very strange happened at that time. Mastodons and
bison unearthed in Siberia and Alaska, believed to be 13,000 years old, appear to
have been 'flash-frozen'. Perfectly preserved, they still had food in their stom-
achs and mouths, apparently still chewing when they were suddenly frozen.
Experts estimate that it would require a drop from 80° to –150°F, occurring very
quickly, for such stomach contents to remain unaffected by decomposing acids.
The food was shown to consist of plants that grow only in the tropics, suggesting that the region was at a warmer position at that time. Ice in this region from
that time shows the distinct crystalline formations indicative of water that has
frozen suddenly, rather than the different patterns that result when ice accumulates slowly in the normal fashion. According to some scientists, a sudden pole-
shift offers the best explanation for these strange phenomena.[5]

Charles Hapgood, who has researched this well, believes that the north pole
was in the middle of Hudson Bay before something caused it to shift to its present location. It is interesting to note that, during the last ice age, the northern
ice cap extended much further south on the American side than it did on the
Russian side. This seems to validate the possibility that the north pole was in
Hudson Bay, which is about the center point of this northern ice cap. Much of
Siberia and parts of Alaska would have been south of the ice line under such
circumstances. (A book by John White, *Pole Shift*, sheds light on a variety of
theories and evidence on this topic.)

Others believe that a **collision with some celestial body** was the cause of past
cataclysms and that another such collision is imminent. In 1908, a small meteorite (70 metres in diameter) exploded in the atmosphere above a remote location
in Siberia called Tunguska. It flattened 2,000 square kilometers of forest. Had it
exploded over Moscow, it would have completely destroyed the city and its residents. In 1989 a much larger asteroid crossed our path, missing the planet by a
mere six hours. Here is what an American House of Representatives committee
said about it, "Had it struck Earth it would have caused a disaster unprecedented
in human history… equivalent to more than 1,000 one-megaton bombs."[6]

In July, 1994, the Shoemaker-Levi comet broke up into 21 fragments as it
pommelled Jupiter, causing weather anomalies and volcanic activity here on
Earth. The Halle-Bopp comet which recently made an appearance (1,000 times

bigger than Halley's comet), is thought to have a large elliptical orbit of about 4,200 years, entering the inner solar system twice per orbit. (Some people believe it was the same star that guided the mysterious Magi to Bethlehem.) The possibility of the Earth being devastated by such a cosmic collision is very real.

Some say that the Earth will be destroyed by *solar flares*. There has been a significant increase in this phenomenon lately. In the late 1960s, David Suzuki led a team of scientists who were observing the sun and issuing urgent warnings that major, devastaing flare activity would occur in 1972, and that it would probably cause a pole-shift. Between August 2 and 7, 1972, four enormous sun-storms took place which scientists felt should have ended all life on the planet. Although there were some effects, all life on the planet did not end. Why it did not is a mystery. Some claim that we were 'rescued' by benevolent extra terrestrials. Prior to the event, there was much written and published about it, but afterward there was what amounted to a media blackout surrounding this mystery.[7]

Despite what seems like a dire situation, many well-informed sources say that there is nothing to fear, that love will save us! Humanity is steadily learning to react to circumstances with a greater dergree of compassion. Thus we are emitting vibrations of a higher frequency. This, combined with other factors, is raising the frequency of the planet, which is creating a slightly different reality. Earth is becoming 'less dense'. Although these circumstances may trigger various earth-changes, it also represents a great opportunity.

Love will change our collective consciousness and we will change our behavior accordingly. Our attitudes toward Gaia, a name we have for the planet, will change. Our very nature will change. This will bring about a mass transformation, a planetary healing. Circumstances on the planet, including the planet's diminishing 'density', will make it easier for individuals to move toward enlightenment. This will result in great numbers of the Earth's population, possibly the entire population, 'reaching enlightenment' as a result of this great opportunity. Some have called this phenomenon *the 'Big Shift'*.

While acknowledging the possibility that the big shift might bring with it some degree of devastation, this section of the book will explore the notion that it has great potential to bring a transformation to a new and glorious reality, to a whole new 'dimension'. Some people believe that every life form on the planet will make the shift. Others say that only those beings who have achieved a sufficiently high level of enlightenment will survive the journey. Perhaps, as greater and greater numbers of people begin to 'enlighten' (a process sometimes referred to as 'the quickening'), it will have an exponential, snowballing effect, taking all of mankind with it. Some say that the 'critical mass' that will trigger this snowballing effect is just over 10% of the population. In other words, if 10% reach an enlightened state, it will have a great effect on the rest of us, creating a momentum that will pull us all toward enlightenment.

There is a question that is often asked. What if the entire population doesn't 'make the shift', i.e. reach enlightenment in time? I would suggest that these individuals would incarnate into new circumstances and continue to 'play the game', as outlined in the previous chapters. Perhaps those circumstances would involve a different planet. Maybe this planet will have its slate wiped clean and a new era, a new projection of souls, a new cosmic opportunity will begin. Perhaps life here will continue with attitudes remaining more or less unchanged, and souls will continue to use these circumstances as a 'learning ground'. In any case, I believe there is nothing to fear. We are all destined to 'get there' sooner or later.

This section will take a look at some of the 'evidence' suggesting, both from the perspective of prophesies old and new as well as that of science, that we are indeed facing some sort of 'big shift'. Before talking specifically about the shift, however, there are some concepts that need to be discussed. Without establishing such a context, this presentation would be far less meaningful.

As we saw in Part one, ***all is energy***. This is a concept that was well known to the ancient sages and, in the wake of Einstein and quantum physics, is being embraced by the scientific community. Most scientists, however, along with the larger 'lay' community, are slow to grasp the enormous implications of such discoveries as they apply to everyday life. The famous equation, $E=mc^2$ suggests that all matter is a manifestation of energy, that what appears to be solid is actually an illusion. Quantum physics recognizes that creation is non-solid and non-continuous, that it is expressing itself in very rapid short bursts of light/energy called 'quanta'. According to scientist/spiritualist and author, Gregg Braden, these quanta are averaged and blended by the human mind into the illusion of a single continuous reality.[8]

Indeed, matter, light, information, sound, and even thought and emotion are said to be forms/expressions/manifestations of energy, measurable in wave frequencies. There are many ways in which energy 'prefers' to behave—these preferences could be called 'laws' of energy. This next chapter will discuss a few of these laws that are relevant to this chapter. It will describe them separately and then bring them together to make some important points regarding the Big Shift. (It should be said that some of these 'laws' that we're about to discuss are not necessarily recognized by conventional science as laws of physics. Maybe someday they will be.)

Chapter 10

THE BEHAVIOUR OF ENERGY

Energy comes from many external sources such as the earth, the sun, other stars, and the galactic center. The Mayans felt that the biggest star in the Pleiades called Alcyon is a major source of energy radiation in the galaxy. Energy from this variety of sources interacts with our consciousness (which is also energy) to create our reality. Our consciousness 'shapes' this energy into the reality that we perceive. From the cosmos we take in the energy of life, something that the Indian traditions call prana and the Oriental traditions call ki or chi, we 'process' it and send it back out to the cosmos. Some of the 'processing tools' are will, intention, attitude, etc, which shape the quality of our thoughts, words and deeds. As described in Part One, the collective consciousness controls our greater reality, while individual consciousness controls our personal realities.

Cymatics, a relatively new science pioneered by Hans Jenny, is the study of how vibration effects form. If one were to place a cookie sheet containing a fine layer of sand upon a hi-fi speaker and then play a note through that speaker, one would find that the sand would arrange itself into a specific pattern. The same note always generates the same pattern. If the note is changed, the pattern will change—the higher the frequency of the note, the more complex the pattern.[9] This seems to agree with mystical thought, which contends that form/geometry generates frequency/sound, which in turn, generates form/geometry. In other words, there is a distinct correlation between frequency and material form. Mystics claim that every possible variation of physical form has its own unique frequency 'signature'.

Studies have been done to show that different emotions generate different measurable frequencies. Using machines similar to those commonly called 'lie detectors', it has been shown that negative, fear-based emotions yield a lower vibration, and that the positive, love-based emotions yield a higher vibration. Simply stated, positive thoughts and emotions vibrate at a higher level than do negative thoughts and emotions. Thus a person whose consciousness is predominantly based in fear will tend to emit vibrations of a lower frequency than one whose consciousness is predominantly based in love. Every individual has a 'signature' frequency, a blend of the fears and emotions that tend to predominate in that individual. Thus, as the individual 'heals', this signature rises in frequency. This is a very important concept and will be discussed further.

If one was to strike a note on a piano, other octaves of the same note as well as harmonic notes would begin to vibrate without having been struck. This is called ***resonance***, and it applies to all forms of vibrating energy, including human consciousness. Thus, if one were in a room full of people who were feeling the emotion of fear, one would tend to resonate with the larger group. One would start feeling fearful as well, without needing to know the source of the fear.

One aspect of resonance that is very relevant to our discussion here is a phenomenon called **entrainment**. If many pendulums of equal length are swinging (vibrating) in unison or 'in synch', and a new pendulum is set in motion at a different frequency, it will eventually entrain or synchronize to the beat of the others. A group of pendulums, or any other type of oscillators, that are all vibrating out of synch will eventually find a common frequency and beat in unison. It's as if nature seeks to use energy more economically. This phenomenon also applies to living bodies. Our physical bodies are affected by the frequencies of magnetic fields, gravitational fields, light patterns and other Earthly pulses. Also, we continually affect each other at a vibrational level. It has been noted that a group of women living together under the same roof will tend to menstruate at the same time of the month. A new woman introduced to this group would soon entrain and thus resonate with the other women.[10]

An interesting aspect of entrainment occurs when two oscillators of similar frequency are vibrating in proximity to each other. The one vibrating at the lower frequency will tend to be pulled up into the higher frequency by the oscillator that is vibrating at the higher frequency. Thus, if all else is equal, someone experiencing the lower emotion of fear would tend to feel more loving when in the company of someone experiencing the higher emotion of love.

In the section on chakras in chapter seven we talked about the tendency of energy to move through the body along pathways called 'nadis'. Similarly, all energy moves in certain invisible 'preferred paths' or conduits called **grids**, which correspond to basic geometric shapes. For each and every expression or manifestation of energy (object, sound, thought, emotion, etc.) there is a corresponding grid. Together they make up what has been called **the matrix** of reality. This has also been called the 'morphogenetic grid'. (Morphogenetic means 'to generate form'.) As consciousness interacts with the matrix it can generate change. In other words, as previously mentioned, we are continually creating reality.

In Part One we talked about the **Law of Octaves**. We saw how, in human history, there have been countless references to the numbers twelve and seven. Strangely, we have tended to honor the number twelve while discrediting the number thirteen, which was deemed to be an unlucky number—Friday the thirteenth, etc. We have chosen not to acknowledge the thirteenth constellation of the Zodiac, Opiuchus the Serpent Holder, a shaman/healer who is said to know the secrets of life. The Mayans knew that this number is very significant, holding the most important place in their sacred calendar and in their number system. Many claim that the number thirteen represents Christ-consciousness—the fourth dimension.

The first fundamental law of the universe is sometimes called the **Law of Three**. It states that all actions and phenomena are the result of the simultaneous interaction of three forces, a positive-male-active-electric force, a negative-female-passive-magnetic force, and a neutral or catalytic force. This trio is evident in countless examples, including atomic structure, which has a neutron and proton making up the nucleus, and negative electrons orbiting the nucleus.

Of course, there are many other 'behaviors' of energy, but we can't discuss them all here. The famous first sentence of the Gospel of John, "In the beginning was the Word, and the Word was with God, and the Word was God", seems to be saying that the universe was created using sound and that God is, in fact, sound. The ancient Hebrew symbol which was translated as 'word', can also mean 'sound'. Sound is vibration, sound is energy. If one 'note' equals one expression of energy, then the universe is an enormous 'chord' of notes, of information/ energy/light, of which we are only able to perceive a small portion. The trained ear of an experienced musician has a greater ability to hear the subtleties and nuances in a piece of music than a novice. As we move toward enlightenment, as we train our awareness, our 'ears' are entraining to hear more and more of the Divine Song of Creation. Many throughout history have felt that the next few years will bring an enormous opportunity for such training.

How do all of these concepts relate to the idea of the Big Shift'? There is a growing awareness that the 'density' of the planet is changing. Due to circumstances such as the position of our planet within the cosmos and the evolution of its consciousness, the frequency of the planet is rising. This affords us the opportunity to rise with it, to entrain to the new vibration, the new reality. Hopefully, this idea will become clearer as the chapters unfold. At this point, before proceeding with a more scientific explanation of this phenomenon, I'd like to take a look at what the prophets have had to say about the Big Shift.

Chapter 11

PROPHECIES

What is a prophecy? Webster's Dictionary defines it as 'a foretelling of what is to come'. Most experts on prophecies would say that a prophetic prediction is not 'written in stone', that it is based on a high degree of probability. If one boards a train bound for Paris, then barring any unforeseen circumstances, it is very likely that one would arrive in Paris. If mankind continues to interact with its environment in the current manner, then any of us could fairly accurately predict what would soon become of us. If prophecies were written in stone, then the entire concept of free will would be called into question. Why bother making choices when our future is already determined?

This classic ongoing philosophical debate between determinism and free will cannot be resolved because both are true. It is part of the paradoxical nature of 'time', which we perceive as linear, but which actually allows for many possible futures to co-exist. Our free will determines which future we will experience, and prophets predict according to the 'time line' in which we currently find ourselves. That time line can be changed if we willfully change the circumstances that define it.

It has been said by mystics throughout the ages that we exist in many dimensions and time-lines simultaneously, learning lessons in all of them until the day when these various aspects of ourselves become aware of each other and come together. Paradoxes such as this, of which there are many, are difficult for our minds to grasp in a conventional way because we are used to thinking in a logical, linear way.

The vast majority of the countless prophecies made about the coming shift have targeted the last couple of decades of the twentieth century and the first two of the twenty-first as being the time in which major changes will occur. I will refer to this period as the *'now-times'*. *At a talk I gave recently I asked the crowd if they felt that our times were, somehow, special. Most felt that they were. While this could be interpreted as an example of narcissism, I tend to feel that their instincts were accurate.* Let's take a look at some of the characteristics of now-times that seem special.

Compared to times past, the **accumulation of information** available to us nowadays is astounding. It is estimated that 4,000 periodicals and up to 7,000 scientific papers are published every day. All of the information that humanity had accumulated from antiquity to 1900, had doubled by 1950. By 1970 it doubled again, and again by 1980. It is currently growing at an enormous rate, so fast that even NASA is about seven to ten years behind in getting its computers up to date. We are out-running ourselves, trying desperately not to trip. And yet most of us pretend that nothing has changed and that life goes on as normal. Life is profoundly different today than it was ten years ago.

Recently there has emerged much new information, many strange **phenomena that challenge our current paradigms** of reality. In 1995 archeologists have discovered in Zaire, ancient tools believed to be 80,000 years old. Indigenous art has been discovered in north-eastern Australia that is 15,000 years older than what was previously believed to be the oldest rock-art on the continent. Authorities are finally starting to admit that many of the ancient stone constructions such as those at Baalbek in Lebanon; Tiwanaku, Chavin de Huantar, and the Inca cities in the Andes; the Nazca Lines; the Mayan, Olmec and Aztec pyramids and structures of Central America; Stonehenge and other circles on the British Isles; Jericho in Israel; and the pyramids and other Egyptian structures at Giza, are much older than we thought. The Sphinx, traditionally thought to be about 4000 years old, shows definite signs of water erosion, which has a much different pattern than wind erosion. It has been 10 to 12,000 years since there was significant water in that region. There is a great deal of evidence to challenge the conventional notion that civilization began approximately 6,000 years ago, or to possibly suggest that some other intelligent group existed before that time. In Book Two we'll look more closely at some of the many enigmas that challenge our current paradigms and some of the 'alternative' explanations that are emerging.

The recent discovery of the Dead Sea Scrolls and other ancient texts such as the Gnostic Gospels, the Book of Enoch, etc, have threatened the Christian Establishment's version of events described in the Bible. There are about fifty gospels, but only four highly edited gospels made it into the Bible. Many Old Testament 'books' were also omitted. Much hidden information about the Knights Templar, the Freemasons, The Rosicrucians, Mary Magdalene and many of the figures during the time of Christ has been emerging of late. This will be discussed at greater length in Part Six.

It is a fact that **weather anomalies** and catastrophes have increased dramatically in the last few decades. 'Munich Re', the world's largest reinsurer, has recently reported that, in the period between the sixties and the nineties, extreme weather incidents and natural disasters have increased by 400%. Even after factoring in inflation rates, claims for property damages have risen by 700%. In 1996 there were four hurricanes in one season; a very rare occurrence. Blizzards, floods, droughts, heatwaves and cold spells, hurricanes and tornadoes, solar flares, volcanoes and earthquakes—all are occurring at an alarmingly increased rate.[11]

One tragic aspect of now-times is that we are witnessing a **massive extinction of species** on the planet. Just how big this extinction will be, remains to be seen. The Global Bio-Diversity Assessment presented by the United Nation's Environmental Program in Jakarta made the startling statement that extinctions are happening at a rate 50 to 100 times faster than previously predicted.[12] Extinctions can have great consequences on life in general, including upsets in the food chain as well as proliferation of insects and germs resulting from fewer natural predators. (See **BOX 8—PAST EXTINCTIONS**)

The now-times are seeing growing numbers of people becoming aware of *a need for change*. More and more alternative communities are being established. There are many new 'paths', teachers and healing techniques available. There's been a huge increase in mysterious 'miracle healings' which defy the explanations of conventional medicine. (Much new scientific evidence re: the power of the mind to effect healing, both in self and others, is coming to light. See the work of Dr. Daniel Benor, *Spiritual Healing*.) More and more people are questioning the efficacy of the conventional medical system, with its dependence on pharmaceuticals. *Newsweek Magazine* recently reported that one third of all Americans are now spending 14 billion dollars per year on **alternative health care methods**. There has also been an increase in new diseases, such as AIDS, Ebola, Legionnaire's disease, West Nile and SARS, as well as new 'conditions' such as fatigue syndrome, allergies, fibromyalgia, new forms of arthritis, etc. New variations of old diseases such as tuberculosis are emerging and antibiotic resistant bacteria are evolving.

We are continually witnessing a **change in tolerances**. Television, movie and book themes dealing with topics such as witchcraft, extraterrestrial life and the 'supernatural', which would have been laughed at or considered 'taboo' only a few decades ago, are now proliferating. Books such as *Conversations With God*, *The Celestine Prophecies* and *Bringers of the Dawn* have been topping the best-seller lists for months. Not long ago such books would have been considered blasphemy or heresy.

Many **unexplainable 'alien' phenomena** such as UFO sightings, reports of abductions and crop circles are on the increase. In the summer of 1995 there were thirtynine new crop circles reported. Since then they are becoming fewer in number, but much more complex in design, as a look at the latest circles will confirm. (see **www.swirlednews.com** or **www.temporarytemples.com**) The translation of ancient Sumerian glyphs and many other sources are producing compelling evidence that we have been visited by extra terrestrials many times in our past and that they played an enormous role in our history. Many of these glyphs demonstrate knowledge of astronomy that modern science has only recently discovered. Glyph translator and researcher, Zecharia Sitchin has spent a lifetime showing that the Sumerian 'gods' are actually a race of ET's called the Anunaki (or Elohim/Nephilim in the Bible). Recent NASA photographs show a 'face' and pyramids on Mars which are laid out according to the same geometric proportions as the pyramids on Earth. There are indeed an ever-growing number of mysteries that are unexplainable by our current paradigms of reality. More on this in later chapters.

> **BOX 8—PAST EXTINCTIONS:**
> There have been five major extinctions of life-forms on the planet including; the Ordovician of 439 million years ago which saw the loss of 85% of all species; the Permian of 250 million years ago which saw the loss of 95% of all species, and most recently, the Cretaceous extinction of 60 million years ago which saw a loss of 75% of species, including the dinosaurs. There have been many lesser extinctions as well. The most recent lasted for about 3,000 years, ending about 9000 years ago and accounting for the loss of 27 genera of larger animals including mammoths, mastodons, sabre-tooth cats, etc. It coincided with the end of the last ice-age. Many feel that another extinction is currently underway.[13]

Reports of *other strange phenomena* are on the rise, including channelings, psychic abilities and intuitive powers. There has been a great increase (especially in Italy) in the number of 'religious sightings', such as visions of the 'Virgin Mother', bleeding and weeping statues and paintings, etc.

Astrologers acknowledge that there have been some *highly unusual alignments* in the heavens recently. On August 11, 1999, there was a solar eclipse during an alignment called a 'grand cross', which formed a circumstance known as the 'points of the Avatar'. (An avatar is defined as a physical manifestation of God.) Another total solar eclipse is due to occur on the thirteenth of November, 2012 (which is thirteen years later), in alignment with Opiuchus the Serpent Holder, considered by some to be the thirteenth constellation of the Zodiac. In 1999 the summer and winter solstices saw the respective poles align with the galactic plane in a way that happens only twice in 26,000 years, causing the planet to absorb a huge amount of energy and marking what some astrologers believe to be the start of the new Aquarian era.

It seems hard to deny that something significant is going on. No matter how one chooses to interpret things, I think most would agree that it is a very dynamic and exciting time to be alive. Many people feel that their 'fears' and 'issues' are being thrown in their face by circumstance at a more intense rate. It seems as though the universe is providing more opportunities for us to heal, encouraging us to deal with our issues now. Now is the time.

John Hogue, who has spent many years examining *prophets and prophecies* of all kinds and has published many books on the topic, has this to say,

> "All prophetic cycles throughout history pinpoint the final years of this century as a turning point or cusp, with prophets of great diversity foreseeing humankind destroyed by an outer fire, or transformed by an inner one."[14]

So many people have made statements and predictions about now-time that they can't all be mentioned. Here is a list of some of the more familiar names and cultures; the Hopi, Lakota, Cherokee, Aztecs, Mayans, Aborigines and many other indigenous cultures rooted in shamanic practices; various writers of the Old and New Testaments as well as the Hindu Puranas and the Buddhist Dharma Pada; writings in stone on walls in various structures such as the pyramids and ancient temples; Nostradamus, George Gurdjieff, Tamo-San, Mme. Blavatsky, Osho, Berosus, Bahaulah, Abdul Baha, Sri Aurobindi, Roger Bacon, Cheiro, Krishnamurti, Mohammed and Y'shua bar Yusef, better known as Jesus of Nazareth; modern psychics like Edgar Cayce, Ruth Montgomery, Jean Dixon and Gordon Michael Scallion.

Many *ancient calendars and traditional cycles* end in now-time. Here is a list of some of them;

- the ancient Egyptian calendars as represented on the pyramid walls
- the Persian Mythratic calendar of 3,000 year cycles
- the last 500 year cycle of the Celts/Druids and the Teutonic Tribes of ancient Germany
- the 7,000 year cycle of the grand calendar of the Qabalistic/Hermetic schools
- the Emerald Tablets of Thoth which is the basis of the Hermetic Sciences of Alchemy, the Freemason Doctrine, the ancient Egyptian Mystery Schools, etc., which says "Mankind is in the process of changing to forms of light that are not of this world."
- the Tibetan traditions which state that there will be only fourteen incarnations of the Dalai Lama (the current one is the fourteenth)
- the Buddhist traditions, in which the Wheel of Dharma requires a new Buddha figure every 2,500 years (Gautama Buddha arrived 2,500 years ago)
- the Hindu traditions say that we are currently at the end of the Kali Yuga, which is the last yuga of a grand cycle (a yuga is a period of time)
- Astrological traditions claim that it takes 25,920 years (twelve ages of 2,160 years) to do a complete rotation through the zodiac. We are currently in the final stages of the Piscean age which is considered to be the final one of the cycle, and are about to enter the age of Aquarius
- the Mayan Tzolk'in calendar, possibly the most sophisticated calendar that we know of, ends in 2,012 (See **BOX 22—MAYAN PREDICTIONS**)
- the Sumerian calendar, also very sophisticated, which is based on the 25,920 year cycle of the Precession of the Equinoxes, divided into twelve eras of 2,160 years (like the astrological zodiac), as well as a cycle of 3600 years which is said to be the length of orbit of the solar system's 'tenth planet', Nibiru.
- many diverse cultures have calendars or other means of referring to the Precession of the Equinoxes. Why were they so interested in this long cycle?[15]

Chapter 12

COSMIC CYCLES AND EARTHCHANGES

Whoever came up with the words 'catastrophe' and 'disaster', both of which contain the root 'astre'(star), knew that cataclysms here on this planet are directly related to our position relative to the stars. Earth is subject to many different cycles, often having to do with its orbits through the cosmos.

Some say that major earth-changes, such as pole-shifts, floods, and the submerging or surfacing of landmasses, have happened often in the history of this planet. There are many theories of why this happens. Some explain it as Gaia, the consciousness of the planet, 'purging' itself of negativity. Gaia's mission, her main purpose, is to produce life and thus provide the opportunity for energy to evolve. She is very patient and loving, but when circumstances develop that threaten her potential to sustain life, then Gaia must take more drastic actions. She cleans the slate and starts again.

Various factors play various roles in these purges. Among those cited as possible causal factors in such cataclysms and earth-changes are: accumulations of ice on the polar caps, collisions with celestial bodies such as asteroids and comets and the effects of technology gone awry, etc. This chapter deals with the notion that our planet is moving through the cosmos according to periodical cycles, and that our position in the cosmos has been and continues to be a key factor triggering earth-changes.

The Earth is subject to many different cosmic cycles. Different positions relative to other cosmic bodies expose us to different strengths of electro-magnetic and gravitational force. Some positions within these cycles cause the planet to come in contact with an increased amount of energy radiation, some positions with less. The amount of energy, as well as the frequency of the energy with which we interact, is a major factor affecting many aspects of life on Earth. Energy from different sources in the cosmos interacts with our consciousness here on Earth. This is the same basic notion that underlies the practice of astrology, which seeks to identify certain predispositions in one's character based on the position of the planet at the time of that individual's birth. Different energies coming in from different cosmic bodies have been said to have their own unique qualities, which somehow imprint upon the newborn personality. These different energies are said to affect us in different ways.

There are several different cycles that affect life here on Earth, some small and less significant and some greater, with greater significance. This chapter will look at a few of them. Probably the most important of these is one that has come to be called the ***precessional cycle***. As we'll see later in the book, the ancient societies were well aware of this cycle. It is approximately 26,000 years in length. In other words, circumstances here on the planet change according to this cyclical pattern, taking 26,000 years to complete (actually 25,920). Different 'ages' within this cycle have different energies, different qualities. If we divide 25,920 by twelve, we get the twelve signs of the zodiac; twelve ages, each lasting 2,160 years. We are said to be currently at the end of the Piscean age, about to enter the age of Aquarius.

It is said that twice in every 26,000 year cycle we are exposed to an increased amount of energy radiation, an accelerated frequency of vibration, which effects our tectonic plates and volcanic activity, climate, magnetic field and other things. It also affects our consciousness and as we shall see, this is key in our exploration of the Big Shift. Earth-changes of varying intensities are said to have taken place roughly every 13,000 years, at which time we are 'predisposed' to cataclysm. There are several different but related explanations for this phenomenon.

In the continual quest for balance, cosmic bodies are revolving around other bodies that have greater gravitational pull. Just as the moon revolves around the earth and the earth around the sun, so does our entire solar system revolve elliptically around an enormous source of gravity, which we'll call the Galactic Center. Scientists have long been aware of this cycle, which is called the *precession of the equinoxes.* Our planet's position in the galaxy changes from year to year. This change has been measured by observing the point on the star map at which our North Pole is pointing. If we started recording the planet's position on the spring equinox of 2004, it would take 25,920 years before the planet would be in the same position relative to the rest of the cosmos. That is, each year at spring equinox, the North Pole would point to a spot in the cosmos just slightly west of the previous year. If one mapped the spots year after year, they would eventually describe a circle on the star map. After 25,920 years, the North Pole would be pointing at the exact spot on the star map as it was in 2004. (For a good explanation of the precessional phenomenon, see **www.shaka.com/~johnboy/Preces.htg/precession**) (See DIAGRAM 6—THE PRECESSIONAL WOBBLE)

During this cycle, as our solar system revolves around the Galactic Center, there are times when our position is such that we are exposed to increased amounts of energy radiation. One theory is that the Galactic Center is an enormous center of energy sometimes referred to as the Black Sun. (See DIAGRAM 7—THE PHOTON BELT) Twice in every 26,000 year period we are closer to this center due to the elliptical shape of the orbit. We are thus exposed to more energy than when we are far from it. Another theory is that there is a 'photon belt' which is perpendicular to the path of our orbit around this great source. We pass through this belt twice per revolution. When we pass through this concentration of photons we are exposed to greater energy—higher frequency.

DIAGRAM 6—THE PRECESSIONAL WOBBLE

The angle of Earth's poles, relative to the rest of the cosmos, changes over the course of 25,920 years.

DIAGRAM 7—THE PHOTON BELT

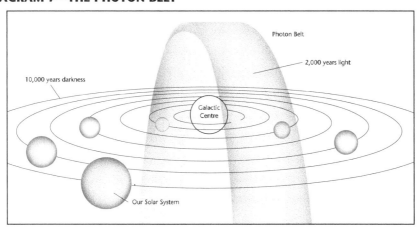

Our solar system passes through the photon belt twice in a 25,920 year cycle.

Whatever the explanation, the important point is that, for half of the cycle the planet is increasingly exposed to more energy and higher frequencies, which cause it to vibrate at a higher rate. The life forms on the planet tend to entrain, to resonate in synch with whatever frequency the planet is experiencing. Thus, as the planetary frequency increases, the frequency of our collective consciousness also tends to increase. Because our consciousness is interacting with more energy, we become more 'enlightened' or 'awakened' during

156 WHY IS LIFE?

this period. The higher vibratory rate also tends to 'shake' the planet, causing many changes in the patterns and 'behavior' of the planet. For the other half of the cycle we move away from the energy source and thus fall 'asleep'. At these times the planet is denser—more stable. In other words, every 13,000 years, the planet is exposed to a greater energy that physically destabilizes it and creates an opportunity for great change.

Many earth-changes, including the 'Great Flood', are said to have occurred 13,000 years ago. The Wisconsin ice age came to an end at that time. We are said to be, once again, on the verge of great change, a new era. We are about to enter the 'Age of Aquarius'. We are entering that part of the cycle that brings higher frequencies. These new circumstances bring great opportunities for us to make enormous advances in our healing, in our evolution. They may also bring cataclysm. However, some information is saying that this particular opportunity is different than the other '13,000 year opportunities'. Some say that, unlike other great transitions in the past, the planet is about to vibrate its way into the fourth realm, into Christ-consciousness, taking many of its inhabitants with it. This is what is referred to as the 'Big Shift'.

There are other 'lesser' cycles such as the 5,200 year, the 500 year and the 20 year cycles, which all seem to be ending in now-time. An important one for our discussion here is the 2,000 year *'magnetic field' cycle* which affects our receptivity to new information. At any given moment there are places on the globe which have a higher or lower degree of electro-magnetic strength, similar to the high and low pressure zones as seen on a weather map. This pattern changes constantly according to set 'rules', and these changes take 2,000 years to complete a cycle. When magnetic strength is low, we are more receptive, more open to new ways of thinking and perceiving.[16] It was 2,000 years ago when Jesus, Mary Magdalene, John the Baptist and a host of other spiritual teachers came to Earth. We are now at the same point in the magnetic field cycle as they were at the time of Christ, a time of great transformation in human consciousness.

There are some significant **solar cycles** that affect life on Earth. Sun spots or solar flares, first noted by the Mariner 2 in 1962, are said to be caused by the sun's irregular spin or rotation pattern. The area of the sun at its poles takes 37 days to rotate, while the equatorial regions of the sun rotate every 24 days. This discrepancy results in a 'twist' in the sun which, as it corrects itself, causes the flares—bursts of radiation which interact with consciousness on our planet. Correlations have been drawn between this kind of solar activity and such things as fertility levels, schizophrenia, biorhythms, hormone production and personality types as in astrological signs. Studies have shown that solar flare activity peaks every 11.5 years, constituting a short cycle that operates within longer cycles. It is said that our sun reverses its magnetic poles every 3,750 years, or 1,366,040 days. (The number 1,366,560 is considered sacred by the Mayans.) These reversals are said to cause mutation in DNA, a phenomenon called 'astrogenetics' by an engineer and computer scientist named Maurice Cotterell in his book, 'The Tutenkhamen Prophecies'. Is it possible that these mutations correlate with sudden proliferations of new species throughout Earth's history, as shown in the fossil records? It has also been suggested that, when these solar reversals occur in conjunction with a 'critical point' of the Earth's precessional cycle, it causes a reversal of the planet's polarity.[17]

Chapter 13

MAGNETICS VERSUS FREQUENCY

There are two key factors that effect life on this (and possibly any other) planet, the strength of the magnetic field and the average frequency at which the planet vibrates. The Earth is an electro-magnetic entity, and so are all of its resident life-forms. Every cell in our bodies has an electrical charge and a magnetic field. The planet's magnetic field shields us from external energy. Without it we would soon fry in the sun's radiation.

Ancient mystery school knowledge tells us that the electrical (male, mental, yang) aspect of our being represents all the information of our true, multi-dimensional reality—the totality of creation. In Part One it was noted that exposure to such a totality of information would cause a type of 'circuit melt-down'. The magnetic (female, emotional, yin) aspect acts as a shield or buffer, allowing us access to only a certain amount of the totality of information. We are thus protected from being overwhelmed by the 'larger truth', for which we are not yet prepared. One must have total mastery over one's fears and react to every possible circumstance with love and compassion in order to be prepared to witness the totality of creation. Thus, lower magnetic strength = less buffer = more information coming in = less amount of time required for thoughts to manifest into reality = more potential for profound change.

The ancient mystery schools of Egypt (consisting of twelve years for the Left Eye of Horus—corresponding to the right brain—and twelve years for the Right Eye of Horus—corresponding to the left brain) are said to have used magnetics in the process of 'training' initiates. It is said that different chambers in various temples and structures were constructed to have varying degrees of *magnetic strength*. The first of the twelve chambers would have the least decrease in magnetic strength and the initiate would be presented with a relatively mild aspect of the human psyche. If the initiate overcame his fear of that aspect and reacted with love, he would pass the test and graduate to the next level of training. He would thus be able to handle increasingly lower levels of the magnetic shielding force. The twelfth and final test is said to have taken place in the 'King's Chamber' in the Great Pyramid, where the magnetic strength was close to nil. Only an initiate with complete mastery over his fears and an ability to sustain a state of love/compassion would survive such a test. With the ability to activate and control his personal electro-magnetic field, he would be placed in the 'sarcophagus' (granite box) for three days (the same amount of time that Jesus is said to have taken before his resurrection), during which he would shift to a higher octave of expression at a cellular level. Hopefully, he would thus ascend into Christ-consciousness.

Magnetic fields are said to accommodate memory. Our personal memories are governed by our personal fields, while our collective memory (sometimes referred to as the Akashic Record) is governed by the planetary field. Memory could be defined as a retained body of finite information, a portion of the infinite whole. Some say that a major Earth-change/cataclysm is accompanied by a collapse of the magnetic field and that whatever happened 13,000 years ago caused the field to collapse for three days, resulting in our collective memory being wiped clean. They say that it signified the end of the Atlantean age and that we lost all language and knowledge from that era, causing us to have to 'start over'.

Scientists are not sure as to the cause of the Earth's magnetic field. We do know that an iron bar with a coil of wire wrapped around it will generate a magnetic field when a current of electricity is sent through the coil. To reverse the direction of the current is to reverse the polarity of the field. Probably the most popular theory about the cause of our field postulates that the planet's solid iron inner core is rotating at a different rate than its mantle/crust, due to the molten, fluid outer core. This would generate an electrical charge, which in turn, would generate a magnetic field. Core samples taken from the ocean floor have shown that there have been many polarity reversals during the planet's 4.5 billion year history. Magnetic strength is a specific quantity, measurable in 'gauss' units. The Earth's field, which has been monitored for about one hundred years, has decreased about 38% to it's present state which has been measured at 8.0×10^{25} gauss units. It is said to have been at a peak about 1,000 years ago according to calculated estimations. Most of this significant reduction has happened in the last few decades. Some feel that this is due to a change in position of the Earth's core relative to the rest of the cosmos.[18]

We have already talked about higher, love-based emotions yielding a higher vibration. One who consistently emits and receives higher vibrations is said to be in a higher state of awareness. *Frequency of vibration* of the planet is thus an important factor affecting our collective consciousness. It is another specific quantity, measurable in Hertz (Hz) units. One pulse or beat per second equals one Hz.

The Earth has a base resonant frequency at which it pulses. This could be defined as the average of all possible frequencies between the lowest parameter and the highest parameter of energy expressible in this reality. (Some say that this is the OM of creation in the Hindu traditions.) All life-forms on the planet would entrain to resonate to the same frequency. Earth's base resonant frequency, until recently, has been 7.8 Hz. Many organizations including military operations have relied on this constant for their transmissions, but have been alarmed recently because the base rate seems to be increasing. The planet's base resonant frequency is also known as the Schumann Resonance, after W. O. Schumann, a German physicist who predicted the increase in vibration back in the 1950s.

There is a well-known series of numbers called the Fibonacci Sequence. It represents a very significant set of ratios to which much of life on Earth conforms. Many growth patterns in nature follow these ratios, which, when used in conjunction with the golden mean rectangle, form the Fibonacci Spiral. (See BOX 9—THE GOLDEN MEAN AND THE FIBONACCI SEQUENCE. Also see DIAGRAM 8—THE GOLDEN MEAN SPIRAL) The pyramids and monuments at Giza are laid out according to this spiral pattern. The previously mentioned morpho-genetic grids are said to conform to this spiral. The sequence is 0, 1, 1, 2, 3, 5, 8, 13, 21, etc. Any number in the sequence is the sum of the previous two numbers. The base frequency of the planet has been almost 8 Hz, which is one of the numbers of the Fibonacci sequence. This frequency is said to be increasing and is thought to be headed for the next step in the sequence, which is that familiar number—13, the number representing Christ-consciousness.

Brain-wave activity is commonly measured in Hz values;

Delta waves range from .5 to 4 Hz—deep sleep,

Theta waves from 4 to 8 Hz—relaxed, barely awake,

Alpha waves from 8 to 12 Hz—awake,

Beta waves from 12 to 23 Hz, high alertness.[19]

As the planet's vibratory rate increases, we will automatically tend *to entrain with the new rate*. When viewed in terms of brain wave activity, the Earth at 8 Hz is in a lower alpha state—a state of being barely awake. At thirteen it would be in the early stages of the Beta state of high alertness. So as the planet enters this new set of circumstances, it is providing us with a big opportunity to move toward enlightenment, to raise our own vibratory rates. This process of entrainment will be easier if we let go of old belief systems and learn to react to different circumstances with, you guessed it, less negative, fear-based emotions and more positive, love-based emotions. We will move into the Alpha state. There will be a mass awakening.

BOX 9—THE GOLDEN MEAN AND THE FIBONACCI SEQUENCE: The Golden Mean, the Golden Section, the Divine Proportion—these are names given to a very special ratio that appears in countless contexts throughout nature. This ratio is represented mathematically as 1:1.618033988749895..., and this number is called 'phi' (not to be confused with 'pi'). Say we had three lines of increasing length, Lines A, B and C. If Line B was 1.618 times as long as Line A and Line C was 1.618 times as long as line B, then these lengths would conform to the phi ratio. Conversely, with diminishing lengths, B would be .618 times the length of C and A .618 times the length of B. With this special ratio, the combined length of Lines A and B would equal the length of C. This ratio can be derived in several ways including mathematically and geometrically. Its most well known derivation comes from the Golden Rectangle. If one had such a rectangle and severed a perfect square from it, one would be left with a rectangle that had the same proportions as the original rectangle.

Phi is known as the Divine Proportion because so many patterns in nature conform to it. For example, the bones of a human hand, from fingertip to wrist, increase in size according to this ratio. Also, the length from wrist to elbow is roughly 1.618 times bigger than from fingertip to wrist. (I say 'roughly' because the phi ratio is an ideal, an archetype, and in nature there is always slight variation.) These proportions can be seen in many body parts, including both the front view and profile of a human face. It also applies to the proportions in other animals, growth patterns in plants, heartbeat patterns, sea-shell spirals and much more. It can even be seen in the DNA molecule, the program for all life. The length of a full cycle of its double helix spiral is 1.618 times greater than its width. Phi can be seen in the distances between planets in our solar system, in the patterns of population growth of many species, the frequencies in the color spectrum and in many musical relationships. The distance between frets on a guitar decreases according to this ratio as one moves up the neck.

Interestingly, humanity has known about this special ratio for thousands of years. It has been used throughout history as an aesthetic standard in art. It is represented in the layout of many great paintings and in the proportions of many works of architecture, such as the Great Pyramid, the Parthenon, the Cathedral of Notre Dame and recently, in the United Nations building. Phi can be found in the Bible. God's instructions to Moses for the building of the Ark of the Covenant (Exodus 25:10) contain strict proportions of width to length, which conform to this ratio. Phi can be seen in God's instructions to Noah regarding the proportions of the ark that he is to build. (Genesis 6:15)

In the 12th century, a mathematician named Leonardo Fibonacci discovered a number sequence that represents the phi phenomenon. It starts with 0 and 1, and each new number in the series is the sum of the previous two numbers, i.e. 0, 1, 1, 2, 3, 5, 8, 13, 21, 34, 55, 89, 144, etc. The further along in the series, the closer the ratio between adjacent numbers approximates the phi ratio. For example, 5 divided by 3 is 1.666..., 8 divided by 5 is 1.60 and 144 divided by 89 is 1.6179...

The Fibonacci Sequence and its offspring, the Fibonacci Spiral, can give us great insight as we continue to unravel the great mystery of life. For more info, an Internet search will yield countless entries; **www.goldennumber.net** is a great place to start.

DIAGRAM 8—THE GOLDEN MEAN SPIRAL

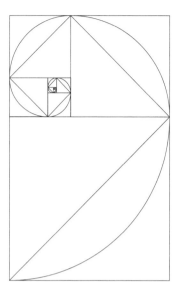

According to Gregg Braden, there is some very interesting evidence suggesting that we are well on our way in the process of entraining to the higher frequency. Scientists have known for a long time now, that we use only about 10% of our brain. The rest seems to be asleep. (We each have about ten billion brain cells, each of which is in relationship with about 25,000 other cells. Therefore, the number of possible relationships between brain cells is a number that is beyond comprehension, larger than the estimated number of atoms in the entire universe! The brain receives about 100 billion sensations per second and fires off 5,000 signals per second. We are aware of only about one millionth of our own cortical signalling.) Similarly, geneticists have isolated the function of approximately 10% of the human genome, but admit to being puzzled as to the function of the remaining 90%.

Dr. Berrenda Fox, Dr. Meg Blackburn, Geoffrey Hoppe, Susanna Thorpe-Clark, Braden and other 'consciousness researchers' are suggesting that, as the frequency of the planet increases and the strength of the magnetic field diminishes, humanity is beginning to *change at a genetic level*. They contend that we are activating more of our DNA and beginning to access more of our mental potential. They claim that researchers are finding new chemical bonds at the DNA level, that they are being found at an ever-increasing rate and are referred to as 'spontaneous mutations'.

According to Dr. Berrenda Fox, geneticists from around the world met in Mexico City a few years back to discuss this phenomenon. They felt that it was prudent to keep this information from getting public attention to avoid widespread anxiety. DNA typically occurs as two strands which form a double helix.

Fox claims to be working with subjects, mostly children, who are developing a third strand of DNA. These subjects exhibit an extraordinary mental capacity as well as psychic abilities. For more information about genetic change check out the following websites:

www.soulutions.co.uk/np_humaneve-8.htm
www.homestead.com/_allaboutlife/files/Dr._Berrenda_Fox.htm
www.luisprada.com/Protected/dna_changes.htm
www.2012.com.au/DNA_upgrades.html

Could it be that these new genetic expressions are occurring because the parameters of possible frequencies that define our reality are broadening? Are different expressions of life occurring because our consciousness—and thus our reality—is expanding. Could it be that we are waking up; entraining to the new, rising frequencies of the planet?

Chapter 14

SYMPTOMS OF CHANGE

Many people are increasingly experiencing strange circumstances and phenomena in their lives. Perhaps, as circumstances on the planet are changing, they are feeling the symptoms of change. Here are some of the more commonly reported symptoms;

- changing patterns of sleep: People are having difficulty getting enough sleep, feeling wide awake when they should be tired, and sleepy when they should be alert. They report a hard time getting to sleep as well as staying asleep. Many wake up in the middle of the night and some feel like their body is 'buzzing'. Some awaken after a good night's sleep still feeling very tired. There has been a great increase in conditions such as 'chronic fatigue' and 'fibromyalgia', which have no perceivable causal agent such as a germ or virus. More people are experiencing muscle stiffness, tension and strange headaches which seem to happen for no reason.
- lucid dreaming: Most people dream during their sleep. Their astral bodies travel and interact with others in the astral world. However, few people remember this activity or relate it to their everyday physical experiences. Increasing numbers of people are now reporting that they are having more vivid dreams, which they can recall in greater detail. Sometimes strange images and settings are returning in 'flashes' during waking hours.
- misperceptions of time: It seems to some people as though time is 'speeding up'. Events seem to fly by. This phenomenon has been referred to as

'the quickening' (a term sometimes credited to radio show host, Art Bell). In regards to the laws of karma, many people feel that their fears and 'issues' are being thrown up in their faces to be dealt with at an increasing rate. Circumstances are arising which demand that one embrace a great deal of change. In other words, opportunities to heal are coming in 'fast and furious'. Those who choose to ignore these opportunities are finding that these issues simply will not go away. Some also report moments when, in states of reverie or stupor, time seems to be suspended. If time is a construct, a product of our collective consciousness, then perhaps our perception of time is shifting along with our consciousness.

- a questioning of the value of important relationships: Many people are feeling a withdrawal or a 'drifting away' from some family members, spouses or friends. This feeling is often accompanied by guilt and anxiety. These people are often attracted to new relationships and have a longing to reinvent themselves.

- unusual memory experiences: Strange, sometimes startling memories drift into consciousness at unexpected times. At other times, names, numbers and otherwise familiar facts seem suddenly inaccessible. Information that one has known for a long time seems to suddenly disappear. The unfamiliar seems familiar and vice-versa.

- shifting values: What once seemed very important no longer seems to matter. Many people feel that what they are doing is not fulfilling them at a deeper level. They feel listless and unsatisfied yearning for something with more meaning. They often feel disconnected to reality, as if they are walking about in a fog. As mentioned previously, more and more people are becoming 'seekers'.

- breakdown of traditional systems and institutions: More and more people are questioning the status quo, challenging aspects of life that were recently considered to be 'written in stone'. Institutions such as the government, the church, the education system, the media and the justice system are increasingly under suspicion. This questioning is sometimes dismissed as rampant cynicism, but actually, it may be the result of an increased awareness and a sense that we are continually being deceived and misled by the authorities. Increase in the number of same-sex relationships and divorce rates is testament to a challenging of traditional marital roles. Some feel that we are moving away from monogamy and there is a great confusion about the nature of relationships and commitment. Many volumes can be (and have been) written about the many facets of life that have been questioned, especially since the decade of the sixties.[20]

Researchers claim that evolutionary changes at the genetic level are resulting in a recognizable list of temporary physical symptoms:
- flu-like symptoms such as fevers, sweating, aching bones and joints

- migraine headaches that are unaffected by pain killers.
- dizziness and a feeling of 'not being grounded'.
- ringing in the ears
- muscle spasms and strange aches and pains, often in the back and neck.
- tingling in arms, hands, legs or feet.
- feeling tired or exhausted with a loss of muscular strength.
- feeling as though one can't get enough breath.
- immune system changes, including allergies.
- wanting to sleep longer and more often than normal.
- nails and hair growing more quickly than normal.
- bouts of depression for no real reason.
- anxiety due to a feeling that 'something is going on', but not knowing what it is.

Could it be that these 'symptoms of change' are the result of humanity entraining to higher vibrations? Is our level of awareness and perception of reality in the process of changing?

Those who suspect that we may very well be resonating at ever higher frequencies may be asking themselves, "what can I do **to facilitate the process of entrainment?**" Of course, there are many ways—as many as there are people on the planet. Some methods, however, are common to many. To more effectively expose oneself to the rising vibration of the planet, it makes sense to be in greater contact with nature. Most of us are always several steps removed from a purely natural environment. In the past sixty years, we are increasingly surrounded by synthetic objects. Our homes, cars, workplaces, etc. are made up of unnatural substances; plastics, paints and lacquers, synthetic fabrics and other manufactured materials come in contact with us continually. These artificial substances do not carry, do not accurately represent the planetary vibrations in the same way as natural substances that are in closer contact with the Earth. Most people who are immersed in the beauty of nature feel more alive, their moods elevated. Natural objects have a 'power', especially rocks and crystals. *Having grown up in Northern Ontario, Canada, I can attest to the fact that the living rock of the pre-Cambrian Shield exudes an enormous energy.*

The next logical deduction is to eat natural foods, drink clean, 'living' water and breath unpolluted air. It's not rocket science, it's common sense—natural products of the Earth will tend to be vibrating in resonance with the Earth. Ironically, our physical bodies are our links to the higher realms. You may have heard the expression, "we are not physical entities having a spiritual experience, we are spiritual entities having a physical experience". As true as this may be, it does not mean that our physical selves are somehow less important than our emotional/mental/spiritual selves. Our bodies represent our point of interaction between the physical, third-dimensional realm and those beyond.

A healthy body will be better equipped to absorb the enlightening vibrations.

Any activity that facilitates our own personal healing will better enable us to resonate with the rising frequencies of the planet. Meditating, practicing yoga, praying, sustaining mindfulness; these are some of the tried and tested methods by which we can self-heal. My favorite is chanting. These methods are all means to an end. Sometimes, however, such practices can start to become the end rather than the means. Some people become so involved in the activity, that they forget the purpose of pursuing the activity, sometimes even to the point of becoming 'snobby'. Any spiritual pursuit that does not result in the participant becoming more compassionate and loving, is not fulfilling its promise. Absolutely any activity that results in an increased capacity to greet all circumstances with love and gratitude, and which does harm to no one else, is a good healing tool. In my opinion, it is very difficult to heal, to move toward enlightenment without, either directly or indirectly, taking a good hard look in the mirror. To heal is to remove fear-based obstacles, to reclaim knowledge and power and to become a better lover.

I believe that great opportunities, such as our current 'Big Shift', have occurred often, roughly every 13,000 years. It is said that the current opportunity is one that is stronger than usual, one that has greater potential for our collective growth, or for our demise. Due to a strange set of circumstances that occurred in the distant past (which will be discussed in the section on 'alternative history'), the planet's vibratory rate was 'turned down' to save it from the crisis that occurred 13,000 years ago. This caused the difference between our current frequency and the one toward which we are moving to be larger than normal. This greater difference could result in a greater 'shaking' of our planet, leading to a more violent set of earth-changes. How can we prepare for this? Is there anything we can do to make these coming changes more positive and less apocalyptic?

On a pragmatic level, it makes sense that we refrain from assisting the cataclysmic potential by weakening and ecologically damaging the planet. If we use our will to change our ways, to become more compassionate in our daily choices, then we will collectively be emitting vibrations of higher frequency. As our collective consciousness awakens and enlightens, then so will the planet, as the two are inseparable. In other words, if we wake up, if we choose to treat the Earth and each other with greater compassion, if we make more love and less war, if we feel less fear and generate fewer negative, lower frequency vibrations, then we will be ready for the changes. If we are collectively generating higher frequencies, then the planet's rate of vibration will be higher by the time we reach that high point in the precessional cycle. Thus the difference will not be so great and the changes will be less violent. The choice is really up to us.

I believe it is important to understand that there is nothing to fear. No matter what happens, the great illusion—the Game—will continue in whatever form. I believe that we are awakening at an ever-increasing rate. More and more people are seeing through the fog and attempting to fill the darkness with light. I joyously antic-ipate the future, whatever shape it takes.

We are truly living in exciting times. I'm sure that most people have an intuitive sense that some great change is just around the corner. Some see it as doom and gloom, while others, myself included, are convinced that a glorious fate awaits us all. Even if we don't experience a global ascension in the 'nowtimes', I'm going to do my best to enjoy the ride, confident that we will get there someday. It's inevitable.

" Lo! I tell you a mystery. We shall not all sleep, but we shall all be changed, in a moment, in the twinkling of an eye."
The Holy Bible, 1 Corinthians 15 : 51

"Soon will the present-day order be rolled up, and a new one spread out in its stead."
—Baha'u'llah, (1863)

"Man is in the process of changing to forms that are not of this world; grows he in time to the formless, a plane on the cycle above. Know ye, ye must become formless before ye are one with the light."
The Emerald Tablets of Thoth

ENDNOTES—PART TWO

1. To read the World Scientists' Warning to Humanity in its entirety, check out **www.worldtrans.org/whole/warning.html**.
2. Jones, P.D. and Moberg, A., 2003: *Journal of Climate*, **16**, 206–223
3. Hogue, John—*The Millennium Book of Prophesy*, HarperCollins Publishing, 1994, New York, p. 74–75
4. Bell, Art and Strieber, Whitley—*The Coming Global Superstorm*, Simon and Schuster, 2001, New York, p. *xv–xx*
5. Doell, Richard and Cox, Allan—*Mining Geophysics,* V. 11, Soc. Expl. Geophysicists, 1967,
6. Hope, Murray—*Atlantis, Myth or Reality?*, Penguin Books, 1991, London, p. 63
7. White, John—*Pole Shift*, A.R.E. Press, 1996, Virginia Beach VA, p. 17–35
8. Hancock, Graham—*The Mars Mystery*, Crown Publishers, 1998, New York, p. 42–43. There is a website devoted to the Tunguska phenomenon—**www.th.bo.infn.it/tunguska**
7. Frissell, Bob—*Nothing in This Book Is True, But It's Exactly How Things Are*, Frog Ltd., 1994, Berkely, CA, p. 157–158
8. Braden, Gregg—*Awakening to Zero Point* , Radio Bookstore Press, 1993, Bellevue, WA, p. 59–64
9. ibid. p. 71
10. Bentov, Itzhak—*Stalking the Wild Pendulum, On the Mechanics of Consciousness*, Destiny Books, 1977, Rochester VT, p. 24–25
11. for more info on extreme weather, including reports from Munich Re and the World-watch Institute, see this NASA-funded website: **www.gcrio.org/CONSEQUENCES/index.htm**, vol 5 no 1
12. Bell, Art and Strieber, Whitley—*The Coming Global Superstorm*, Simon and Schuster, 2001, New York, p. 150
13. ibid. p. 169
14. Hogue, John—*The Millennium Book of Prophesy*, HarperCollins Publishing, 1994, New York, back cover
15. ibid. This information comes mostly from Hogue's work, plus various other writings I've encountered.
16. Braden, Gregg—*Awakening to Zero Point* , Radio Bookstore Press, 1993, Bellevue, WA, p. 20—information about the declining magnetic field can be found in the work of McDonald, K.L. and R.H. Gunst, *Earth's Magnetic Field 1835* to *1965*, ESSA Tech. Rept. U.S. Dept. Com., 1967
17. Cotterell, Maurice—*The Tutankhamen Prophecies,* Headline Books, 1999, London. This is a summary of Cotterell's views as expressed in pages 236–338
18. Braden, Gregg—*Awakening to Zero Point* , Radio Bookstore Press, 1993, Bellevue, WA, p. 19. A search on the Internet will yield a great deal of info to corroborate the idea that the magnetic field is diminishing and the Schumann frequency is on the rise.
19. ibid. p. 63
20. ibid. p. 46

BOOK 2

QUESTIONING
THE PARADIGMS

or

'Is Someone Pulling the Wool Over My Eyes?!'

*W**hy is life? As you may have gathered, I am pretty well convinced that the purpose of life, the reason why most of us are on the planet at this time is to pur-
sue* **enlightenment.** *That is, to learn all the lessons of this third-dimensional level
of the Game so that we'll be ready to move on to the next level. I believe that, in order
for an individual to achieve enlightenment, s/he must have evolved to the point where
each circumstance is greeted with love/compassion/gratitude/joy and positivity, and
not with any degree of fear/anger/self-pity and negativity. In order to arrive at such a
state of mind an individual comes to the realization that we are all the same, cut
from the same fabric, and so there is no need to judge anything or anyone. One comes
to the realization that we create our own reality, that we are immensely powerful
beings who have gone through a temporary period of forgetting. One seeks to remove
all obstacles to this process of realization, of becoming whole, of healing. An individual seeks to heal, using whatever methods s/he chooses.*

*Any effective healing method involves some form of self-examination. One may
well understand the way that the universe works in theory, but until this knowledge
is applied to one's actions on a daily basis, healing will be limited. Knowing that one
is a parcel of divinity is only a step in the process of behaving like a parcel of divinity. Knowing why one does the things one does leads to greater control and wiser choices. Digging out our hidden motives and examining the underlying intention behind
our actions is necessary in order to understand the power of our intent and to learn
to use that power wisely. Healing requires honesty, a willingness to examine the long
list of rationalizations that most of us have to justify our actions. Through self-examination, one begins to make better and better decisions in life until, ultimately, all
decisions are made in love. In other words, to heal is to know oneself.*

*What is true for the individual is also true for collective humanity. The human
collective is evolving,* **the collective is healing.** *This healing happens as the collective seeks to know itself. In order to heal we must be willing to look into the dark corners of our collective soul. We must know ourselves thoroughly. It is important to
examine our past actions in a sincere and honest way, unafraid to confront hidden
motives and rationalization.* **It is important to question the bodies of knowledge, the accepted paradigms that shape our attitudes, govern our
daily actions and direct our collective evolution.**

*There are many such paradigms and any book that sought to examine them all
would soon become a large encyclopedia. In this book I have focussed on several of
the bodies of knowledge, belief systems and attitudes that I feel are holding humanity back from its progress down the path to enlightenment.*

Our **ruling paradigms** *are often built from information that serves the interests of a particular group of people, a political agenda. The clearest example is
the paradigm of history, which as we all know, is written by the victor. In other
words, the official account of history is shaped by the interests of the elite group
who is occupying the place at the top of the social heap. It is then fed to the mass-*

es via the mass media, the education system and other tools that are firmly in the grip of the ruling elite. This body of knowledge becomes the ruling paradigm, the base from which the ruling elite can justify further decisions and actions.

History is only one category. There are religious and philosophical paradigms. The story of Jesus and the tenets of Christianity, for example, are firmly entrenched in our collective psyche, although there is a growing body of information that seriously challenges these belief systems. This religious paradigm has been used to justify actions all through history. The philosophies of democracy and communism are examples of concepts that have become paradigms. They have been used to justify a host of questionable actions in our recent history.

Under the vast umbrella of science or academia there are many paradigms, accepted bodies of information on a wide variety of topics. Although it may sometimes be more difficult to recognize, these paradigms also serve the ruling elite and exert a great influence over society. For example, the paradigms of knowledge regarding human physiology, which underlie and shape our attitudes toward medicine and the health care systems, generate huge profits for the pharmaceutical corporations. They also offer the ruling elite, in the form of health organizations and licensing bodies, enormous control over the health and welfare of the entire population.

The accepted schools of thought, the paradigms of knowledge, are usually taken for granted, absorbed without question into our collective lifestyle. It usually takes a huge, irrefutable upheaval for old-school thought to be displaced. Even when newly accepted theories completely pull the rug out from under established paradigms, as did Einstein's, it takes a long time for the ramifications of such revolutions to actually infiltrate and effect our daily lives.

For the most part, the ruling elite do not encourage the questioning of established paradigms. That is putting it mildly. In the not-so-distant past, such a questioning was called blasphemy or heresy and was usually punishable by death. Most information that has challenged our paradigms gets ignored and pushed aside. When it refuses to be ignored it is often scoffed at, even to the point of having to withstand organized debunking campaigns. In the past, revolutionary thinkers like Galileo or Giordano Bruno paid dearly for the advances they sought to bring to mankind. Many things have changed since then. Although in more modern times it is unlikely for scientists to be killed or jailed for their views, there have been cases of scientists losing their jobs or enduring derision and public humiliation as they courageously fought to bring forth some new idea or to challenge the old paradigms. (We'll mention a few such cases later in this book.)

This is not to say that old paradigms shouldn't be honored and respected. Humanity's collective knowledge grows in increments and most paradigms represent a positive step down the path. In most cases the old paradigms have served humanity well for a time, even if they have served some elite group to a much greater degree. But when we cling to them, or when certain factions persist in using them to further their personal gain, to the detriment of the pursuit of truth and the well being of mankind, then the old paradigms no longer serve us.

One can hardly blame the establishment for clinging to their paradigms and thus, to their expertise. A great many jobs and social positions are dependent upon that expertise. There are families to feed and chests to thump. Over many years the mountain of information that becomes an accepted paradigm accumulates one layer at a time. Challenging such a mountain becomes very difficult. Any new information or evidence that threatens it is usually swept aside, rather than destroy the entire mountain and its host of experts.

At a much higher level, at the very apex of the pyramid of world social structure, the 'power elite' are very much invested in maintaining the status quo. When one is presiding; when one's social position is at the top of the heap, with all its power, prestige and privilege, why rock the boat? Why fund research unless it is going to further one's own position? Why encourage the schools to present a more accurate portrayal of reality if that information threatens to take the reigns of power from your hands? Why own huge media conglomerates unless you can control the information that is being dispensed? There has always been an ongoing struggle between sincere educators, journalists, scientists, etc., and the ruling powers of the day. Some try to tell the truth by operating outside the system, but most try to do so while remaining within the system. In most cases it is difficult to operate outside the system and still be able to feed one's family.

Increasingly, many people feel that the power elite has willfully suppressed information that could have benefited all of mankind, in order to ensure its own wealth and power. Some of the more widely spoken allegations contend that those who control the world's energy resources, in the form of fossil fuels and electricity, have suppressed knowledge that could have provided the world with **free energy**. (See **BOX 8—FREE ENERGY; TESLA AND SCHAUBERGER**) Many people feel that there exists a great deal of technology designed to make life easier for one and all, but that inventions have been suppressed, patents bought up, because powerful corporations have feared losing profit potential and power. It is, after all, very difficult to challenge the status quo in a way that does not result in a redistribution of wealth. And so, the wealthy resist change. It has been that way throughout our known history.

However, it is human nature to seek knowledge. No matter how often we become sidetracked, no matter how many obstacles are in our way, humanity will not be deterred and will relentlessly seek the ever-elusive 'truth'. We instinctively know that the path to the next level involves self-examination. We must somehow come to **a state of knowing**.

As I have said earlier, researching and writing this book is one of the ways that I seek to better know myself, to attempt to better understand 'what is really going on'. Since childhood I have been instinctively suspicious that there was more going on than met the eye. As I grew older, I felt that there was much that we were being taught that *was mistaken and that there was even important information being kept from us. I was born to a tough and difficult father who planted the seeds of anger in me at an early age. Those seeds were further nurtured by a growing awareness of the atrocities that had been committed by mankind over the years. The anger was accompanied by guilt at the knowledge that our 'prosperity' had come largely by means of war, deceit, thievery, genocide, slavery, and other forms of exploitation. In my late teens and early twenties (I am currently fifty) I started snooping out information about social injustice and the dirty dealings that went on behind the scenes. I had a low opinion of humanity. I walked around seething.*

*It is only in the last ten years that I am getting a grip on my anger. A wise man taught me to forgive myself and all the stupid things I've done over the course of my life by getting me to realize that I was **doing the best I could with what I had at the time**. As this realization settled into my mind, I felt a great weight fall off of my shoulders. Soon the **forgiveness** began to spread. I soon realized that the same thing could be said of all of humanity. We have made many stupid mistakes throughout the course of history. In order to forgive ourselves we must take an honest look at ourselves, acknowledge the mistakes, take responsibility and move on.*

*Forgiveness and healing will not come about by pointing fingers elsewhere. It is easy to blame **the ever-changing power elite**, the infamous 'they'. The truth is, persons from any strata of society could have been slotted into positions of power and made the same mistakes. Our ruling elite are holograms, fractals, smaller versions of the prevailing collective attitudes. The darkest element of society is an extreme representation of the dark shadow that runs through all of us. If the collective darkness becomes lighter, then that extremely dark faction will also become lighter. It helps to have an understanding of what the power elite have done and are doing. But, rather than become bogged down with blame and judgement, it makes more sense to me to attempt to peel back the layers, to strip away the veils of deceit, misinformation and mistake, and to try to see what is underneath.*

*Throughout the ages, people have sought to disempower each other. This is partly due to the misguided notion that 'the pie is only so big and so I'd better get as big a piece of it as I can'. Often one's self-worth is wrongly measured by comparing one's lot in life to that of one's neighbor, so that those in better social positions can feel superior to others. Thus, groups have sought domination over other groups in a quest for external (false) power and wealth. Even within these groups, members have sought power over each other. To disempower a group of people is to control them. This has been developed to a fine art, and as Machiavelli pointed out, there are many effective ways for the ruling elite to maintain control over the masses. Such ways could be called **controlling devices**. I'm sure that these devices are implemented both calculatedly and inadvertently. Many of the belief systems that have been drilled into us have been used as controlling devices. (See* **BOX 11—MACHIAVELLIAN CONTROLLING DEVICES**)

BOX 10—FREE ENERGY; TESLA AND SCHAUBERGER: Some researchers claim that there exists the technology to provide the world with free energy. They say that such knowledge has been suppressed by the corporations who have made fortunes selling energy, i.e. electricity and fossil fuels. There are many web-sites on the subject, such as **www.free-energy.cc/**, **www.colossus2.cvl.bcm.tmc.edu/~wje/free-energy**, **www.educate-yourself.org/fe/**.

"Everything is spinning. Everywhere there is energy. There must be a way of availing ourselves of this energy more completely." These are the words of Nikola Tesla (1856—1942), a brilliant scientist and inventor whose accomplishments are as great as any in history. Before Tesla electrical power was provided with direct current, a very inefficient method. He brought us alternating current, making electricity widely available, and showed us how to harness the power of Niagara Falls. He also invented radio transmission, remote control, neon and fluorescent lighting, the Tesla Coil, and much more.

Tesla's biggest ambition was to provide the world with an inexhaustible supply of free energy, which he believed could be harnessed from the ionosphere and 'broadcast' to the world without the enormous grid of power lines that we use today. Tesla insisted on continuing research in this direction even though his financial backers refused to fund it. He locked horns with Thomas Edison, J. P. Morgan and George Westinghouse—all powerful financiers who had made fortunes with Tesla's inventions. During repeated self-funded efforts to explore the possibilities of free energy, the potential in high frequency sound emissions, resonance and other interesting fields of study, Tesla's work was thwarted and sabotaged. He died penniless, a broken man.

As a child Tesla claimed to have had 'otherworldly experiences' during which he saw visions and strange lights. He claimed that his ideas came to him in visualizations which he later analyzed and constructed. In mid-life Tesla became deeply interested in eastern mysticism, and was inspired by the teachings of Swami Devekananda. In Tesla's words, "Exploring the akash and prana is the only pursuit modern science should take." (This info from "Tesla, Master of Lightning", a movie shown on PBS, produced and directed by Robert Uth.) For more info on Tesla, checkout these web-sites: **www.teslatech.info**, **www.sftesla.org**, and others.

Another brilliant scientist and naturalist, an Austrian named Victor Schauberger (1885—1958) was also convinced that it was possible to harness free energy. He was well versed in the Pythagorean idea that all of creation is a manifestation of sound and that all matter could be understood in terms of the proportional relationships of integral numbers. His research, which started with a study of the dynamics of flowing water, eventually came to the attention of Hitler and he was recruited to help with the development of flying saucer-type craft called 'Foo Fighters'. After the war he was taken to America under the supervision of Karl Gerscheimer and Robert Donner where he was kept against his will. Every effort was made to acquire his scientific knowledge. When Schauberger eventually became uncooperative, he was returned to Linz, Austria, where he mysteriously died five days later. According to friends he was heard to say repeatedly in his final days, "They took everything from me—everything. I don't even own myself." (For more info on this topic, see 'Living Water, Victor Schauberger and the Secrets of Natural Energy', by Olof Alexanderson, and 'Living Energies, An Explosion of Concepts Related to the Theories of Victor Schauberger', by Callum Coates.)

Many religions, despite what may have been noble intentions in the beginning, and despite the fact that many individuals working within these religious systems may have noble intentions, soon become controlling devices for some elite groups. In Book Two we will look at some of the forces that shaped our western religions and some of the consequences. We will see how sex has been vilified, rather than promoted as the great healing tool that it is. We'll see how the ancients, including the founders and followers of Tantra, viewed sex. We'll look at ways in which the female aspect of humanity has been squelched and at how the resulting imbalance has disempowered us. We'll try to look at other accepted, established belief systems and the ways they've clouded our vision. We'll weigh some of the evidence that suggests that we would probably be wise to relax some of these old beliefs.

In Book Two, I will attempt to share, to introduce (as opposed to thoroughly examine) some of the information that I've encountered in the process of peeling back the layers. This will cover a lot of ground and thus, a detailed examination would extend well beyond the confines of this book. Wherever possible, I will attempt to point out where further information could be had. (I will continue to use italics when I am clearly presenting my own beliefs and opinions.) I will attempt to draw attention to those subject areas that I feel represent the more formidable obstacles to humanity's quest to know itself. In what ways have we been unable to see clearly? In what ways have we been duped? What keeps us from becoming fully empowered?

The information introduced in Book Two will challenge the status quo. Some of it will be in direct opposition to the mainstream paradigms; some will be elaborations or tangents on newly emerging accepted ideas; some of it may even be misinformation. All of it has helped me to liquefy my belief systems, to open my mind and to get to know myself a little better. Perhaps it'll do the same for you.

BOX 11—MACHIAVELLIAN CONTROLLING DEVICES: In 1513 AD, a political philosopher named Niccolo Machiavelli wrote 'The Prince', a book that outlines the most efficient methods by which a ruler could acquire and maintain power. These methods are often cunning and underhanded, devoid of ethics or morality. Today, one can interpret the adjective, 'Machiavellian', as describing any ruthless and deceitful means by which a ruler maintains control and power. It is not hard to see such a list of controlling devices at work today, diverting attention from the real enemy and keeping the majority from taking power away from the elite few. A list of points of advice given to some ruling elite could read as follows:
- keep factions of the populace fighting amongst themselves; emphasize the differences rather than the similarities between belief systems and ideologies.
- keep the masses impoverished, focussed on the struggle to make a living.
- prevent the masses from recognizing the real source of it's problems by keeping them in poor health, by promoting values which keep the masses too busy to see clearly, by constantly creating 'red herrings' and directing the attention of the masses away from important concerns.
- stay out of sight; have puppets and fall-guys to do your dirty work.
- create problems and then profit by selling the solution.
- control the way people think by promoting certain mindsets, ideologies and bodies of 'knowledge'. Discourage anything that questions such doctrine.

The list could go on and on. If explanations and examples embellished each of these points, this little box could easily become a long essay.

Part Three

The Origins of Man

"The sunset for the empire of science has arrived."
—*Huston Smith*

*B*efore launching into this next chapter, I think it's important to say a few words about the world of **science**, which has often been called the new religion, and scientists, who have been referred to as the new priesthood. The 'scientific era' has been underway for about 500 years during which it served humanity well, helping to pull us out of the dark ages of paranoia and superstition, and into the age of reason. I agree with a growing number of scholars such as Huston Smith and Dr. John Mack, Professor of Psychiatry at Harvard Medical School, who believe that this scientific age is about to end. Although that may seem a bold statement, I am not saying that the field of science will be no longer, but rather that it will cease to be the dominant way in which we glean our knowledge. Society has placed a great faith in science as our guiding light and the solver of all of our problems, similar to the faith placed in the 'churchianity' that dominated our consciousness a few hundred years ago. That faith will be replaced by the awareness that the scientific method is just one of many by which we'll come to know our universe.

Don't get me wrong, I have nothing against scientists, some of them are amongst my favourite heroes. I believe that most of them, fresh out of school, start off with a genuine love of life and a curiosity about the workings of the universe. The best of them are blessed with inspiration, with 'muses' similar to our best artists. That idealism, however, is often replaced with the realization that, rather than working for the good of humanity, they will likely be employed (either directly or indirectly) by a corporation, working for the good of its profit-making potential. If all research was funded by objective, impartial sources, what a different world it would be.

Despite being employed by those who seek to maintain the status quo, many scientists bravely speak out against it. Groups such as the Union of Concerned Scientists are often issuing warnings regarding the actions of governments or the ways that corporate actions are hurting the environment. Scientists often suffer the indignity of having their research manipulated in the interests of some corporations' profit potential. There were examples of this that came to light during the class action suits against some of the tobacco companies. I once attended a meeting during which a senior scientist, who had been employed by the department of government that tests new food products, was moved to tears as he told how he had resigned his position in disgust. He referred to the testing process as a sham and was appalled at the way that research was misrepresented. In the past, the work of great scientists such as Darwin has been manipulated to justify the economic policies of the ruling elite.

But I'm digressing, that's not the point I'm trying to make. Science continues to search for a unified model of the universe, that is, a provable theory that explains everything, both in the macro-world and in the micro-world, thus rendering our universe a safe and predictable place. What is the substance common to everything? What exactly are nuclear, gravitational and electro-magnetic forces? I do not believe that it is possible to determine the true nature of reality using the scientific method, which relies on some sort of observation based on the five senses. I believe that reality is intangible, ineffable and beyond the five senses. What if, as many ancient mystical writings contend, the primal substance of the universe is consciousness itself? Is reality being thought or imagined into existence? I believe that the true nature of reality is unobservable from our five-sensory, physical perspective and that science will ultimately prove its worth by bringing us to that conclusion.

Thinking and perceiving in the linear, logical way in which we have become accustomed, can only take us so far. Our best scientists, a good example being Einstein, have been 'lateral' thinkers who receive inspiration in much the same way as do mystics and artists. Some of the newest theories, at least in physics, seem to be going in a direction that will soon bring them into the realm of mysticism. I believe that this trend will grow and that many branches of science will start to pay heed to what the mystics are saying. This will result in researchers applying the scientific method to premises and theories that develop from suggestions from the world of mysticism. It will also result in an awareness that some things are just not scientifically testable.

One of the dilemmas of modern science, in my view, is that it has become a multifaceted mosaic, a collection of sharply focussed areas of specialization. Most scientists spend their careers examining a very narrow, specialized aspect of reality, to the point where it becomes difficult to put the pieces together into a coherent whole. While most would acknowledge that such focussed scrutiny is necessary, it seems to me that we need another branch of science that seeks to examine the whole. We need scientists who can step back and view the mosaic in its entirety. The difficult question in such an endeavor would be, who would fund it, who would employ such a scientist?

Another dilemma (one that is more relevant to this book) is the tendency to examine new information using old assumptions. Often such assumptions lie at the very core of an accumulated body of knowledge—at the very base of the mountain of information that has become a paradigm. Here's an example. Assumptions are made in all fields of science, and archeology is certainly no exception. In assessing the Mayan civilization, conventional science tends to assume that, because they were a culture that did not use iron or bronze, with no knowledge of the wheel, they must be 'primitive' and basically, belong in the same category as other primitive societies. The fact that they had one of the most sophisticated calendars ever known on Earth and that they had extensive knowledge of the workings of the solar system and beyond, without the use of a telescope—none of these amazing discoveries seems to prompt the establishment to look beyond the paradigms.

Maybe the Mayans come from another planet. Maybe they are leftovers from Atlantis or Lemuria or some other advanced, ancient society. Maybe the knowledge and stone structures were only inherited by the group that has come to be known as the Mayans—maybe it originates from some much older civilization. So engrained are the old paradigms that it's hard to resist rolling one's eyes at such possibilities, even though there is more than enough evidence to merit an investigation into such suggestions. Very few research projects are done with a completely open mind, devoid of all preconceived notions and assumptions, where even the most remote theories are treated fairly.

Assumptions are made continually in the world of science. In examining our very ancient past, for example, we assume that certain factors that define our existence today were also in place then. For example, we assume that the strength of the planet's gravitational pull has always remained constant. We assume that the laws of physics, that is, the laws governing our ability to observe the physical world, have always been the same. If consciousness shapes reality, then maybe such 'laws' have changed with our changing consciousness. While I admit that it is difficult to progress in the pursuit of knowledge without using such assumptions as a sort of 'toe-hold', it seems even more difficult, ultimately, if these assumptions are never questioned.

In the NASA project known as the Search for Extra Terrestrial Intelligence (SETI), over 100 million dollars in ten years was spent sending capsules into space, sending radio waves, etc, in an attempt to make contact with whatever other intelligent life may exist out there. Again we have made assumptions. We are assuming that these life forms are going to communicate with us via some medium and language that is familiar to us. What if they are already trying to communicate with us in their own way? What if they don't even use words, but use symbols and pictographs like the ones in crop circles? Trying to communicate with us could be the equivalent of humanity trying to communicate to a colony of ants. How would we do it? Maybe the Great Pyramid was an attempt to get through to us. Maybe their attempts to contact us are right in front of our noses. What if it is less important to them to communicate with us in the way we imagine? Maybe they prefer to drop hints and clues rather than approach us directly, based on an awareness that it is better for us to accumulate our own experiences, use our own will, etc. In any case, the point is, we can't assume to know what their methods and motives might be.

I believe that we would be wise to open our minds and to re-assess the information we already have. I believe we should stop making unchallenged assumptions and dismissing investigations because they are outside our old paradigms.

Who are we? Where did we come from? These are questions that mankind has grappled with for a very long time. As we move toward enlightenment, toward graduation day, these issues seem to take on a renewed urgency. Many people are no longer satisfied with the traditional answers to these questions. Neither the religious explanations, nor those provided by science seem to make complete sense.

For many centuries, in conjunction with the teachings of organized religion, the dominant point of view in western culture was that the universe, including mankind, had been created by 'God'. This mysterious entity, this 'supreme being', had taken a lump of 'clay' and 'breathed life into it', creating a new class of being that would exercise dominion over all the other creatures. This new species was said to have been created 'in the image of God', and was meant to serve, worship and obey God.

With the cultural revolution known as the Age of Reason (approximately 500 to 600 years ago) came a dissatisfaction with such simplistic views. Explanations based on the blind faith of religion came to be replaced by explanations based on scientific observation. The scientific viewpoint that began to prevail seemed to be the exact opposite of the old creationist paradigm. It seemed to be saying that there was no supreme intelligence, that all of creation came into being due to some 'cosmic accident'. This is in line with the 'mechanistic view' of the universe as a giant machine in which each event follows logically from some other event; that every effect is the logical result of some cause. According to this view, the universe came into being after an event called the 'big bang'. It did so in a completely predictable way, according to the chemical reactions that took place due to certain laws of physics. At some point these chemical reactions just happened to produce conditions that caused the arrival of 'life'.

According to this dominant paradigm, life began to evolve into a wide variety of forms, becoming ever more complex as time went on. This evolution was driven by certain laws, mechanisms, ways in which nature was predisposed to behave. These mechanisms were completely logical and, with enough of an understanding, scientists could determine and possibly even predict the course of this evolution of life. After great volumes of information were gathered, a picture that was acceptable to science began to emerge. The ***conventional overview of the history of life***, including the development of mankind and civilization, goes something like this:

- 4.5 billion years ago; Earth was newborn, a lifeless lump of space dust.
- 3 billion years ago; the first traces of life in the form of bacteria and algae made an appearance
- 530 million years ago; after having stayed virtually the same for a very long time, life began to appear in many diverse forms of flora and fauna. This era is known as the Cambrian Explosion.

- 190 million years ago; the first dinosaurs made an entrance, ruling the planet for 125 million years.
- 60 million years ago; relatively suddenly, the dinosaurs went extinct. A diverse variety of mammals made a relatively sudden appearance and began to dominate.
- 6 million years ago; the first of the early hominids (defined as bipedal ape-men) began to appear.
- 2.5 million years ago; hominids started using the first simple, stone tools.
- 800,000 years ago; this marks the beginnings of *Homo erectus*
- 200,000 years ago; *Homo sapiens* makes an appearance. He differs greatly from *Homo erectus*, with a much larger brain size. The first religious artifacts, cave paintings and evidence of a shamanic lifestyle emerges at this time.
- 70,000 years ago; this is the Neanderthal period.
- 40,000 years ago; the Cro-Magnon period.
- 30,000 years ago; Neanderthal man becomes extinct. The debate still rages about whether Neanderthal was the ancestor of Cro-Magnon. Some say that DNA testing has proved that they were not the ancestors of Cro-Magnon, but rather co-existed with them for a while, and then Cro-Magnon began to dominate and Neanderthal died out.
- 15,000 years ago; Asians cross the land bridge at the Bering Strait and populate North America.
- 13,000 years ago; the ice age ends and the Wisconsin ice field retreats.
- 11,000 years ago; agriculture emerges in the middle east. Jericho, the oldest town is established.
- 9,000 years ago; the town and culture of Catal Huyuk is established in what is now Turkey.
- 6,000 years ago; the first great civilization is established at Sumer, in Mesopotamia.
- 5,000 years ago; the dawn of the great Egyptian civilization.

Science felt no need to consider notions of 'supreme beings' or creative intelligences. It sought only to understand the mechanisms underlying the existence of our universe. It considered information gleaned only through scientific methods. Science has contributed greatly to our growth as humans, to our understanding of the nature of reality, to our ability to answer questions such as, 'who are we—where do we come from?' However, many people (myself included) are beginning to feel that a more accurate answer to these questions will come from some kind of marriage of the scientific views and the idea that the universe was created by some form of 'superior intelligence'. They further feel that the clues leading to such an understanding may be outside the realm of science; that all pertinent information may not be scientifically testable.

Chapter 15

DARWINIAN SKELETONS IN THE CLOSET

Questions of human origins are very delicate and have always elicited impassioned responses. When Darwin suggested that humans and modern apes were descended from a common ape-like ancestor, it created an enormous furor of protest, especially from the religious establishment. Nowadays, however, the suggestion that maybe we didn't evolve from some ape-man seems to get a similar response.

The Darwinian theory of evolution and it's driving mechanism, ***survival of the fittest/natural selection***, have become fully entrenched in modern western thought. It has become the new paradigm. The familiar chart representing the evolution of man with a series of steps, starting with a small ape-like creature and ending with Cro-Magnon and modern man, hung in many classrooms for many years. Another familiar chart is the one depicting the evolutionary journey of the horse, from a small dog-sized mammal to its present form. In the minds of most people these Darwinian notions of evolution, driven by the process of natural slection, have come to represent the accepted orthodox view of human origins.

Before we proceed, it is important to ***define the terms 'Darwinism' and 'Darwinian'***. Similar to the way in which Christianity has come to represent teachings that were not taught by Christ, Darwinism has come to embody information that did not necessarily come from Darwin. For example, contrary to popular perception, he did not introduce the term 'survival of the fittest'. Some people feel that such a term represents a good example of the way that scientific theories become distorted, possibly for political and economical motives. Some of the evolutionary concepts that have filtered down into the common consciousness differ from those that were offered by Darwin. For our purposes in this book, the term Darwinism will refer to the modern body of theories that derive from Darwin's work and from those scientists, like Richard Dawkins, who have embraced and added to his ideas.

It is also important to keep in mind that Darwinian concepts, such as natural selection, are theories and as such, are works in progress. Nothing is conclusive, nothing written in stone, and yet these ideas have become firmly entrenched in the human psyche and in the minds of many scientists. Eminent scholars such as Dawkins and Sir Julian Huxley have gone on record with their opinions that Darwin's ideas have become less like theory and more like unquestionable fact. However there are some, including prominent scientists, who are less convinced.

Before we take a look at some of these dissenting views, let's concisely review the modern theory of natural selection, which has grown from Darwin's ideas. It basically states that **random mutations** would occur in a species and, occasionally, this would result in a more efficient version of that life-form, one that was better equipped to feed itself, to procreate or to in some way survive and thrive. This new and improved version would then out-compete its immediate ancestors. The less efficient version would become extinct as the new form became dominant. In this way life has evolved slowly and gradually, over 3 billion years. This is true of all life, from the simplest microorganisms to the sophisticated life forms, including man, that exist today. Implicit in the title of Darwin's book, 'The Origin of Species by Means of Natural Selection', is the contention that the existence of all species can be attributed to this process, this mechanism of nature. The simple logic of this theory was very attractive and it fit neatly within the prevailing mechanistic view.

I remember feeling uneasy about the notion of natural selection when I first heard about it back in high school. Parts of it just didn't make sense to me. I could see that certain species could evolve in this fashion, or that an established species could gradually change in this way. The part of the theory that made the least amount of sense to me, was the idea that whole new species or new animal types could come about in this manner. How could natural selection explain the transitions between species? Until a wing became fully formed, a process that would take millions of years, it would be neither a wing nor a leg—an appendage which would be of limited usefulness. How could such an appendage provide this pre-bird-like creature with an advantage that would be 'selected' in the 'survival of the fittest' sense? This is only one of many possible examples.

Among scientists, even those that embrace the idea of evolution, there has been much **controversy** regarding this theory. At the same time that Darwin published his paper on natural selection, an essay purveying virtually the same theory was released by Alfred Russel Wallace. Both were published by the Linnaeus Society. Shortly thereafter however, Wallace reneged, saying that there were too many human behaviours that had nothing to do with survival, i. e. the human capacity for art, music, humor, compassion, passion and self-sacrifice. He went on record that he believed in a hierarchy of spiritual beings or forces that affected life and its evolution, a remark that quickly earned him the cold shoulder of the scientific community.[1]

Even within the modern academic establishment there are eminent scientists who seriously question aspects of Darwinian theory and the evidence that is used to support it. One of the key bodies of evidence is the fossil record, which according to some prominent scientists, fails to support the concept of natural selection. Stephen J. Gould, professor of zoology and geology at Harvard pointed out in 1977 that the fossil record offers no support for the notion of gradual change. It shows that, in Gould's words, "In any local area, a species does not arise gradually... it appears all at once and fully formed."[2]

David Schindel, professor of geology at Yale pointed out in 1982 that there are no fossils of the 'transitions' on record. For example, no one has ever found the fossil remains of a giraffe with a medium sized neck. This is true even though palaeontologists and geologists have exerted a great deal of effort to find such fossils, which would do much to validate the theory. The fossils uncovered and documented by science form a large and impressive record, with fossils having been found for 97% of all existing orders of land vertebrates. Rather than supporting the idea of gradual change due to the process of natural selection, the fossil record suggests something quite different.

What is apparent in the fossil record is that distinct animal species seem to come into existence rather abruptly, with no trace of the 'transitional' body forms that would imply a gradual evolution. The fossils show only minor changes occurring gradually within an established species. In the animal kingdom, 37 phyla all came into being relatively suddenly, about 530 million years ago during a period that has come to be called the 'Cambrian Explosion'. The fossil record suggests that about twelve groups of mammals first appeared at about the same time around 55 million years ago, on several different continents. Distinguished academicians like Gould, Schindel, and professors Niles Eldredge, Steven Stanley and Jeffrey Levinton are saying that the fossil record does more to disprove than to support the claims of Darwinian theory.

The idea that random mutations can lead to an improvement in the species has also been called into question. Each human cell contains 23 pairs of chromosomes which consist of approximately 100,000 genes. The genetic code is a very complex set of instructions and even the slightest variation can result in a large amount of change. If such a gene pool were compared to a 100,000 word essay, there is a very slim chance that randomly replacing a few words would result in a better essay. Computers have been used to actually figure out the chances of achieving such a feat. Using the old 'monkey at the typewriter' analogy—how long would it take a monkey, randomly typing one letter per second, to produce a twelve letter word of any kind? The answer is 17 million years. The number of years to produce a sentence that makes sense is so large it is beyond our ability to conceive. If mutations are a key factor in the evolutionary process, then it seems likely that something other than random chance is involved in the creation of such mutations.[3]

One new theory reported by Maurice Cotterell suggests that cosmic radiation in the form of a stream of quarks could cause the mutations. Occasionally, a quark would collide with DNA, causing it to change. It further postulates that, during certain points in cosmic cycles, when the planet is in a particular position in the cosmos, it is bombarded by vastly increased amounts of such radiation. This implies that, at such times, the increased radiation would cause a much higher incident of mutation, possibly leading to an explosion of evolutionary change. Although this is an interesting theory, it is probably untestable.[4]

Some scientists feel that attempting to explain **human evolution** poses more problems still. Professor Gould uses the expression, "the awesome improbability of human evolution."[5] There is still a good deal of controversy amongst scientists regarding human origins.

Almost all important fossil finds have occurred in Africa's Rift Valley, which runs from Tanzania through Kenya and Ethiopia before meeting with the Red Sea. In 1974, anthropologist Donald Johanson found the fossilized bones of an early hominid that came to be known as Lucy, but is officially dubbed *Australopithecus afarensis*. He claimed, amidst much excitement, that it was the elusive 'missing link'. Famous anthro-exploring family, the Leakeys, disagreed and a well-known feud began. They insist that there is no fossil proof showing man's gradual evolution from 'apedom.' In 1978, Mary Leakey found a series of fossilized footprints in Laetoli, North Tanzania which show an anatomy virtually identical to that of a modern human foot. Interestingly, these footprints are thought to be 200,000 years older than Lucy. In the early 1990s, the oldest bipedal fossils, thought to be 4.4 million years old, were found and given the name *Ardipithecus ramidus*. Older yet, the fossil remains of a chimp-sized bipedal found in the same area are thought to be about 5.5 million years old and have been given the name *Ardipithecus ramidus kadabba*.[6] More recently, the skull of a bipedal homonid was found in the desert area of central Africa in the country of Chad. Nicknamed the Toumai skull, it has been given the classification, *Sahelanthropus tchadensis*. It is raising eyebrows because it is even older, estimated to be 7 million years old.

Many palaeontologists have gotten very excited about these developments, arguing that a clear lineage from 'primal ape' to man is becoming evident. Others point out that there is no evidence to suggest that these different finds represent one continuous lineage. There have been many hominid lines that seem to have gone extinct, including *Australopithecus robustus*, *Homo habilis* and, more recently, Neanderthal man. Indeed all the fossil finds could represent 'branches of the hominid evolutionary tree' that went extinct. Who's to say that any of them represents the actual ancestor of mankind? Even Johanson says of the various finds, "...you're not taking into consideration that these could be twigs on a tree. Everything's been forced into a straight line."[7] Clearly the verdict is still out regarding the fossil proof of human origins.

Despite this however, the notion that man and ape descended from an ape-like ancestor, due to the process of natural selection, has taken a very firm foothold. One of the more popular theories contends that the hominid line branched from the line that also produced chimpanzees about 6 million years ago. At some point they began living to a greater degree on the savannah, where an ability to stand on two feet in order to see over the grasses, was 'selected' by nature as being advantageous to survival. Of course, cleverness was also a trait that was selected. This notion seems to make sense and has been widely embraced, becoming something of a paradigm. However, good arguments have been made that seriously question this model.

According to Michael Baigent in his book, 'Ancient Traces', some scientists are saying that there are many human traits, characteristics not found in any other primates, that are very difficult to explain in terms of natural selection. Some feel that a slow, bipedal ape would not have succeeded because it would have made too easy a snack for savannah predators. Relative hairlessness, fragile skin and a perspiration system unique to the human ape seem particularly ill-suited for life on the savannah. Baigent suggests that these traits are more suitable to life in the water and that many human characteristics have more in common with aquatic mammals than with terrestrial primates. Humans are the only primates with a descended larynx, a layer of fat beneath the skin and an ability to consciously control our breathing process—traits that we share with aquatic mammals. Baigent makes a case that humans could have descended from a type of 'water-ape'.

Noted scholar and linguist, Noam Chomsky has declared that it is highly unlikely that natural selection could have produced the complex voice-box required for human speech.[8] The degree of sophistication of speech that would necessitate the physiological development of such a complex apparatus seems far greater than what was needed for the simple task of survival. In other words, why would such a complex larynx evolve when it was far more than what was needed at the time? The same question has been posed regarding brain size. The size of the brain cavities in these early fossils imply a brain that was grossly overqualified for the job of survival. Why did such a brain develop? Distinguished scientist, Roger Penrose, does not believe that natural selection could have resulted in the human brain, with all its complexities.[9] These are only some of many quandaries faced by scientists as they try to explain human evolution in terms of natural selection.

One area about which scientists are greatly puzzled is that of **human sexuality**. Human sexual behaviour is very different from that of other animals. Extended foreplay which includes kissing, stroking and fondling, extended copulation and female orgasm are all aspects of sexuality unique to humans. It is difficult for some scientists to see how the development of these behaviours could have enhanced survival on the African savannah. For example, during the regular 'doggy-style' copulation practiced by most animals it is much easier to be on the alert for predators. The face to face copulation practiced by humans seems dangerous, especially if it takes a longer time.

Humans are much more sexually active than most animals. Human females are available and willing to have sex at all times, unlike most animals that confine their activities to certain times of the year. This results in many copulations that are 'wasted' in a procreative sense, a phenomenon that we share with dolphins and whales, but with very few other species. In proportion to body size, human males have extra-large sex organs. Human females, unlike most animals, are equipped to derive physical pleasure from sexual encounters. Physical traits such as hairlessness, combined with erogenous zones and skin that is very sensitive, a vaginal angle that accommodates face to face copulation, and other sexual characteristics seem to have been designed to accommodate pleasure, emotion and the expression of affection and love. The purely practical, procreative, survival based functions of this design seem secondary.

Without belaboring the point, I think it is obvious that there is much about the Darwinian theories of evolution that are still very much up in the air. They are theories, works in progress, and certainly ongoing research will shed more and more light on the matter. We need to ask ourselves, does Darwinism deserve to be the only game in town? Does it deserve to be the pillar of scientific orthodoxy that it has become? The concept of natural selection is certainly valid and does not deserve to be discarded, yet it seems inadequate to completely explain the process of evolution, especially as it pertains to humans. Scientists such as Chomsky, Gould, Schindel and others, cannot account for the amount of change in human evolution in the past 6 million years, claiming that it should have taken 25 million years. The enormous amount of change that has occurred in the past 200,000 years, including a large increase of brain size, the development of complex language and culture, etc, defies explanation within the current paradigms. Are there other factors at work?

There is a growing body of scientists, academics, philosophers and theologians who are promoting the ***theory of an 'Intelligent Designer'*** as a factor in the evolutionary process. Reports on this movement have recently appeared in Time Magazine, the New York Times and other publications. Although traditional Darwinists dismiss them as 'creationists in disguise', the ID group are clearly not related to the dogmatic creationists of old. They do not try to define the intelligent designer or to call it 'God'. They merely point out that natural selection alone cannot account for the emerging evidence; that the new religion of Darwinism is not providing the answers to the mysteries of evolution; that even if the universe does operate like a huge machine, there must be some type of 'force' or 'intelligence' that designed it .

In the past century there have been theories besides Darwin's that have had things to say about evolution. One of these is ***Chaos Theory***, developed by

Gaston Julia circa 1920, and Dr. Edward Lorenz and Dr. Benoit Mandelbrot in the early 1960s. To state the gist of this theory it is necessary to oversimplify and to try to put into words something that is usually described mathematically. It points out that there are sequences in nature that appear to be disorderly or chaotic—displaying no precisely measurable pattern. The shapes of snowflakes, weather patterns, the turbulence in flowing water and waves breaking on a beach are all examples of systems that appear to have no precisely repeating pattern of behavior. When viewed over long time periods, however, these sequences do occur in ordered, measurable patterns. Research has shown that such sequences display an ***underlying order***.

This is only testable using computers, capable of plotting and graphing the huge volumes of data representing these sequential movements, which would otherwise require far too much time. This data, when plotted in diagram form, would yield cyclical patterns, but ones where the ends of the circle do not meet, but rather, spiral on indefinitely. This implies that cycles do repeat themselves, but without ever coming full circle to the points at which they began, because there is no beginning and no end. These plotted diagrams form images which contain *fractals*, a term coined by Mandelbrot. They are smaller images within a larger image which are exact duplications of the larger image. These larger images are, in turn, exact duplications of even larger images, etc. Thus, ideally, these images would regenerate indefinitely into both micro and macro infinity. The concept of fractals seems to be yet another confirmation of the famous Hermetic axiom, 'as above, so below.'

Some well-known examples of these fractal images are the Julia set, the Mandelbrot set and the Sierpinski triangle. Fractals also appear in depictions of the 'flower of life' and other examples of sacred geometry, which have been getting much attention lately. (See **BOX 4—SACRED GEOMETRY**)

In 1991, Dr. Robert Wesson, in his book entitled 'Beyond Natural Selection', claims that we would do better to seek an understanding of the ways in which greater systems evolve, rather than focussing on the evolution of individual species. Does environmental change come about because of the evolutionary cycles or patterns of the larger ecosystems, of the Earth itself? Wesson suggests that, as described in Chaos theory, systems swing from chaos to order and then 'cascade' back to chaos, then begin moving again toward order. This pattern of evolution, this orderly sequence of change, applies to all types of systems. Just like the sequence of waves breaking on a beach, any system goes through a series of changes, which if observed and graphed over a long period of time, would yield an orderly, spiral, fractal pattern.

A species is a system unto itself, but it is also a sub-system, a product of the greater system of which it is a part. Change within the greater system triggers change in the sub-systems, and vice-versa. For a system to remain stable, it is dependent on initial conditions within the greater system remaining the same. The slightest change in these initial conditions cause the system to begin to collapse, to cascade into chaos. There is a constant interaction between developing systems and their environmental systems—any change in the environment triggers change in the systems. Evolution, which could be described as a series of changes, happens in conjunction with the environment. Natural selection may play a role in determining whether a species succeeds or not, but the actual arrival of the species, according to Wesson, owes more to the chaotic effect of changes in surrounding systems, which constitute the environment. Evolution progresses like an ebb and flow.

Wesson further says, "Evolution can be conceived as a goal directed process insofar as it is part of a goal-directed universe, an unfolding of potentialities somehow inherent in this cosmos."[10] In other words, systems evolve in this pendulum-like manner according to a predetermined plan, an underlying order as represented by the previously mentioned spiral patterns. This implies an 'intelligent designer'. Could this intelligence be the same web of consciousness, discussed in Part One, of which we are all a part? Could it be that the machinations of evolution as purveyed by Darwinism exist as part of this design?

(For a good discussion of Chaos Theory in general, see the work of Nobel Prize winner, Ilya Prigogine and Isabelle Stengers, 'Order Out of Chaos, Man's Dialogue with Nature', Bantam Books, New York, 1984. An excellent website on the topic, with good pictures of fractals, is **www.mathjmendl.org/chaos/**, by Jonathan Mendelson and Elana Blumenthal.)

Another relatively new area of investigation relevant to the concept of evolution is one regarding *morphogenetic fields*. In plain English that translates as force fields that generate form. A force is an intangible, unexplainable power that has no observable substance, but which exerts an influence that can be observed. Science still does not know what magnetic or gravitational force actually is. Just as a gravitational or an electro-magnetic field possesses a mysterious ability to exert causal effect on the universe, morphogenetic fields, it is postulated, exert forces which cause primal substance or particles, if you like, to arrange themselves into specific forms.

The *organistic view* postulates that the morphogenetic field of any particular system generates a set of instructions which determine the qualities of that system. The morphogenetic field of any species, for example, contains the blueprint for the form and behavior of that species. This is much the same as saying that the collective consciousness of a species contains a template for the form and behavior of that species, and that any change in the species is preceded by a change in its collective consciousness. This would agree with ancient mysticism, which contends that all objects have a type of consciousness. The consciousness of a diamond crystal, for example, contains the blueprint that determines the crystalline pattern in which diamond particles will arrange themselves. *(I believe that the more evolved the entity, the further along it is in the Game, the greater the potential for variation from the template. In other words, the greater the role played by free will, the greater the potential to intentionally alter the blueprint.)*

This differs from the traditional mechanistic view that the universe is a giant machine, behaving in a predictable way according to predetermined laws. Within this mechanistic view is the notion that a living organism is a chemico-physical machine and that all aspects of life can be explained in terms of physics and chemistry. An organism takes form and behaves according to a set of instructions that are present in the DNA, in the genetic code. It implies that this very complex code came into being because the requisite conditions just happened to be present, leading to the chemical reactions that brought about life. In other words, the miracle of life was some kind of cosmic accident. The organistic view implies that nothing was accidental, that the DNA code and any other blueprint that may exist are part of a grand design, a grand intelligence.

The problem with this theory is that, although it seems to make sense, it is very difficult to test scientifically. In his book written in 1995 entitled 'A New Science of Life', Rupert Sheldrake sites some ways in which it has been tested. For example, tests have been done on rats to see if the consciousness of one group of rats can influence the consciousness of another group. Similar to the '100 monkey phenomenon', these tests show that a group of rats will more easily learn a task if a previous group of rats at a different time and place have been taught the task. The new group of rats seems to resonate with the energy of all 'ratness', including the change that occurred in the earlier rats. Sheldrake calls this phenomenon ***morphic resonance***. He admits that although the tests bear interesting results, there is nothing resembling a definite proof of morphic resonance.[11]

This 'organistic' view implies that there is a force field or collective consciousness at work and that it is subject to change, to evolution. This dovetails with chaos theory, and even with Darwinian theory, in that it suggests that a system, in this case a species, reacts to/evolves in conjunction with its environment. Rather than being driven solely by the laws of natural selection, this suggests that change occurs from some sort of learning, which further implies that some kind of decision was made in the collective consciousness. The fossil record seems to show that evolution occurs in abrupt bursts during which great numbers of species go extinct or come into being, rather than in a slow, continuous process of change. These bursts of change seem to happen in conjunction with environmental change. What triggers these environmental changes? Could these changes be part of a larger pattern, some sort of design? Is this design an accident?

As must be obvious by now, I tend to believe that Darwinism and the mechanistic view are simplistic ways of understanding the workings of life in our universe. I don't understand the futile argument between the Darwinists and the Creationists. I don't see that the two points of view are mutually exclusive. Even if the universe could be seen as a giant machine, who or what designed and created it? How did it come to be? It seems obvious that many of its workings are unobservable using merely the five-sensory scientific methodology that we have grown to depend on. I believe that, to achieve a greater understanding of this great machine, we must open our minds and hearts and refuse to cling too tightly to any explanations.

That is not to say that the ideas of Darwinism are irrelevant. It seems clear to me that natural selection plays a significant role in the process of change, but that surely there are many other factors influencing the origin and evolution of species, many of which are probably outside the realm of pure science. I feel that, if we are to achieve a better understanding of human origins, we must look beyond the Darwinian paradigms. We must ask ourselves, are these old paradigms continuing to serve us? Are they serving the few? Are they getting in the way?

A good question to ask oneself is, 'why has the philosophy of natural selection become such a tenacious, almost dogmatic paradigm?' The answer could be that the power elite have used and promoted this tenet of Darwinism to ensure their position at the top of the heap. In other words, it was manipulated and taken out of context in order to justify the economic actions of the wealthiest faction of society. It dovetailed nicely with the Protestant work ethic and the new capitalist philosophies emerging in the 1800s. The work ethic basically states that hard work is good for the soul and that economic success is equivalent to a predestination for eternal salvation. Economists like Adam Smith and Thomas Robert Malthus promoted the notions of government non-interference, called 'laissez-faire', and the uneven distribution of labor. It was deemed healthy for the overall economy that there be a class system of those that are wealthy and those that are not.

By appropriating the concept that it was natural law for the fittest to survive, to be selected, the new economic elite created the impression that they were operating with the scientific seal of approval. It seems obvious that this economic movement, which became known as 'Social Darwinism', was a misinterpretation of scientific theory in order to gain economic advantage. This quote from 'Darwinism and the Division of Labour', by Robert M. Young seems to sum it all up:

"The tremendous vogue of Darwinism provided both a rationalization for competitive struggle and a warrant for using scientific concepts to justify particular forms of social and economic relationship. Only the fittest survive, and those who do survive must therefore be fit. This slogan was placed on the banners of imperialists as well as on those of the most ruthless industrialists."

The masters of the industrial revolution, the new power elite, feel entirely justified in their relentless and ruthless pursuit of profit. According to their distorted logic, such behavior is completely natural—they were simply 'out-competing' the less fortunate and being selected by nature to survive. There came to be little room in this equation for compassion. Even abhorrent human behavior like slavery and the conquering and subsequent genocide of native populations could be rationalized. It could all be explained as the superior white race out-competing these lesser races—something that is a natural process.

Are we being manipulated to embrace the notion of 'survival of the fittest' because it has become such a convenient rationalization for the ruling elite?

Chapter 16

EXTRA TERRESTRIAL SKELETONS IN THE CLOSET

Whenever there is serious talk about extra terrestrial life forms (ETs) or non-physical entities, it is often greeted with rolling eyes and a scoffing tone. Even those who do believe in such things tend to keep it to themselves to avoid derision. This is starting to change, however and recent polls have found that about 50% of the American population, including many notable scientists, astronauts, etc., feel that there is intelligent life on other planets. Many feel that it is far more logical, given the number of stars in the universe, that we are not alone, nor are we the most advanced life form in the universe.

Terrance Dickinson, an astronomer who writes for the Toronto Star points out that, according to current scientific estimations based on the work of astronomer Edwin Powell Hubble, there are about ten billion, trillion stars in the universe. This is a number too large to comprehend. If each star was represented by a grain of sand and the sand was loaded into haulage cars on a freight train, how many cars would it take to contain ten billion trillion grains of sand? If you were standing at the side of the track watching the train go by at the rate of one car per second, how long would you be there? The answer is—three and a half years! Imagine that! It would take three point five years to watch the passing of a train big enough to haul that amount of sand. That is a heck of a lot of sand—an incomprehensible number of stars.

Back in the mid-twentieth century, Hubble (after whom the Hubble Space Telescope launched in 1990 was named) had access to the best telescope of his day. He was determined to learn more about the numerous spiral swirls that were faintly observable in the night sky. He found that each swirl was a galaxy like our own Milky Way, containing billions of stars. Those galaxies at the furthest edge of our observational capabilities are moving away from us at speeds that approach the speed of light. Galaxies that are moving away from us at lightspeed are unobservable because their light cannot reach us. So there are even more galaxies, even more 'grains of sand' that we cannot observe. The universe is indeed, staggeringly large. Two thirds of its star systems are older than ours. Surely there must be life in a great many places.

This is what the great scientist and educator, Carl Sagan had to say about it; "It seems the height of human arrogance to imagine that this planet is the only inhabited world." In their book, *Intelligent Life in the Universe*, Sagan and co-author, I.S. Shlovski say that there could be as many as 50,000 to 1 million civilizations in the universe more advanced than ours.[12]

There is a growing body of evidence suggesting that life on this planet has been greatly influenced by life on other planets. Some factions of science believe that life first happened on Earth due to a chance electro-chemical reaction, occurring under conditions that just happened to be conducive to life. Some people, including scientists, believe that life could not have developed by 'accident', and that perhaps it arrived in germ form on an asteroid, or was seeded by intelligent life-forms. Some astronauts, including Buzz Aldrin, have publicly stated that they believe in extraterrestrial life. Astronaut Gordon Cooper is convinced that they visited Earth in the past.[13] Francis Crick, one of the discoverers of the DNA double helix, believes that the highly complex DNA constituting the primitive life forms of 3 billion years ago, could not have developed here in so short a time. He says that science should seriously consider the possibility that, "a primitive form of life was deliberately planted on Earth by a technologically advanced society on another planet."[14]

Some people believe that extra terrestrials (ETs) have played a huge role in human evolution, affecting us in ways ranging from the manipulation of our genes to the teaching of computer technology. Back in 1968, Erich Von Däniken published his book, *Chariots of the Gods*, which asked the question, "Is God an astronaut?" Although it was widely read and made the author a millionaire, it was totally scoffed at and dismissed by the academic establishment. He had traveled the globe, digging out ancient artifacts from many diverse sources, which looked suspiciously like spaceships and astronauts. For example, ancient Hebrew statuettes called 'malachim' depict demi-gods or ambassadors that look very similar to modern descriptions of ETs known as the 'Greys'.

While admitting that some of his claims may seem far-fetched and somewhat sensationalistic, I believe that much of Von Däniken's research is fascinating, relevant and at least worthy of further study. (See **BOX 12—EZEKIEL**) In fact, there has been a good deal of subsequent research on the subject, most of which is somewhat more thorough and scholarly. This next section will take a look at some of the information that has become available, mostly in the past fifty years, which may shed some light on ET activity in our past.

In the 1950s, French anthropologists Marcel Griaule and Germaine Dieterlen were studying and living with an African tribe near Timbuktu, just south of the southwest corner of the Sahara. The people of this tribe were known as *the Dogon*. After a few years, when the anthropologists had won their trust, the Dogon began to show them their sacred artefacts and ceremonies, things that had been with the Dogon for centuries. The Frenchmen were shocked to see depictions of strange flying craft and information about the solar system and the star system of Sirius; information that the Dogon could not possibly have gained themselves. They knew, for example, that Sirius was a binary star system, with one bright giant called Sirius A, and one extremely dense white dwarf called Sirius B. So dense is Sirius B, that one cubic inch of its matter would weigh 2000 pounds on Earth. The Dogon knew this. They knew the amount of time it takes for these two stars to orbit each other, which is 50.1 years. How could they know this kind of information? The dwarf emits almost no light and is completely invisible to the human eye and science has only been able to observe it very recently, since we've had a satellite telescope out beyond our atmosphere.

The Dogon worship a deity they call *Nommo*, the leader of a group whom they claim arrived a long time ago in a spaceship. They are described as amphibious creatures who lived in a water-hole of their own making, emerging to teach the native people about astronomy and certain technologies.

In the mid-1960s, an American scholar named Robert Temple became fascinated by the work of Griaule and Dieterlen. What made little sense to him was that a group of ETs would come to Earth and make contact with a small, remote tribe, leaving the rest of the world's population alone. After seven years of extensive research he published his book, *The Sirius Mystery*. Temple succeeded in tracing the cultural lineage of the Dogon back to ancient Egypt, showing that the Egyptians had extensive knowledge of Sirius as long ago as 3200 BC. He dug up ancient references to legends of a strange race of amphibians that had helped bring civilization to the ancient Sumerians. The Babylonians had a god named *Oannes*, who was depicted in ancient artifacts as a strange fish-man.[15]

Temple's work is extensive, thorough and seems very convincing. Why is it not more widely known? Why didn't the media jump on such a fascinating story? It seems at least worthy of further discussion and research.

About 100 years ago, an archeologist named Sir Leonard Wooley was excavating sites in what is now Iraq, in the region between the Tigris and Euphrates rivers which has been named Mesopotamia. He uncovered several layers of civilization, the oldest of which went back to 4500 BC, making it the oldest sophisticated civilization to be unearthed so far. This civilization is known as

Sumer. Large stepped pyramids called ziggurats were found, which are similar to the Step Pyramid of Djoser at Saqqara, Egypt. Mountains of clay glyphs, cylinder seals and ancient texts containing enormous amounts of information about many aspects of life in Sumer were also found.

> **BOX 12—EZEKIEL:** There are many references in the Bible, including several in Exodus, that can be interpreted as descriptions of advanced weaponry or the take-offs and landings of flying craft. By far the most graphic and detailed of such descriptions can be found in the Book of Ezekiel, which is 48 chapters long. In 1968, in reaction to Von Däniken's 'Chariots of the Gods', a NASA engineer by the name of Joseph Blumrich, who had been awarded the Exceptional Service Medal, began to study Ezekiel from an engineer's perspective, with the intent of showing the world that Von Däniken's views were ridiculous. Instead, he became convinced that its descriptions were about some sort of space-craft, and has published a book, 'The Spaceships of Ezekiel', detailing his findings.[16] Other Biblical references that sound like descriptions of rocket launchings can be found in stories involving Moses and Elijah.

Scholars, such as Sumerologists Arno Poebel in 1914, Thorkild Jacobsen in 1940, and Henri Frankfort in 1950, set about the arduous task of deciphering and translating this information. It revealed a society of breathtaking sophistication, one that seemed to arrive relatively suddenly. Cities such as Uruk (considered the oldest city on Earth), Ur and Eridu contained relatively luxurious houses that speak of a comfortable standard of living. Many of civilization's 'firsts' happened in Sumer, such as; writing, school, congress, libraries, proverbs, cosmogony, historians, the wheel, money, taxation, laws, social reform, medicine, surgery and much more. It also marks the first production of bronze, a fairly complex operation requiring a mix of 15% tin to 85% copper. Tin, a difficult metal to extract, does not naturally occur in Mesopotamia.[17] This degree of sophistication seems to have come out of nowhere, with no evidence of an incremental accumulation of such knowledge that surely would have taken many centuries. How can we account for this abrupt arrival of culture and technology?

One of the scholars chosen to translate Sumerian cuneiform writings was a man named Zecharia Sitchin. He began to note that a great deal of it, in fact a disproportionate amount of it, dealt with information about the cosmos, flying chariots and a race of 'gods' called *the Annunaki*. Throughout Mesopotamian art there are many depictions of stylized rockets, fiery landings, battles in the sky, planets, etc. Sitchin began to see connections with Biblical stories in the Old Testament, especially in Genesis. In the original Hebrew text the Annunaki are referred to as the Nephilim or the Elohim. (In the modern version of the Bible, the word 'Elohim' has been replaced by 'God' or 'the Lord God'.) Even though these terms are used to denote God in the singular, they are definitely pluralized words. The Bible also makes mention of a group called 'the Watchers', who appear in the Book of Daniel and in the apocryphal Book of Jubilees.

"Behold a watcher and an holy one came down from heaven."

—*Daniel; 4:13*

Sitchin began to cross-check Sumerian information with the original Hebrew Old Testament texts, even the ones that weren't selected for inclusion in the Bible. He also began to research other ancient cultures, looking at the Sumerian writings from many perspectives. He found that the Genesis stories such as; the seven days of creation, Adam and Eve, Noah, the Tower of Babel, etc., come directly from old Mesopotamian texts like the Enuma-Elish, the Epic of Gilgamesh and the Atra Hasis. In the older accounts, however, the stories are longer and more detailed than the Biblical versions. We'll take a closer look at some of this stuff in a later chapter.

A year before the unmanned spaceship, Voyager 2 flew by and photographed Neptune in August, 1989, Sitchin accurately predicted what it would look like based on Sumerian information he had encountered. These predictions appeared in several magazines in the US, Europe and South America. There is a great deal of knowledge about the solar system, and other things that the Sumerians shouldn't have had, that Sitchin has uncovered. He has released many fascinating books on the subject, coming to some very startling conclusions about humanity's origins.

I'll now present an encapsulated account of Sitchin's views regarding the Annunaki. Bear in mind that, what may seem quite far-fetched when presented in skeletal form, is backed up convincingly in Sitchin's books by volumes of evidence and research. He claims that, according to the Sumerian writings, the Annunaki came to Earth about 400,000 years ago to mine gold, mostly in South Africa where, it is said, there can still be found old mine-shafts containing bones that have been dated to 150,000 years ago. They came from a planet named *Nibiru*, the tenth planet in our system, which has a strange, highly elliptical orbit that brings it close to the inner planets every 3600 years. (See **BOX 13—THE TENTH PLANET**) The familiar symbol of the winged disc, examples of which have been found in numerous ancient cultures, is said to de a depiction of Nibiru.

BOX 13—THE TENTH PLANET; There has been a good deal of talk about a tenth planet recently. In 1981, the US Marine Observatory speculated on the existence of a tenth planet that was affecting the orbit of Pluto. In 1983, the infrared space telescope, IRAS, spotted something that could be a new planet. In 1987, NASA officially admitted the possibility of a tenth planet which they call Planet X. The Sumerian and Babylonian accounts of the size, orbit and directional location of Nibiru, fit the NASA description of the hypothetical Planet X. One might feel that it would be impossible for there to be life on a planet whose orbit takes it so far from the sun. When flying by Neptune in 1989, the Voyager 2 observed that Neptune radiates three times as much energy as it receives from the sun. Could this energy be coming from some sort of 'gate' in the planet? Could a similar situation exist on a planet named Nibiru?[18]

The grand leader of this mining project was named *Anu*, who resided mostly on Nibiru, coming to Earth every 3600 years. On Earth, his two sons, *Enki and Enlil* were left in charge, with Enlil holding higher rank. There was an ongoing rivalry between the two. After 200,000 years of mining, the Annunaki decided that life would be much easier if they had slaves, so they genetically manipulated some native hominids and thus created the first man. Enki and his partner, Ninkhursag, were in charge of this project and grew to love their creation, while Enlil maintained a colder, more utilitarian disposition toward the new slaves, who were known as the Adama (the word adama means earth/clay/dust). Over the years there was some genetic experimentation, sometimes yielding Adama that were too smart to be slaves, and sometimes too stupid to be of use. Eventually they got it just right.

Although operations were going on elsewhere, the Annunaki lived in a lush, fertile section of Mesopotamia named E.Din. The Adama that lived and served in this area were eventually given by Enki (also known as Samael/Ea/the Serpent), the secrets of the *tree of knowledge of good and evil*, the ability to procreate. The Sumerian writings imply that, before this occasion, the Adama were 'mules', incapable of reproducing. Enki, who is often depicted in Sumerian glyphs holding a vial of liquid, had offered mankind the ability to procreate, via another genetic manipulation. The ancient word, 'hu', means color/vibration/god. Man had now become 'hu'man, made in the image of the gods.

This new, improved version of humanity was known as 'Adapa the Adama'. It is interesting to note that this expression appears in the ancient Sumerian text, the Enuma Elish, as well as in the Egyptian archives of Amenhotep III.[19]

Enlil did not approve of this turn of events, in fact he was very angry and banished mankind from E.Din, sending him to fend for himself in the surrounding hills. Enlil was upset that the Adama could now reproduce, and was worried that they would learn from the *tree of life*, the secrets of immortality, becoming equal to the gods. From this perspective, the following Biblical passage suddenly makes much more sense;

> "Then the Lord God said, 'behold, the man has become like one of us, knowing good and evil; and now, lest he put forth his hand and take also of the tree of life, and eat, and live forever'—therefore the Lord God sent him forth from the garden of Eden, to till the ground from which he was taken. He drove out the man; and at the east end of the garden of Eden he placed the cherubim, and a flaming sword which turned every way, to guard the way to the tree of life."

Genesis; 3-22

This is a very significant passage in the Bible. What is one to make of this? Does the flaming sword represents all the ways in which mankind has been held back from discovering (remembering) its true nature, its divine potential? Has Enlil/Jehovah, referred to in this Biblical passage as 'the Lord God', been keeping humanity down all these years? Is the true friend of man actually Enki, the Serpent, whom the Bible has vilified? This is exactly what is being stated by Sitchin and other researchers, whose views we will discuss in a moment. These are also the views held by Gnostics around the time of Christ, as expressed in recently discovered Gnostic texts. In 'On the Origins of the World', Yahweh is portrayed as a false God, hiding the real God from view. In 'The Testimony of Truth', Genesis is presented from the Serpent's point of view.[20]

Enki is said to have given 'civilization' to mankind, to have given knowledge which was written on 100 discs, and to have established 'kingship'. In those days, the king/priest was the one who was the most scientifically knowledgeable, serving and guiding the people down the path to enlightenment.

To continue with our story, mankind went forth and multiplied over the centuries, or possibly millennia. Sitchin claims that the old texts indicate that both the Annunaki and the humans were **preoccupied with sex**, and that the Annunaki regularly had sex with the humans. This would throw some light on a passage of the Bible that has been baffling scholars for years;

> "the sons of God saw that the daughters of men were fair; and they took to wife such of them as they chose....The Nephilim were on the Earth in those days, and also afterward, when the sons of God came in to the daughters of men, and they bore children to them. These were the mighty men that were of old, the men of renown."
>
> —*Genesis; 6-2*

According to Sitchin, this activity, this mixing of genes was also offensive to Enlil, who decided in conjunction with the Assembly of Gods, to allow the humans to be culled by the coming deluge. Again, it was Enki to the rescue. He arranged for Ziusudra/Utnapishtim/Noah to escape the flood in a strangely shaped 'ark', taking with him the 'seed' of all creatures. After the flood, according to the Bible, Noah's three sons are said to have fathered the various races, Shem being the source of the Semitic peoples, Ham the African , and Japheth the Indian and far eastern races. Science, however, claims that racial diversity has existed for about 135,000 years. But, if there was a great flood, didn't all of humanity die in it? Alford claims that racial traits were 'saved' in test-tubes in the ark. Other sources say that, even though the consequences of the deluge were great, many life forms survived, including many humans.

After the flood, new instructions regarding sexual intercourse were issued, instituting two different kinds of sex, one for procreation, the other for pleasure. (Non-procreative sex played a big role in the cultures of ancient man and we will take a look at this in a later chapter). Also, humanity's lifespan was reduced. Before the flood, even according to the Bible, the average age was close to 1,000 years. After the flood, lifespans became much shorter. Abraham lived to the age of 175 years, and subsequent Biblical characters lived ever-shorter lives. (The shorter life spans could also be explained as being the result of the new denser circumstances on the planet after the flood and the 'fall of man', although this is not part of Sitchin's theories. The next section will explore this idea further.)

Inspired by Sitchin's work, many other researchers, such as; Alan Alford, Laurence Gardner, Father Charles Moore, William Bramley and David Icke have gone on to write about the Annunaki, whom they claim are a race of 'reptilians'. There is also channeled information from Barbara Marciniak and others that refers to such extra terrestrials. Bramley and Icke claim that, behind virtually every government and religious movement throughout history, the hidden elite consisted of a hierarchy of 'reptilians' who quietly pulled the strings. In their view, these creatures continue to control events in the modern world. They say that these entities somehow feed on negative energy, so that their agenda generally involves trying to ensure that humanity remains disempowered, mired in fear and negativity. (Regular human food can be thought of as a form of energy. Is it possible that some entities can live on food that is a non-physical, non-material form of energy?)

In his book, *The Biggest Secret*, Icke claims that they are still very active today, and that they have the ability to 'shape-shift' from human form to reptilian form. Some of the most powerful people in the world, including members of the British royal family are, according to Icke, reptilian shape-shifters.

As outrageous and far-fetched as this may sound, there are a great many mysterious references to reptiles, including serpents and dragons, throughout all cultures going back through history. There are many ancient depictions of humanoid reptilians, including one that is holding her baby in a typical 'Madonna and child' pose. In a cave near Casares, Spain, there is a cave drawing that looks suspiciously like reptilian humanoids. These drawings are said to be 15,000 years old.

Interestingly, the dragon is considered a positive symbol of goodness and wisdom in most cultures worldwide, except for the Judeo-Christian traditions which see it, and the serpent, as symbols of evil. The Chinese and Tibetans revere their dragons and in the traditions of many native American cultures, the plumed serpent in the form of Quetzalcoatl, Kulkulkan, Viracocha and others are credited with having brought wisdom and knowledge. The Celts had their Pendragons and the Egyptians, who prized crocodile fat (messeh) as a spiritual ointment, established the Dragon Court in 2170 BC. Amongst Australian Aborigines, the Rainbow Serpent is credited with creation, while in Africa such entities as Kush and Dumballah Wedo are revered.

In his books, 'Gods of the New Millennium' and 'The Phoenix Solution', Alan Alford presents a vast amount of information, expounding on Sitchin's work and claiming that the gods (Alford does not use the term Annunaki) have been manipulating mankind, to our detriment, for millennia. According to Alford, much of history and many of our great mysteries can be explained in terms of the ongoing rivalry between the lineage of Enki and that of Enlil. While contending that there were no violent confrontations before the flood, he shows evidence suggesting that tensions mounted after the deluge until, by the time of the Sumerian civilization, the gods were engaging in all out war. Two key players were Marduk, an Enki-ite and Inanna, an Enlil-ite.

Alford contends that highly sophisticated weaponry was used in these altercations, citing a collection of Sumerian 'lamentation tablets' describing what sounds like a **nuclear holocaust** and fall-out. The famous Biblical devastation of Sodom and Gomorrah, as described by these tablets, could be interpreted as the result of a nuclear explosion. Even the Bible's account could be interpreted as such. The site of the two cities, which is thought to be a shallow section of what is now the Dead Sea, still emits radio-activity, as does Jebel Barkal, a 'sacred' mountain in the Sudan. Here one can see blackened rock faces and rubble in what appears to have been a large explosion. A third suspected site is in the Sinai, where there is a blackened scar that is anomalous to science. Alford claims that this was once the site of a 'space-station' that was destroyed in one of the wars.

Archeologists and scholars have often puzzled over the sudden demise of Sumer and Akkadia and the sudden appearance of Assyria and Babylon, around 2000 BC. Alford claims that Sumer met its end due to nuclear fallout, and that Abram, the Enlil-ite patriarch who was to become **Abraham**, was warned by Enlil and left the Sumerian city of Ur to settle in Canaan. In a Sumerian poem entitled, 'The Curse of Agade', there is the story of the leveling of Agade, the capital of Akkadia, which brought an end to that society.

I have run across several postulations claiming that nuclear explosions have occurred in the distant past, in the Sahara and Gobi deserts. Brad Steiger claims that fused glass has been found there as well as in Gabo, Africa, the Mojave Desert, Iraq and the Euphrates Valley. This is the same glass, caused by the super-heating of naturally occurring silica that can be found in the deserts of New Mexico as a result of nuclear testing.[19]

In an old epic poem from India called the Mahabharata, there is a description of what sounds like a flying saucer dogfight (involving Vishnu, Nara and Narayana), complete with nuclear explosions, fallout and ray-gun weaponry. Dr. Robert Oppenheimer, who helped create the first atomoc bomb, was familiar with the Mahabharata and held similar beliefs that it was describing a nuclear explosion.[22] Similar accounts can be found in some translations of the Hindu Vedas, particularly the Srimad Bhagavatam and the Hymn to Vata. Ancient skeletons discovered in India gave off fifty times the normal levels of radio-activity.[23]

The Sumerians also had a great and mysterious knowledge of astronomy, with a very sophisticated calendar and number system. (See **BOX 14—THE SUMERIAN NUMBER SYSTEM**.) Like the Egyptians and many other cultures, they display an obsession with information relating to the zodiac and the Precession of the Equinoxes. Alford states that the first known references to these things are those found in Sumer and he postulates that the Sumerian gods were the ones to institute them. He claims that Anu, in an effort to stave off conflict between the Enki and Enlil lineages, divided the precessional cycle of 25,920 years into twelve eras of 2,160 years, so that the two lineages could take turns being the boss in Mesopotamia. Thus, the Enlil-ites would rule for one zodiacal period of 2,160 years, and then the Enki-ites for the next period. Alford claims that the number twelve became sacred because of these eras, and also because Nibiru was honored as being the twelfth major cosmic body in the solar system, counting nine other planets, the sun and the moon. (The moons of other planets are considered to be true natural satellites. Our moon, which is much bigger than all other moons in proportion to the host planet, is enigmatic and thought to once have been a planet unto itself.) *I believe that the number twelve is special for deeper, meta-physical reasons, which have to do with the sub-structure of the universe.*

> **BOX 14—SUMERIAN NUMBER SYSTEM;** Our numbers are based on the decimal system, probably because we have ten fingers. The Sumerian system was sexagesimal, based on the number 6, in combination with the decimal system. 360 degrees in a circle and 60 minutes on a clock are remnants of this system. This comes from the ratio between a Nibiru year which equals 3,600 Earth years, and a precessional or zodiacal period which is equal to 2,160 years. This ratio, 3,600/ 2,160, reduces to 10/6. Their mathematical tables are based on the number 12,960,000 and its factors. This number, when divided by 500, equals 25,920 which is the length of a complete precessional cycle. The 10/6 ratio is very close to the golden mean ratio, known as 'phi', which is 10/6.18.[24]

Alford thus claims that many of the enigmatic astro-observatories which we will discuss in the next chapter, were built by the gods who needed to accurately measure the precessional cycle to know when their ruling term was due. He says that most of these structures were designed by Thoth, a god who was an impartial pacifist, and built by a crew led by the god, Ishkur. This crew is said to be a genetically constructed race of Negroid giants, roughly nine feet tall and facially resembling the statues on Easter Island and the large stone heads of the Olmecs. These giants were experts at stone masonry and had the use of advanced powered tools. Alford points out that there are many references to giants in the Bible, the most famous being Goliath. He postulates that groups of giants known as the Kassites, the Rephaites, the Anakim and the mysterious Olmecs all came from this ancient race of stoneworkers.

Alford takes a stab at establishing a new chronology of events which succeeds in reconciling the differences between Biblical time scales, Sumerian and

Babylonian king lists, anthropological information and records of pre-flood gods and dynasties as recorded on the Turin Papyrus and the Palermo Stone, and by Manetho. (See **BOX 15—ANCIENT DYNASTIES**) He does this by assigning the precessional period of 2,160 years to a unit of time which appears often in Sumerian records, called a 'sar'.

Alford feels that these 'gods' and thus all the 'dragon' stuff, are 'badguys', the source of all of our problems, oppressing mankind for millennia. He claims that they left the planet at the start of the Piscean age, just before the time of Christ, and that they are due to return shortly, in the age of Aquarius. He thinks of them as a form of anti-Christ and warns that we must be on guard for their return. There are others, however, who feel that this group are benevolent to mankind and anticipate their return as being akin to the second coming of Christ, the return of the messiah.

> **BOX 15—ANCIENT DYNASTIES;** The dominant academic paradigm claims that Egyptian civilization began circa 3113 BC with the first pharaoh, Menes. There is some information that seems to challenge this claim. In the third century BC, an Egyptian priest/historian by the name of Manetho compiled lists of all the kings and pharaohs. Like many ancient historians, he regarded the gods as having lived real lives. The first dynasty includes Ptah—9000 years, Ra—1000 years, Shu—700 years, Geb—500 years, Osiris—450 years, Seth—350 years and Horus—300 years for a total of 12,300 years. The second dynasty includes Thoth, Maat and others and totals 1,570 years. The third dynasty includes 30 demi-gods and totals 3,650 years. The fourth dynasty is considered to be a period of chaos during which there was no ruler, lasting 350 years. At this point we have the first pharaoh, Menes, who began ruling in 3113 BC, which is the same year that the Mayan calendar begins. Although archeology has confirmed Manetho's more recent king lists starting with Menes, scholars dismiss the older lists, relegating them to myth.[25] Mesopotamian texts say that Thoth ruled circa 8,700 BC and that Ptah = Enki, Ra = Marduk. An ancient Egyptian document now in a museum in Turin, Italy, called the Turin Papyrus, mentions 9 dynasties of kings before Menes, and claims that Egypt was ruled by 'gods and demigods' prior to that. Currently in a museum in Palermo, there is a document called the Palermo Stone, which mentions 120 kings before Menes.[26]

Another author who has written extensively on the Elohim/Nephilim/Anunnaki in his books, 'Bloodline of the Holy Grail' and 'Genesis of the Grail Kings', is Sir Laurence Gardner, who has a string of titles behind his name. He is an internationally known sovereign and chivalric genealogist, holding the following positions: Prior of the Celtic Church of the Sacred Kindred of Saint Columbia, Chevalier Labhran de Saint Germain, Preceptor of the Knights Templar of Saint Anthony, Presidential Attaché to the European Council of Princes and Chancellor of the Imperial and Royal Court of the Dragon Sovereignty. He is attached to the Royal House of Stewart, is the Jacobite Historiographer Royal and is a Fellow of the Society of Antiquaries of Scotland.

Some of the ways in which Gardner differs from Alford and Sitchin have to do with the chronology of events, which we will not discuss here. The key difference is that, unlike Sitchin and Alford who never mention the concept of enlightenment, Gardner feels that the Annunaki/reptilians are 'goodguys' who brought us culture, technology and methodologies to facilitate our spiritual progress. He claims that the 'Adapa' referred to earlier, was the start of the true king line, the original royal *'dragon' bloodline*, which started with Qayen (Cain), the first son of Enki and Eve. Gardner claims that, for whatever reason, the Roman/Christian church, via the Bible, has distorted this truth (as well as many others) and made Adam's son, Seth, the father of the Hebrew lineage. He goes to great pains to demonstrate this, claiming that this 'pure' bloodline runs from Qayin, through to David, Jesus, the Merovingian kings of France, etc. He strongly implies that the true descendant of Jesus should shortly appear upon the world stage to lead us through the end times.

As well as examining ancient texts, many of Gardner's contentions come from his knowledge of etymology, the examination of word origins. The words 'king' and 'queen', for example, are derived from Qayin. The word 'ritual' comes from 'ritu' which means red gold, which means blood. This brings us to one of Gardner's more interesting topics.

Over many centuries before the flood, the process of enlightenment was assisted by the ingestion of **menstrual blood**. This was known as the 'starfire' tradition. Rich in melatonin and other hormones, menstrual blood contains the chemical information of life, having the power to stimulate the pineal gland/crown chakra, long considered to be the seat of the soul. The female genital organ is the first flower (from the word 'flow'), and is symbolized in the lotus and lily. The kings, under the supervision of Enki, were treated to Anunnaki menstrual blood, which, according to Gardner, was of superior potency. This ritual ingestion, as well as other sacred sexual activities was practiced for many years, until it was outlawed by Enlil during the days of Noah.

In the days after the flood the practice continued despite the ban, especially in areas where Enlil had less control. The Hebrew lineage, which had started with the patriarch, Eber, several generations before Abraham, was strongly aligned with Enlil and had to be secretive about the continued practice of the starfire rituals. When the Annunaki left Mesopotamia during the time of the destruction of Sumer (about 2000 BC), the more potent menstrual fluids became unavailable to the kings and Enki came up with another means of facilitating enlightenment.

A method of processing gold into its 'highward' state was developed. This involves some form of combustion that transforms the metal into a *'white powder gold'*, which when ingested, also stimulates the pineal gland/crown chakra. This was the science that became known as **alchemy**, which later became mistaken for the process of attempting to turn base metals into gold. The changing of lead to gold was meant as a metaphor, symbolic of the transformation of ordinary states of consciousness into the elevated consciousness of enlightenment. The word 'alchemy' comes from 'al khame' which means 'overcoming blackness, bringing light'.

The powder was pressed into a conical, 'shem'-shaped loaf, which was known to the ancient Egyptians as 'shem-an-na' or to the Hebrews as 'shew-bread' or 'manna'. In Egypt the powder was also called 'schefa food' and in its pressed loaf form, was known as the legendary **Philosopher's Stone**. There are at least two reference to the white powder in the Bible. Exodus 32:20 refers to the golden calf that the Hebrews made and worshipped while Moses was up the mountain. Moses then "burnt it with fire and ground it to powder, and scattered it onto the water, and made the people of Israel drink it." In Revelation 2:17, God says, "To him who conquers I will give some of the hidden manna, and I will give him a white stone..."

In 1904, Egyptologist Flinders Petrie discovered the Sinai Mountain Temple at Serabit, which had been built circa 2600 BC, and had been lost for the past 3000 years. In it he found two shems, a crucible and mounds of white powder, much of which is now in the British Museum. White powder is also said to have been found in the so-called 'sarcophagus' in the King's chamber of the Great Pyramid. (We'll speak more of this later). According to an electrical engineer named Preston Nichols, who was involved in the Philadelphia Experiment and the Montauk Project, the Egyptian mystery schools were designed to balance the left and right brains of the initiates. When this state of balance was achieved, a white powder was emitted by the pineal gland. It has also been said that monks in prolonged states of meditation emit small amounts of white powder in the forehead region.

According to Gardner, rendering gold into its highward or high-spin state is a process that is partly physical, partly meta-physical, and involves getting the electrons in a gold atom to spin at a higher rate. All the platinum group of metals have the capacity to achieve a high spin state. Iridium in a high spin state is said to stimulate serotonin production in the pituitary gland/brow chakra. Gardner says that 95% of a human brain's dry weight is carbon, and the rest is iridium and rhodium. He sites several other relevant attributes of the platinum group and their effects on DNA. (Gardner got much of this info from a researcher of ancient alchemy, David Hudson, who operates through the Ramtha School of Enlightenment. For more info re: white powder gold, and many related subjects, see **www.halexandria.org**)

In 2170 BC, 39 men and women formed the **Great White Brotherhood** in Egypt. Although it may sound like another name for the Ku Klux Klan, it has nothing to do with race, and is also known as the **Dragon Court**. To the Greeks it became known as the Therapeutae, to the Hebrews it became the Essenes/Nazorenes, and to the Europeans it became the Roscrucians. Secret societies like these, as well as the Knights Templar, the Sons of the Priory of

Sion and the Freemasons, have been guarding the secrets of the white powder and other forms of magic/alchemy for all these years. (See **BOX 16—MASONS, TEMPLARS AND THE SECRET SOCIETIES**)

BOX 16—MASONS, TEMPLARS AND THE SECRET SOCIETIES:

Much has come to light regarding the secret societies over the past few decades thanks to several publications, including the bestseller, *The Holy Blood and the Holy Grail*, by Baigent, Lee and Lincoln. This information is gaining a larger place in the public consciousness, as witnessed by the success of Dan Brown's novel, *The Da Vinci Code*. According to researchers, powerful secret organizations have been quietly pulling the strings behind most of the historical events throughout history. These groups, mostly somewhat affiliated, are usually structured in levels, with the lower levels being unaware of the identity and true motives of the upper levels. The identity of those at the very apex of the pyramid remains a mystery. Opinions vary as to their intentions. Some claim that they are good-guys, guarding and preserving important information, while others regard them as evil incarnate, selfishly manipulating toward their own ends.

THE KNIGHTS TEMPLAR—Established in 1118 AD by French noblemen, the Templars originally answered only to the Pope. They headquartered in Southern France and became affiliated with the Cathars. They are credited with starting the first banks. Over the next two centuries they became extremely wealthy and powerful, eventually falling from grace at the Vatican. In 1314, their Grand Master, Jaques de Molay was slowly roasted to death and the Templar wealth was seized by the French monarchy. The Templars fled, went underground and eventually merged with the Freemasons, Rosicrucians, etc. It is said that they guarded secrets about Mary Magdelaine, Jesus, John the Baptist and the Holy Grail. They, like most secret societies, were greatly concerned with magic, alchemy and other 'occult' pursuits that were considered heretical by the establishment.

THE PRIORY OF SION—Said to be the smaller group that led the Templars, this society is thought to still exist today. Over the years many famous individuals have served as Grand Master of the Priory, i.e. Leonardo Da Vinci, Robert Boyle, Isaac Newton, Victor Hugo, Claude Debussy and Jean Cocteau. Some believe that they are dedicated to the restoration of the Merovingian Dynasty, thought to be of the same bloodline as Christ.

THE ROSICRUCIANS—Also concerned with magic and Hermetic wisdom, this group was/is dedicated to the union of pagan and Christian mysteries, symbolized by the rose and the cross.

THE FREEMASONS—Although the earliest lodges appeared circa 1640 AD, Freemason iconography suggests that it goes back to ancient Egypt. The earliest Freemasons were ancient architects who preserved sacred knowledge by incorporating sacred geometrical proportions and symbols into the temples and monuments they built. In today's world, this organization is very powerful and most world leaders, including all of the American presidents, are 33rd level Freemasons. One of the key Mason symbols, the pyramid capped with the all-seeing eye, can be found on the back of any American dollar bill.

The word 'grail' comes from 'sangreal' = sangre réal = blood royal. For Gardner, the **Holy Grail** symbolizes the vessel, the womb that holds the true kingly bloodline of the Dragon lineage. Thus, the quest for the Holy Grail is the quest for the rightful heir to the throne, the descendant of Jesus. (The question of whether Jesus had offspring will be taken up in a later chapter). Although Gardner's book is chock-full of fascinating information, it seems designed to convince us that some sort of new messiah is about to enter the world stage. Many people have a difficult time with this notion, particularly David Icke, who has accused Gardner of working for 'the reptilians', if not actually being one himself!

*I believe that it is entirely possible, maybe even probable, that ETs interacted sig-nificantly with mankind in the past (and probably in the present). Such an idea does not seem far-fetched to me. In an age when the ability to clone and to manip-ulate DNA is already here, I find it within the realm of possibility that ETs could have tampered with our DNA in the past. I admit that such a suggestion makes more sense to me than the idea that humanity evolved into its current complex form **entirely** due to natural selection.*

Temple, Sitchin, Alford, Gardner et al, present reams of very compelling and convincing evidence, although none of it, in my opinion, represents concrete, definitive proof. Ancient glyphs and texts must be difficult to decipher and the process must surely be subject to a certain amount of personal interpretation. Some of the glyphs, however, require very little deciphering, as they are clear depictions of the planets of our solar system, recognizable by the accurate num-ber of planets and their relative sizes. Again, it seems clear to me that there is more than enough worthwhile information here to challenge the paradigms of human origins. These seemingly far-fetched lines of thought definitely deserve further investigation.

It seems to me that mankind has a tendency to look at things in black and white, preferring to take either one side of an argument or the other. There are several clas-sical debates, such as 'determinism vs. free will' in the field of philosophy, or 'nature vs. nurture' in the field of psychology. In the latter, one side will argue that behavior is inherited, while the other side argues that it is learned. It seems obvious to me that both are true; behavior is both learned and genetically inherited, with probably a few other factors thrown in. Most of these classical 'either-or' debates seem to be exam-ples in which both sides of the argument are partially true. I believe that nothing is black and white. I believe that most phenomena have many causal factors, and that in many cases these factors are not mutually exclusive.

In much of the alternative information that I read, I find the same tendency to argue in favor of either 'black' or 'white'. While I do feel that Sitchin and Alford have made a major contribution to our understanding of mankind's origins, they can't seem to resist the temptation to come up with the explanation to end all explanations. Can every ancient mystery be explained in terms of the Anunnaki and the desire of the gods to take turns ruling? Even though I consider Sitchen, Alford and like researchers to be my personal heroes, I would love to see them examine the same information from more of a metaphysical, spiritual perspective. I believe that, even though the picture they paint is far closer to the truth than the official line, it is still part of the 'maya', the cosmic illusion, and is a very small fraction of the total picture.

Even if one chooses to buy the idea of a race of reptilian shape-shifters, taking a stand as to whether they are goodguys or badguys also seems to me a pointless endeavor, which could almost be interpreted as racism. Surely any race of beings, whether extraterrestrial or not, would consist of individuals making bad decisions as well as those making good ones, with the majority of individuals making a mixture of both types of decisions. They, like us, have a variety of motives. I personally believe that there are and have been many different races of ETs, possibly including those known as the Anunnaki, interacting with us in subtle and not-so-subtle ways, all playing the Game at their own level. This would include those levels of consciousness that have come to be called angels or archangels. Any form of consciousness, even those that are non-physical, are by definition, ETs. I believe that most of them are more aware than are we, of the cosmic cycles and the coming shift, the laws of energy and the workings of the Game. I believe that their actions have both helped and hindered mankind throughout the ages. While it is, no doubt, prudent to be vigilant and aware, to view any one race as the 'evil enemy' is, in my opinion, folly. At the risk of sounding like a broken record, I believe that the only good course of action is one based on love and compassion. We must feel that way for everything and everyone, even for those who may have hurt all of humanity.

I am grateful for the wealth of information provided by Sir Laurence Gardner, however I must say that I am not comfortable with his obsessions regarding a 'truly royal' bloodline. If one believes in reincarnation, which seems to be the case with Gardner, then why are bloodlines important? Does a soul always incarnate into the same bloodline? I doubt it. I believe that the entity that was Jesus, for example, has incarnated many times in different racial forms and cultures in an attempt to assist humanity. Looking for a new messiah who is of the same bloodline as Jesus seems to me to be foolish and dangerous.

Chapter 17

ATLANTEAN AND LEMURIAN SKELETONS IN THE CLOSET

There are many stories and theories about incredibly advanced civilizations that have come and gone in eras before the one we are currently enjoying. There is information on societies with strange names, such as Dar, Mu, and Gondwanaland, and even a civilization that once existed on Mars. By far, the most commonly known of these lost empires, is the one called *Atlantis*.

There has been a great deal written on Atlantis, with a wide range of theories based on different types of research as well as psychic or channeled information. Some of the key researchers are: Ignatius Donnely, Lewis Spence, Otto Muck, A. Braghine, Andrew Tomas, Charles Berlitz, Col. W. Scott-Elliot, Jergen Spanuth, Robert Scrutton and others. Some of the key channels are; Edgar Cayce, Helena Blavatsky, Rudolph Steiner, Tony Neate, Dion Fortune, Christine Hartley, Daphne Vigers, Frank Alper, Gordon M. Scallion, Drunvalo Melchizedek and others. If one wanted to read only one book on the subject, offering a variety of theories and a thorough presentation of information regarding this fascinating story which has such a firm foothold in the human psyche, I would recommend 'Atlantis, Myth or Reality?', by Murry Hope.

Many cultures over the years have made reference to some large island or advanced society that was destroyed in the distant past, with various themes of cataclysm, angry gods and/or misused technology. Some northwest African tribes have legends of places called Atarantes and Atlantioi. The Berbers from the region now called Morocco spoke of a place called Attala, rich in gold and silver, which will rise again. The Celts of Gaul, Ireland and Wales claim that their ancestors came from a place to the west known as Avalon, which is also the name of an island in the Arthurian legends. The Basques of northern Spain say they descended from Atlaintika. The Phoenicians spoke of an island of great wealth called Antilla. There are Arabian legends of Ad and Indian writings of the white islands of Attala. The Mayans, Aztecs and other Native American tribes claim that they originated from a land to the east, which they refer to as Aztlan. The Norse or Scandinavian legends tell of the origin of the Frisian race as coming from Atland.[27] Of course, Atlantis was referred to by the Greeks, and one very famous Greek actually wrote about it.

A highly respected scholar, one who was not known to lie or exaggerate, was the famous Greek philosopher *Plato*. His accounts are based on information brought to Greece from Egypt two hundred years earlier, by Solon, a revered warrior and national hero. It would be unthinkable for Plato to utter falsehoods in Solon's name. Plato describes Atlantis as a mighty and aggressive power whose empire extended into Europe and North Africa, and whose advances were thwarted by ancient Athens, thus saving its people from slavery. Atlantis consisted of two large islands located 'beyond the pillars of Hercules', which most scholars have interpreted as meaning beyond Gibraltar. Described as an impenetrable fortress with many impressive canals, bridges and temples, it was said to be rich in food, wood, gold, silver and a mysterious metal called orichalcum.

Plato says that God initially gave the lands of Atlantis to Poseidon, who begot children with mortal women. He then divided the land into ten parts, one for each son, making the oldest son, Atlas, the king. Eventually, after violent quakes and floods, Atlantis sank into the sea, 9,000 years before Plato's time. (This makes puzzling Plato's claim that Athens defeated them, as it would not yet have existed.)

Many *possible locations* have been theorized regarding Atlantis. In 1450 BC, at the time of the decline of the Cretan civilization, there was a volcanic explosion on the nearby island of Santorini, devastating most of the island. Galanopoulos and Marinatos, two Greek archeologists, tried to make a case that this was Atlantis and, although it is unlikely, this theory has helped to foster the booming tourist trade that exists there today. Another contender is the ancient city of Tartessos (Tarshish in the Bible), a society of sea traders that mysteriously disappeared.

Scandinavian researcher, Jergen Spanuth has purported that Atlantis lay beneath the North Sea, where divers have found what appears to be the remnants of rock walls. The mythical land of Hyperborea was said to have been in the North Sea. An old text called the 'Oera Linda Book' claims that the predecessors to the Frisians were a tall, blond, blue-eyed people from an island called Atland, who later mixed with native Scandinavians, Germans and Magyars. Perhaps it was these people that attacked Athens and were defeated, as in Plato's account.

Some say that perhaps the area of the Yucatan Peninsula and Central America could be Atlantis. There are many similarities in the art, culture and science that came from societies that pre-date the Mayan and Aztec civilizations, that are very similar to that of ancient Egypt, including calendars and pyramids. The area of Tiwanaku, high in the Bolivian altiplano, near the shores of Lake Titicaca, is another proposed possibility. Researcher, Arthur Posnansky has provided convincing evidence that the entire area was once at sea level, citing the many old shells from salt water marine life that have been found there, as well as what appear to be old wharves and harbors with strand lines from tide activity. The reed boats that were used in the area are almost identical to the ones used in ancient Egypt.

A Canadian husband and wife research team called the Flem-Aths, elaborating on the work of Charles Hapgood, has published a theory that Atlantis could have been in Antarctica, before a pole shift caused its current frozen circumstances. Ancient maps (which we will discuss later in the book) show that it was once ice-free.[28] Sediments taken from the Ross Sea during the Byrd expedition of 1949 suggest that warmer conditions prevailed there until 4000 BC.[29] Other contenders for the location of Atlantis are Brazil, east Africa and the Sahara Desert. Some are of the opinion that the lost continent could actually be the lost planet of Atlantis, or that the Atlanteans came from some doomed space-place to settle on the island continent. By far, the most popular theory is that it existed in the mid-Atlantic, somewhere between the Azores and the West Indies.[30]

At this point it may be wise to take a look at some of the *evidence for the existence of Atlantis*. We won't look at all the evidence pertaining to all the different theories, but will look at some of the evidence suggesting that it may have been located in the mid-Atlantic. There is an 'underwater island', a raised area 9,000 feet above the ocean floor, the peaks of which form the Azores, St. Paul's Rocks, Ascension Island and Tristan D'Alunha Island. The contention is that this underwater island could once have been above water.[31]

The proponents of the 'continental drift' theory point out that, if the continents are pushed together so that we can approximate how they would have looked when it was one large land mass called Pangea, we can see that the continents of South America and Africa nestle together nicely. However, where North America and Europe come together, there is a hole right around the proposed Atlantis location. If one visualizes a large island in this location, then the puzzle pieces of the Pangea picture come together more neatly.

Most of the theories of Atlantis' demise say that, during the cataclysm, there was much volcanic activity. Is there evidence of this? During the laying of the trans-Atlantic cable, volcanic rocks were found on the ocean floor about 1,000 miles north of the Azores. It was shown to be a vitreous form of lava that had been ejected above ground. Lava ejected below water shows a distinctly different form. A later Soviet expedition led by Dr. Maria Klenova confirmed this, dating the lava as being about 15,000 years old.

In 1882, Captain David Robson and the crew of the S. S. Jesmond of the Queen's Merchant Marine observed a strange sight just southwest of the Azores. The water had become muddy, with a great number of floating, dead fish and smoke coming from an area where, according to the charts, there was no landmass. Approaching this spot, they saw what appeared to be a newly arisen piece of ocean floor. A boarding party went ashore and reported that there was no sand and no signs of life, only volcanic rubble and debris, some of which looked like the remains of rock walls. They also found bronze artifacts, such as swords, rings, mallets and carvings, as well as fragments of vases, jars and bones, including a skull, much of which they took with them to New Orleans. The entire story was reported in the 'Times Picayune' of New Orleans. Unfortunately the ship's log was destroyed in the London blitz of the Second World War. The artifacts have also gone missing.

Around the same time, Captain James Newdick of the steamer, Westbourne, en route to New York saw the same 'island'. His story was reported in the New York Post in April 1882. Several other vessels reported seeing muddy water and floating fish. Pilots flying over this area have reported that, on clear, calm days when sunlight conditions are just so, they can see vague underwater shapes that look like human habitations. Some have explained this sudden temporary rise of the sea-bottom as being due to pressure from gas pockets just below the Earth's crust beneath the ocean floor.

In 1974, there was a Russian deep-sea expedition headed by Professor Andrei Akstonov aboard the research vessel, Academician Petrovsky. They succeeded in taking many photographs of what appear to be stone blocks, masonry and stairs. During the well publicized 'Bimini Discoveries' of the 1960s, a palaeontologist, geologist and underwater archeologist by the name of Dr. Manson Valentine found a series of large, rectangular stones connected in straight lines and other non-natural architectural patterns. A large grooved building block and a stylized feline head were successfully brought to the surface.[32]

This is not a complete list of evidence, nor is any of it conclusive. However, there is enough to suggest that more research is definitely warranted. It is strange that there is always plenty of money to be spent on the military and other things, but none to fund important research such as this. There are people who believe that the American government is aware of many other anomalous findings on the ocean floor, which they have chosen not to share with the public.

Now we'll take a look at *various theories regarding the demise of Atlantis*. Most opinions claim that it happened in a series of events that spanned about 2,000 years. Some cite three distinct phases of destruction, the first two having more to do with quakes and volcanoes and the third having to do with flood. Some of the phenomena commonly cited as being characteristic of the Atlantean cataclysm are; fire and volcanic activity, flooding, objects falling from the sky, including 'black rain', dramatically worsening climatic change and the sinking of land masses.

Otto Muck believes the demise was caused by a giant asteroid that struck the planet in the waters near Puerto Rico. Other opinions have stated that a large meteor struck near the city of Charlestown, South Carolina. Yet another theory proposed by Hans Hoerbinger says that the cataclysm was caused by a shift in the position of the moon, or by the first appearance of the moon. One of the theories of the moon's origins contends that it was once a small planet equal to Earth in age which, due to some circumstance, was 'captured' by

Earth's gravity. Many tribes such as the Chibchas of Columbia, the African Bushmen, the Mayans, the Tupis and the Aravac have legends of the recent appearance of the moon. In ancient Greece the moon was called Selene and several Greek legends speak of the 'Preselenites', people who lived before the arrival of the moon.[33]

The ancients were well aware of the cosmic cycles and of the effect of the position of other cosmic bodies relative to Earth's. For example, the work of a German scientist, Rudolph Toaschek suggests that Uranus exerts a certain kind of pull on the Earth's crust. In the number of quakes that have occurred over the past 49 years, 39 of them have been in locations which had Uranus positioned directly above.[34] The planet's position in the precessional cycle of 25,920 years at the time of the Atlantean cataclysm is said to be a key factor. Another factor would be the pull exerted by the sun and moon when in alignment, as in eclipses. The ancients appear to have been aware of this force. The Babylonians knew of the eclipse cycle, which they called the 'Saros Cycle'; a solar eclipse occurs every 18 years, 11 and ⅓ days, or 223 lunations.[35] Egyptians had recorded 373 solar and 832 lunar eclipses and their tidal effects on the Nile. That represents 10,000 years worth of observations! These ancient peoples obviously assigned great importance to such events.

Some theorists believe that there was a change in the planet's orbit, that we were slightly closer to the sun before the Atlantean event, taking 360 days for a complete revolution. I've run across information from a variety of sources referring to this idea. Many ancient societies including those of the Indus Valley, Egypt, Babylon, China and Rome at the time of Romulus, had 360-day calendars, usually divided into twelve months of 30 days. The stone circles of Avebury in England are said to represent a 360-day calendar. The Incas and the Aztecs had 360-day calendars. The Mayans, who knew the periods of revolution of all the planets to an uncanny degree (which according to Professor H. Ludendorff of the Astrophysical Observatory, must have taken a very long period of observation), had a 360-day calendar to which they added 5.25 days at a later time. There are also Greek and Egyptian myths regarding the adding of extra days. This seems to validate some of the claims of channeled information, which says that somehow, about 13,000 years ago, the Earth became denser, requiring a longer time to orbit the sun.[36]

One of the more interesting theories contends that our planet has undergone periodic pole shifts, whereby the north and south axis on which the planet spins is in a different location than the one we take for granted. The last time the poles changed position is thought to be right at the time of the sinking of Atlantis. Geologists are puzzled by scars from ice sheets that have been found in parts of the globe that are currently tropical. For anyone desiring to get a handle on the many different pole-shift theories, I recommend a book by

John White called *Pole Shift*.

One of the main purveyors of this theory is Charles Hapgood, a Harvard educated teacher, who claims that there have been three shifts in the past 100,000 years. In the first of these three positions, the north pole was in Canada's Yukon Territory. In the second position, the one that would have been in place in the Atlantean era, the north pole is said to have been in the middle of Hudson's Bay. If you check this on a globe map, you can see that a good deal of Antarctica would have been in a temperate zone and that Atlantis, if it was in the mid Atlantic, would have been closer to the equator, which would have been important during the ice age that prevailed in Atlantean times. The first two positions also explain why the northern ice cap of the last glaciation was so lopsided, reaching as far south as Philadelphia on the American side, but only to the north coast of Siberia on the opposite side.

Two star maps at the tomb of Senmouth, the Papyri of Harris, Hermitage and Ipuwer and the famous Denderah Zodiac all allude to the world having 'turned upside down'. Ancient Chinese records as reported by Jesuit missionary, M. Martini, suggest the same thing. There are some interesting legends that may shed some light on the pole shift theories. In the Egyptian legend of the twin lions Tefnut and Shu, they are depicted seated back to back with the disc of Ra supported between them. The lions represent fear on the one hand, and desire on the other. The disc represents reason and self-control, which holds the lions in place. If the lions move, the disc is displaced, symbolizing a pole shift and the effect of consciousness (fear and desire) on the circumstances of the planet. In a Hopi legend, Poquanghoya and Palongawhoya, who are the guardians of the north and south poles, allow the poles to slip to destroy the evil of the Second World.[37]

Who were **the people of Atlantis**? What did they look like, what was their language, lifestyle, religion and customs? What of the legendary technology of this reputedly advanced empire? Most of the information which addresses these questions comes from sources that are not hard science, such as myths and legends, oral traditions, ancient texts and psychics.

One of the most frequently mentioned physical traits of Atlanteans is height. They are said to have averaged seven feet tall, with heights of nine feet not being uncommon. There have been a fair number of tall skeletons found throughout the world, including Java, China, South Africa and recently in North America. We'll speak more of this in a subsequent chapter. As previously mentioned, there are many references to giants in mythology and ancient writings including the Bible.

There is said to have been three main races in Atlantis, the White race, the Red race and the Semitic race. Some contend that all five races were represented. Others say that they were predominantly red or golden skinned with blue eyes. Native Americans, Egyptians, Phoenicians and all original Mediterranean people other than Semites were considered red-skinned, with typically sparse facial hair. The white-skinned faction are described as blue-eyed, tall and heavily bearded, the same description given in Native American legends of gods who brought knowledge; Quetzalcoatl, Viracocha, Kukulcan, Bochica, Zamna, Zume and Tupan.

Many traditions say that the Atlanteans had a common language and the Hopi say that they 'understood each other without speaking'. Such telepathic ability is often cited, especially in the early years which are said to be as far back as thirty or forty thousand years before the cataclysm. This ability diminished as the years went by and a verbal language developed. Many linguists claim that the many languages around the world today probably descended from one common language. It is interesting to note that there are many similar words with the same meaning in cultures all around the globe. Father, for example, is taita, aita atta, atey, atya, tatay and aht. The Fijian, Roman, Aztec and Slovakian word for father is the same, tata. In both Egyptian and Quechuan (Amerind), the word for high mountain is andi. There are also many ancient town names in the old world that are similar to ancient town names in the new world. Did this ancient common language come from Atlantis?

Many aspects of Atlantean life are said to have changed dramatically from the early days to the latter days. In the early days they tended to be more right-brained, gentle, artistic and naturalistic. It was a polygamous, mostly vegetarian, theocratic society with equality of the sexes, where psychic abilities were nurtured and trained. Children were selected early for vocation. The state provided for the needs of all, and retirement came early. In the latter stages it became more left-brained, aggressive, hedonistic and power-hungry. The practice of religious blood sacrifices became more common, as did the dependence on external technology. By the end, there was a strict caste system in place. Many speak of two competing mind-sets operating in the final days, the more spiritual versus the more materialistic, much like it is in our society today.

There is a fair bit of controversy regarding the technologies that had been developed by the final days. Their technology came from a different angle than ours. They harnessed energy from solar and cosmic rays, from the Earth's magnetic field, and from the ionosphere, which was then transmitted using a 'broadcasting' technique, so as not to require cables. This is similar to the ideas that Nikola Tesla was trying to develop in the latter part of his life. They used crystals to amplify, store and reflect energy. The main crystal is said to be underwater somewhere in the Bermuda Triangle, causing 'rifts in the space-time fabric' which result in the mysterious disappearances of planes and boats and other strange phenomena in the region.

Some say they had anti-gravity technology, using magnetics and sonics. As

Tesla proved, all objects have a 'keynote', a maximum frequency at which the object vibrates, which the Atlanteans manipulated to various ends. There are claims that they had flying machines, advanced weaponry and the ability to move large objects.

In the field of medicine or healing, they are said to have been very sophisticated, with advanced knowledge of surgery, psychology, bionics, psychic healing and genetic engineering. There are many legends of the chimeras, the 'half man, half beast' entities that they created, and some claim that the Minotaur, the gryphon, mermaids and other mythical beasts were genetically engineered by the Atlanteans. The Mayan mural of Bonampak shows a collection of strange humanoids with various beastly body parts.

Another area that eventually got them in trouble, according to researcher Mark Hammons, was the manipulation of weather and tampering with natural forces. They are said to have staged, for entertainment, artistic displays of violent weather, using lightning, high winds and volcanic activity. Hammons says that they accessed energy by tapping into gas pockets or bubbles beneath the Earth's crust, which eventually led to uncontrollable eruptions. It is generally said that they got carried away with their technology to the point that it became a factor in the cataclysmic ending of their civilization. Just prior to the final days, the more spiritual, psychic faction began to make preparations, bringing sacred knowledge to the colonies to be preserved in buildings, stone texts, etc. Some of the knowledge was hidden or coded, to be accessed at a time when the new era would be ready. Like the Excalibur story, the sword (representing knowledge) could only be pulled from the stone by one with the correct attitude and level of wisdom.

Ancient civilizations in North, South and Central America, the West Indies, North Africa, the Canary Islands, Egypt, Greece, Sumer and Tibet, are said to have been *Atlantean colonies*. Many of these cultures had similar beliefs regarding the immortality of the soul and similar practices regarding the embalming and mumification of their dead. It is interesting that a list of ancient cities from Asia Minor—Chol, Colua, Zuivana, Cholina, Zalissa—have almost exact counterparts in Central American cities that existed before the arrival of the Spanish—Chol-ula, Colua-can, Zuivan, Colina, Xalisco.[38] The Egyptian and Mayan societies are particularly good candidates for such a claim, in that they have so many things in common. Both cultures had solar, lunar and Sothic (pertaining to Sirius) calendars, extensive knowledge of astronomy, mathematics, geometry, etc. Both built pyramids and stone texts with similar markings. Many Egyptian gods, including Thoth, Osiris, Isis, Horus, Bast and others, are considered to be Atlanteans. Ra and Ptah are thought to be both Atlantean and Lemurian.

That makes for a nice segue into the next section. After Atlantis, the next most well known of possible 'lost' civilizations is one that has come to be called **Lemuria**. Another name, and one that I believe to be more accurate, is **Mu**, but for our purposes in this book, I'll use the former, as it is the more popular.

Considered to be a series of many islands in the Pacific that predated and then overlapped the time of Atlantis, Lemuria sank slowly into the ocean over the course of thousands of years. Probably the chief authority on this subject was the explorer/researcher, James Churchward, who refers to Lemuria as the 'motherland', claiming that it was the predecessor to virtually all other civilization on the planet.

Churchward found two sets of ancient **Naacal** tablets in a Hindu monastery near Tibet, circa 1900. A high priest of a college temple in India taught him how to read the Naga language of Burma/Tibet, and to decipher its symbols. Much of his work involves the translating of this symbology, most of which can be found in cultures around the globe. He claims that these symbols, such as the circle, the equilateral triangle, various crosses (including the Swastika), squares, winged discs and serpents (including the feathered and seven headed types) originate in the motherland. He shows examples of artifacts from various cultures that seem to be referring to the demise of Lemuria.

Churchward believes that the civilizations of the Pacific rim, including Indonesia, Malaysia, China, Japan, Hawaii and the many islands of the South Pacific, are all remnants of colonies of Lemuria. The Aborigines of Australia and the Bushmen of South Africa are said to be direct descendants of Lemurians, with a highly right-brained, 'dream-time' type of consciousness. Native populations of the north-western corner of South America as well as those of the south-western USA and western Canada are thought to have been from the motherland, and there is a growing body of evidence to challenge the accepted paradigm that all Native Americans entered from Europe via the land bridge at the Bering Strait, and then populated the entire two continents. Alternative theory suggests that the native Americans from the northern regions of North America are more like the 'yellow' races of Asia and probably did come over on the land bridge. However, native Americans from South and Central America, as well as the southern part of North America, bear little resemblance to the Asians and are said to be of the 'red' race that came from Lemuria at an earlier time.

By way of **evidence regarding Lemuria**, Churchward gives many examples of ways in which the information on his tablets accords with that of ancient Hindu writings, such as the Rig Veda, Manarva Dharma Sastra and the Aitereya-A 'Ram-'Ya. He claims that writings from the Burma region and other regions of the South Pacific are also in accord. Ruins and remnants of stone structures, walls, roads and statuary from islands such as Easter, Mangia, Tong-Tabu, Madrone, Mariana and others, are similar to ruins found on the Burmese peninsula, such as Angkor Vat and Angkor Thom, as well as Mayan ruins on the Yucatan such as Uxmal. Churchward gives specific examples of these similarities.

Churchward also cites a discovery made by archeologist, William Niven at a Mexican excavation. Below 30 feet of gravel and volcanic ash, Niven uncovered parts of a lost city. He found artifacts with designs resembling those of China, as well as bones, arched doorways and things made of iron. This came from strata that were at least 15,000 years old. Churchward claims that the facial features of many of the figurine artifacts represent all racial types, and that necklaces were found made of jade which is not a naturally occurring mineral in that region. Churchward expresses amazement that the site was not completely excavated and that science showed no interest in it.

As further evidence, Churchward cites old coral reefs that have been found at depths of 1800 feet. Coral cannot grow in water deeper than 150 feet. He also points out that the flora and fauna of Hawaii is the same as that of locations as far away as Easter Island.[39]

Another piece of evidence discovered recently, which I'm sure would have delighted Churchward, is located 75 miles southwest of Okinawa near the Japanese island of Yonaguni. Underwater structures were discovered there which, according to Dr. Masaki Kimura, were not naturally made. In April, 1998, a Boston University professor of geology named Robert Schoch went on record saying he thought it looked like the side of a stepped pyramid. Other smaller stone structures were found nearby. Dr. Teruaki Ishii of Tokyo University says that the land beneath this structure sank into the waters at least 10,000 years ago.

Yet another enigmatic site can be found on the island of Ponape in Micronesia. Known as the ruins of Nan Madol, they largely consist of large, log-shaped beams of basalt that weigh up to 50 tons each. The entire city contains approximately 450,000 tons of basalt! In the same area, carved right into the coral reef is an extensive system of underwater tunnels. How this was achieved is anyone's guess.[40]

In order to talk about **the people of Lemuria**, we must refer to channeled or psychic information. Most sources describe a people who were highly right-brained, who were very much connected to the Earth and its natural rhythms. A highly psychic people, they practiced shamanic techniques for astral travel and altered states of consciousness. They lived an idyllic lifestyle with no currency, no land ownership, in extended families that were governed loosely by a group of volunteers. Life was simple and easy, with all needs provided by nature.

There is controversy as to whether there was **contact between Lemuria and Atlantis**. Some say they were uninterested in each other and had no contact, while others say that Lemuria and Atlantis merged with each other, eventually forgetting the right-brained ways and becoming more and more left-brained. Yet others explain that Lemurians migrated to many places including Atlantis, when they realized that their homeland was slowly sinking. Some opinions offer that Poseidon, the founder of Atlantis, was actually a Lemurian patriarch.

In various readings, I've come across mentionings of other ancient civilizations about which very little is known. There is said to have been populations of entities in various overtones of third dimensional Earth for 500 million years. These populations existed for long periods of time which I'll refer to as 'grand eras', which divided up into shorter periods. For example, we are said to be the third wave of a grand era that started with Mu or Lemuria. According to a Hindu writing called the Bhagavata Purana, we go through immense cycles of time called yugas. We are currently at the end of the Kali Yuga, the last of four, which total 4,320,000 years. Maybe the yugas are the equivalent of these grand eras.

Some of the beings in past eras would have been barely perceivable to us in this reality, and are sometimes called 'shadow people'. They existed in a different overtone of this realm. (The same is sometimes said of Atlantis and Lemuria.) There are legends of civilizations living in the region of the Sahara and Gobi deserts that became very technically advanced and eventually succumbed to nuclear war. Traces of radioactivity have been found in the desert, but were dismissed as unexplainable. There are also legends of societies with strange names, such as ***Dar, Zu and Ur***. It is said that these names are based on the predominant sound made by these entities.

There is a fair amount of information about a civilization that existed at some time in the distant past, on ***Mars***, the red planet of war. More than any other planet, Mars is deeply ingrained in the human psyche. Stories and legends about it abound. H. G. Wells wrote about the two Martian moons, Deimos (panic/flight) and Phobos (fear), before they were officially discovered by scientist, A. Hall, in 1877. Jonathan Swift also refers to them in 'Gulliver's Travels'.

There are several interesting little tidbits about Mars. In the Celtic cultures, Mars was known as Camul. 'City of Camul' was Camulodunum, which became Camelot, of the Arthurian legends. The name of the Egyptian city, Cairo, comes from the Arabic, El Kahira, which means Mars. The archeologist, George Hunt-Williamson, who was the inspiration for the Indiana Jones character, was obsessed with ET stuff, to the point that it got him fired. One of his finds, in the Monastery of Seven Rays in the Andes, was a pot with the map of Mars' surface in the design. The Third Reich, also obsessed with anything metaphysical or paranormal (See **BOX 17—THE NAZIS AND THE OCCULT**), found similar items in Tibet and the adjacent Chinese province of Shensi, the location of the Pyramids of Shensi.

Like Earth, Mars is said to have had a different orbit at one time. It was 720 days, exactly double Earth's old orbit, which took 360 days. Something happened to Mars that caused its orbit to take it a little further from the sun and reduced its year by 33 days. It is said that the red planet once occupied the 'cradle orbit', the distance from the sun most conducive to life as we know it, until some occurrence displaced it.

March, named in honor of the red planet, used to be the first month of the year, thus September and October were the seventh and eighth months, as their names imply. Mars' orbit brought it close to Earth twice per year, on March 15 and October 26. If we add 5.25 days to March 15, we get March 20, the feast of Ishtar, which became Easter. 5.25 added to October 26 results in October 31, which became Halloween. One Martian day equals 24.62 Earth hours. When experimenting with people in flotation tanks, which were the rage a while ago and which had the effect of causing people to recall 'primal' memories, researchers found that some people's bio-clocks reverted to 24.62 hour days.[41]

> **BOX 17—THE NAZIS AND THE OCCULT:** Not many people are aware of the connection between the Nazi movement and the occult. They were obsessed with 'mystery school' information and the acquisition of sacred 'power relics' such as the Holy Grail and the Ark of the Covenant. Hitler did not commence his military aggressions until he had possession of the 'Spear of Longinus'; an ancient artifact once owned by Charlemagne that was said to have some sort of magical power. Both Hitler and Himmler were very well versed in scripture and mystical writings. The Nazis conducted extensive archeological searches, especially in Tibet and the Chinese province of Shensi. They also thoroughly researched anything that could be considered paranormal, enlisting the services of such noted magicians as Aleister Crowley.
>
> The Nazi movement had its roots in mystical organizations. An enigmatic character and a General in WWI, Karl Haushofer was an occultist who spent much time in Tibet and was a member of the Bon priesthood. After WWI he formed two societies, the Thule Society (Thule was the main city of Hyperborea, the mythological home of the ancient Aryan race), and the Vril Society (Vril, which means 'psychic energy', is said to be the language of the ancient Atlanteans.) The Thule Society was split into two parts, an esoteric branch led by Rudolph Steiner, and an exoteric branch of industrialists and bankers that was eventually led by Hitler, who drove Steiner out of Germany. The Vril Society supervised the construction of strange 'flying saucer'-type craft called 'foo-fighters'. Some believe that they received information for this construction from a group of ETs called the Aldeberans. The goal of Haushofer and his associates was to bring a new order of 'spirituality' to the world that was to last for 1,000 years. They backed the German war effort until Hitler started rounding up and killing Jews. They felt that Hitler was out of control, that the movement had gone astray and they withdrew support.
>
> After the war the extensive Nazi files, chockfull of all sorts of wild and wonderful info, went to the CIA. Some people (including myself) believe that the upper echelons of most power elites throughout history, at levels above that of political leaders and public figures, are well aware of magic and many other strange things talked about in this book. (For more info on this topic, see *The Occult Conspiracy*, by Michael Howard, *Nazis and the Occult*, by Dusty Sclar, *The Spear of Destiny* by Trevor Ravenscroft and *The Black Sun*, by Peter Moon.)

According to channeled information, reptilian life forms occupied Mars about 18 million years ago, during the time that 'shadow people' occupied Earth. They lived in two continent/cities and had vast canal systems. At first they were very spiritual, peaceful and right-brained. They got progressively more left-brained and war-like. Eventually, marauders from the Plieadean star system came in search of minerals, so the Martians set up a force field which kept the Plieadians out. It also had the effect of keeping the Martians in. This beam stayed in place for eons, till the Martians took it for granted and forgot how to turn it off. The desire to space-travel made them attempt to disengage the field, but something went wrong. For 65 years the planet was bombarded by its own devise, destroying the planet and most of its population. Some of them, however, managed to escape by travelling through time and arriving at Earth about 65,000 years ago. They 'invaded our evolutionary pattern', began to incarnate here, eventually competing for control in Atlantis.

Mars is still very much a mystery. New controversy rages about a huge stone face and pyramids on the face of Mars that were photographed by NASA. We'll take a look at that in a subsequent chapter.

Before giving my opinions on 'life before the flood', I would just like to stress a point made earlier in the book. The main function of becoming aware of the previous information is to liquefy old beliefs, not to find a new set of beliefs on which to cling. There is not much to be gained by replacing old dogma with new dogma. Knowing with certainty whether civilizations existed in Atlantis, Lemuria or Mars, is not as important to me as knowing with certainty that the reality which we all take for granted, and the paradigms that we've been fed are incomplete and inadequate.

Having said that, I'll stick my neck out and say that I believe there is a very good possibility that some type of advanced civilization, which had a profound influence on our current situation, did once exist. I am more reluctant to try to define or name them. Perhaps Atlantis and Lemuria and maybe even civilizations on Mars did exist. There is certainly enough information to warrant a sincere investigation. The existence of advanced ante-diluvian societies, as well as some type of interaction with ET groups certainly helps to explain the mysteries and enigmas that we'll look at in the following chapters, which completely defy the accepted paradigms.

What I feel instinctively as well as logically, is that life on this planet, and probably everywhere, follows an inbreath—outbreath, ebb and flow pattern as alluded to in chaos theory. Systems move back and forth between chaos and order. Even patterns that appear chaotic, however, have an underlying order. The pendulum starts at one extreme and then swings over to the other extreme. I believe this swinging back and forth happens in the evolution of most systems, and yet I believe that consciousness or free will has the power to change that tendency. The extremes at either end of the

pendulum swing are forms of imbalance and, as noted earlier, I believe that all sys-
tems naturally seek balance or homeostasis.

I believe that all the eras of civilizations discussed above, as well as the one we
currently find ourselves in, could be thought of as a great 'opportunity', a larger sys-
tem going about the business of experiencing all that the third realm has to offer. The
process of this experience is such that it starts off in a state of imbalance, whereby
the predominant consciousness is extremely right-brained. Then the pendulum starts
to swing until it reaches the opposite extreme, a left-brain imbalance. The pendulum
would then start swinging back toward center again, toward a state of balance, except
that the very nature of left-brain imbalance makes that unlikely. The aggressive,
materialistic, technological and largely non-compassionate nature of the left-brain-
dominant consciousness tends to bring the entire population to the edge of the abyss,
as it is today. Whether the entire era comes to a cataclysmic end, depends on whether
the collective consciousness succeeds in seeing through the fog of illusion in time to
avert such a fate.

This fate may sound scary, but it just means that the circumstances on Earth
would change and the players would find some new place, some new opportunity to
continue playing the Game. And even if the big system goes over the edge, as it sup-
posedly did in Atlantis, the many smaller systems within the large system need not fol-
low. In other words, every individual is a smaller system, experiencing its own ebbs
and flows, creating its own realities and, possibly, achieving its own balance. Some
people, including myself, believe that our current era/opportunity will not repeat the
mistakes of Atlantis, but will succeed in achieving collective balance this time around.

Needless to say, the above explanation is a gross oversimplification. Part of the
wisdom of the expression, 'as above, so below', implies that there are systems within
systems within systems, all interacting in a complex web of illusion. There are many
spectrums of duality with extremes at either end, which need to be balanced before
unity can be perceived.

Some quick thoughts about imbalance—I believe that most people don't think of
extreme right-mindedness as an imbalance, but rather, as an idealized lifestyle of
peace, love and plenty, living in harmony with nature and spending a lot of time in
the astral realms. Even if that is an accurate description, it still is an imbalance in
terms of playing the Game and experiencing all that this dimension has to offer. If
our mandate, in the physical realm, is to experience all there is to experience at this
level, then part of that would include suffering and the types of experiences which are
characteristic of left-brain imbalance. Every soul must learn, (or remember), how to
love in every circumstance, not just in idyllic circumstances. Balance comes after a
wide variety of experiences.

At this time, the current opportunity, the current projection of souls playing the
Game on this planet have, for the most part, collectively experienced both extremes.

I believe that it is not useful to pine for the idyllic lifestyle, the memory of which is imprinted in our sub-conscious minds. It is time to move on, to achieve balance.

After spending some time thinking about human origins, maybe we can ask ourselves the following brief quiz. Did humanity achieve its current form and culture by a) evolving according to natural selection as part of an elaborate machine? b) being genetically manipulated and handed knowledge by ETs? c) inheriting knowledge and form from previously existing civilizations of Earthlings? d) none of the above e) all of the above. For me the most attractive of these five options is e), all of the above. I believe we are a sub-system, part of a huge ordered system that includes many types of intelligent life.

*Attempting to unravel history and to get a grip on reality is a joyous adventure. Looking toward the future is even more exciting! By examining our origins we may better understand who we were, and thus who we are. We will have a better idea of where we're going. I believe that, by opening our minds and our hearts, by asserting the power that is our birthright, we will be better able to see through the maya, the illusion. By clinging to **no** particular belief regarding human origins we can clear the way for knowledge, which I believe resides deep down in our bone marrow. We will achieve a better understanding. We will find balance and vault forward into a glorious and exciting unknown.*

ENDNOTES—PART THREE

1. Cerminara, Gina—*Insights for the Age of Aquarius*, Quest Books, 1973, London, p. 183–184
2. Baigent, Michael—*Ancient Traces*, Penguin Books, 1998, London, p. 30
3. ibid. p. 24–36
4. Cotterell, Maurice—*The Tutankhamen Prophecies*, Headline Books, 1999, London, appendix 1
5. Alford, Alan—*Gods of the New Millennium*, Hodder and Stoughton, 1997, London, p. 23
6. Time Magazine, July 23, 2001. *One Giant Step for Mankind*, M. Lemonick, A. Dorfman
7. ibid. p. 54–55
8. Alford, Alan—*Gods of the New Millennium*, Hodder and Stoughton, 1997, London, p. 61
9. ibid. p. 22–23
10. Wesson, Robert—*Beyond Natural Selection*, Cambridge MA, 1993, p. 294 as reported by Baigent, Michael—*Ancient Traces*, Penguin Books, 1998, London, p.38–39
11. Sheldrake, Rupert—*A New Science of Life*, Park Street Press, 1981, Rochester, VT, p. 186–191, 95–107
12. Cerminara, Gina—*Insights for the Age of Aquarius*, Quest Books, 1973, London, p. 23
13. Sitchin, Zecharia—*Genesis Revisited*, Avon Books, 1990, New York, p. 132
14. ibid. p. 152
15. Temple, Robert—*The Sirius Mystery*, Destiny Books, 1976, Rochester, VT
16. Alford, Alan—*Gods of the New Millennium*, Hodder and Stoughton, 1997, London, p. 27–28
17. ibid. p. 169–71
18. Sitchin, Zecharia—*Genesis Revisited*, Avon Books, 1990, New York, p. 314–332 and Alford, Alan—*Gods of the New Millennium*, Hodder and Stoughton, 1997, London, p. 231–235
45. Gardner, Laurence—*Genesis of the Grail Kings*, Bantam Press, 1999, London, p. 108
46. Freke, Timothy and Gandy, Peter—*The Complete Guide to World Mysticism*, Judy Piatkus, Inc., 1997, London, p. 103–104

47. Dunn, Christopher—*The Giza Powerplant*, Bear & Company, 1998, Santa Fe, NM, p. 245
48. Hogue, John—*The Millennium Book of Prophesy*, HarperCollins Publishing, 1994, New York, p. 4
49. Hope, Murray—*Atlantis, Myth or Reality?*, Penguin Books, 1991, London, p. 97
50. Sitchin, Zecharia—*Genesis Revisited*, Avon Books, 1990, New York, p. 212–218 and Alford, Alan—*Gods of the New Millennium*, Hodder and Stoughton, 1997, London, p. 179–182
51. Alford, Alan—*Gods of the New Millennium*, Hodder and Stoughton, 1997, London, p. 455
52. Wilson, Colin—*From Atlantis to the Sphinx*, Virgin Books, 1997, London, p. 93
53. Hope, Murray—*Atlantis, Myth or Reality?*, Penguin Books, 1991, London, p. 6–8
54. Wilson, Colin—*From Atlantis to the Sphinx*, Virgin Books, 1997, London, p. 115–119
55. Hope, Murray—*Atlantis, Myth or Reality?*, Penguin Books, 1991, London, p. 147
56. ibid. p. 49–64 (most of the information in the last several paragraphs comes from this source.
31. Donnelly, Ignatius—Atlantis, the Antediluvian World, Rudolph Steiner Publications, 1971, New York, p. 46–49
32. Hope, Murray—*Atlantis, Myth or Reality?*, Penguin Books, 1991, London, p. 71–87, 232–233
33. ibid. p. 111–116
34. ibid. p. 150
35. ibid. p. 127–128
36. ibid. p. 151–152
37. ibid. p. 122–123
38. Donnelly, Ignatius—Atlantis, the Antediluvian World, Rudolph Steiner Publications, 1971, New York, p. 178
39. Churchward, James—*The Lost Continent of Mu*, Ives Washburn Inc., 1931, New York
40. Bell, Art and Strieber, Whitley—*The Coming Global Superstorm*, Simon and Schuster, 2001, New York, p. 49–55
41. Moon, P. and Nichols, Preston—*Pyramids of Montauk*, Sky Books, 1994, New York

Part Four

An Alternative History

Most of us in the modern western world have been fed an 'official line' regarding the history of life on Earth. The establishment-approved, scientifically backed version of 'how things are', is virtually the only interpretation we are exposed to in our educational facilities and the mass media. Other versions of history, such as those deriving from the traditions of indigenous peoples, which have been passed down for millennia, largely via the spoken word, are tolerated only as myth, legend and cute little stories. Channeled or intuition-based information is ignored and often ridiculed, even though much of it, from a broad range of sources, seems to be telling a very similar story which dovetails with most indigenous accounts. As the book proceeds, it will attempt to present evidence/information that may encourage us to rethink the conventional stories we've come to accept and to entertain the possibility that there's much more to our history than meets the eye. This next section, in a playful way, offers an alternative version of our history.

Chapter 18

EARTHSCHOOL VOLUNTEERS

Earthschool, like many other places in the universe, was established to provide a place for energy to experience third dimensional, physical lessons. In other words, Earth's job is to create life and the circumstances of life so that, according to the laws of karma, one has the opportunity to learn/remember and thus evolve. It is said that there are many other planets in the universe where the frequency, due to their position in the cosmos, is just right for experiences of the physical kind. The higher entities, aware of this mysterious need for energy to keep evolving toward a more perfect perfection, have always been around to facilitate the process.

This book has already looked at some of the evidence regarding the contention that we have interacted with a great variety of entities throughout our history, including the present. Some of them are said to be from planets, solar systems and galaxies other than our own, while others are past graduates of Earthschool. Many do not exist in physical form and are operating at higher levels of the Game; existing as expressions of energy at higher frequencies. (Angels and gods are, by definition, ETs.) Sometimes they guide us from beyond and sometimes they feel it necessary to actually take on form and 'descend' to Earth. They come here voluntarily, that is, they do not need to incarnate here to learn lessons. They come to serve mankind, to help us play the Game, and so they are often referred to collectively as *'volunteers' or 'facilitators'*.

Advanced entities understand that they must not interfere in the evolution of less advanced life-forms, much like the 'prime directive' in the Star Trek television series. We must progress because of our own free will, experiencing all there is to experience and thus, little by little, remembering our own divinity. It's not that they are 'forbidden' to interfere; they also have free will (for the most part) and would reap the appropriate karmic repercussions from any such actions. More advanced consciousness simply understands that it is in the best interests of everyone involved that learning proceed at its own pace, according to the consequences of free will. Thus, we receive help only indirectly and only if we ask for it. Free will is crucial, for without it we would be denied the opportunity to truly experience. Unsolicited assistance comes most often in the form of teachings, which we are free to accept or reject.

It is said that there have been about twenty different races or civilizations of ET's that have had significant interaction with humanity throughout the ages. Most of these civilizations have been more advanced than our own. Some have helped human evolution, some have hindered. There have also been ETs who are perhaps not as evolved as us, but who have different technology than us, that have played roles in our history. We shouldn't jump to the conclusion that, because an ET group has somehow acquired the ability to space-travel, they are more advanced than us in terms of having accumulated experiences in the Game. By the same token we should not assume that western society, with its technology of gidgets and gadgets, is more advanced than some 'primitive' society living in simple harmony with nature.

Whether these advanced entities are more or less evolved than us, they too are going about the business of experiencing the Game at their own level, which sometimes involves making 'poor' decisions. Some of these decisions, the ones involving humanity, have affected us in various ways. In any case, of the civilizations that have interacted with us, some are more evolved than others. The lesser-evolved ETs tend to be more like the aliens in flying saucers depicted in sci-fi movies. The more advanced races have no need for 'spacecraft' or any other type of technology. They do not exist in the physical realm. They have no need for anything external to themselves. Their flights are fuelled by love-power!

Chapter 19

A NEW LOOK AT HISTORY

This next part may seem a little far-out to some, especially those that have not been exposed to this type of information before. This overview is quite different than the typical, accepted views of the genesis and development of life on Earth. It is taken from an assortment of sources, including various indigenous traditions or 'mythologies', channelled information, the writings of Doreal and the teachings of Drunvalo Melchizadek. A word of warning—this is a brief overview and not much effort has been made to offer 'evidence' to support these ideas. Also, many words have been used only due to the lack of a better word, and are usually in quotation marks. Much of the information in this chapter will be expanded upon throughout the rest of the book. If this account seems too far-fetched for you, please try to remain light-hearted and open-minded to it. Just try to enjoy it, rather than to be constantly deciding whether to 'buy' this strange tale. Anyway, the alternative history of life on Earth goes something like this.

Although some say that there has been intelligent life on various dimensional overtones of Earth for 500 million years, the oldest Earth-civilization about which I'll comment at this point, is called **Gondwanaland.** It existed approximately 200,000 years ago on a land mass just west of what is currently South Africa. Souls were happily evolving there for many years with the assistance of two immortal volunteers, Ay (male) and Tyia (female). People lived much longer lives back then and the planet was not as 'dense' as it is today. A 'mistake', of which we'll speak more later, took place which contributed greatly to the 'predicament' we are in today. Anyway, some earth-changes took place and Gondwanaland sunk. Some people survived and eventually ended up in Africa and in Lemuria.

Lemuria was a series of many islands in the Pacific ocean that existed for thousands of years. Life was good there; people lived a relatively peaceful life with little or no dependence on external technology. They were a people who started off with a predominantly right-brained, more intuitive type of consciousness. Ay and Tyia were there to help establish the Naakal Mystery School, and a great many willing souls were assisted into Christ-consciousness (about one per year). Approximately 80,000 years ago, Lemuria went below the sea. Some survived and went to the Americas, Africa and Australia and an island/continent in the area just east of what is now Florida. We're not sure what it was called at the time, but it has come to be known as *Atlantis*.

Atlantis consisted of one large landmass and ten islands. One thousand immortal/ascended beings went there with the intention of attracting souls to incarnate there and establishing 'mystery schools' and other forms of guidance to help the process of evolving souls. After a time, along with the regular terrestrial group, two new 'soul-pools' (sometimes called 'projections') saw an opportunity and decided to 'relocate' to this fresh version of Earth. The first was a group from the realm of Hoova, which came to be known as the Semites. When they began to incarnate here, they brought positive knowledge to this planet because they had a greater awareness of their own godliness. The second group was from Mars, the doomed planet of war.

Up until this point in the Atlantean era, the world was populated by predominantly right-brained, highly intuitive societies who lived in harmony with nature and depended very little on 'external technology'. The Martian group was the total antithesis of this. They were almost totally left-brained and this imbalance had brought about the destruction of their own planet because of their unwillingness to choose 'paths of the heart'. They had become more and more dependent upon external technology while notions of love and compassion became more and more foreign. They had brought about the destruction of Mars by trying to technologically create a vehicle into the next realm, rather than creating an internal vehicle fuelled by love-power.

So powerful was the Martian presence in Atlantis that it further tipped the scales in favor of an unbalanced, left-brained consciousness. It became increasingly difficult to assist souls into the next level and it has been said that it took approximately 20,000 years to 'graduate' the first one. In the 60,000 years of Atlantis' existence, it is thought that only about 600 souls graduated into Christ-consciousness. To make a long story short, they became a very technically advanced civilization which fell once again into the trap of trying to artificially create an inter-dimensional vehicle using crystals.

This caused a 'tear' in the 'dimensional fabric' or 'energy matrix' of the planet. Combined with other factors such as the alignment of celestial bodies and the precession of the equinoxes, this tear caused not only the sinking of Atlantis, it also created a situation that threatened the very existence of the planet. The magnetic field collapsed for three days, causing the Earth to lose its collective memory. All knowledge was now gone. Ascended beings and advanced life forms from all over the cosmos came to Earth's assistance.

Using a technique similar to acupuncture on a global scale, they collectively succeeded in lowering the vibratory level of the planet, thus saving it from shaking itself apart as it approached that phase of the 25,920 year cycle which exposed it to increasing energy. Earth 'fell' into a denser state; stabilizing a few 'sub-realms' or 'overtones' lower in the third realm. This greater density, this greater mass in turn caused our orbit around the sun to change from a more harmonious 360 days (a multiple of twelve), to 365.25 days. It now took an extra 5.25 days to orbit the sun. Some say that this increased mass may have caused an increase in gravitational force, possibly affecting the rate at which time passes. From this point on, life on this planet would become subject to conditions of increased density. The length of life spans would decrease (as noted in the Bible). Consciousness would change. A new variation of physical, third dimensional laws would preside.

This new variation, this increased density would become even further accented as the planet moved into the darker portion of the precessional cycle. Souls incarnating here would have a more difficult time to 'see the light', would 'fall asleep' and become in effect, 'stupider'. Usually, greater wisdom and compassion are achieved in the latter years of life, so that shorter life-spans meant a reduced opportunity to enlighten. Although souls were still inclined to come to Earth because of its unparalleled beauty, they became 'trapped' here, incarnating over and over and failing to learn the lessons of this level. This caused a type of 'bottle necking' in the evolution of energy, the processing of souls in this part of the universe.

This phenomenon, this fall into a denser reality, is what is often referred to as the *'Fall of Lucifer'*, or the Fall of Man. It is said that there have been many such 'falls' throughout the universe. In our classic mythology, God's most brilliant angel decides to become God's equal by using his head instead of his heart. In the ensuing calamity he falls from grace and becomes the leader of the 'dark forces', whose role it is to tempt us away from the path of love. The myth thus attempts to personify, to put a face on the concept of fear/evil/darkness.

I don't believe there is actually a 'devil'. There is only negative energy attracting negative energy. There are only poor choices being made in ignorance, attracting the requisite consequences. There is no right or wrong, no good or bad. The polarity spectrum between fear/evil and love/good is merely a construct, an illusion. What we think of as 'evil' or the 'dark forces' is actually a pool of negative energy whose 'task' is to offer us opportunities to have experiences that would otherwise not be possible. In other words, 'evil' offers us a particular type of experience, a special opportunity to make choices. We need fear/evil/darkness in order to fully experience love/good/light. We need the yin to know the yang. Ultimately, however, there are no such dualities. It is our task to remember that there is really no polarity or duality, only unity. There is no me, no you. We are all one. (Please pardon this little aside—I couldn't resist.)

The fall of man occurred in conjunction with cataclysm and great planetary change, including earthquakes, volcanic eruption, the shifting of continental plates, giant storms and what has come to be called *the Great Flood*. Such legends and stories have been recounted by almost all cultures around the globe, including the one that produced the Biblical Genesis account. Many researchers now believe that the flood happened roughly 13,000 years ago. Conventional science cited this as the same general time in which the last ice age, which has been named the Wisconsin ice age, came to an end. During the ice age, which lasted about 100,000 years, a greater amount of the planet's water existed in the form of ice-sheets gathered at the poles, covering most of the northern hemisphere, and thus the ocean levels were much lower than they are today. The research of Dr. Bruce Heezen, an oceanographer working out of Columbia University, suggests that the oceans rose by about 300 feet after the ice-sheets melted. At the same time, many species became extinct. Scientists have discovered more than 116 sites, on the highest points of plateaus, containing huge piles of mammoth and rhinoceros bones from that era, suggesting that they were seeking refuge from floodwaters.[1] Many people no longer view the flood as mere myth.

Before the Great Flood, Atlantis had established outposts or colonies in such places as the Andes Mountains, the Yucatan peninsula, the Himalayas and Egypt, which was known at that time as Khem. After the fall and the temporary collapse of the magnetic field, these colonies forgot most of the knowledge they once had. It was back to primitive tribal living; hunting and gathering, huddling near the fire, etc. At this point a very right-brained/feminine/intuitive/yin type of consciousness predominated. It was a time of matriarchy, when mankind lived in close contact with the Earth, in harmony with nature. Feminine, maternal qualities were seen as responsible for the bearing of new life and were highly valued. There was little need for external technology. They relied on the tribal shaman for leadership, there was less individual ownership and blood lineage was less important.

This predominantly 'female' consciousness would gradually begin to swing to a more left-brained mentality, embracing a more agricultural lifestyle. This started with nomadic animal husbandry and then settled down to a lifestyle based on the harvesting of crops. Land ownership became increasingly important, which led to the need to capture or protect large tracts of land. War became a way of life, and with it, the development of more and more external technology. With an increased emphasis on ownership of property, inheritance and blood lineage became more important. Humanity became more and more dominated by this 'male' consciousness and eventually the patriarchy would be in complete control.

At some point during this transition, in an effort to restore previously held knowledge and to facilitate the evolution of human consciousness, 'civilization' was more or less handed down to mankind by 'volunteers' or other life-forms. They became relatively advanced societies virtually overnight. Great civilizations such as Sumer and Egypt blossomed suddenly, with very sophisticated knowledge and codes of behavior. Some say that the volunteers were mainly interested in guiding mankind along the path to enlightenment and they provided mankind with sophisticated spiritual methodologies, which became the mystery school traditions. Teachings were offered which encouraged love and compassion, balance and insight. These early civilizations were theocracies, with the entire society being spiritually motivated and concerned with the quest for enlightenment.

Differing points of view contend that alien life forms established these institutions and traditions for more sinister reasons. They were more interested in manipulating and supressing mankind for their own selfish reasons. Probably both of these perspectives contain some truth. These points of view will be discussed in other parts of the book. For now I'll present this alternative history with the contention that there was at least one group of volunteers that cared a great deal about humanity and acted with positive motives.

Because of the effect of the new density on the mental capacity of humanity, much of this handed down knowledge and guidance would soon became distorted, misunderstood and misused. At their request, parts of humanity were periodically given 'refresher courses' of knowledge and technology, which again would soon deteriorate and be forgotten. Often volunteers were sent down (prophets, leaders and teachers) to offer guidance. Many of them were 'deified' and their teachings often degenerated and became distorted. Messages such as 'love is the only way' and 'you are the creator of your own reality' were often manipulated by power-hungry monarchs and priests. Although there were factions of society that continued to understand these philosophies of compassion, for the most part people were taught to fear 'God', to accept dogma and suffering. Instead of counting on the abundance that the universe provides, societies went to war, plundering, looting, raping and enslaving. This process took place over thousands of years to many different cultures.

Before the flood the Atlanteans had little need for language, as we know it. They communicated more telepathically in picture flashes; similar to the way that dolphins and whales are said to communicate. (See **BOX 18—DOLPHINS AND WHALES**) After the flood, language was established and information was passed on verbally from generation to generation. When the consciousness was predominantly right-brained, language was less linear, more pictorial and story-like. As consciousness became increasingly left-brained, the correct meaning of more abstract, pictorial language became more susceptible to misinterpretation. Writing was introduced as a way of more accurately preserving knowledge. The earliest writing started as picture glyphs, evolving into symbols and eventually into letters and complex word structures. This evolution followed the change in consciousness from a more pictorial, lateral, intuitive way of thinking to the linear, logical thought processes that dominate today.

BOX 18—DOLPHINS AND WHALES; Many people feel that, along with their long acknowledged intelligence, there are some things about whales and dolphins that are very special. Some of the 'alternative' things that are said about cetaceans are:

- They think in a way that is much more 'right-brained' than do humans. They communicate in 'sound pictures' that can transmit large amounts of information in one flash.
- They have heightened psychic abilities, including telepathy and a capacity for astral travelling. They can access other realms or dimensions.
- They are in communication with other consciousness systems, other lifeforms.
- They are 'guardians' of our planet, providing a much-needed balance to the prevailing 'left-brained' consciousness.
- Many current cetaceans are incarnations of souls that were at one time Atlanteans.
- Being in their presence helps humans to develop their right-brain capacities.
- Their collective consciousness houses, fully intact, the memory of the entire history of life on Earth.

Interestingly, some of these views are reflected in the movie, Star Treck IV, The Voyage Home'. It is also interesting that cetaceans spend an extraordinary amount of time engaged in sexual union. (For more info on this topic, see the work of Joan Phillips Ocean, MSW—**www.joanocean.com** and Ilona Selke—**www.livingfromvision.com**)

Immediately after the fall, there was a great deal of concern among the volunteers about the new circumstances of Earth. It was agreed that a good course of action would be to attempt to have the entire planet raise into the next realm, rather than the lengthier process of teaching and graduating individual souls. This is only possible if the collective consciousness of the planet and its inhabitants succeeds in raising its base vibratory rate to a sufficient level to take advantage of the next great cyclical opportunity. To do this it was necessary to establish a new 'Christ-consciousness grid' around the planet. All expressions of energy; all dimensions of reality need a corresponding conduit or grid. The higher vibrations of Christ-consciousness needed the appropriate pathways, which would accommodate their 'expressibility'. Such conduits usually 'grow' in a gradual, natural way. In this case, however, it was decided to construct the grid more quickly in the hopes that the planet would be ready for the next 'cosmic opportunity', the next 'big shift', the point in the cycle when enormous amounts of energy would again interact with the Earth.

In a section of 'The Emerald Tablets', Thoth, an immortal being who had been volunteering in Atlantis for thousands of years, tells the story of coming to **Egypt** with Ra, Araaragot and other immortal, ascended volunteers. The native population was soon rendered awestruck by some displays of 'magic' and superior technology. The 'invaders' thus became 'gods', even though they taught that there was only one God-force. They soon built the Great Pyramid.[2] (It is very doubtful that they used slaves pushing enormous stone blocks up wooden ramps.) It is interesting that the Greek name for Thoth is Hermes, related to the word 'herma' meaning a 'pile of stones'.[3]

The Sphinx had been built thousands of years earlier, before the flood. (More on the Sphinx and the pyramids later.) Beneath the Sphinx is the Hall of Records where the entire history of life on Earth is said to be written on tablets. There is also a vast chamber which exists in a different dimensional overtone than ours; a different third dimensional sub-level. It is called the Hall of Amenti and is said to contain the 'flame of life'. It can be accessed by a human placed in the granite box in the King's Chamber of the Great Pyramid for three days, but only if that person is fearless and filled with love.

Egypt was established by Ra as the 'male' point of the new grid. Thoth founded the great civilization at Lake Titicaca in the Andes, which became the 'female' point in the grid. (Some people feel that tribes such as the Incas, who came much later, merely inhabited the amazing Andean stone structures, and that they were actually built by some earlier civilization.) Araaragot went to the Himalayas and started the Tibetan culture, making it the 'child' point of the grid. (See BOX 19—LEY LINES)

Thoth, also known as Chiquetet Arlich Vomalites (Atlantean), Tehuti (Egyptian), Hermes (Greek), Mercury (Roman) and Enoch (Hebrew), is a volunteer who has played a major role, serving on Earth for many thousands of years. He is said to have written 36,525 scrolls of wisdom[4] (note that this number equals 100 times the number of days in the year), which were hidden at various locations around the globe, to be found at different times according to humanity's readiness to embrace the knowledge they contained. Thoth wrote the 'Emerald Tablets', known to the ancient Assyrians as the 'Table of Destiny', and referred to in the Bible as the 'Tables of Testimony'. He is known as the most powerful of all sorcerers, the source for most forms of alchemy and magic. These ancient writings contain the secrets of magic and guidelines for achieving enlightenment. According to the Bible, they were given, along with the Ten Commandments, to Moses who placed them in the Ark of the Covenant. The Church has chosen to focus on the 'commandments' and has completely ignored (some say supressed) the tables.

In shamanic traditions, those entering a deep trance seeking alternative realities encounter a large, looming entity sometimes known as the Dweller on the Threshold. If the traveler reacts to this presence with fear, then s/he is not allowed to enter. If the traveler recognizes the entity as yet another illusion of the Game, choosing to react with love/compassion, then s/he gains entrance. This entity is considered to be another aspect of Thoth. He is also called the Scribe because he is said to have brought writing, which was now needed in an attempt to regain and preserve knowledge that was wiped out of the collective consciousness by the collapse of the magnetic field. This collective consciousness is sometimes called the Akashic record. Before the flood, this record was commonly accessed in telepathic, psychic ways.

Thoth, his son Tat and a group of ascended volunteers went to the Hall of Amenti and formed the Tat Brotherhood. They then assisted the Egyptian people to embrace 'civilization'. In this context, civilization refers to sets of skills and regulations that would assist the newly emerging consciousness facilitating the tendency for humanity to live together in large groups in a relatively cooperative manner. The volunteers were aware of the natural swing from right to left-brained consciousness and sought to facilitate this transition in a way that would preserve sacred knowledge.

> **BOX 19—LEY LINES;** Throughout the planet there are energy conduits, pathways or meridians which are sometimes referred to as 'ley lines' or 'dragon lines' to the Chinese and 'song lines' to the Australian Aborigines. These are similar to the meridians of a human body referred to in the science of Acupuncture. Points at which several of these lines intersect are known as 'power spots' or 'vortices'. Certain types of buildings constructed at such spots act in a way similar to acupuncture needles, balancing the flow of energy. There are currently 83,000 'sacred sites' or power spots on the Earth's grid system, which took the next 13,000 years to establish. Many famous landmarks such as Stonehenge and many temples, etc. are located at such sites.

The Mystery Schools of the Eyes of Horus were established in an attempt to balance the right eye/left brain and left eye/right brain aspects of consciousness and to open the chakras. The messages of love were once again taught. Pharaohhood was instituted for the preservation of this knowledge. Egypt was once a society whose sole purpose and focus was to facilitate the process of enlightenment. Generally speaking, the awareness of our Earthly quest for enlightenment was far more widespread then than it is now. This awareness deteriorated throughout the ages, but has started to make a comeback in recent times.

As the sacred knowledge deteriorated, the mystery schools and the Pharaohs acquired their own distorted agenda. The new density of the planet as well as the effect of the precession of the equinoxes (our solar system moving away from the Galactic Center) caused us to distort the teachings of love and to embrace fear. The planet was 'falling asleep'. Sacred teachings all over the world have been, until very recently, squirreled away in monasteries and temples, no longer available to the common man. Much of it was encoded or shrouded in mystery. This was done according to motives that were both noble and not so noble. Some feared that this sacred information would be diluted, distorted and misused, while others simply wished to hoard it.

It was understood by many groups and individuals throughout history that mankind's 'purpose' was to seek enlightenment. Some of these groups knew that this process was meant for humans in all walks of life, while others felt it should be reserved for some sort of elite, whether it be the nobility, the priesthood or whomever could afford the latest 'new age' miracle cure. Many 'methodologies' for achieving this goal would eventually venture off course, often becoming empty rituals. Most often the missing ingredient was love/compassion. In many cases the motives for enlightenment became diluted or distorted. For example, enlightenment became synonymous with immortality, which was sought due to a fear of death. Initiates often sought some kind of super-power, i.e. magical facility or siddhic power, which would make them superior to their fellow humans. Alchemy, which has been misinterpreted to be an endeavor to turn lead into gold, was originally meant to be a methodology by which ordinary, human consciousness (symbolized by base metals) could evolve into divine consciousness (symbolized by gold).

Many of humanity's mysteries, whether they be enigmatic writings or various stone structures, make much more sense when viewed in light of this quest for enlightenment. Much of the accomplishments of ancient man were based on such motives. Unfortunately, academia has had little time for such notions. Whenever archeologists encounter what seems to be a 'religious' motive, it is usually dismissed as primitive superstition or fertility rituals or something to do with the planting of crops. For example, many of the various stone structures including Stonehenge, have been found to be astronomical observatories, capable of detailed and complex observations. These observations often pertain to the Precessional Cycle and the corresponding astrological insights, which affect the enlightenment process. This type of thing is usually explained as knowledge pertaining to the planting of crops. This explanation is also given for the many complex ancient calendars. That such detailed information is needed to plan sowings and harvestings seems a little ludicrous.

Anyway, back to our story. Around 1355 BC, it was felt that Egypt was sufficiently 'off course' as to require an ascended master to incarnate and move among the people. His name was **Akhenaten**, the Heretic Pharaoh.

The Tat Brotherhood asked Ay and Tyia (remember them?) to parent a body that would be inhabited by an advanced soul from the Sirius star system. The child grew up to become Pharaoh Amenhotep IV who soon changed his name to Akhenaten. Together with his wife, Nefertiti, he was part of the eighteenth dynasty of Egypt. They were definitely making a new fashion statement at the time—depictions of them show two very tall beings with large, bulbous heads and strange, androgenous shapes. Some sources claim that the unusual appearance of the royal couple is because they were ET's or possibly the product of an alien 'seeding'.

Great changes were brought about during their reign. The people were taught to access prana (the healing energy of love/life) from the sun (the Aten) and to think in terms of 'unity' rather than 'duality'. The priesthood, with all its rituals and dogma, was dissembled and the army was not allowed to wage war. The people were not pleased with these messages of peace and love because they treasured their traditions and they admired their powerful army who were usually out there conquering, pillaging and bringing home the spoils. Another part of Akhenaten's role, which he accomplished, was to restore as much knowledge as he could to the Akashic record, which is the collective knowledge of all who incarnated on Earth since the record had been wiped clean. With the mystery schools back on track and new techniques in place, about 300 souls achieved Christ-consciousness.

Around the same time, according to Doreal of the Brotherhood of the White Temple, Egyptian 'pyramid priests' were dispatched to certain parts of the world bearing the wisdom of Thoth. They settled in South America amongst a group that had retained some memory of the ancient knowledge of Atlantis. This group became the Mayans, who eventually settled in the Yucatan. They recorded amazing information in their 'codices' and built awesome structures, including pyramids. Like other cultures, however, the Mayans went through some periods when the great wisdoms were ignored by the ruling elite, while smaller groups secretly made efforts to preserve the ancient wisdom.

Some schools of thought say that Akhenaten was the same entity as the one who was to become known as Moses. They say that he taught the Hebrews about unity consciousness and the underlying oneness of all things. At that time, the Hebrews waffled between worshipping a pantheon of Sumerian gods, and worshipping only one of these gods who was once called Enlil/El/El Shaddai, whom they renamed YHWH/Yahweh/Jehovah. They claim that the Hebrews, like everybody else, came to distort and misinterpret the information about 'one God', and began to exclusively follow the will of the entity they called Jehovah. (See Part Six for more on Akhenaten and Moses.) Another school of thought claims that Akhenaten was not Moses, but that he had a great influence on Moses, and that after a short reign, he went on (either in that incarnation or in a new one) to establish the Essene Brotherhood.

There is much controversy about *the Essenes*. Scholars and interpreters of the Dead Sea Scrolls cannot agree as to who they were and what they stood for. The information I've read says that, despite what their outward function seemed to be, their main mission was to prepare for the next phase. This involved the incarnation of a highly evolved soul whose mission was to bring a strong message of love to the world and to do further crucial work to the 'Christ-consciousness' grid. This was, of course, *Jesus the Nazorene*.

Most of us are familiar with the Jesus story and the beautiful message he brought to us. Some of us are also aware that the institution that bears his name, Christianity, came to have very little to do with those teachings. Once again the cosmos sent us an entity bearing the truth and once again that truth has been distorted. Jesus taught us unconditional love, compassion, tolerance, joy, freedom of thought, etc. The church, while paying lip service to these things, taught us 'fear of the Lord', adherence to dogma, intolerance and suffering. One of its more powerful doctrines was one that denied and disempowered the feminine aspect of our human consciousness. By vilifying sex, downplaying the role of Mary Magdalene and many other important women, blaming Eve as the bearer of temptation and by virtually enslaving womanhood, they effectively 'took the goddess' out of the equation. It's only been a few hundred years since women have been deemed by the church to even have a soul. As we move toward enlightenment, this imbalance will be/is being corrected.

There is a great deal of mystery and controversy about the details and circumstances surrounding the life of Y'shua bar Yusef, better known as Jesus the Nazorene. A great deal of 'new' information has recently come to light in the wake of the discovery of many ancient texts including many Gnostic scripts; hidden volumes found in ancient Egyptian libraries such as the one at Nag Hamadi, as well as the Dead Sea Scrolls. There are as many as fifty gospels, yet only four were selected for inclusion in the New Testament. There are many Old Testament 'books' that were excluded. Some say that there were many 'messiahs' 2,000 years ago, that have similar legacies of miracles, virgin births and ascensions, etc. Some say that there was no historical Jesus, that the whole story is a myth or worse—a conspiracy. The Pleiadians, as channelled by Barbara Marciniak, say that Jesus was a 'committee' of like-minded entities with the same mission.

Some say that Mary Magdalene played an equally important role and that she initiated Jesus with sacred sexual rites, etc. Some say that, as well as bringing us a wealth of teachings, he also completed an important 'section' of the Christ-consciousness grid, which made it no longer necessary for us to get prana solely from the sun. From this point on we could get it from the Earth as well. Jesus 'brought down the Holy Spirit'. Despite the multitude of perspectives, it seems clear that once again we have had the message of love delivered to us and that, somehow, that message went astray. Between the time of Jesus and the present, for the most part, humanity entered a deep sleep. This is especially true of western culture. We forgot about the quest for enlightenment. Aside from the odd exceptions, humanity largely forgot about its own inner, magical power to affect our reality; forgot about compassion and other key components of the Game. Although, in the last hundred years or so we are slowly awakening, our history from this era is shrouded in fear.

Fear is the root of all negativity. Whenever we think a negative thought, say a negative word or do a negative deed, we are pumping negative energy into the morphogenetic grid. This heavy, dark energy causes the world to become more dense. The 'forces of darkness' have used a wide variety of devices to try and keep the majority of humanity disempowered in a futile effort to hoard power. In their imbalance, they have a distorted notion of what power is, focusing on external, five-sensory, survival-based power rather than internal, multi-sensory, abundance-based power.

Throughout the ages that portion of society that dominated, that sat at the top of the heap—the power elite—has changed faces many times. Whether they be pharaohs or any other type of monarch and their associated aristocracy, or popes with their priesthood, or wealthy bankers and merchants with their subservient governments, their actions are based on much the same motives. The seek to retain their position at the top of the heap. The best way to do this is to empower themselves and to disempower the masses. Institutions like the organized religions, governments, corporations, media, medical establishments, banking systems and war machines are tools of the power elite who attempt to keep the masses in the dark and thus control them. It has been that way for ages.

As recently as one century ago the masses were much more securely under the thumb. Lately, however, the power elite increasingly sees that control slipping away. The firm grip that they had in the dark ages is no longer. Their attempts at spreading 'globalization' and 'free trade' by pushing through (often in sneaky, covert ways) various trade agreements and by establishing non-elected governing bodies like the World Trade Organization, are acts of desperation. Thinly veiled aggression, often under the guise of 'bringing freedom' to some part of the world that happens to have valuable resources, is explained by huge, elaborate propaganda machines. That is because the people of today demand to know the reason for such actions. In terms of the evolution of human consciousness, things are improving daily. In the past no such explanations were requested by the masses and the power elite simply did as it wished. The masses lived in fear and were firmly under control.

Nowadays, by controlling the news media, the power elite goes to great lengths to try to reign in the power of our collective will. They are well aware of the power of consciousness. They know that no amount of technological weaponry could control us if our vision was clear and our will united. They are desperately trying to regain control. Their actions are based on misguided and imbalanced notions of what power actually is. In many ways, they are the most soundly asleep entities on the planet— remnants of that ancient imbalanced 'Martian' consciousness. The 'forces of darkness' will awaken, however. They too will become enlightened. All we need is love.

Love is the root of all positive energy. Whenever we feel, think, say and do positive things, we are pumping positive energy into the grid and the world becomes more enlightened. Thus do we create our own reality. During the beginning of the last decade Thoth left the planet. He did so because he said that, for the first time since before the flood, there is more positive energy on Earth than negative and that this energy will snowball. The 'quickening' is upon us, the Big Shift is just around the corner.

Although it may seem to those of us who watch the nightly news that just the opposite is true, we must remember that it is the people most heavily invested in the old fear-based ways who make and present most of what we call 'the news'. Ninety percent of the media is owned by huge corporate conglomerates, the new power elite. They can best manipulate and control us by feeding us bad news and keeping us mired in fear. But these efforts are failing. In terms of our continued progress and evo-lution toward a more compassion-based consciousness, it's all good news.

Everywhere I look I see people seeking. Books like 'Conversations with God' and other 'spiritual' books are topping the best-seller lists for months. Television and movie themes are increasingly dealing with the 'supernatural'. Our tolerances continue to change. A few centuries ago, I would have been risking my life to write a book like this. To question authority in any way was to be put to death. Human consciousness is indeed evolving. Great beings are here doing wondrous work. Volunteers are everywhere. 'Spirit' misses no opportunity to express itself. Recently, the new grid for Christ-consciousness was completed and many believe that our time here is not long. There is much 'evidence' (both scientific and non-scientific) to suggest that the planet's base vibrational frequency is rising and that the magnetic field is diminishing. We are recording drastic increases in weather anomalies, solar flares, seismic activity and other phenomena. Prophesies both old and new from diverse sources, from every culture and corner of the globe are saying that now is the time. Get ready for the big shift!

Needless to say, the preceding history is far from a complete picture. Many important chapters of our history are not dealt with, such as the history of the Far East, the heritage of our various indigenous peoples, etc. Much of the information that I've attempted to deal with is only scratching the surface. We'll attempt to look more closely at some aspects of this story and some of the substantiating evidence as the book proceeds. It is not, in my opinion, just a wild and fanciful tale. The story I've recounted here is an overview, a blend of several versions of roughly the same story. There are many interpretations of this history, many smaller points of disagreement, but the larger points, which differ so much from the established, 'official' view, are much the same.

Most of the 'establishment' information we have been fed is, I believe, greatly incomplete and highly inaccurate. There is a great deal of compelling information that the schools and the media do not present—stuff that the establishment does not want us to see. I believe that, as we awaken, more and more alternative information is becoming available. These writings represent a part of my version, my outlook on things, as well as some information that I neither believe nor deny. I truly hope that you do not take my word on it (or anybody else's, for that matter) and that you see fit to investigate, both inwardly and outwardly, for yourself. Find out what rings true for you. I hope to continue to dig out information that assists me in my quest for 'truth', despite its ever-changing nature. I'm quite sure that truth will always be stranger than fiction.

ENDNOTES—PART FOUR

1. Bell, Art and Strieber, Whitley—*The Coming Global Superstorm*, Simon and Schuster, 2001, New York, p. 79
2. Doreal, M.—*The Emerald Tablets of Thoth the Atlantean*, Alexandrian Library Press, p. 3–4
3. Gardner, Laurence—*Genesis of the Grail Kings, Bantam Press*, 1999, London, p. 305
4. ibid. p. 221

Part Five

Mysteries and Enigmas

Have you seen the latest crop circles? They are absolutely astounding. There have been over 1,000 crop circles reported over the past 11 years, but one of the most impressive, which is being referred to as the mother of all crop circles, occurred on Milk Hill in England on August twelve, 2001. It is immense. It covers 700,000 square feet of field (four acres), and contains no less than 400 perfect circles of various sizes, set in a perfect, complex, swirling pattern. Like all crop circles, it occurred overnight; one day it was not there and the next day it was. Some of the more recent crop patterns are even more amazing. If you'd like to have a look at them just go to **www.cropcircleconnector.com** or **www.temporarytemples.co.uk** on the Internet.

If this incredible work of art was made by a couple of hoaxers, or even a whole team of them, dragging planks with ropes, I'll eat every hat I own! When is the last time you've seen a crop circle on the front pages of any newspaper? Why were the media and other institutions so intent on keeping this information suppressed, to the extent that they organized a debunking campaign and got the world to believe that two guys from the local pub were doing these crop patterns as a hoax? Even the slightest investigation into the crop circle phenomenon would convince anyone of the ludicrousness of such a claim.

The crop circle phenomenon is only one of a growing number of mysteries and enigmas, which are completely unexplainable within our currently accepted schools of thought. There are also countless mysteries in our past—structures built with seemingly impossible precision and various enigmas that defy our paradigms about what life was supposed to be like back then. The 'establishment' explanations for most of these enigmas, old and new, are becoming embarrassing. One can't help but feel that the authorities are attempting to cover them up or sweep them under the carpet. Are we being deceived?

In Part Five we'll look at a wide variety of paradigm-challenging puzzles, from a variety of ancient stone structures such as the Great Pyramid, Stonehenge and others, to fossilized human footprints, to unnatural structures on Mars.

Chapter 20

MISCELLANEOUS ODDITIES

For much of the following information, we owe a debt of gratitude to Dr. Richard Thompson, a well educated American scientist, and writer Michael Cremo. Their 1993 release, *'Forbidden Archeology'*, which took ten years to research, reports on a collection of controversial archeological finds that challenge the accepted paradigms. They have been ignored by the academic community. We'll take a look at a few of them now.

In July, 1989, at an excavation in the North Jordan Valley, an archeologist, Professor Naama Goren-Inbar, found an *ancient plank*. It was flat and smooth with one side dressed to a high polish. One of its edges was perfectly straight and beveled. According to carbon dating, this plank was 500,000 years old!

In the diggings that went on during the *California goldrush*, human remains and many artefacts such as spear and arrow heads, knives, mortars and pestles, dishes, bones, etc. were found in strata that were hundreds of thousands of years old. ('Strata' refers to layers of Earth deposited at a certain time. Scientists can tell the approximate age of a stratum.) A report in the London Times in 1851 told of an iron nail found imbedded in stone. In 1899 the Smithsonian Institute did an investigation. They admitted that some of the artifacts, found at depths of 2,000 feet in ravines or hundreds of feet down in mine shafts, could not be accounted for within current paradigms.

At Table Mountain, near Yosemite National Park, a skull, a mastodon tooth, a mortar, a marble bead with a hole drilled through it and other anomalous items were found in gravel beds considered to be 53 million years old. The strata above these finds were undisturbed, suggesting that they were not buried at a more recent date. Twenty-six other mine sites yielded similar finds.

In 1891, near Morrisville, Illinois, a delicate gold chain was found imbedded in a chunk of coal considered to be about 300 million years old. It was made of eight-carat gold, a further anomaly, since fifteen-carat gold normally represents the least level of purity at which gold is produced. There have been other similar finds in coal, such as old nails, etc.

There have been several *fossilized human footprints* that also defy explanation. In 1938, Professor Wilbur Burroughs, head of biology at Berea College, found such a print in an ancient beach. In the bed of the Paluxi River in Texas, several fossilized footprints were found in 1969. The footprints disappeared under some layers of rock, which were removed to reveal more footprints, a total of fourteen. In the same fossilized mud, from the same time period, there are 134 dinosaur footprints. There have been other fossilized human prints found around the world, but none as old as these. Even more astounding than this, fossilized shoeprints have been found, including the one found by geologist, John Reid in 1922. When studied under a microscope, stitching could be seen. This print is thought to be 250 million years old! In 1968, in Antelope Springs, Utah, another shoeprint was found in shale which dates to 500 million years ago.

At an excavation in Suffolk, England, called the Red Crag, which was part of the sea 2.5 million years ago, archeologists found several sharks teeth which had holes drilled in them as for a necklace. The holes were filled with the same fossilized red clay in which they were found. In 1875, in Italy, Professor Capellini of Bologna University found fossilized whalebones in strata from 2.5 million years ago. The bones bore unmistakable butchering marks that had been made by a sharp knife. There have been other similar marks found on the fossilized bones of a rhinoceros and a sea cow. Many tools have been found at sites in France and Spain, the age of which also defies explanation. Fossilized human skeletons very similar to that of modern man have been found by Professor Guiseppe Ragazzoni and colleagues whose studies showed them to be 3–4 million years old. Thompson and Cremo's list goes on and on.[1]

A strange machine-like object called the **Antikythera Computer**, now in the Museum of Athens, was found in a shipwreck in the Mediterranean Sea. The ship sank in 82 BC. This complex gizmo consisted of forty cogwheels made from metal two millimetres thick, certainly beyond the capabilities of humanity at that time, according to currently accepted thought. It is thought to be a calendrical sun/moon computing device.[2]

And then there are the maps. From the research of Charles Hapgood we are told of the **Piri Re'is** map from 1513 AD, the **Oronteus Finaeus** of 1531 AD, and various other maps called **Portolans**, which show the world as it was before ice covered Antarctica. The shorelines of Antarctica are accurately depicted. We have only acquired detailed knowledge of this coastline recently, using technology that could 'see' through the two-mile thick sheet of ice that currently encompasses the continent. The Piri Re'is map also shows the Azores at their correct latitudes and longitudes, but shows them as a group of 17 larger islands, rather than the nine that we know of today. Mapmakers of the 1500s certainly shouldn't have had this kind of information. Could this map be a copy of one that was made when the water levels were much lower or at a time when Antarctica was ice-free?[3]

In a cave in southern Illinois, thousands of ancient artifacts were found depicting Egypt-like scenes, Roman clothing, African (Senegalese) faces and other images that make no sense according to current paradigms. These artifacts are at least 2000 years old and are thought to have come from Mauritania in North Africa.[3] Even more enigmatic are the contents of a cave recently discovered near Manti, Utah. Ancient boxes were found containing metal plates on which were writings in a style very similar to that of the Mayans. Also found were several red-haired mummies that were nine feet tall.[5]

Some researchers have paid a dear price for work that challenges the accepted views. While many have been dismissed, ignored or ridiculed, some have lost their jobs. Thomas Lee, a Canadian archeologist working for the National Museum of Canada in 1951, was excavating a site at Sheguindah, on Manitoulin Island in Lake Huron. He found dozens of stone tools that were dated at between 65 and 125 thousand years of age. This challenges the current paradigm, which claims that all native Americans descended from Asians who came to America via the Bering Strait land bridge approximately 15,000 years ago. Over the years, about 100 geologists and archeologists visited the site, many of them corroborating Lee's findings. Despite this, the establishment refused to consider his work and eliminated his publication possibilities. Lee's artifacts disappeared. Lee and his immediate supervisor, museum director Dr. Jacques Rousseau, who stood up for Lee, were fired.[6]

Chapter 21

MYSTERIES IN STONE

There are thirty-three limestone quarries in the American state of Indiana. Most of America's limestone comes from there. It is a major industry in Indiana, using all the modern quarrying technology including huge trucks, cranes and heavy machinery. Merle Booker, technical director of the Indiana Limestone Institute of America estimated that it would take all thirty-three quarries about twent-seven years just to cut the amount of limestone (131,467,940 cubic feet) used in the construction of *the Great Pyramid at Giza.* Weighing about 7 million tons, which is the equivalent of thirty Empire State buildings, the 2,500,000 stones of the Great Pyramid were cut and then transported many miles from the quarry to the building site, where they were hoisted as high as 480 feet and assembled with incredible precision. This is an unimaginably large amount of stone. If made into a wall three feet high and one foot thick, this amount of stone would create a wall long enough to cross America from the east coast to the west and back![7]

Conventional Egyptology would have us believe that this was accomplished in twenty years, by 100,000 slaves laboring without the assistance of the wheel. They are said to have used sleds for transportation, and to have built enormous ramps up which the stones, the biggest of which weigh fifty to seventy tons each, were dragged and manipulated into place. No trace of these ramps, which would have been marvels of engineering unto themselves, has ever been found. What would these ramps and sleds have been made of? Wood was and is a rare commodity in that part of the world, consisting largely of soft palm trees and some scattered acacia trees.

If the enigma of the labor aspect seems somewhat implausible, please consider the engineering aspects. These huge blocks were cut so that they fit together perfectly. In the inner chambers there are mammoth fifty to seventy ton blocks of very hard granite, from a quarry 600 miles to the south, which fit together so well that a razor blade cannot be inserted in the seams. The degree of precision is astounding and would be very hard to duplicate even with today's technology. Edges run absolutely strait for hundreds of feet, thicknesses are completely uniform, and some surfaces are polished and perfectly flat. All of these inner chambers and passageways would have had to have been planned and cut before assembly!

The casing stones, which formed the outside covering, were appropriated by Arabs to help rebuild Cairo over 1000 years ago. Consisting of 115,000 blocks of polished white limestone weighing ten tons each, this outer casing was put together with high precision, resulting in a flat, uniform surface. The entire pyramid sits on a thirteen acre square platform which is perfectly level. Anyone who has ever tried to lay a patio stone in their back yard will tell you how difficult a task this is. I could go on and on, but without belaboring the point, the Great Pyramid is an astounding marvel of engineering.

There are many **peculiarities in the dimensions and layout** of the Giza pyramids that suggest some hidden meaning. Here are some examples:

- In 1864, John Taylor discovered that the perimeter of the base of the Great Pyramid, in proportion to its height, seems to form a pi ratio. (Pi is the ratio of the circumference of a circle to its diameter. Thus, if the square base were shaped like a circle, then that circumference would be in pi ratio to the height, which is equal to the circle's radius. In other words, the Great Pyramid is equivalent to half a sphere. This results in the sides rising at a 51° angle, which is very steep and difficult to construct. The lesser pyramids are not so steep, except for the Mayan 'El Castillo' pyramid at Chichen Itza which also has this ratio in its design.[8]

- The ancient Egyptians used an inch that is .001 inch larger than a British inch. There are 25 such inches in a cubit. The perimeter of the base of the Great Pyramid is exactly 36,525 of these ancient inches. Divide this number by ten and we have the number of days in a year. If the axis running through the center of the planet from north to south were divided by 500 million, it would equal one of these Egyptian inches.[9]

- There are other astounding correlations between this pyramid and the Earth. If it were a perfectly equilateral pyramid, the angle of the sides to the base would be 60°. But in fact, the Great Pyramid is 'squashed', that is, the angle is 51.51° and not 60°. The Earth is not a perfect sphere, but is also 'squashed' to a tangerine-like shape. In other words, if a perfectly equilateral pyramid were placed inside a sphere so that all the corners were touching the inside wall of the sphere, and then it was compressed to the same degree as the planet, then it would be just like the Great Pyramid! The degree of 'squashedness' of the Earth corresponds to that of the pyramid. This suggests that the builders were aware of the dimensions of the planet![10]

- There used to be a casing of white limestone on the outside of the Great Pyramid. There were enough of these stones to fill 22 acres. Almost all of these are gone now, having been taken around 1220 to help rebuild Cairo, which had been destroyed by an earthquake. Historian Abdul Latif was the last to see and write about the casing stones. He says they fit together, virtually seamlessly, and that there were many hieroglyphics carved into them, enough to fill 10,000 pages. Herodotus testifies to having seen these inscriptions. The Coptic papyrus from the monastery of Abu Hormeis has the following passage: 'In this manner were the pyramids built. Upon the walls were written the mysteries of science, astronomy, geometry, physics and much useful knowledge, which any person who understands our writing could read.' We can only wonder at the information these writings would have yielded. Our ability to decipher such writing has only been gained recently with the discovery of the Rosetta Stone in 1799. The stone bore parallel inscriptions in Greek and Ancient Egyptian, allowing us to translate the hieroglyphics.[11]

- Robert Bauval has been one of the key proponents of the idea that the Great Pyramid is aligned to certain stars. The shaft that goes out from the King's chamber is aligned with Orion, while the one from the Queen's chamber points at Sirius. The three pyramids at Giza are laid out in exactly the same shape as the three stars of Orion's belt, with one of the pyramids being significantly smaller than the other two in the same way as the stars. When these stars are directly over Giza, they are not a perfect reflection of the pyramid layout, but are tilted. Using a computer to calculate the effect of the precessional movement, it was shown that the last time that the pyramid layout was a perfect reflection of the three stars was in 10,500 BC. At that time, the Sphinx would have been facing the sunrise at vernal equinox. 10,500 BC is a time that was called 'zep tepi' by the Egyptians, which translates as 'the first times'.[12]

- The four faces of the Great Pyramid are aligned exactly with the four directions, north, south, east and west.
- The three pyramids are also laid out according to the proportions of a Fibonacci spiral within a golden mean rectangle (See **DIAGRAM 8—THE GOLDEN MEAN SPIRAL**). According to Drunvalo Melchizedek, the Christ-consciousness grid that surrounds the planet is shaped like a Fibonacci spiral, with its starting point at Giza.[13]

Conventional Egyptology would have us believe that the precision of the Great Pyramid was accomplished using copper hand tools and primitive instruments such as plumb-lines and water levels. The experts tell us that the engineers living in Egypt around 2800 BC were capable of this high level of craftsmanship and calculation, and yet they still hadn't figured out the wheel. The degree of precision with which the Great pyramid was constructed is significantly greater than that required in the building codes of today. This precision is more reminiscent of a tool or instrument than a building. Why was this degree of perfection required by these ancient builders? This question has stumped most Egyptologists, but some have offered that it was some kind of fluke or accident!

They say that this extra-ordinary feat was carried out under the order of a relatively insignificant pharaoh named ***Khufu***, (Cheops in Greek), to serve as his tomb. If this were the case, then surely a larger ego has never walked the face of the Earth. Strange then, that he would not have left his 'signature' on the structure. When, around 820 AD, an Arabian Caliph named Al Mamoun led the first known entry into the Great Pyramid, he found no treasure, no statue or tribute to Khufu. In fact, no evidence has ever been found showing it to be a tomb. Conventional Egyptologists insist on the tomb theory based on very sketchy evidence. A cartouche bearing Khufu's misspelled name (Raufu) was claimed to have been found inside the Great Pyramid by an Englishman, Colonel Richard Howard-Vyse in 1835. This cartouche, which was shown to be fraudulent in 1980, is the only scrap of evidence supporting the tomb theory.[14] Most tombs, including Tutenkhamen's, have been found in non-pyramid structures in the Valley of the Kings, hundreds of miles away from Giza. According to American Egyptologist, Dr. Mark Lehner, none of the other eighty pyramids in Egypt show any indication that they were intended as tombs, and yet this misperception persists.[15]

DIAGRAM 9—INSIDE THE GREAT PYRAMID

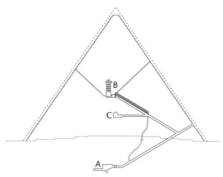

A. Subterranean Chamber. B. King's Chamber, containing the granite box that has come to be called the 'Sarcophagus'. C. The Queen's Chamber.

A great deal of alternative research and postulation has been put forth in the past 100 years which attempts to explain why, when, how and who built this amazing structure. In my opinion, most of these alternative explanations are more convincing than the conventional theories. Unfortunately, much of this work has been ignored by academia. There is almost a religious fervor around the defense of the old Egyptology paradigms. Why do the 'experts' pretend to have the answers to the riddles of the Great Pyramid when it seems obvious to anyone who does even a little research in this area that there are huge pieces of the puzzle missing? We will take a quick look at some of this alternative information, but for those of you who find this subject as fascinating as I do, I recommend a deeper investigation into the work of the researchers mentioned in this chapter. I will try to present the various theories about the Great Pyramid by examining the questions: why, how, who and when.

If we can set aside the idea that it was a tomb, then **why was the Great Pyramid built?** What was the function of such an incredible structure? Let's take a brief look at some of the many opinions regarding this question.

- Some, including Robert Menzies, adhere to the 'pyramidology' theory, whereby the Great Pyramid as well as others, are instruments of prophecy. Hieroglyphics etched in the stone, as well as measurements and proportions, are said to date Biblical events and to predict significant events in history. According to 'futurist', G. M. Scallion, the pyramid time record ends in 1953, which is said to be the start of a period known as 'the choosing'.
- Much has been made fairly recently, of the notion of 'pyramid power', whereby the actual pyramid shape somehow generates sub-sonic waves of energy which have the capacity of making wine age better, maintaining the sharpness of razor blades, inhibiting the decay of dead flesh, etc. It is said to have several medical applications, influencing the lifespan of bacteria and affecting human brain-wave activity.

- In 1883, Richard Anthony Proctor suggested that it was an astronomical observatory. He was not the first to make this claim, however. In 400 AD, the Byzantine philosopher, Proclus, proposed the same notion.[16]
- Alan Alford contends that, among other things, the Great Pyramid has served as a prison of the god, Marduk/Ra who was battling with Ninurta. He also feels that it was a navigational beacon for incoming ET craft, pointing out that, with the white casing, it would have been highly visible from a distance. He also claims that the many empty niches in the pyramid once housed large crystals, with names such as; the 'Sham' (destiny stone), 'Gug' (direction determining stone), 'Su' (vertical stone), 'Kashurra'(awesome pure which opens stone), 'Sagkal' (sturdy stone in front), and 'Ul' (high as the sky stone).
- Some people have suggested that the pyramid is some kind of time machine or star-gate, and that the amplification of certain frequencies could cause 'portals' to open.
- Several opinions contend that the Great Pyramid was once used as an energy generator/power plant. Edgar Cayce's readings on Atlantis describe similar power plants. The most convincing argument in that department is provided by Christopher Dunn, an engineer much experienced in the field of high-tech tools. He claims that the pyramid is tuned to the planet's base resonant frequency, the Schumann Resonance, that it is a harmonic integer of the planet. Earth produces a very low frequency note, which is said to be F#. (It is interesting that many indigenous flutes and musical instruments are tuned to F#.) This note is amplified by the structure and converted to electricity. He suggests that this is achieved by the huge blocks of granite in the pyramid's interior. Granite is 50% quartz, which has the ability to transduce sound vibration into an electrical current, as in a crystal microphone or Piezo-tension transducer. This is called the piezoelectric effect.

  Dunn points out that the huge granite beams above the King's chamber are dressed on all but the top side, which was chipped away until the beams were precisely tuned. An acoustic analysis of the Great Pyramid was done by acoustic engineer and NASA consultant, Tom Danley. It was said that the pyramid had a sonic 'purpose', and that an F# note is always present in the pyramid shafts. The granite box in the King's chamber, known as the Sarcophagus, has been shown to be tuned to A440. (I'm not sure if this is significant, but A is the third note in an F# minor chord.) Dunn claims that microwaves enter the chamber via the north shaft, pass through the granite box which acts as a lens which concentrates the microwaves into maser beams. (A laser beam consists of concentrated light waves, while a maser is concentrated microwaves.) The mazer beams are then shot out through the south shaft to some receiver—possibly a satellite, which he suggests could have been called the 'Eye of Horus'. Dunn sites a good deal of technical evidence to make his point. It is interesting that other Egyptian structures also seem to have something to do with sound. The two Obelisks at the Karnak complex are made from one solid piece of pink granite weighing 143 and 320 tons. When struck these monuments produce a deep, low-pitched note.

Alford also believes that the building was used as a power plant, claiming that hydrogen was extracted from water in the Queen's chamber, and then burned for electricity in the King's chamber. Psychic, Gordon M. Scallion claims that the Great Pyramid once contained volcanic gases, which were harnessed for power.

• Edgar Cayce said that the Great Pyramid was a temple of initiation. Many psychics and mystics are of the opinion that it once housed great crystals and that it was part of an elaborate mystery school which was divided into two parts, taking twelve years each to complete. The school of the Right Eye of Horus focussed on left-brain 'mind' issues, involving the learning of cosmology, sacred geometry and other information. For the next twelve years the initiate attended the school of the Left Eye of Horus, which dealt with right-brain, 'emotional' issues, involving the development of intuition and other psychic abilities, as well as the overcoming of fears. Twelve different chambers in various temples were designed to bring in certain energies, to house different ratios of magnetics/frequencies that corresponded to twelve different basic fears, one for each of the twelve chakras. The King's Chamber was the last step in a process by which the initiate achieved unity consciousness, overcame fear, discovered his/her true identity, gained complete control of self and achieved Christ-consciousness. The initiate was sealed in the granite box for three days, where s/he was subject to conditions of elevated frequencies and greatly diminished magnetic strength. If the initiate could control all thoughts and emotions and maintain a state of grace with no fear or doubts, s/he would experience life in the next dimension. The Queen's Chamber was then used as a place to stabilize.[17]

The next big question is, ***how was the Great Pyramid built?*** Conventional Egyptology says that it was built in twenty years by 100,000 slaves. According to the calculations of a civil engineer named P. Garde-Hanson, for this to be true, 4,000 blocks per day or 6.67 blocks per minute would have been installed with perfect precision.[18] That it was done using ropes, sleds, ramps, hammers and copper cisels adds to the incredulity of such a feat. Let's set aside this seemingly remote possibility and take a quick look at some of the alternative ideas.

• In 1986, a chemist named Joseph Davidovits argued that this enormous structure could have been poured into place, using forms and geopolymers. A chemical analysis of the pyramid limestone showed that it was different than other types, containing a phosphate called brushite, which is not typically found in limestone.[19]

- One widely held notion is that the pyramid was built using an anti-gravity device or some methodology that defies gravity. There are several versions of this idea. Laurence Gardner suggests that the white powder/high spin gold has some anti-gravity properties used to move the stone blocks. Scallion had psychic visions of dirigibles in the sky hauling stones with the assistance of men on the ground who were spinning slings with cups attached to the ends. These devices gave off a loud, high-pitched sound, which he claimed had some anti-gravitational capacity. An eccentric Latvian-American by the name of Ed Leedskalnin claimed that he knew the secret of creating anti-gravitational forces, which he harnessed to move the huge stone blocks used to create his Coral Castle in Florida. (See **BOX 20—THE CORAL CASTLE**) He was very guarded about this knowledge, however, and in 1952 he died with it. Those who investigated his workshop after his death found no written information, but they found many magnetic devices. The concept of defying gravity may seem a bit far-fetched, but science admits that it still does not know what gravity actually is. A good deal of channeled information claims that UFO's do not use rocket technology, but rather, some form of anti-gravity technology.

- It is feasible that the pyramid stones (and other huge stones) were moved using some form of telekinesis. Some people feel that human psychic powers were much greater and more common back in matriarchal times when 'right-brain' consciousness predominated. Telekinesis is the ability to move objects using the power of the mind or will. This ability is very real and has been extensively tested in the lab in modern times by institutions such as the British Society for Psychical Research, and especially by Russian researchers. One Russian subject, Nelya Mikhailova, can move small objects at will under the strictest laboratory conditions.[20]

- Christopher Dunn seems convinced that high tech power tools were used. He says that, to achieve the degree of accuracy seen in the Great Pyramid, one would need ultra-sonic cutting and drilling equipment, guided by computer. He examined blade and drill marks on pyramid stone and claims that it bears a close resemblance to the marks made by ultra-sonic tools. He believes it to have been impossible to make such marks using hand tools, even if steel and diamond cutters were available. If the Egyptians had power, it seems to me that we would have found some tool or piece of electrical cord or something. The only evidence is a wall carving at Dendera in the Temple of Hathor which shows two Egyptians holdings what looks like large light bulbs attached to cords and insulators.[21]

There are many other enigmas in ancient Egypt, other than the Great Pyramid, which seem to have been made with power tools. Thousands of large bottles made of solid stone have been found, many of which are in the Cairo museum. The body of a typical bottle is hollow, round and squat, with a long, perfectly drilled out neck. How something like this could have been made from solid stone using hand tools completely defies explanation.[22] At the Temple of Serapeum in Saqqara, there are narrow tunnels carved into solid bedrock, which contain twenty-one perfect granite boxes with lids, each of which weighs 100 tons! How were such things placed in there when there is only room for a few bodies?[23] Another compelling question—how were the many dark interiors in the pyramids and structures throughout Egypt lit? There are no soot marks, no evidence on the walls and ceilings that torches were used.

> **BOX 20—THE CORAL CASTLE:**
> "I have discovered the secrets of the pyramids, and have found out how the Egyptians and the ancient builders in Peru, Yucatan, and Asia, with only primitive tools, raised and set in place blocks of stone weighing many tons!" These are the words of an eccentric Latvian, Edward Leedskalnin, who created in his backyard a large complex of quarried, sculpted, coral blocks which came to be called the Coral Castle. He achieved this in the thirty years prior to his death in 1952. No one knows how he moved his collection of stone, which totals 1100 tons, the largest block weighing 30 tons. One can still visit the Coral Castle at its current location in Homestead, Florida. Interestingly, it was once located in nearby Florida City. When Leedskalnin decided to move, he transported all of the heavy blocks with a flatbed truck. Nobody knows how he managed to load and unload these huge blocks without the use of any heavy equipment. He claims that he did it using some form of 'levitation' based on vibration and magnetics. He said that "all matter consists of magnets which can produce measurable phenomena, and electricity." However he did it, his secret died with him. (For more info on this subject—'The Enigma of Coral Castle', by Ray Stoner or **www.labyrinthina.com/coral**)
> There are also reports of a Canadian scientist, John Hutchinson, who has used some sort of electro-magnetic device that resulted in some very anomalous phenomena. He has been video-taped levitating several heavy objects including a sixty pound cannon-ball.(for more info see: **www.geocities.com/ResearchTriangle/Thinktank/8863/main** or **www.rumormillnews.com/hutch**)

- Graham Hancock writes that, according to Jewish Talmudic/Midrashic sources, the Egyptians had a tool/device called 'the Shamir', which could cut even the hardest stone without heat or friction. It is said to have been stored in a lead basket wrapped in wool, implying that it may have been radioactive.[24]

This brings us to the question, ***who built the Great Pyramid?*** Convention says that it was commissioned by the pharaoh Khufu, and that it was designed by a guy named 'Imhotep the Builder'. Again, let's set that possibility aside and look at some other ideas.

- Graham Hancock feels that it was built by some unidentified ET group trying to warn us of a celestial collision that is pending. He suggests that the pyramids on Mars are also warnings. Writers such as Sitchin, Alford and Dunn suggest that it was probably built by the Anunnaki, (Alford does not use the word Anunnaki) who also created Cydonia on Mars.

- According to Murry Hope, an Arab historian from the ninth century named Ibn Abd Hokum wrote that the pyramid was built by Surid Ibn Salhouk, an Egyptian king living 300 years before the great flood.[25]

- When all the continents were together as Pangea, the area at Giza was at the center of the landmass. It is said that there has been activity there for millions of years, with civilizations such as Zu, Ur and Dar. Probably the most popular alternative opinion is that the pyramid was built by Thoth, an Atlantean god who helped colonize this area, and a handful of his cohorts. As pointed out in **BOX 15—ANCIENT DYNASTIES**, many texts and legends suggest this. According to the 'building texts' found in the Temple of Edfu, it and other structures were built by the 'seven sages', 'builder gods' who were survivors of a great flood and who came from an island. A fourteenth century Arab scholar by the name of Ibn Batuta writes that 'The pyramids were constructed by Hermes to preserve the arts and sciences and other scientific acquirements during the Flood.'[26]

Thoth has also been mentioned by many psychics and channels, including Drunvalo Melchizadek. Alford names Thoth as the builder of the pyramid and other structures around the world, claiming that he was also a Sumerian god. Some say that, having set the standard with the Great Pyramid, Thoth trained Imhotep the Builder, often referred to as Thoth's successor, who then built some of the subsequent pyramids. It is interesting to note that the newer pyramids are not nearly so complex and impressive as the Great Pyramid and that the knowledge of pyramid construction seems to have deteriorated over the years. Whoever he was, Thoth/Hermes is referred to by countless diverse sources as an entity that has played a great role in our history.

Lastly, let's take a look at some views addressing the question, **when was the Great Pyramid built?** The current paradigm offers that it was built in 2500 BC, some 600 years after the Upper and Lower Nile were united under the leadership of Menes, the first pharaoh. Other sources feel differently.

- The oldest estimate comes from an Arab writer named Abu Zeyd El Balkhy who translated and interpreted some ancient texts. He claims it was built 73,000 years ago.[27]

- On the 'Tablet of Menes' (3313 BC), there is a glyph which shows the pyramid in the background, yet it was not supposed to have been built for another 600 years.[28] A stone text called the 'Inventory Stele', now in the Cairo Museum, tells of repairs to the Temple of Isis (also at Giza) which is referred to as the 'mistress of the pyramid'. These repairs were done by Khufu, suggesting that the pyramid was already there.[29] As already noted, a ninth-century Arab historian, Ibn Abd Hokum, says that the Great Pyramid was built by Surid Ibn Salhouk, a king who lived 300 years before the Great Flood.[30] The most popular alternative theory is that the Great Pyramid was built around 10,500 BC, during the time known as 'zep tepi'. Before leaving this segment, let's take a look at another very famous Giza enigma, **the Sphinx**. Traditional Egyptologists say that it was made by the pharaoh Kafre (Chefren in Greek), circa 2500 BC. Recently, however, so much strong evidence has emerged to challenge this idea that even conventional science is admitting that it could be much older. In the early 1990s, a geologist by the name of Robert Schoch presented the results of his studies that showed that the erosion visible on the Sphinx came from water, not wind and sand. The marks made by water erosion are distinctly different than erosion from wind-blown sand. The question is, how long has it been since there was significant water in that area?[31]

Some say that the Sahara was green and fertile as recently as 3500 BC. A radar scan conducted on the space shuttle Columbia in 1981 shows buried river systems in the Sudan, suggesting that the area was once green.[32] The erosion on the lower part of the Sphinx seems to suggest that it was submerged in water for a significant period of time. Was it there during the flood?

Egyptologists contend that the face of the Sphinx is that of Kafre. Detective Frank Domingo of the NYPD, a forensic artist and expert on facial structure, was asked to compare the face of the Sphinx to that of a known statue of Kafre. In his opinion, the two are not alike.[33]

Alternative theories about the Sphinx seem to more or less agree that it is older than the pyramids. There is considerably more erosion on the Sphinx, which Egyptologists tried to explain by claiming that it was made from softer stone than the pyramids. It was proven, however, that they are made from the same limestone. Most alternative theories also seem to agree that Thoth had something to do with the construction, or at least, the planning of the Sphinx. They also seem to accord with the idea that there is a secret chamber under it called the Hall of Records. Some say it is beneath the right shoulder, others that it is under and between the front paws. The Hall of Records is said to contain the complete history of life on Earth and the answers to the many mysteries. Prophecies say that we are going to discover this chamber very soon, as the right shoulder collapses. Authorities have been working desperately to keep the Sphinx in a good state of repair.

Some opinions purport that the Sphinx was once a female, with breasts that were later removed by a pharaoh who tried to make it look like himself. Graham Hancock offers the idea that this monument, which would have been half lion, half woman, was meant to signify the passage from the age of Virgo to that of Leo, an event that occurred about 12,000 years ago. Other views contend that it was made as a tribute to Bast, the goddess of witchcraft and sexual magic who presided over the sexual experiments in Atlantis that yielded the 'chimeras'. (Under her matriarchal rule, parental lineage was not a question, as the identity of a child's mother is always obvious. It only became important, as the patriarchy took over, to know the identity of the father, thus determining rightful bloodlines. This led to the institution of monogamy. Thus, a child born out of wedlock, whose paternal lineage was in question, was called a bastard, in memory of Bast.[34])

Another very old temple called *the Oseirion*, also made of 'Cyclopean' blocks, was discovered in the 1920s. Till that time, it was covered in sand. The Sphinx itself was buried up to the neck until 1817. How many other ancient structures remain undiscovered beneath the desert sands?

So what are my own opinions regarding the Great Pyramid? Again, rather than arriving at conclusive answers, it seems more important to be asking better questions. It seems obvious to me that, whatever the 'truth' may be, the conventional viewpoints are sadly lacking.

I do feel inclined to believe that the Great Pyramid was built just before or after the flood, by some previous civilization, (Atlanteans if you like), or volunteer 'gods', in an effort to preserve knowledge. Some, including Alan Alford, believe that it was the first Egyptian pyramid, and that the other lesser pyramids came later, possibly built by pharaohs trying to recapture the glory of an older age. It seems that, the newer the pyramid, the more poorly it was constructed, with far less precision and complexity. I tend to agree with this position.

In terms of the function of the Great Pyramid, I believe it was designed to do many things. It seems questionable that the Anunnaki would have built it as a power plant. If they were advanced enough to come to Earth in spaceships 300,000 years ago to mine gold, then surely they would have had a simpler way of harnessing energy than to go through the enormous effort of building such a pyramid. Perhaps it was not an enormous effort. That implies some very advanced technology. Or possibly it served many functions, which justified such an effort. I believe the prime purpose of this great structure was to help humanity in the process of enlightening, to preserve in the minds of humans, the knowledge of who we are and what we are doing in this dimension. I believe that, all through history, there have been pockets of awareness, groups of people who have known of our quest for enlightenment, who have kept this knowledge preserved while the bulk of humanity was sound asleep. I believe that the power elite has always had more access to this knowledge and that, with the odd exception, they have kept it from the masses because they did not have a clear understanding of its essential message.

At this point, I would like to quote Gordon Michael Scallion from his book, 'Notes From the Cosmos'.

"The Great Pyramid's purpose, as constructed, was multiple in design. Bending time was its focus, so as to provide a process for initiation. However, the manner in which this was accomplished provided other benefits for its people.

These varied from increased crop yield, weather control, a form of electrical power, and a learning institute for the study of the heavens—astronomy, astrology and cosmic forces, mathematics, chemistry, inner world dimensions and the seven levels of initiation. All were part of its design."

What do you think?

The Sphinx is surely a wonderful mystery. The Great Pyramid is an enigma of huge proportions and is probably the best known of a whole category of anomalous structures, which I've called 'mysteries in stone'. Lesser known examples can be found all around the world, defying conventional academic explanations. Attempts are sometimes made to cram the information regarding these anomalies into the confines of the old paradigms, but often it is a poor fit with most of the questions remaining unanswerable. As a result, we tend to hear little about them in school or in the mass media.

What **enigmatic qualities** do these stone structures have in common? In many cases there are precision cuts and fittings, straight edges, precisely drilled holes and 'inside' cuts which seem impossible without power tools. These cuts are often in very hard rock such as granite, porphyry and andesite and are considered by the current paradigms to have been built by societies that had yet to discover bronze. Often these structures consist of huge, 'Cyclopean' blocks weighing as much as 800 tons each! How were such stones moved from quarries that were sometimes hundreds of miles away, often through precipitous mountain passes? One is forced to ask why they would go to the trouble of using such mammoth stones when smaller stones could be used to make, for example, an equally effective wall. In many cases these structures have been found to have mysterious and apparently meaningful functions such as alignments with stars and other celestial bodies.

It is very difficult to determine the age of these sites. Only organic matter can be dated by radiocarbon technology and other similar methods and so, since rock cannot be dated, the age of stone structures is estimated based on whatever organic matter is present at the site, or whatever civilizations were known to have lived at the site. There is a serious flaw to this method of dating. There is nothing to prove that some civilization inhabiting a particular site, leaving behind organic evidence, is the group that actually built the site. For example, in 1532 AD when Francisco Pizarro's conquistadors plundered the Inca empire, they were awe-struck at the incredible stonework amongst which the Incas lived. They found no stone-craftsmen, however, no written records, no evidence that the Inca people had actually built the structures. It was assumed that they had built it because it challenges the accepted paradigms to a greater degree to think that some previous society may have been the builders. There is some convincing evidence to suggest that many of the stone enigmas were built much earlier than what is usually contended.[35]

One reason that some researchers have come to this view is due to a method called *'archaeo-astronomy'*. After 100 years of derision this method has gained respectability largely due to the work of Sir Norman Lockyer, who studied temples and cathedrals from around the globe and noted that they were aligned, in some way, to significant celestial bodies. Some stone structures have been found to be aligned to certain stars during key days such as the spring or fall equinox or the summer or winter solstices. In some cases these alignments are off by a bit. Using computers, researchers have traced the map of the heavens back to a time in the zodiacal cycle when the alignment would have been dead on. In this way they have come to a probable construction date. There are other non-scientific methods such as the examination of myths, legends and 'circumstantial' evidence.

So at this point, let's take a little global tour to look at some of these stone anomalies. A more detailed account of these mysterious structures, as well as some great photos, can be found in Alan Alford's book, 'Gods of the New Millennium', but we'll take an abbreviated look at them here. Let's start with the largest cut stone blocks that we know of on this planet. At **Baalbek** in Lebanon there is a platform that has been built upon many times, the age of which nobody knows. Nine blocks weighing 300 tons each make up huge walls, but the biggest blocks make up what is called the Trilithon. Somehow, hoisted twenty feet in the air onto a wall, there are three blocks weighing 800 tons each. There is no machine in the world, at present, capable of lifting these monoliths. But that's still not the biggest. In a nearby quarry sits the 'stone of the south', a dressed block weighing 1000 tons! That's equal to the weight of three 747 jets![36]

From here it's off to Bolivia, 13,000 feet up in the Andean plateau, to the ancient site of **Tiwanaku** on the shores of Lake Titicaca. This site features a huge man-made mound inside of which there is a strange, over-engineered water conduit which has been precisely cut in hard andesite. Another sophisticated, over-engineered, underground water system can be found 10,000 feet up in a remote corner of the Peruvian Andes, at a place called **Chavin de Huantar**. The function of these water conduits is a mystery. At a place just outside of the Tiwanaku complex called Puma Punku, there is a 100-ton block with perfectly straight grooves and perfectly drilled holes through it. A large temple called the Kalasasaya has astro-alignments that date it to before 10,000 BC.[37] Interestingly, two statues have been found here that are reminiscent of Oannes, the Babylonian fish-god. They are humanoid with fish scales. There are also carvings of elephant and hippo-like creatures called 'cuvieronius' and 'toxodons' which have been extinct since about 10,000 BC.[38] (There were also ancient stone carvings of the headdresses of Mayan priests found in the ruins of Palenque, depicting the head of an elephant. Interestingly, in Plato's description of Atlantis he mentions the presence of elephants.[39])

Some researchers feel that Tiwanaku and Lake Titicaca were once at sea level. There is evidence of old wharves and harbours and strand lines from tides. In the lake, many salt-water shells and fossils have been found. The reed boats used on this lake have been found to be almost identical to the ones used in ancient Egypt. Alford contends that, based on the research of Arthur Posnansky and others, there is evidence to suggest that Tiwanaku was a center for the production of bronze, circa 4050 BC.[40]

While in Peru, let's check out the Inca structures which conventional opinions claim were built between 1100 and 1532 AD. In the city of *Cuzco*, which has survived earthquakes that have leveled other towns, there are enormous walls with huge, precision cut stones that fit together perfectly, so that a razor blade would not fit in the seams. At *Sacsayhuaman*, walls made of huge stones, the largest of which weighs 120 tons, have been placed on sheer cliffs. A monument known as the Inca's Throne was precision carved into the living rock, with straight edges and polished surfaces. The famous site of *Machu Picchu* was built on a thin ridge, well hidden from view, amongst precipitous mountain peaks. There is much precision cutting with strange niches, ledges and windows. The stone here was quarried miles away. How it was transported along difficult mountain passes is anyone's guess. The temple of Intihutana is an astro-observatory that has been dated to 2200 BC.[41]

Not far from here, in the Andean foothills, one can find the mysterious *Nazca Lines*, a series of geoglyphs that are only visible by air. The lines in these glyphs can run very straight for considerable distances; a task that would be very difficult without the perspective attained by being in some sort of flying craft. Amongst the glyphs are 300 stylized animals, some as long as 90 feet. There is, amongst the surrounding craggy rocks, a flat, very straight wedge-shaped strip that runs for 30 miles! It looks very much like it could be some kind of landing strip. Conventional paradigms say that these geoglyphs were made by the Nazca Indians, around 500 AD.[41] Local legends say that they were always there. A Spanish magistrate, Luis de Monzon, was told in 1586 that, long before the Incas, came a 'saintly' people called the Viracochas and that the Nazca Lines were made in their honor.[43]

In the South Pacific, 2300 miles west of here, we can find *Easter Island* with its strange crop of stone heads. On this small, 45 square mile volcanic island, there are 300 of these standing statues, called 'moai', and there are another 400 unfinished moai in a nearby quarry. The biggest of these weigh up to 89 tons. Most of them are standing on stone platforms and are wearing 'hats' that weigh ten tons. The only known inhabitants of this island were a very primitive tribe who spent most of their time trying to eke out a living on this barren and desolate island. How they had the time or skills to carve and erect so many massive statues remains a mystery. Alford contends that they were made by the same team of giant stonemasons, products of the genetic manipulation of the Sumerian gods, that made the stone structures of Machu Picchu, Cuzco, Tiwanaku, the Nazca Lines and others.[44]

Let's double back now, towards Central America and Mexico's Yucatan Peninsula, to take a peek at the *Mayan structures*. In remote jungle locations, completely engulfed in vines and foliage, archeologists have uncovered amazing cities, such as; Uxmal, Cichen Itza, Mayapan, Palenque, Copan and Tikal. These sites contain incredible works in stone, including the Acropolis at Copan and the enormous El Castillo Pyramid in Chichen Itza. There were also amazing depictions intricately carved in stone and numerous painted hieroglyphics among the ruins. One of the more incredible carvings is the Coffin Lid at the tomb of Pacal Votan in the Temple of Inscriptions at Palenque. This amazing work is rife with meaning, showing the five ages of the sun. The Mayans believed that the four previous ages ended in cataclysm and that the age we are about to enter is the fifth and final. The most compelling form on the lid is a depiction of what appears to be a man at the controls of a complex machine. I have come across several interpretations of this structure, and though they are somewhat different from each other, they all marvel at the craftsmanship and they concur that something very strange is being depicted.[45]

Even more impressive than the buildings and artifacts is the *extensive knowledge* that the Maya recorded. Unfortunately, much of that knowledge is gone, thanks to an overzealous Spanish bishop, Diego de Landa. In 1562, he made it his mission to gather and destroy all the Mayan texts and artwork that he could find. Some books, usually called 'codices', survived this gargantuan act of stupidity, an act that overshadows the fact that de Landa felt great remorse and spent the latter part of his life collecting and preserving Mayan treasures.[46] Texts such as the Troano Codex, the Chimalpopoca Codex and the Popul Vuh contain astonishing information, including facts about our solar system. There is especially extensive information about Venus, including its 540-day cycle around the sun. The cycles that were recorded would have taken thousands of years of observation. Calculations were done to extreme accuracy. For example, it was recorded that the Earth took 365.2420 days to orbit the sun. The moon's orbit around Earth was noted as 29.528395 days! This degree of accuracy far surpassed any western knowledge at the time.

They had a very *sophisticated three-tiered calendar* which started in 3113 BC, (the same year cited as the start of the Egyptian civilization), and ends on December 21, 2012 AD. (See **BOX 21—MAYAN PREDICTIONS**) Their calendar had twelve months of thirty days and a thirteenth month of five days, allowing for the 'leap year' effect. It also included a long count that could record a period of 63 million years, called an 'alautun'. Their number system, which accommodated the calendar, was also very advanced, based on the number thirteen. Its system of dots and dashes is virtually identical to the dots and dashes used in the Chinese I Ching.[47]

One must ask the questions; Where did this information come from, since the Maya had no system for measuring time, no instruments such as telescopes for seeing into space? Why did a primitive, Stone Age, agricultural society need this sort of information and this degree of accuracy? As Alford points out, the typical explanation that they needed such information to know when to plant and harvest crops is ludicrous.

Some interesting tidbits: in the Mayan codices, there are accounts of a great catastrophe that occurred in 10,500 BC, and of a great island continent in the Atlantic that was destroyed by flood. There is a Mayan word, 'oaana', which means 'he who lives in water'. This is reminiscent of the Babylonian 'fish-god', Oannes. There is another Mesoamerican god named Itzamna, whose name also means 'He Whose Home is Water'. A nickname of the Nepalese Hindu god, Narayan is also 'He Whose Home is Water'. There is a Mayan relief that depicts a man with a rope through his tongue, exactly as it is done in Hindu traditions. The Hindu epic 'Ramayana', tells of an ancient sea-going people called the Nagas, who populated India. The Mayans have a similar myth of a sea-going troop of priests called the Naacal who spread wisdom around the globe.[48]

BOX 21—MAYAN PREDICTIONS: The Mayans, the Aztecs and other indigenous cultures have several calendars of incredible complexity and accuracy. One of these is called the Tzolk'in, based on the cycle of the Pleiades, which has proven very prophetically accurate. It predicted that April 21st, 1519, would be a day when life would be completely changed for native Americans. It was right. That was the day that Hernando Cortez and his men arrived in the 'new world'. This sacred calendar comes to an end on the winter solstice of 2012 AD. Many would-be prophets have cited this as the day the world will end. Mayan elders, however, are quick to point out that this is not so, that this day signifies the end of one era and the beginning of a new era. We are about to enter the fifth 'ajaw', or 'sun'. They say that four suns have already passed, each with its own 'element', fire, earth, air and water. The first ajaw was of feminine energy, the second was of masculine energy, the third feminine, and the fourth and current ajaw is of masculine energy. Each ajaw is 5,126 years long, thus the current era started in 3113 BC, which is also the date given as the start of the Egyptian civilization. The fifth ajaw will be a balance of masculine and feminine energies, its element, ether.

According to Mayan elder and spokesperson, Carlos Barrios, "At sunrise on December 21, 2012 for the first time in 26,000 years, the sun rises to conjunct the intersection of the Milky Way and the plane of the ecliptic." This circumstance will usher in a new energy, a higher frequency that will signify a great change in human consciousness. It will be an era of harmony.

For more info on Mayan wisdom, check out; www.sacredroad.org

The El Castillo Pyramid has the same 'pi' proportions as the Great Pyramid at Giza. According to Arthur Posnansky, the great Mayan pyramid at Cholula, near Mexico City, is three times as massive as the one at Giza. Covering 45 acres, it is thought to be the largest building on Earth.

Maurice Cotterell believes that the number 1,366,560, which was sacred to the Mayans, referred to the number of days between reversals of the sun's magnetic field, which he goes to great lengths to explain. He also believes that the soul that incarnated as Lord Pacal is the same soul as that of Egypt's pharaoh, Tutenkhamen, and shows how both leaders came to deliver the same message of monotheism and sun worship. He claims that the solar flare cycles, which have a great effect on humanity, are encoded in both tombs, as well as references to the significant numbers, 144,000 and 666. (See **BOX 22—144,000, 666 AND OTHER SPECIAL NUMBERS**) Cotterell points out that Tutenkhamen's wet nurse as well as the architect of his tomb, were both named Maya. Gautama Buddha's mother's name was also Maya, which is a Sanskrit word meaning 'illusion'. Is all this a coincidence?[50]

For a more in depth look at the Mayan mystery, check out the work of Charles Brasseur, Desire Charnay and Augustus Le Plongeon, as well as the more recent work of Maurice Cotterell, José Argüelles, Humbatz Men (**www.mayamystery.com**) and Judith Bluestone Polich (**www.web-of-light.com**).

Another amazing civilization in this region was that of *the Aztecs*, whose city, Tenochtitlan, was the biggest city in the world at the time of the Spanish invasion. Just north of Mexico City exists the amazing site of *Teotihuacan*, meaning 'the city where men become gods'. Incredible stone structures abound in this eight square mile site, including the Pyramid of the Sun (212 feet high), the Pyramid of the Moon (140 feet high) and the Temple of Quetzalcoatl. These three buildings are laid out like the three pyramids of Giza, and are aligned with Sirius and the Plieades. There are subterranean aqueducts, passages and chambers, some walls of which are made of mica, which comes from Brazil! The faces on pottery found there shows racial diversity.

The Aztecs occupied this area from around 200 BC, but even some conventional archeologists acknowledge that some of the carbon dating suggests that Teotihuacan existed in 1400 BC. Local Indians say that it was there when the Aztecs arrived. The Aztecs said that it was built by Quetzalcoatl in 3113 BC, that civilization began in 20,238 BC, and will end on December 24, 2012.[51]

There is controversy about whether the Aztecs built Teotihuacan, but if they didn't, is there another group who could have done it? Some feel that it could be the work of a mysterious society that thrived in this area at a much earlier time. They were called *the Olmecs*. Very little is known about them, as their ruins are mostly in swampland—very difficult to excavate. They are thought to have lived around 1500 BC. They left behind a strange collection of sixteen heads carved in stone, each of which weighs about thirty tons. The

facial features on these heads appear to be from many races and Alford suggests that they may represent the Kassites, that race of giant stoneworkers created by the Sumerian gods.[52]

I've run across several mentions of the Olmecs in various readings, the gist
of which is that they were very ancient, very advanced, and that they originated elsewhere. Scallion says that they came from what is now the Gobi
Desert about 54,000 years ago. A Spanish priest living and working in Mexico
City in 1697, Don Carlos de Siguenza, who was also a scientist and historian
capable of reading the native hieroglyphics, said that they came from the sea
to the east. In fact, he believed they came from Atlantis.[53]

The next stop in our 'enigmaquest' is the British Isles. Next to the structures
of Giza, one of the most famous mysteries is the one at **Stonehenge**, 80 miles
south west of London on the Salisbury Plain. The outer circle consists of 80
'bluestones' weighing four tons each, which were quarried in the Prescelly
Mountains in Wales, 250 miles away. The inner circle is made up of fifty sand-
stone posts and lintels, weighing up to fifty tons each, which came from
twelve miles north. Laid out according to sacred geometry, with many cosmic
alignments, this arrangement of stones has been shown to be an astro-observatory of sun and moon cycles. (Nineteen-year moon cycles are very complex
and difficult to observe.) The site of Stonehenge is said to be in a globally
unique position, both for astro-observation, and for ley lines, which converge
in a unique and powerful way in this region. It has been suggested that whoever built Stonehenge may have been from elsewhere, having sought out the
ideal spot. According to conventional views, there was no one living on the
Salisbury plain capable of such a structure 5,000 years ago, which is the currently accepted age of Stonehenge.[54]

We must again address the question; why would primitive people go
through the trouble of such a project? Why did they need to make such complex astronomical observations? I've run across many opinions, often from
chanelled sources, saying that Thoth was the mastermind behind the construction of Stonehenge and other enigmatic structures. Alford also believes
this and sites an ancient Egyptian text that mentions Thoth at Stonehenge.[55]
(For more info on Stonehenge, check out the work of astronomers Gerald
Hawkins and Sir Norman Lockyer, philosopher/geomancer John Mitchell and
archeologist Richard Atkinson.)

Equally ancient and enigmatic are the sites of Avebury, Silbury Hill and
Glastonbury, also built on ley lines. Although less awesome than Stonehenge,
the stone circle at **Avebury** is said to predate Stonehenge by 2,000 years.
Consisting of stones, the biggest of which are 60 tons, the circle looks something like the ancient symbol of a solar disc being crossed by a serpent. Not far
away is the huge man-made mound of **Silbury Hill**, which has been dated to

2600 BC. Its purpose is unknown, but the notion that it was an ancient gravesite has been disproved. An ancient place of pilgrimage, **Glastonbury** is reputed to be the site of a church built by Joseph of Arimithea during the time of Christ. He is said to have planted the Glastonbury Thornbush, which botanists confirm as being a species unknown in Europe. It is a species native to the Palestine region. Legend says that here lies the grave of King Arthur and that the Holy Grail is buried here.

The area within the triangle formed by these three sites is steeped in folklore, with many tales of dragons and serpents. Some say it is a dimensional gateway. William Blake believed that it was the site of the post apocalyptic 'New Jerusalem', as mentioned in Revelations in the Bible. It seems to me that, for whatever reason, this portion of the world holds some great significance. The same view must be held by whomever or whatever formed the crop circles, as the majority of them have occurred in this same region.[56]

Chapter 22

THE CROP CIRCLE MYSTERIES

Probably the most mysterious and newsworthy phenomenon of recent times is the ever-evolving story of the crop circles. They first started appearing in the early 1980s in farmers' fields of wheat, corn, barley, rye, rapeseed and oats; areas where the crops had been flattened in circular patterns forming designs that can best be seen from above, as in an airplane. These designs became more complex and appeared more frequently, peaking in 1991. Since then they have diminished in numbers, but have increased drastically in scale and complexity, many of them hinting at some hidden meaning. The early ones were collections of circles forming symmetrical patterns; the later ones were huge picto-graphs, sometimes resembling exotic-looking insects (called insecto-graphs), well-known symbols and complicated geometrical patterns.

There have been occurrences of these enigmatic images in countries all over the world, including Ireland, Sweden, the Netherlands, Germany, Belgium, France, Italy, Spain, Switzerland, Rumania, Hungary, Bulgaria, Czechoslovakia, Turkey, Afghanistan, Egypt, Australia, New Zealand, Japan, Brazil, Puerto Rico, Mexico, the USA and Canada. The majority of crop circle patterns have occurred in England, mostly on ley lines such as the St. Michael Line, which runs from Glastonbury to Avebury. Criss-crossing this line (in the same way as the twin serpents of the Caduceus or the Hermetic Staff of Asclepius, and the Ida and Pingala in yoga) is the Mary Line, the intersection points acting like Earth chakras.

For some strange reason, there has been a great deal of energy expended in an effort to draw public attention away from the crop circles. Unfortunately, these efforts have been very effective, especially the ones that claim that the circles are *mere hoaxes*. So successful was this debunking campaign that even to this day, when crop circles come up in any given conversation, most people dismiss them as having been made by a group of hoaxers with no motive other than to 'put one over' on society. In 1991, a great deal of media attention was given to a pair of beer-drinking pub crawlers named Dave and Doug, who claimed to have made the patterns by flattening crops with boards which were dragged about on ropes. The media let out a collective sigh of relief that the mystery had been solved, and virtually no further coverage was given to the phenomenon, continuing into present time. Since the 'Dave and Doug confession', there has been an increase in counterfeit crop circles. It is widely believed amongst crop circle researchers that hoax groups have been secretly recruited, funded and trained.

Dave and Doug must certainly manage to get around. As previously noted, crop circles happen all over the world. They must also be incredibly gifted artists to produce these remarkably beautiful designs, which are accomplished, without discovery, in the dead of night. That the media could be convinced of their story is truly ludicrous. One quick glance at one of the hoaxed circle patterns is all that one needs to see the difference between them and the real thing. Why did such a denial occur? Who is behind the propagation of this hoax explanation? Crop circle researchers believe that M-15 (Britain's version of the CIA) was involved, as well as the governments of America, Germany and the Vatican.[57]

Authentic crop circles have many *characteristics in common*. Here is a list of such characteristics:

- The circles and other forms within the patterns have crisp, sharp edges. Lines are usually perfectly straight, with circles, ovoids, triangles and other geometrical forms that are often perfect. Hoaxed circles are sloppy, irregular and simple in design.
- The stems of the crops are bent, not broken, usually at the point where they meet the ground. They are laid down in interwoven patterns, with layers criss-crossing each other, and in spiral patterns with different lay directions, both clockwise and counter-clockwise. Hoaxed circles have stems that are broken at various locations along the shaft of the plant and lay on the ground in haphazard ways.
- All of the patterns appear overnight with no one witnessing the process. They are said to happen in an instant. It is hard to imagine that hoaxers could accomplish this in complete darkness and never be discovered.
- Some of the circles are as big as 60 meters in diameter; some of the patterns as long as 200 meters.

- Electro-magnetic 'noises', such as a 5 KHz. buzzing have been recorded at some sites.
- Using computers, the geometric ratios of crop patterns have been translated into diatonic ratios, as in musical scales. When notes are then assigned to correspond to these ratios, it results in a strange, unfamiliar, yet beautiful music. The same process applied to man-made circles results in noise. Research pioneered by Dr. Gerald Hawkins, and then continued by Paul Vigay, shows that crop circle ratios were perfect integers corresponding to the major scale. The chances of this being a coincidence are 1 in 400,000.
- Years later, long after the crop has been harvested and the pattern thus erased, the sites can still be found by dowsers.
- Radioactivity has been measured within the circles.
- Dogs sniffing within the circles have become sick and vomited.
- Many dead houseflies have been found stuck to the kernels of the crops. Usually they are found with their proboscis stuck to the kernel of grain, with all of their legs flayed out as if in some kind of spasm.
- A strange, white, jelly-like substance has been found at some sites. Similar stuff has been found at UFO sightings. It sublimates quickly, but when some successfully reaches the lab, it is found to be an unknown sugar-like substance.
- The ground within many circles is found to be dry while the surrounding ground was wet. This suggests that the ground was heated, causing the crops to become pliable at ground level and fall.
- Crop circles have often been formed during a night when strange sounds and rumblings have been reported. 20% of all crop circle events have been preceded by reports of UFO sightings in the area. Some of these are small, football sized discs of light.[58]

Some researchers have spent considerable effort trying to unravel the *hidden meaning* potential of some of the circle patterns. In general, it has been noted that the pictographs consist of images that are similar to Native American symbols, Jungian archetypical symbols, ancient Sumerian, Egyptian, Celtic and Oriental symbols, mystery school and secret society symbols, sacred geometry and mathematical equations. At this point we'll take a look at a few *specific patterns* and their 'translations'.

- The Mandelbrot Set pictograph occurred in a wheat field south of Cambridge, England on August 13, 1991. This image is a fractal, a representation of a mathematical formula devised by chaos theorist Benoit Mandelbrot, which is generated with a computer. As mentioned earlier, chaos theory suggests that there is order behind all apparent chaos. For this design to appear in a crop field is quite remarkable.[59]
- The Flower of Life pictograph appeared in a field near Hungerford in

August, 1994. This ancient symbol has been found in old Chinese artifacts, Egyptian stone engravings and in various sites around the world. It is a symbol of sacred geometry that speaks of the holographic nature of the universe. (As above, so below.)

- The image which occurred in July, 1992 at Milk Hill, is not a graphic symbol but rather, it appears to be some kind of script. It bears resemblance to Hebrew script which reads, "the Creator wise and kind". It also resembles ancient Sumerian cuneiform script for "Din Gir", which means "fiery chariot of the gods". This is the same insignia reportedly filmed on the side of a UFO at the Holloman Air Force Base in New Mexico.[60]
- The Barbary Castle pictograph located at Swindon in Wiltshire in June, 1991, was known as the 'mother of all pictographs' in its day, but has been dwarfed by some of the more recent occurrences. It is still huge, covering 10,000 square meters. It is similar to many ancient symbols depicting trilogies, as well as the Rosicrucian symbol of godliness, alchemical and Qabalic symbols. It incorporates the sacred geometrical platonic form, the tetrahedron. Many of the angles measurable in this image are identical to angles found in the monuments on Mars, which will be discussed in one of the following sections.[61]
- The Litchfield pictograph happened in 1995 in Hampshire, England. According to information channeled by G. Michael Scallion, the central circle represents Earth and the seven concentric rings represent the seven levels of consciousness; the seventh being the collective consciousness or Akasha. The broad squiggly area surrounding them represents the electromagnetic field with the break representing the coming period of interruption in the field.
- The pictograph at Telegraph Hill near Winchester was also interpreted by Scallion's channeled entities. Again, the central circle is Earth being orbited by the moon and showing the moon's most extreme magnetic effect points.
- The Cowdown pictograph near Andover also has a central Earth circle surrounded by concentric rings representing the dimensions or levels of consciousness. The zigzag lines radiating out from center illustrate the notion that actions on the physical plane affect all the higher dimensions of the planet.[62]
- Some of the pictographs from 2001, including the one at Milk Hill mentioned at the beginning of Part Five, are truly astonishing. On August 17, two remarkable crop images happened near Wherwell, again in Hampshire. One is a pixilated face staring up into the sky, framed by a rectangle. It is done in a 'dot-raster' technique, which is usually used by printers. It is eerily reminiscent of the face on Mars. It is virtually impossible to imagine this image being done by hand. The second image is even more remarkable.

Appearing in the same field at the same time, it is the exact replica of a digitally encoded schematic beamed into space on November 16, 1974 from the Arecibo radio telescope at Puerto Rico. This schematic was broadcast as part of NASA's 'Search for Extra Terrestrial Intelligence' (SETI) in the hopes of communicating with some ET life form!

- The year 2002 yielded another amazing array of designs. The most noteworthy of these is another face that appeared near Sparsholt (aka Crabwood), close to Winchester, Hampshire, UK on August 15th, 2002. This face, done in a 'line-raster', is more defined than the one in 2001 and looks much more distinctly like the face of an ET. In the bottom right of the formation is a disc containing what looks like some sort of code.[63]
- The crop-circle season of 2003 saw another amazing batch of designs, but none of them are as noteworthy as the ones already mentioned.

So what is to be made of this amazing phenomenon? *How can we explain it?* What is going on? There are several theories.

When Hopi elders were shown photos of pictographs, they immediately recognized some of the symbols. They became distraught and emotional, claiming that the images were messages of distress coming from the consciousness of the planet.[64]

Isabelle Kingston is a psychic who has accurately predicted the location of certain crop circle patterns. She claims to be in touch with a group called 'the Watchers', known to the Egyptians as the 'Neteru', and that they are helping to prepare Earth for a new era, a new frequency. They do this by 'charging the ley lines' with crop circles formed by earth/akashic energies, which are manipulated and facilitated by the Watchers. Many of the planet's key ley lines are located in England.[65]

According to information channeled through psychic and futurist, Gordon Michael Scallion, non-physical entities called 'Etherians' are working in conjunction with Pleiadians, Sirians (the root races of Earth) and other intelligences to send us messages designed to awaken us to changes, responsibility, divinity and the knowledge that we are not alone. This must be done in a way that does not interfere with our free will, does not spoon-feed us the answers, but assists us in discovering them for ourselves. Scallion claims that the circles are made with "highly charged particles of light, so compressed as to emit strong gravitational and magnetic fields" that move "in stylus fashion". These "small spheres of red plasma" are robotically guided to produce symbols, which are the language of the higher mind. In accordance with the philosophies of Carl Jung, these 'archetypical' symbols can subliminally or sub-consciously communicate massive amounts of non-linear information in an instant.[66]

Experiments done with diviners suggest that crop circles discharge pent up earth-energy, possibly resulting from the increase in the planet's base resonant frequency. Cambridge University biochemist, Rupert Sheldrake, refers to this as some form of 'Earth acupuncture'. He also has suggested that the morphogenetic field (the consciousness of Earth) is accessing symbols from the Akasha (the collective consciousness of humanity) in an effort to communicate with us.[67]

Some opinions hold that the Annunaki, the Elohim, or whatever name one wants to use, are preparing us for their return. It has been suggested that the only thing preventing ETs from contacting us directly, is that it would cause an enormous upsurge of low frequency 'fear-energy', which is definitely not what the planet needs at this time. Crop circles are examples of efforts being made to prepare the human consciousness, so that the thought of ET entities conjures up feelings of love, rather than fear. At that point, help can be directly asked for, and thus provided without interfering with our free will process.

Chapter 23

UFOs, LIVESTOCK MUTILATIONS AND ABDUCTIONS

There have been countless books written on this subject, ranging from well-researched journalism to ridiculous sensationalism, and I will not spend much time writing about it here. For a well-rounded overview of various cases, check out 'The UFO Encyclopedia', by Margaret Sachs, 'Above Top Secret', by Timothy Good, and 'Alien Identities', by Richard Thompson.

Most people regard this phenomenon as belonging to modern times, but there is actually a *history of UFO reports*. Strange sightings in the skies, which have recently been dubbed 'unidentified flying objects', have been reported for thousands of years and historical references to them can be found in several old texts. Here is an example of an excerpt from writer, Julius Obsequens in 216 BC, from his book, 'Prodigorium Liber':

> "Things like ships were seen in the sky over Italy....At Arpi, a round shield was seen in the sky....At Capua, the sky was all on fire, and one saw figures like ships...."

Similar accounts came from Cicero, the Roman statesman, and many occurred at the time of Charlemagne, when even human abductions were reported. As previously mentioned, countless references in ancient Mesopotamia, Egypt and the Americas, including several from the Bible, could easily be interpreted as being about strange flying craft. For a more thorough accounting of ancient UFO sightings, please refer to the works of Harold T. Wilkins and Jacques Vallee.[68]

Although the majority of sightings do not get reported, hundreds of claims of some type of contact with a UFO are reported each year. Of these reports it is said that about 90% are explainable phenomena, 2% are hoaxes, and about 8% are unexplainable and appear to be extra-terrestrial.[69] Probably the most well known and irrefutable UFO incident is the one that took place at **Roswell**, New Mexico, in July, 1947, where many witnessed a UFO crash in the desert and the government cover-up that followed. I saw a TV documentary that showed a movie in which a group of white-coated doctors are doing an autopsy on an alien corpse retrieved from the Roswell crash. It had the delicate, thin, grey body, bulbous head and large, almond-shaped eyes that have become typical of most mental images of an ET. Some have claimed that the movie was probably produced using high-tech, Hollywood special effects, but tests have shown that the celluloid came from the 1940s when such special effects were unheard of and highly unlikely. So many reputable people have spoken up about what they saw and about the government threats and bullying in the ensuing cover-up, that the Roswell incident has become very difficult to deny.[70]

According to several inside whistle-blowers, an incident took place at the **Holloman Air Force Base** in New Mexico on April 25, 1964, which was recorded on film. The footage shows a UFO landing at the base, three ETs emerge, are greeted by military personnel and escorted into an office building. It is said that they met with President Dwight Eisenhower at a subsequent landing at the Edwards Air Force Base. A drawing of the ET looks very similar to the image on an ancient artifact from the Assyrian city of Kachu. The insignia on the side of the space-craft looks like the ancient Sumerian symbol 'Din-Gir', which translates as 'righteous ones in fiery chariots'. This same image occurred in a crop formation at Milk Hill in July, 1992.[71]

In 1994, the FBI had accumulated about 24,000 reports of cases of **livestock mutilations**, mostly cows and horses. These reports have many **characteristics in common:**

- The carcasses have had organs removed, most often reproductive organs, with what appears to be laser cuts.
- Many of the carcasses have broken bones, as if they had been dropped from a height.
- Mutilated bodies are often marked with potassium and magnesium powder, which is visible under ultra-violet light.
- Circular 'landing marks' are often found nearby. Reports of mysterious lights, sounds and sightings often accompany the mutilations.

Professor David Jacobs of Temple University has studied 300 cases of **human abductions** in America between 1986 and 1991. The 'abductees', whose memories were accessed under hypnosis, report the same fundamental pattern.

They claim to have been given medical examinations, to have had sperm and eggs taken from them, given short explanations and then told to forget. Some claim to have been shown live embryos growing in laboratory settings. Some examinations of abductees have discovered small implants under the skin or in the brain, which can be seen with x-rays. Alleged abductions from other parts of the world report similar circumstances. The common denominator with these reports is that the abductors were obsessed with functions of reproduction.[72] The most common criticism of these claims by doubters, is that people under hypnosis are highly susceptible to suggestion and that memories can just as easily be some one else's ideas.

Some compelling information about ETs and government cover-ups, etc, has come from 'insiders'. A former member of American Naval Intelligence, Bill Cooper, in his book, 'Behold a Pale Horse', claims that the 'power elite' has been co-operating with a race of ETs since the '40s, trading permission for the abductions and livestock experiments in ex-change for technology, especially computer technology. (People involved with the Philadelphia Experiment and the Phoenix Project say that ETs provided information about anti-gravity, free energy, mind control and time travel.) Cooper puts the finger on specific government offices and projects designed to mislead the public and to thwart investigation into this phenomenon.[73]

Another insider is Bob Dean, an officer in NATO's Cosmic Top Secret Level, who claims to have been privy to many cases of UFOs and even of ET carcasses found in Europe in the 60s. He believes that many different races of ETs have been interacting with humans for thousands of years. Some of them are benevolent and some are here for reasons that are more self-serving.

Drunvalo Melchizadek tells of the 'Greys', a race of ETs that came to Earth because their survival was being threatened by their own left-brain imbalance. They had forsaken 'heart' knowledge for 'brain' knowledge to the point where they lost the ability to procreate naturally. They came to this planet to research the reproductive process and possibly to find a new home. These ETs had made agreements with the secret governments of several countries, including the US, Russia and Germany at the time of Hitler, trading for technology. They were highly manipulative, but were prevented from doing too much damage by other ET races, and were turfed out of here in the early 1990s. Drunvalo claims (*and I tend to believe*) that there are a great many races and types of entities who are 'parked' in the overtone above ours, patiently watching, interested to see how we will react to the enormous change that is coming our way.[74] They are not alarmed or worried. They know that, whatever move we make, the Game will continue.

Chapter 24

MARS, VENUS AND THE MOON

There is a fair bit of controversy about Mars these days, mostly due to the contention that NASA has photographs of some strange, apparently artificial ***monuments on Mars***. In 1976 the Viking 1 began to orbit the red planet, taking many photographs of its surface. Several of these photos reveal structures that appear to be artificial. Some of them look similar to some of the Inca walls. Others look similar to the Nazca lines, long, straight patterns etched into the planet's surface.

The most enigmatic photos were taken at a site on Mars that has been named Cydonia. Several of the landmarks in this region seem to be artificially constructed. They consist of the ruins of at least seven ***pyramids*** of varying sizes and a mysterious face that stares out into space. They are within close proximity to each other and appear like they could have been a part of some ancient city. The largest of the pyramids, which has been named the D & M pyramid, is five sided and is ten times the height and one thousand times the volume of the Great Pyramid at Giza. These pyramids are said to be made up of significant angles, both in their structure and their layout. These angles are said to correspond with the angles in the Barbary Castle crop pattern that appeared at Swindon, Wiltshire in June of 1991, as well as other crop circle patterns. They also correspond to some of the angles and proportions of the Giza pyramids.

The mysterious ***face on Mars*** has gained a fair amount of notoriety. It is a two square kilometer mound of dirt that looks much like a face staring upward from the surface of the planet. A crop pattern that appeared on August 17, 2001 near Wherwell in Hampshire is a depiction of a face looking straight up from the Earth's surface, which resembles the face on Mars.

When these photographs first surfaced they received a flurry of attention at a NASA press conference, but were quickly dismissed by Nasa officials as being insignificant. A few years later two scientists, Vincent DiPietro and Gregory Molenaar got their hands on the photos and began their own investigation. They got no support from NASA and it seemed to them that there was some sort of a cover-up regarding the face and pyramids. After the initial interest, very little further reporting appeared in the press. However, many scientists including Carl Sagan went on record saying that further investigation was warranted. It was suggested that any future mission to Mars include detailed high-resolution photos of the structures at Cydonia. If subsequent missions to the red planet have secured such photos, the authorities have made no mention of it to the public.

The mission of Viking 1 was to take many photos, partially for the purpose of determining a good location for the landing of Viking 2. Before the discovery of the face and pyramid structures, Cydonia was recommended as a place where there was a good chance of finding signs of life and water. After the controversial photos were discovered and then dismissed by NASA as being a "trick of lighting and shadow", it was decided not to have Viking 2 land at Cydonia. It was decided that it would land in a relatively insignificant region for no particularly good reason. It seems reasonable that even the remotest possibility of artificial structures on Mars would have been motive enough to merit a landing at Cydonia.

Up until the year 2000, the Russians and the Americans have sent a total of thirteen probes to Mars. Out of that number, eight have been unsuccessful for varying reasons. Such a poor success rate in itself is something of an enigma. Many of these failings have occurred under strange circumstances. On March 27th, 1989, the Russian probe 'Phobos II' was beaming pictures of the Martian surface back to Earth when it suddenly went blank and was never heard from again. The last images before blackout showed a large, dark, anomalous object in the space between the probe and the planet surface. The probe was in the process of telecasting the image of a strange marking on Mars that resembled some kind of a runway. To some investigators, these circumstances suggest the possibility that the Phobos II was shot down. In 1992, the 'Mars Observer', a probe that was equipped to take high resolution photos of the Martian surface, was reported by NASA as having gone missing just before its scheduled arrival. In 2000 another Martian probe went missing. Some investigators find these incidents suspicious.[75]

For more information on the monuments of Cydonia and other related mysteries, I recommend 'The Monuments of Mars' by Richard Hoagland, and 'The Mars Mystery' by Graham Hancock.

Somewhat less controversial and less publicized are the enigmas associated with *the Moon*. According to researcher William Bradley, photos of six mysterious pyramid shaped spires on the surface of the Moon were taken by the 'Orbiter 2' on November 22, 1966. The discovery of the pyramid shapes, which were arranged in a purposeful geometric pattern, was reported in the *Washington Post* and the *L. A. Times*.[76]

Our Moon is by far the biggest, in relation to the size of the host planet, than any other planet in our solar system. It is also the only moon of the inner planets, as the moons of Mars are thought to be asteroids that have been caught and set in orbit by the planet's gravity. There is controversy as to the origin of our Moon, some claiming that it could be a piece that was broken off of Earth or born of the same cosmic dust cloud as Earth. Others saying that it is more likely a small planet unto itself which has been captured by Earth's gravity. Sitchin claims that the Moon has been shown to consist of a different chemical makeup than Earth. He believes that, although it may be related, the Moon was not born of the Earth.

Researcher David Hatcher Childress has many strange things to say about the Moon in his book, 'Extraterrestrial Archeology'. Amongst them is the claim that, when the Moon was struck by the spent components or stages of the Oppollo craft, it emitted a mysterious ringing sound that lasted for up to four hours. Some have offered the possibility that the Moon is hollow. Hatcher says that moon rocks have been found to contain a form of iron that does not rust, something that is unheard of. He says that high radioactivity has been recorded there. He points out that there is relatively little dust on the lunar surface, thousands of years of accumulation rather than millions. He reports that strange domes, streaks and lights have been observed in a lunar crater called the 'Plato Crater', which seem to appear and disappear. There are also reports of other strange and unnatural structures that resemble walls, domes, platforms, etc.[77]

Zecharia Sitchin believes that the Anunaki took advantage of the reduced gravity of Mars and the Moon to dock their larger ships, so that they could access Earth in smaller craft.

Finally, a few words about **Venus**. It is the only planet in our solar system to revolve in the opposite direction. Scientists speculate that some great collision may have caused this retrograde motion, which is very slow, taking 243 Earth days for one rotation. Venus was very important to the ancient Mayans, who had recorded a good deal of information about it. According to channeled information, there are three pyramids and a sphinx-like structure on the face of Venus. Its thick, impenetrable atmosphere makes it very hot and inhospitable to life as we know it. However, it is said that there are entities living there called the Hathors. Some describe them as physical beings, fourteen feet tall, living in a higher overtone of the third realm. Some say they are a nonphysical, very advanced and beautiful race of Christ-conscious beings living in the fourth realm. They exist in a constant state of love.

So what do we make of all of this? Fossilized shoeprints, the wonders of the Great Pyramid, the amazing crop circles, monuments on Mars—it's enough to make your brain rattle!

I guess it's safe to say that my opinion lies somewhere between the eye-rolling naysayers and the wide-eyed embracers of anything weird. I have to make the point, yet again, that it is less important for me to have all the answers or to have staunch opinions, than it is to recognize that we know very little with certainty. I feel comfortable with the opinion that our dominant paradigms are inadequate and are holding us back. I believe that, if the establishment funded some truly open minded and sincere research, with no hidden agenda, we would learn some things that would rock our world. *I believe that our collective evolution toward enlightenment will be greatly facilitated if we pull our collective head out of the sand. I also believe that, if we demand answers and refuse to accept lies and deceit, the power elite will be forced to show us the information that we already possess.*

I admit that I do tend to believe that there have always been forces at work, intelligences if you like, that are trying to send us messages. They do so in a variety of ways and from a variety of perspectives. Most of these forces, the advanced ones, send us messages with an attitude of playfulness and genuine curiosity. Whether we accept these messages is totally up to us, they are not worried. From their perspective and their level of awareness, they are observing us with great compassion and interest, wondering what we're going to do next. The great experiment of life, the Game, proceeds at its own pace.

ENDNOTES—PART FIVE

1. White, John—*Pole Shift*, A.R.E. Press, 1996, Virginia Beach VA, p. 99–102, and Wilson, Colin—*From Atlantis to the Sphinx*, Virgin Books, 1997, London, p. 100–104
2. *Ancient America Magazine,* Vol. 4, Issue # 30
3. *Ancient America Magazine,* Vol. 4, Issue # 28
4. Baigent, Michael—*Ancient Traces*, Penguin Books, 1998, London, p. 103–106
5. Dunn, Christopher—*The Giza Powerplant*, Bear & Company, 1998, Santa Fe, NM, p. 55–59
6. Wilson, Colin—*From Atlantis to the Sphinx*, Virgin Books, 1997, London, p. 74–75
7. Dunn, Christopher—*The Giza Powerplant*, Bear & Company, 1998, Santa Fe, NM, p. 132–133
8. Moon, P. and Nichols, Preston—*Pyramids of Montauk*, Sky Books, 1994, New York
9. Wilson, Colin—*From Atlantis to the Sphinx*, Virgin Books, 1997, London, p. 63 and Hope, Murray—*Atlantis, Myth or Reality?*, Penguin Books, 1991, London, p. 251
10. Wilson, Colin—*From Atlantis to the Sphinx*, Virgin Books, 1997, London, p. 81–87
11. Frissell, Bob—*Nothing in This Book Is True, But It's Exactly How Things Are* , Frog Ltd., 1994, Berkely, CA, p. 45
12. Wilson, Colin—*From Atlantis to the Sphinx*, Virgin Books, 1997, London, p. 66–72 and Alford, Alan—*Gods of the New Millennium*, Hodder and Stoughton, 1997, London, p. 123–131
13. Dunn, Christopher—*The Giza Powerplant*, Bear & Company, 1998, Santa Fe, NM, p. 6
14. Wilson, Colin—*From Atlantis to the Sphinx*, Virgin Books, 1997, London, p. 75–76
15. Dunn, Christopher—*The Giza Powerplant*, Bear & Company, 1998, Santa Fe, NM, a summary of Dunn's views.
16. Hancock, Graham—*The Sign and the Seal*, Doubleday Canada, Ltd., 1993, Toronto, p. 311
17. Dunn, Christopher—*The Giza Powerplant*, Bear & Company, 1998, Santa Fe, NM, p. 106–108
18. Cerminara, Gina—*Insights for the Age of Aquarius*, Quest Books, 1973, London, p. 198
19. Dunn, Christopher—*The Giza Powerplant*, Bear & Company, 1998, Santa Fe, NM, p. 231
20. ibid. p. 168–172
21. ibid. p. 96
22. Hancock, Graham—*The Sign and the Seal*, Doubleday Canada, Ltd., 1993, Toronto, p. 369–370
23. Hope, Murray—*Atlantis, Myth or Reality?*, Penguin Books, 1991, London, p. 252
24. ibid. p. 251
25. Dunn, Christopher—*The Giza Powerplant*, Bear & Company, 1998, Santa Fe, NM, p. 5

26. Alford, Alan—*Gods of the New Millennium*, Hodder and Stoughton, 1997, London, p. 134
27. Wilson, Colin—*From Atlantis to the Sphinx*, Virgin Books, 1997, London, p. 53–54
28. Hope, Murray—*Atlantis, Myth or Reality?*, Penguin Books, 1991, London, p. 252
29. Alford, Alan—*Gods of the New Millennium*, Hodder and Stoughton, 1997, London, p. 276
30. Hope, Murray—*Atlantis, Myth or Reality?*, Penguin Books, 1991, London, p. 62
31. Wilson, Colin—*From Atlantis to the Sphinx*, Virgin Books, 1997, London, p. 54–56
32. Moon, P. and Nichols, Preston—*Pyramids of Montauk,* Sky Books, 1994, New York
33. Alford, Alan—*Gods of the New Millennium*, Hodder and Stoughton, 1997, London, p. 144–148
34. Cremo, M. and Thompson, R.—*Forbidden Archeology,* San Diego, 1993. A summary of the work of Cremo and Thompson as reported by Baigent, Michael—*Ancient Traces*, Penguin Books, 1998, London
35. Alford, Alan—*Gods of the New Millennium*, Hodder and Stoughton, 1997, London, p. 94–95
36. ibid. p. 74–80
37. ibid. p. 80–92
38. Wilson, Colin—*From Atlantis to the Sphinx*, Virgin Books, 1997, London, p. 149–150
39. Hope, Murray—*Atlantis, Myth or Reality?*, Penguin Books, 1991, London, p. 180
40. Alford, Alan—*Gods of the New Millennium*, Hodder and Stoughton, 1997, London, p. 473–475
41. ibid. p. 92–101
42. ibid. p. 101–107
43. Wilson, Colin—*From Atlantis to the Sphinx*, Virgin Books, 1997, London, p. 162–164
44. Alford, Alan—*Gods of the New Millennium*, Hodder and Stoughton, 1997, London, p. 483–488
45. Cotterell, Maurice—*The Tutankhamen Prophecies,* Headline Books, 1999, London p. 9–11
46. Wilson, Colin—*From Atlantis to the Sphinx*, Virgin Books, 1997, London, p. 135 and Alford, Alan—*Gods of the New Millennium*, Hodder and Stoughton, 1997, London, p. 155–156
47. Wilson, Colin—*From Atlantis to the Sphinx*, Virgin Books, 1997, London, p. 164–165, and Alford, Alan—*Gods of the New Millennium*, Hodder and Stoughton, 1997, London, p. 157–158, and Cotterell, Maurice—*The Tutankhamen Prophecies,* Headline Books, 1999, London, p. 8–9
48. Wilson, Colin—*From Atlantis to the Sphinx*, Virgin Books, 1997, London, p. 126–132, and Alford, Alan—*Gods of the New Millennium*, Hodder and Stoughton, 1997, London, p. 547
49. Wilson, Colin—*From Atlantis to the Sphinx*, Virgin Books, 1997, London, p. 153
50. Cotterell, Maurice—*The Tutankhamen Prophecies,* Headline Books, 1999, London. A summary of Cotterell's views.
51. Wilson, Colin—*From Atlantis to the Sphinx*, Virgin Books, 1997, London, p. 154–159 and Alford, Alan—*Gods of the New Millennium*, Hodder and Stoughton, 1997, London, p. 466–469
52. Alford, Alan—*Gods of the New Millennium*, Hodder and Stoughton, 1997, London, p. 469–473
53. Wilson, Colin—*From Atlantis to the Sphinx*, Virgin Books, 1997, London, p. 122
54. Alford, Alan—*Gods of the New Millennium*, Hodder and Stoughton, 1997, London, p. 148–152
55. ibid. p. 377–379
56. Heseman, Michael—*The Cosmic Connection,* Gateway Books, 1996, Bath UK, p. 9–15
57. ibid. p. 28–32
58. These characteristics are summarized from the work of Heseman (ibid.) and Haselhoff, Eltjo—*The Deepening Complexity of Crop Circles,* Frog Ltd, 2001, Berkely
59. Heseman, Michael—*The Cosmic Connection,* Gateway Books, 1996, Bath UK, p. 38 –39
60. ibid. p. 114–115
61. ibid. p. 38, 111–112, 133–135
62. Scallion, Gordon-Michael—*Notes From the Cosmos*, Matrix Institute, Inc., 1987, Chesterfield NH, p. 218–230

63. This information comes from the following web-sites; **www.cropcircleconnector.com** and **www.temporarytemples.co.uk**

64. Heseman, Michael—*The Cosmic Connection,* Gateway Books, 1996, Bath UK, p. 123

65. ibid. p. 95–114

66. Scallion, Gordon-Michael—*Notes From the Cosmos*, Matrix Institute, Inc., 1987, Chesterfield NH, p. 218–230

67. Heseman, Michael—*The Cosmic Connection,* Gateway Books, 1996, Bath UK, p. 93

68. Bramley, William—*The Gods of Eden* , Avon Books, 1990, New York, p. 11

69. ibid. p. 11

70. Thompson, Richard—*Alien Identities,* Govardhan Hill Publishing, 1993, Badger, CA, p. 103—110

71. Heseman, Michael—*The Cosmic Connection,* Gateway Books, 1996, Bath UK, p. 114–115

72. ibid. 120–122

73. Frissell, Bob—*Nothing in This Book Is True, But It's Exactly How Things Are* , Frog Ltd., 1994, Berkely, CA, p. 2–3

74. From 18 hours of video—Flower of Life Workshop—Drunvalo Melchizedek

75. Hoagland Richard C.—*The Monuments on Mars*, Frog, Ltd, 1996, Berkely, CA Hancock, Graham—*The Mars Mystery*, Crown Publishers, 1998, New York. A summary of the work of Hoagland and Hancock.

76. Bramley, William—*The Gods of Eden* , Avon Books, 1990, New York, p. 59

77. Childress, David Hatcher—*Extraterrestrial Archaeology*, Adventures Unlimited Press, 1995, Stelle, Ill., p. 33–45

Part Six

Bible Roots and Western Religion

Chapter 25

LEVITICUS AND THE HOMOSEXUAL

A few years ago there was an interesting story circulating on the Internet. It had to do with an American radio personality whose name I'll refrain from mentioning. She was the host of a phone-in talk show on which she dispensed advice. One day she was questioned as to what the Bible had to say about homosexuality. Was it something that was considered wrong according to the Bible? In her response she said that, according to the Bible, homosexuality is an abomination and cannot be condoned under any circumstance. That's what was written in Leviticus 18:22. In response to this advice, a man named Jim wrote a letter, which was posted on the Internet. This is what it said.

Dear Dr. Radio Host:

Thank you for doing so much to educate people regarding God's Law. I have learned a great deal from your show, and try to share that knowledge with as many people as I can. When someone tries to defend the homosexual lifestyle, for example, I simply remind them that Leviticus 18:22 clearly states it to be an abomination. End of debate. I do need some advice from you, however, regarding some of the other specific Biblical laws and how to follow them.

1. When I burn a bull on the altar as a sacrifice, I know it creates a pleasing odor for the Lord (Lev.1:9). The problem is my neighbors. They claim the odor is not pleasing to them. Should I smite them?

2. I would like to sell my daughter into slavery, as sanctioned in Exodus 21:7. In this day and age, what do you think would be a fair price for her?

3. I know that I am allowed no contact with a woman while she is in her period of menstrual uncleanliness (Lev.15:19-24). The problem is, how do I tell? I have tried asking, but most women take offense.

4. Lev. 25:44 states that I may indeed possess slaves, both male and female, provided they are purchased from neighboring nations. A friend of mine claims that this applies to Mexicans, but not Canadians. Can you clarify? Why can't I own Canadians?

5. I have a neighbor who insists on working on the Sabbath. This is clearly in violation of the wise Laws and ordinances listed in Exodus 21 through 23. Am I morally obligated to kill him myself?

6. A friend of mine feels that even though eating shellfish is an abomination (Lev. 11:10), it is a lesser abomination than homosexuality. I don't agree. Can you settle this?

7. Lev. 21:20 states that I may not approach the altar of God if I have a defect in my sight. I have to admit that I wear reading glasses. Does my vision have to be 20/20, or is there some wiggle room here?

8. Most of my male friends get their hair trimmed, including the hair around their temples, even though this is expressly forbidden by Lev.19:27. How should they die?

9. I know from Lev. 11:6-8 that touching the skin of a dead pig makes me unclean, but may I still play football if I wear gloves?

10. My uncle has a farm. He violates Lev. 19:19 by planting two different crops in the same field, as does his wife by wearing garments made of two different kinds of thread (cotton/polyester blend). He also tends to curse and blaspheme a lot. Is it really necessary that we go to the trouble of getting the whole town together to stone them? (Lev.24:10-16). Couldn't we just burn them to death at a private family affair like we do with people who sleep with their in-laws? (Lev. 20:14)

I know you have studied these things extensively, so I am confident you can help. Thank you again for reminding us that God's word is eternal and unchanging.

Your devoted fan, Jim.

Next time you're in a hotel room, look in the drawers and, sure enough, you will likely find a Bible. To this day we use them to swear oaths of truth in our courts of law. At any given moment one could probably find, on some television channel, an evangelist waving a Bible and professing it to be the word of God. As demonstrated in the above story, some very questionable advice and guidance is being dispensed because of some strange Bible passages or quotes taken out of context. These quotes are often a part of some list of rules and ordinances, many of which are just plain ludicrous. Can the Bible really guide us in some of the pressing issues of our day?

There is no question, it is a very powerful book that has played an enormous role in our history and is deeply engrained in the western psyche. Wars have been and are being fought based on ideas and information first encountered in the Bible. This book and the religions surrounding it have exerted an iron grip of control over the minds and wills of a large percentage of the world's people. The leaders of some of the world's most powerful nations, including the USA, constantly pay lip service to this book. Very few westerners today have belief systems that have not been significantly influenced by it. And yet, very few of us know much about the book. Its history, its origins, and many aspects of it, including the history of its associated religions, remain a mystery.

Of all of the talks I've given in the past, this topic always fills me with a certain amount of trepidation. There is usually a palpable amount of tension in the room. Sometimes, about thirty minutes into the presentation, a disgruntled Bible enthusiast has left frowning, appalled that any-one would question it in any way. I've received the odd letter of indignation, several days after the talk. This occurs even after I've explained, ad nauseam, that I'm not there to change anybody's belief systems, to try to win anyone over to my way of thinking, or to make any definitive statements about the Bible. All I do is present a wide range of information, much of which has come to light in the past 100 years, that is different to the unquestioned, widely held views of most people. It is designed only to provoke thought, to satisfy my own desire for understanding and to share my thoughts and beliefs. Some people simply do not want to see such information.

For the most part, everyone in the western world has some sort of strong belief about the Bible in which they are heavily invested. Any questioning of this view makes many people very uncomfortable. It is remarkable that a piece of writing with such a huge influence in our lives is so seldom questioned or examined. Many people still adhere to the notion that this 'word of God' is unquestionable, and that to challenge the Bible is blasphemous and heretical. On the other hand, many people are curious about the roots of this great work. Many have instinctive feelings or suspicions that all is not as it seems regarding this book.

I remember attending catechism class in the earliest years of public school. I remember the first time I was introduced to the concept of 'fear of the Lord'. We were told that it was a good thing to have a healthy fear of the Lord. I remember having a strong reaction in the pit of my stomach at the time. Something did not feel right about that statement. How could there be anything to fear from a God who was all-loving and all-knowing?

All these years later, after the research I've done and the hours I've spent contemplating, I have some serious questions regarding the Bible and its associated religions. I have to ask, are these things aiding mankind or are they hindering our progress toward enlightenment?

At this point, I'm going to stick my neck out and make this declaration. I believe that there are a great many profound nuggets of wisdom, as well as useful historical information and clues to the many mysteries, that can be found in the Bible. It has been said by Qabalists that there are four levels of meaning to the Torah, the first five books of the Old Testament; the literal meaning, the allegorical meaning, the Hermeneutical meaning, and the mystical meaning. There is important information in the Bible that is encoded in various ways, such as numerologically. If we could access such information in a reliable way, I believe it would be of great benefit to mankind. However, I also believe that the Bible has been used, throughout its existence, as a tool to manipulate and control the masses. With that end in mind, it has been edited, misinterpreted and mistranslated to the point that it now contains a good amount of misinformation, nonsense and outright lies. I believe that it has come to be very difficult to distinguish between the wheat and the chaff.

I believe it has also suffered distortion of 'truth' or original intent due to honest misunderstanding and the inherent difficulties and pitfalls of rendering a compilation of ancient texts, written by many hands, into a comprehensive package. With all of these multi-motivated distortions, it is hard to know whether the Bible was ever a useful tool to help humanity move toward enlightenment. Whether it is a useful tool in the modern era is even more questionable. (I believe this to be true of most, if not all, of the 'bibles' of the other major religions. Although I may refer occasionally to the other religions, this chapter mostly deals with the Judeo-Christian traditions with which I am more familiar.)

Earlier in the book I said that I believed that the discipline of science may be of limited use because of its insistence on proof as provided by the five senses. Certainly the opposite can be said of the discipline of religion. It would be of much more use to humanity if we did insist on a bit more evidence regarding the information in the various bibles, and especially the interpretations of such information, which have been presented as unchallengeable truth by the religious organizations.

This part of the book will take a look at the Bible and the roots of western religion from the traditional viewpoint, the scholarly/academic viewpoint and the alternative viewpoint. The Bible is a compilation, a collection of shorter books from a variety of sources, which we'll attempt to uncover. How was it compiled, who compiled it and why? These questions will be applied separately to the Old and New Testaments. Where did the Genesis stories come from? Who was Moses? What was the Ark of the Covenant? How does the latest body of archeological evidence fit with the information and history presented in the Old Testament? It will also look at a variety of information about life at the time of Jesus, including the roles of Jesus, Mary Magdalene, John the Baptist, the Essenes, the Romans and other characters. What happened in the centuries after Jesus? How did religion become organized? What is the history of the Christian Church?

Hopefully, after this examination, we'll be able to determine for ourselves whether the Bible and its religions are useful to us in our quest for enlightenment.

Chapter 26

THE INHERENT DIFFICULTIES OF UNDERSTANDING THE BIBLE

Before jumping in, I thought it would be wise to take a look at some of the pitfalls inherent in the process of trying to make sense of a work like the Bible. I recommend a delightful book by Gina Cerminara, 'Insights for the Age of Aquarius', which takes a thorough look at these problems. Any body of writing is wrought with obstacles, which make it difficult for the reader to glean the pure message intended by the author. A philosophy that analyses these difficulties is known as General Semantics, pioneered by Alfred Korzybski in the early 20th century. Cerminara applies this system to the Bible. This is not the place for a detailed examination of all the obstacles to communication, but in the following brief section, I will try to summarize some of them.

Even with the best of intentions and the best of circumstances, tests have demonstrated the ***difficulty of communication*** in general. The movement of words from person to person naturally results in the distortion of meaning. Tests done by William Stern in 1902 showed that a number of observers reporting on the same event would invariably yield an equal number of different accounts. The accuracy of any report depends on the ability of the reporter to perceive, interpret and then retain a body of information.[2]

In the world of religion, most texts are collections of the 'reports' of the teachings of a third person, often hundreds of years after the fact. Tests have shown that significant distortion of the meaning of a body of information takes place immediately after a 'reporter' has been exposed to the information. How much meaning is lost after many years have gone by? The teachings of Jesus, Buddha and Mohammed, for example, all exist in writing due to the reporting of others, usually after a significant amount of time.

As already mentioned, the integrity of a body of information becomes threatened by the **compilation process**, in which someone else decides which portions are kept or rejected. Almost all of the world's religions have undergone this process. The Sikh Bible consists of the teachings of Granth Sahib as assembled by Guru Arjan. In Jainism there are two branches, each with a distinct collection of texts. A year after the death of Mohammed, Muslim leader Abu Bekr compiled his teachings from those followers who could remember Mohammed's words. Twelve years later, Caliph Othman revised them and destroyed all previous compilations. A collection of Gautama Buddha's sayings known as the Dhammapada was compiled many years after his death by the Indian monarch, Asoka. The Pali Canon, a collection of Buddhist scriptures from oral traditions was put together about 500 years after the fact. The list goes on and on.[3]

Another problem is **distortion by omission**. There are, for example, many more gospels than the four that appear in the New Testament. Many of these have been collectively called the Gnostic Gospels. (More on this later.) In the Essene Gospel of John, Jesus extols the virtues of vegetarianism. In the Gospel of the Holy Twelve, he demonstrates and calls for kindness to all animals. The omission of these and many other teachings, including the deletion of all references to reincarnation, resulted in a significant misrepresentation of Jesus' message. Despite the fact that most great teachers, such as Jesus and Buddha, treated men and women equally, many religions have chosen to omit from their scriptures anything that was written by a woman.[4]

The original intent of the source of a message can be referred to as 'meaning'. We'll now show several ways in which meaning can be lost as it travels from the source to the recipient. A particular statement can have meaning that corresponds to the time in which it was written. We are all familiar with the statement, "If you drink, don't drive." We all know what it means, but hundreds of years from now, someone reading such a statement out of **time context** may ask, "Drink what? Drive what?" Someone may then interpret that it means that one should not drink any type of beverage while driving a golf ball or a nail. What is common knowledge in one era may be totally unheard of in another.[5]

There are other ways in which the context is crucial to the meaning. A great teacher would not give the same advice to a humble person that s/he would to an arrogant person. The group of sayings called the Beatitudes that Jesus is said to have given in the Sermon on the Mount can be very controversial and open to interpretation. For example, "Give to them that ask of thee" may be good advice to someone lacking in the virtue of generosity, but it is hardly good advice to someone who is gullible and of whom others are always taking advantage.

Scholars now believe that it is most likely that the Sermon on the Mount never occurred and that the beatitudes are a collection of Jesus' sayings that came from a variety of contexts, that is, they were said to different groups of people at different times and places. The meaning of such a saying would be much clearer if the correct context were known.[6]

Another pitfall is the tendency of the message recipient to look for a **hidden meaning**. While I'm sure that many passages of Biblical texts do have hidden meanings, the interpretations of such meanings are highly subjective and can vary widely. There is also the distinct possibility that hidden meaning could be assigned to passages where there were none. Anyone familiar with the Peter Sellers movie, 'Being There', will remember the scene during which Sellers' character, Chancey Gardener, responds to a question by saying, "There will be growth again in the spring." He was a simple gardener who was talking about the growth of plants, while those around him assigned great meaning to what they thought was a comment on the economy.

A great deal of meaning can be distorted by the use of *simple punctuation*. Take the following sentence, for example; 'The boy says the teacher is a fool.' With the addition of two simple commas, the meaning of this sentence can be completely reversed; 'The boy, says the teacher, is a fool.' In the Bible, during the Last Supper Jesus says to the Apostles, "Drink ye all of it". Because of the absence of a comma, this statement could have two completely different meanings. Is he referring to all of the wine, or all of the Apostles? (Drink ye, all of it.-or-Drink ye all, of it.)

Ancient Hebrew was always written with no vowels and no punctuation! There are many words, with diverse meanings, which share the same consonants, but different vowels. In English, for example, BLD could be build, bold, bald, blood or bled. What an enormous opportunity for misinterpretation and mistranslation! Hebrew scholars called Masoretes, faced with the task of translating the Hebrew texts of the Old Testament, had to decide where the vowels and punctuation were supposed to be. This was no small task.

In the part of the Bible that says that Eve was made from Adam's rib, we have a very important passage whose meaning was dependant upon which word the Masoretes chose. The Hebrew word for 'rib' was tzadi, which would have been written as TZD. The word for 'side' was tzad, and would have been written the same way. The statement that Eve was made from Adam's rib, something that many women find to be demeaning, could have had a completely different meaning. Perhaps it was saying that females are one 'side' of a two-sided being.[6]

This leads us into the other difficulties in the ***translation process***. The oldest texts are mostly written in Hebrew or Aramaic, and were then translated into Greek and Roman before the subsequent translation into French, English, Spanish, etc. Even with the best intentions, it is easy to mistranslate or misinterpret. In many cases a word can have several possible meanings. For example, the ancient word for 'word' can also mean 'sound'. Thus, the opening line in the Gospel of John, "In the beginning was the Word...", could be interpreted as saying that creation started with sound or vibration. Another example is the Hebrew word, 'naggar', which can mean 'carpenter/craftsman/learned man/magician'.[7] So was Jesus a carpenter, or was he a magician? The original meaning of words can change or be changed over time. The Greek word 'harmartolos', which means 'sinner' was once used to describe someone who did not follow Jewish law, but has now been broadened to mean someone who acts against God's wishes. Which is it?[8]

One of Jesus' most famous beatitudes, "The meek shall inherit the earth", is fraught with interpretive problems. The original Aramaic word for 'meek' can have many meanings, ie; poor in spirit, tranquil, dispassionate, humble, wise and even debonair. Even if we accept the choice of 'meek' as being the right one, what exactly does 'meek' mean? Even that meaning is open to subjective interpretation. And what of 'inherit the Earth', what does that mean? Wouldn't one be more interested in inheriting heaven? What seems like a straightforward statement, then, is actually full of controversy, completely subject to a variety of interpretations.[9]

This section was meant to show that there are many obstacles to the accurate communication of the information in the Bible, even if there is an honest intent to do so. As we shall see, however, there is a great deal of evidence to suggest that the information in the Bible was willfully distorted and altered many times, in many ways, by many people.

Chapter 27

CHURCH HISTORY AND THE COMPILATION OF THE BIBLE

The five oldest known copies of the Bible are very different from the newest ones. According to Australian researcher, Tony Bushby, who wrote 'The Bible Fraud', there are approximately 4800 significant differences between them. Some of these represent major changes. Many familiar concepts such as the Immaculate Conception and Virgin Birth of Jesus, and the Resurrection are not present in the old Bibles. This section will discuss the process that brought us the Bible that we know today, looking at the ways it was altered and edited and at the key people involved in the assembly of Biblical information. First we'll look at the Old Testament and then the compilation of the New Testament in conjunction with the history of the Christian Church.

The process of *compiling the Old Testament* began around 600 BC, while the Jews were captive for 50 years in Babylon, under the rule of King Nebuchadnezzar. Archeologists now believe that most of the Old Testament, particularly that which has come to be called the Deuteronomistic history, was written in the few decades preceding the Babylonian conquest during the reign of the Judaite king, Josiah. Instrumental in the process of compilation were two men, Nehemia and Ezra. After Babylon, the Hebrews were conquered by the Persians, the Syrians, Alexander the Great and Rome. It is said that the Old Testament was compiled in an effort to centralize belief systems that were suffering from the diversification resulting from the foreign occupations. It appeared as a single book only after 70 BC.

While most traditional views state that the Pentateuch or the Torah (the first five books) were written by Moses, there is growing evidence that this is highly unlikely.[10] Much of Genesis, which contains the stories most familiar to us, came from Babylonian stories that originated in Sumer. Excavations of Mesopotamian sites over the past 100 years have yielded mountains of clay texts that have shed much light on the origins of many Bible stories. Many of the cities mentioned in Genesis, such as Ur, have been excavated and shown to be Sumerian. Usually found in the form of clay glyphs and cylinder seals, texts such as the Sumerian 'Enuma Elish',[11] the Akkadian 'Atra Hasis Epic'[12] and the Babylonian 'Epic of Gilgamesh'[13] contain stories very similar to the ones in Genesis.

Much of the Old Testament is derivative of Egyptian texts, such as the 'Book of the Dead', 'The Wisdom of Ptah-Hotep', the 'Pyramid Texts', 'Coffin Texts' and 'Table of Destiny'.[14] The Ten Commandments are virtually identical, although much less detailed, to 'Spell # 125' in the Book of the Dead.[15] Many of the sayings attributed to Jesus, including 'the Lord's Prayer', can also be found in this book. Psalm 104, which speaks of the virtue of monotheism, is very similar to the Hymn of Bulak, written by Akhenaten.[16] The word 'amen', which ends many Christian prayers, is the name of an Egyptian god. (Possibly, at a time when knowledge was purer, prayers were ended with the sound of OM, a mantra which has a similar vibratory quality to Amen.)

In fact, Egypt has had a great influence on Judeo-Christian tradition, which has virtually shaped western culture. The era in which the Israelites lived in Egypt is traditionally portrayed as a time of slavery, but many scholars contend that, in many ways, the Hebrews came of age and prospered within the borders of Egypt, in a region called Goshen. For much of this time the rulers of Egypt were the Hyksos Kings, a group of Semitic nomads from the coastal regions of Canaan who were related to and lived much like the Hebrews. It is believed that the Hebrews prospered under their rule, falling into slavery only when the 18th dynasty took over, just prior to the time of Moses. A different view, originating with the ancient historian Manetho, holds that the Hyksos themselves were the Semites that left Egypt in the original Exodus story. In other words, the people that the Bible calls the Israelites were the same people as the Hyksos who ruled Egypt for hundreds of years. (More on this later.)

Many scholars claim that many of the Sumerian stories and the Egyptian writings were tailored to fit Hebrew beliefs and customs at the time of the compilation. For example, the earliest references to God in Genesis are clearly pluralized words—the Elohim and the Nephilim. The Bible clearly makes it sound as though this group is speaking as a single voice. An example of this can be found in Genesis 26, "Then God said 'Let us make man in our image, after our likeness..." By the time of the compilation, the notion of one God was firmly established and it was blasphemy to speak of a group of gods. The Sumerians, from whom the Hebrews were descended, worshipped a pantheon of gods as did the early Hebrews.

It has been further suggested that the compilation was affected by the political motives of the Hebrew ruling faction. *That doesn't seem too far-fetched to me. The ruling classes are continually jockeying for position, competing for power and ways of retaining dominion over the masses. Even in modern times, they are constantly exercising editorial power and deciding what information the public will be given access to. Would it have been any different then?* A great number of ancient Hebrew holy texts were not includeed in the compilation, including the 'Book of Jasher', 'Book of Jubillees', 'Book of Enoch', 'Book of the Lord', 'Book of the Wars of Jehovah', etc.

The greatest amount of compiling, editing, doctoring and institutionalizing of the Bible happened after Jesus, during the first few centuries of the Christian church, headquartered in Rome, which grew into a hugely powerful organization that virtually ruled the western world until quite recently. This group of self-proclaimed emissaries of God ruled with such an iron fist that to question them or their doctrine would literally result in being branded a heretic and put to death. Even many devout Christians would not deny that, for most of its existence, the Christian church was more of a political power than purveyors of the wisdom of God. The degree to which official church accounts differ with the teachings of Christ and the events surrounding his life, as well as events from the Old Testament, has become much clearer in the past 100 years or so, largely due to the availability of new information.

Independent scholars have been scrutinizing the **Apocrypha**, the name given to the large collection of pertinent books and texts that were not included. Most of us take the four gospels of the New Testament for granted, not realizing that, aside from these highly edited texts, there are about fifty other gospels. Many of these were discovered in 1945 in a small village in upper Egypt called Nag Hamadi. Most of these scrolls, known collectively as the **Nag Hamadi Library**, were purchased by the Carl Jung Foundation. Within this collection are the **Gnostic Gospels**, which includes such works as the Gospel of the Infancy of Jesus, the Gospel of Truth, the Gospel of the Egyptians, the Pistis Sophia, the Essene Gospel of John, the Aquarian Gospel of Jesus the Christ, the Gospel of the Holy Twelve, the Gospel of Philip, of Peter, of Mary Magdalene, of Thomas, and many more. (Much of the contents of the Gnostic Gospels are presented verbatim in the following website: **www.thenazareneway.com**)

Even though there are some inconsistencies within these gospels, there are many commonalities. The Gnostics, based largely in the multi-cultured, cosmopolitan Egyptian city of Alexandria, collected many of the texts written by people who came in direct contact with Jesus and his teachings, but were excluded from the Bible. Some of the common beliefs held by many of these works were that Jesus was human, that he didn't die on the cross and that he was married to Mary Magdalene and had children. These gospels indicate that Magdalene and many other characters who were marginalized by the Church actually played a big role in the 'Jesus movement'.

Another source of challenge to traditional church doctrine was the discovery of the **Dead Sea Scrolls**, which were found between 1947 and 1951 in caves near the Dead Sea in Israel, by the ruins of the Essene center known as Qumran, which thrived at the time of Jesus. The scrolls are original versions of ancient texts, some of which became part of the Bible, some of which chronicle life at that time. The Book of Isaiah, for example, is thought to have been written in 100 BC and is the oldest copy of a Bible text yet discovered. It is assumed that the Essenes hid and preserved these texts. Most of these scrolls are in the hands of the Vatican and the world still waits, after fifty years, for their publication. Are they worried? Why are they taking so long? Fortunately, some of the information in the Scrolls has leaked out; some text has been photographed and translated independent of Vatican control. It seems that some of it is in accord with the Gnostic viewpoints. (For more information on the controversy of the Vatican's reluctance to release this important information, I recommend 'The Dead Sea Scrolls Deception' by Michael Baigent and Richard Leigh.)

Before going through the chronology of key events in the compilation process of the New Testament and the history of the early Church, allow me to present a ***simplified overview***, according to the opinions of many researchers, of how and why the Church came into being. The ruling elite of that era were the Romans who, basically, controlled the conquered people with a small garrison of troops stationed at each population center in its vast empire. The Roman Empire was, at the time, by far the largest in recorded history, engulfing land as far north as the British Isles, the north coast of Africa and Asia Minor. Whenever necessary, larger armies were deployed to squash rebellions and uprisings. At some point, they began to realize that it was more efficient to control people with belief systems. At that time, without the transportation and communication that we enjoy today, each town had its own dialect and, similarly, its own version of a religion. There was not the unification and organization of religion that we know today. Different religions and belief systems abounded. There were even several versions of a newly growing movement called Christianity.

Somewhere along the way, it dawned on the power elite that one unified belief system could be very advantageous in the quest to control the masses. One priest collecting tithes could replace a large number of hungry horses and soldiers. The Roman Empire set out to become the Holy Roman Empire. The title, Pontifex Maximus, which used to belong to the Caesar, was now applied to the Pope, who was referred to as the Pontiff. The Romans had always had difficulty getting people to deify Caesar. They needed a central figure who could be convincingly deified, around whom a whole new theology could be developed. They needed someone who could be portrayed as a miracle worker, and not just a sayer of wise things. While looking around for a good vehicle to appropriate, they noticed a fledgling movement that was growing quickly, the belief systems of which could be tailored to meet the religious tastes of a wide variety of people.

Systematically, the 'official' Christian doctrine was constructed using a combination of respected ancient text, various 'paganisms' from other belief systems, some of the teachings of this guy, Jesus the Nazorene and some of the accounts of his cohorts. Then a complex mess of rules, regulations and 'sins' were introduced, designed to keep the people subservient and subject to the authority of the Church. People were taught that to break these rules was to defy the will of God. All interaction with God now had to happen under the supervision of a hierarchy of priests who were God's 'Earthly emissaries'. Church doctrine was preached and enforced at every turn.

At first many of the people, both subjugated and free, resisted this imposition of religion, choosing to do things their own way. Systematically, the Roman Church began to crush these groups and all competition. Groups were branded as heretics and given the option of joining the fold or being killed. Many chose death. We have all been made aware that the earliest Christians were persecuted, fed to lions, etc. According to a historian named Gibbon, who did the number crunching, 2000 Christians lost their lives before the Romanization. Between then and now, however, an estimated ***25 million people were put to death*** for the crime of directly or indirectly opposing the will of this organization!!! That is a staggering statistic.[17]

Thus, over the years, almost all voices of dissent were silenced and the official church doctrine became ever more firmly implanted in the collective mind of the western world. Armed with the 'irrefutable word of God' and led by an 'infallible' Pope who was the sole earthly representative of God's will, the Roman Church became an immensely powerful entity with enormous control over the destiny of mankind. Such power was unprecedented in the known world. Was it used for the betterment of humanity, or was it used to suppress and disempower the masses, for the benefit of an elite few?

Although many of us are vaguely familiar with the concept of 'inquisition' and witch burning, few really know what it meant. Why are we not taught more about this in school and in the media? Why won't the Catholic Church of today (as well as many other religious organizations) come clean and perhaps make a new start? If it has the welfare of humanity as its highest motive, is it not necessary to tell the truth, or at least as much of the truth as possible? I believe that we would benefit greatly by shaking off the yoke of dogma and beginning, en masse, to ask difficult questions and to demand responsible leadership. We can then decide for ourselves which aspects of religion are useful and worth keeping, and which need to be changed.

So how did the Roman Church become such an enormously powerful institution? Who were some of the key players in this process? How did the Bible evolve into the text we know today? Let's now take a look at the ***compilation of the New Testament***, in conjunction with the ***history of Christian religion***.

One of the largest and most controversial characters of the post-Jesus era is **St. Paul**, whose many letters or epistles take up as large a chunk of the New Testament as do all the gospels combined. In fact, his words are much better represented than those of Jesus. Paul was an Orthodox Jew who came from the Greek city of Tarsus in Asia Minor. As the story goes, before the 'road to Damascus' incident when his name was still Saul, he was a persecutor of Christians. After his conversion he changed his name to Paul and went about spreading 'the word'. But whose word was he pushing? In the opinion of most modern researchers, he did much to move the doctrine of Christianity away from Jesus' teachings and to distort the story of his life. An Arabic text from the fifth or sixth century AD, discovered in a Christian monastery in 1960 by Professor Schlomo Pines, denounces Paul and his followers who "..have abandoned the religion of Christ and turned towards the religious doctrines of the Romans."[18]

Paul is credited with the earliest efforts to deify Jesus, calling him the 'Christ', a Greek word meaning 'king'. Even 'Jesus' is the Greek translation of the Jewish name, 'Issua' or 'Yssua' a derivation of the name 'Joshua'. Here is an example of Paul's words.

> "Christ was truly God...So at the name of Jesus everyone will bow down, those in heaven, on earth and under the earth. And to the glory of God the Father everyone will openly agree, 'Jesus Christ is Lord!' "
>
> —*Philippians 2:6-11*

Paul did much to marginalize the role of females in the Jesus story and to suppress the feminine in general. Here are a couple of quotes by Paul;

> "Wives submit to your husbands, for the husband is the head of the wife as Christ is the head of the Church."
> "But I suffer not a woman to teach, nor to usurp authority over the man, but to be in silence."[9]

He also brought in many paganisms, mostly from the worshippers of Dionysus (also known as Bel), the Greek god who dominated the religion of Tarsus. Like many other god-figures popular at the time, such as Horus and Mithra, he is associated with a virgin birth, was born on December 25th (traditionally celebrated because of the winter solstice—the rebirth of the sun), died and was resurrected. Many of the titles of Jesus, such as the Vine, the Only Begotten Son and the Saviour, were also titles held by Dionysus.[20]

So, who was Paul? Even though he often spoke of love, it is said that he greatly distorted the message of the Jesus movement. The Gnostic gospels make it clear that he was involved in power struggles with Peter and especially with James, Jesus' brother. (James was a key player, although virtually ignored by the Bible and the Church. More on him later.) Barbara Theiring, in her book 'Jesus the Man', claims that Jesus accompanied Paul, guiding his teachings until Jesus' death circa 65 AD.[21] Some scholars portray Paul as misguided but well-intentioned, while others claim he was tantamount to a Roman spy. There is definitely controversy surrounding him and his epistles. According to linguistic experts working with the assistance of computers, only five of the fourteen epistles credited to Paul seem to have actually been written by the same hand.[22]

Cyprian, the Bishop of Carthage circa 250 AD, promoted the idea that only Christians could achieve salvation. He discouraged people from thinking for themselves, advocating the strong guidance of the priesthood.[23]

The next major figure was the Roman emperor, **Constantine**, who made Christianity the official religion of Rome by issuing the 'Edict of Milan' in 313 AD. Unlike typical Hollywood portrayals, he was hardly a religious man, but rather, a ruthless, ambitious man of war. He started the process of outlawing the 'heathen' faiths and crushing the competition. He did much to give Christianity mass appeal, taking aspects of Sol Invictus (the previous official

Roman religion), Mithraism, the Goddess based religions and others, and injecting them into the new Church. An edict passed by Constantine in 321 changed the Christian sabbath from Saturday, the traditional Jewish sabbath, to Sunday, that of Sol Invictus. The birthday of Jesus was later changed from January 6 to the established Sol Invictus feast of Natalis Invictus, which means 'rebirth of the sun', on December 25. This date, representing the winter solstice, was celebrated by many pagan cultures. The idea of a baby in a manger in a stable comes from Horus; changing water to wine comes from Dionysus; the idea of healings and raising people from the dead comes from Aesculapius; resurrection from a rock tomb comes from Mithra. Many of these aspects of Christianity are shared by several of the Pagan faiths.[24]

Constantine did much to alter the Bible. He ordered it translated into Greek by scholars who were not totally familiar with the subtleties and nuances of Aramaic and Hebrew. Texts were also manipulated intentionally. Christian stories were altered to show Romans in a favorable light, while at the same time vilifying the Jews. A good example of this is the 'Pontius Pilate story'. By all historical accounts Pilate, like the Romans in general, was a brutal, intolerant ruler. Even the slightest hint of insurrection was quickly squashed. It is highly unlikely that he would have 'washed his hands' of Jesus, leaving his fate to the Jews, who unanimously screamed for his death. Furthermore, crucifixion was a Roman sentence given to transgressors of Roman law. Transgression of Judaic law was punishable by stoning, which the Jews were free to implement without Roman approval.[25] This 'hand washing' propaganda, combined with the fact that the Romans never did succeed in getting the Jews to join their new religion, has caused the Jewish people to be persecuted and degraded over the centuries.

In 313 AD, Constantine convened the *'Council of Nicea'*, which indoctrinated the 'Nicene Creed'. This established that Jesus Christ was officially the son of God. The concept of the Holy Trinity, one that excluded a female component, was also decreed.[26] Constantine is also credited with instituting the feudal system which, like the Indian caste system, was designed to keep the elite in power and the masses subservient.[27]

In 379 AD, Emperor *Theodosius the Great* passed the eighteen Laws of Obedience, including the Theodosian Code, which decreed the death penalty for those not accepting the Nicene Creed.[28] Many non-Roman Christians like the Gnostics and the Arians were killed at this time. Many pagan temples were shut down or destroyed.[29]

One of the most heartbreaking of human crimes was committed by Theodosius' army, in conjunction with Cyril, the Archbishop of Alexandria. At that time, the most multi-cultural and sophisticated city in the western world was Alexandria in Egypt. *The Library of Alexandria* contained incredible records of antiquity; historical, scientific and literary records that had been gathered over the course of 700 years. Luciano Canfora, author of 'The Vanished Library, a Wonder of the Ancient World', says that it contained over 200,000 scrolls![30] In 411 BC, these works were denounced as heretical and burned! (A quantity of books was also burned by the Muslim leader, Omar I, who said, "If these books agree with the Koran, then they are unnecessary; if they do not agree with it, they are pernicious".)[31] In those days, most texts were unique, with no copies, so all that information is lost forever. This boggles the mind. It is thought that these texts included information on alchemy and Hermetic magic, geometry, mathematics, science, history, etc. Answers to many of the questions and mysteries talked about in this book, including human origins, the various laws around the workings of energy, etc, could possibly have been recorded amongst these texts.[32]

Books from Plato's Academy and Aristotle's Lyceum were also burned and these great centers of learning were closed down.[33] Even the development of science or any knowledge that did not agree with Christian dogma was considered heretical. Over the centuries, many scholars and scientists were targeted. Copernicus (1543 AD) was silenced and Galileo (1632 AD) was persecuted and imprisoned, despite his great reputation and contributions to humanity, for daring to suggest that the universe did not revolve around the Earth.[34]

According to Bushby, many Jewish texts were also targeted by the Roman Church because they did not agree with Church doctrine. Circa 1415, Pope Benedict XIII seized and destroyed all copies of two ancient texts called the 'Mar Yesu' and the 'Book of Elxai'. Pope Alexander VI tried to destroy all copies of the Talmud around 1500 AD. Although thousands were burned, many survived. Many thousands of old, original Hebrew scrolls were also burned, circa 1550.[35]

Three dudes who contributed greatly to church doctrine were *Augustine, Ambrose and Jerome*. Augustine was the first to put forward strong anti-sex 'guidelines' claiming that it was sinful to have sex for reasons other than procreation. He did much to promote 'fear of damnation' and the notion that non-baptized babies that died could not go to heaven. Ambrose, the Bishop of Milan, is considered to be the unofficial founder of the Inquisition, which actively sought out 'disbelievers', who were then tortured and/or put to death. Under his guidance, things really began to get bloody.

Eusebius Hieronymus, a Roman who eventually came to be known as St. Jerome, presided over the 'Council of Hippo' in 393 AD and the 'Council of Carthage' in 397 AD, decreeing that all psychics, channels and mediums be put to death. It was largely here that the books were chosen and texts compiled into the New Testament. These texts were manipulated, edited, translated and interpreted in a way that kept them in line with the newly emerging doctrine. The concept of the Trinity, for example, was injected into the Gospel of John.

This was only the start of this process, and manipulations occurred periodically. For example, at the Second Synod of Constantinople in 553 AD, convened by the Emperor Justinian, all references to reincarnation were deleted from the Bible.[36] Here is a quote from Eusebius, according to Bushby, " It is an act of virtue to deceive and lie, when by such means the interest of the Church might be promoted."[37]

Many learned people lived in Alexandria at that time and it was a center for the pursuit of knowledge. There were many mystical traditions and belief systems, including the Hermetic sciences of magic and alchemy. To the organized Church it was a hotbed of heresy, a threat to their quest to bill themselves as the great authority on all things religious. One of the most learned and respected persons at the time of the library burning, was a woman named Hypatia who, in the process of being put to death, had the flesh torn from her body.[38] There were many hideous executions, particularly under the reign of **Justinian**, Emperor of the Eastern Roman Empire around 550 AD, who is responsible for the death of hundreds of thousands of pagans and heretics.[39]

Among Bible scholars it has become common knowledge that the Bible was deliberately manipulated, and this has been proven by researchers who have discovered letters and other 'smoking guns'. One such letter, and an older Bible with a different version of the Gospel of Mark, was found in an ancient library at Mar Saba by Professor Morton Smith of Columbia University in 1958. The letter was written by Bishop Clement of Alexandria who was explaining why a certain section was being removed from the Gospel of Mark. One of the lines in the letter says, "Not all true things are to be said to all men". The section removed had to do with the story of Lazarus who, according to the traditional line, was brought back to life by Jesus. The deleted story was about how Jesus, over the course of six days, put Lazarus through a mystery school ritual initiation involving a 'death and rebirth'. Information referring to sexual rituals was also removed.[40]

Let's spend some time talking about the **Gospels of Mark, Luke, Matthew and John**, which are said to have been written after the Jewish revolt and subsequent sacking of Jerusalem in 70 AD, several years after the teachings of Jesus. These writings, which often contradict each other, have caused much confusion. There is disagreement about Jesus' last words, which differ in each gospel. According to John, the crucifixion happened before Passover, while the others claim it was the day after. Old Bibles have been found in which there is no mention of the Resurrection in Mark's gospel. It does appear in newer versions, however. According to Matthew, Jesus' family was aristocratic, a direct descendant of David, and the Magi that came from the East to worship the newborn Christ did so in a house and not a manger.[41]

Most of us have been led to believe that these gospel writers were Apostles, people closely affiliated with Jesus. This was not the case. Mark was a disciple of Paul, and probably never knew Jesus. Luke was a Greek doctor who wrote for the Romans. Matthew basically copied Mark, but in Greek, and was also not a disciple of Jesus. Their gospels were written long after the fact. The gospel of John surfaced about 100 AD, and is considered the most controversial of the Bible gospels. The actual writer is said to be unknown and was given the name 'John' at a later date. This gospel is notably different from the others and is considered to be more mystical and reliable, although still highly edited.[42]

One of the more mysterious books of the Bible is the **Revelation to John**, in which we get a description of the Apocalypse. Much of this work is difficult to make sense of and many feel that there is a great deal of wisdom and magic encoded in its words. There are many allusions to special numbers such as 144,000, 666, 7 and 12 and to 'songs' that contain certain powers. (See **BOX 22— 144,000, 666 AND OTHER SPECIAL NUMBERS**) One curiosity is the scroll mentioned in Revelation chapter five, on which all the visions and revelations are written. In early translations this 'scroll', which is said to be tiny, is eaten by John. Some scholars contend that it could have been some sort of psychotropic drug, and that the visions were revealed in a state of altered consciousness.[43]

As well as the numerous pagan cults and religions, there were many **heretical Christian groups** who did not see things in the way that the Roman Church insisted. **The Gnostics**, a large group with many sub-sects that were based mostly in Alexandria, saw Jesus' teachings from the perspective of the mystical traditions of Egypt, Greece and the Far East. Much of it is rooted in Hermetic magic. The word 'gnostic' comes from the root 'gnosis', a Greek term which means 'to know intuitively and deeply'. Such knowledge is held in all levels of the being, body, soul and spirit, and is usually acquired in a trance-like or altered state of consciousness. The Gnostics believed that it was possible to know God directly, without the need for intermediaries such as priests, and that we are all of divine nature. They did not believe one needed to grovel before God's feet. Within most Gnostic societies women had a role, officiating at ceremonies alongside men.

An early Gnostic teacher living circa 150 AD was Valentinus, a very influential leader who had important people, including Ptolemy, among his followers. He claimed to have a body of text that contained the secret teachings of Jesus. Another notable leader at the same time was Marcion, whose writings referred to the difference between Old Testament law and New Testament love. Yet another leader was Basilides, who wrote twenty-four commentaries on the gospels, claiming that Jesus' crucifixion was fraudulent.[43]

BOX 22—144,000, 666 AND OTHER SPECIAL NUMBERS: There are many numbers that are considered to be 'special' or 'sacred'. They appear repeatedly in sacred texts, ancient measurements, calendars, etc. As previously noted, the numbers '7' and '12' are very special. Two other very special numbers are 666 and 144,000. In the Book of Revelation, 666 is said to be the 'number of the beast'. There are many theories about this number and an Internet search will yield an enormous number of opinions. It truly is a fascinating number with many mathematical peculiarities. For example, the sum of all numbers from 1 to 36 (also a special number) equals 666. If we multiply 6x6x6, we get 216. Add a zero to that, and we have the length in years of a precessional or astrological 'age'. (Zeros added to the end of a number do not change its significance.) While modern popular culture has interpreted this to be the number of the devil or Satan, it is thought by many scholars to be referring to humanity in its physical manifestation. Carbon, which is the basic element of all earthly life forms, has 6 electrons, 6 protons and 6 neutrons. The number 6, as in the six faces on a cube, is said to be symbolic of the 6 directions of the 3-dimensional realm; up, down, left, right, forward and backward.

According to Revelation, 144,000 refers to the number of individuals (12,000 from each of the twelve tribes of Israel) that will be saved or protected. The square root of 144 is that special number, 12. Also, the 12th number in the Fibonacci sequence is 144. Gematria is the ancient system whereby each number has a meaning or a corresponding letter. The gematric meaning of 144 is 'light'. It is thought by some that 666 refers to man in his physical state, while 144,000 refers to 'ascended' man.

Researchers have compiled lists of words with special gematric meanings. Interestingly, the same gematrically significant numbers, such as 36, 108, 144, 216, 396, 576, 864, 1296, 2304, 2592, 3024, 3456, 5184, etc., appear in a wide variety of seemingly unrelated contexts. They appear in Roman weights and measurements, in Sumerian and Mayan calendars, in the measurements, angles and geographical positions of ancient structures such as Stonehenge and the Great Pyramid, in geometrical relationships and in many ancient texts. Almost all of these special numbers are multiples of 9. The sum of the digits in all multiples of 9 is 9; i.e., 18, 1+8=9; 27, 2+7=9; 2160 (astrol. age), 2+1+6+0=9; 25,920 (precessional cycle), 2+5+9+6+0=18=1+8=9, etc. Interestingly, the tangents of these significant numbers are always either 3.077683537 or 0.726542528. If we multiply these two numbers together we get 2.236067977, which is the tangent of the earthly speed of light! (Light travels slightly slower through our atmosphere than in a vacuum.) You can check this astounding 'coincidence' yourself—get out your calculator.

The zodiacal number 2160 appears in many contexts. It is the sum of all the corner angles in a cube. The Babylonian 'maneh' (measuring volume) equals 21600 'um'. The Egyptian 'schoenus' (distance) equals 216000 inches. 3000 Roman 'libra' (weight) equals 2160 pounds. The earliest bushel is 2160 cubic inches. Astonishingly, the diameter of the Moon is 2160 miles! If you don't believe it, look it up! Somehow the ancients had a lot of knowledge that, according to current paradigms, they shouldn't have.

Some researchers, astounded by the high degree of 'coincidence' in historically significant numbers, have suggested that these sacred numbers allude to the order that underlies all of creation. They cite it as evidence that the universe is the product of an intelligent design. This view is in contrast to the current scientific paradigm that suggests that life on Earth is the result of a long chain of accidents

As well as the Gnostics, there were other major groups of non-Roman Christians. Nestorius, the Bishop of Constantinople in 428 AD, who declared that Jesus was not God, but rather, a very special human, was labeled a heretic and banished to the Egyptian desert. Nestorian Christianity continued to grow, however, and eventually it merged with the Egyptian Church to become *the Coptic Church*, which is a brand of Christianity based in Egypt and

Ethiopia that still exists today.[44]

The **Celtic Church of Ireland** was a blend of pagan and Christian beliefs that endured until it was dissolved at the Synod of Whitby in 664 AD. The island of Ireland was a safe haven for free-thinkers during the first few centuries of the Roman Church, being far enough removed from the rest of Europe to avoid persecution and oppression. It became a center of higher culture, civilization and learning, until it was infiltrated by the Roman Church, who quietly took over. Many texts were subsequently destroyed, although it is believed that some texts were hidden away and may some day come to light. An old Celtic saying—"The Celtic Church brings love, while the Roman Church brings law."[45]

Two of the largest heretical groups were the **Manicheans**, led by Mani, and the **Arians**, led by Arius. These two leaders were put to death in the third century AD; Mani was skinned alive and beheaded. These groups had much in common with Judaism, and they regarded Jesus as a great teacher and messenger, but not as divinity incarnate. The Koran of Islam, which mentions Jesus in a reverential tone many times, is in accord with these views. Despite persecution and great loss of life, these huge movements persisted for centuries, and some of their beliefs survived and were adopted by many populations including the Cathars.

In the south of France, with Toulouse as its center, is a region known as the Languedoc. Notable as a center of alchemy, this region is home to many strange legends and pagan art. A large percentage of the powerful Knights Templar came from here, as did a large number of the 'Holy Grail' stories. Living for hundreds of years in this region were a group of Christians known as **the Cathars**, a powerful and prosperous people who refused to recognize the Pope's authority. They viewed the Roman version of Christianity as being overly concerned with pomp and wealth, differing greatly with the true teachings of Jesus. They were pacifists and vegetarians who believed in reincarnation, equality of the sexes, simple living, sex with birth control and the idea that God could be known directly, without the need for intermediaries. (They also had some strange beliefs; that the world was intrinsically evil and that the physical body was a 'filthy envelope of flesh' in which we are trapped, enduring until the day of release.)

In 1209, Pope Innocent III ordered the Albigensian Crusade, and over the next 30 years the Cathars, every man, woman and child, were systematically slaughtered. This amounted to over 100,000 lives lost. The considerable wealth and properties of the Cathars were confiscated. An entire people was eradicated. This process was assisted by a Church representative named Dominic Guzman, founder of the Dominican order. This monastic order became the overseers of the Holy Inquisition in 1233.[46]

(For a thorough account of the atrocities and 'ridiculosities' of the Popes over the years, check out 'The Vicars of Christ', written by former Roman Catholic priest, Peter da Rosa.)

In the 16th century came *the Reformation*. While this movement did result in a decentralizing of power away from Rome, it certainly did not result in the distribution of that power to the masses. It definitely did not generate what I believe is the true message of Jesus, that we are all inherently divine, powerful beings, cut from the same fabric, in the process of trying to see through illusion and discover our true identities. The message continued to be distorted, both in a deliberate political way, and by means of genuine misunderstanding.

Martin Luther (1483–1546) and other reformers took issue with the concept of indulgences, whereby money was given to the Church in return for the absolution of sins. Unfortunately, it was not the absurd notion that one could purchase salvation that troubled them. They believed that we have no control over salvation, that it could not be achieved through our own efforts, and that whatever fate was bestowed upon us was God's will and therefore, each person deserved whatever circumstances befell them. John Calvin (1509—1564), who believed in predestination, took this a step further, implying that the elite were those favored by God before birth. This led to the rich being able to justify their exploitations and to turn their backs on the less fortunate. One could say that this was/is a major factor in the growth of the ever-widening chasm between the rich and the poor.[47]

The Calvinists were very intolerant, advocating death to all heretics. Women who practiced ancient wisdom, using old remedies, methods and rituals, were branded as witches and burned at the stake, their knowledge dismissed as evil superstition and old wives' tales. Calvinism led to Puritanism and the stifling notion that just about any activity other than endless toil was tantamount to sin. Oliver Cromwell, the first Puritan 'dictator' of England, claimed that the Jews had 'fallen from grace' and that the English Puritans were the new 'chosen people'. They glorified war as something that was expected by God. War was a permanent inevitability, a constant struggle against Satan.[48]

In 1607 a major revision of the Bible was initiated by order of King James I of England. Under the direct supervision of the attorney general, Sir Francis Bacon, the scriptures were overhauled and 'protestantized'. Bacon, a very powerful and influential man, is one of history's controversial figures. (See **BOX 23— SIR FRANCIS BACON**)

One large and powerful group of people with unorthodox ideas are *the Mormons*. Due to the 'angelic' visitations and visions experienced by their leader, Joseph Smith, they have an unusual body of beliefs. They believe that there are many inhabited planets in the universe and that God lives near a star named Kolob. They believe that people from the Palestine region were brought to America by strange flying ships in ancient times, which is also alluded to in the Tower of Babel story. Native American legends also speak of this phenomenon, as in the idea of the 'thunderbird'. The Innuit legends say they were brought to the north in large metal birds. In the Book of Mormon 3 Nephi 8:5—23, there is a lengthy description of an ancient American city being wiped out in punishment. It sounds very much like an nuclear holocaust, complete with radioactive fallout. (As reported earlier, there are several works in various ancient texts, including the Bible, that also describe what sounds like large bombings.)

Most people are not aware of the extent of the size and power of the Mormons. They are over 6 million strong and own great tracts of land and big businesses. There are many Mormons in top levels of the CIA. One of the more interesting ongoing projects of the Mormon Church is the compilation and maintenance of the world's largest genealogical library. Their aim is to know the genealogical lineage and ancestry of not just Mormons, but all families. This ongoing endeavor produces over 60,000 rolls of microfilm per year, warehoused in a huge vault in a mountain near Salt Lake City.[50]

BOX 23—SIR FRANCIS BACON: Bacon was a controversial figure in history—a brilliant scholar who was well educated in almost every field, he had many links to several secret societies and was well versed in ancient mysticism and the occult sciences. He is said to have been the highest executive of the Rosicrucians in Britain at that time. Some say he was a 'good guy', bringing great wisdom to mankind. Some even credit him with having written all the Shakespeare works. Others contend that he was a 'bad guy', working secretly for the power elite, seeking to control the masses. Some of the philosophies he advocated were questionable. He believed that mankind should know nature in order to control her. Nature must be "hounded in her wanderings"... "bound into service"... made a "slave" and "put in constraint". Science is meant to "torture nature's secrets from her". Bacon's choice of words, with their violent, sexist overtones, is a little alarming. As Fritjof Capra points out, Bacon's views helped to shape the dominant, patriarchal attitudes toward science and reflected the intolerance and cruelty of the witch-hunts of the era.[49]

We can see the incredible odyssey taken by Jesus' message of love and the incredible array of deeds, including some of history's most atrocious crimes, that have been done in his name. The small sketch provided here only scratches the surface. There have been other atrocities, such as the Crusades, the wars, the missions and the genocide of native populations that were done in his name in two millennia of darkness. I believe that, in order to move away from that darkness, we must be able to look at our past, learn from it, forgive and move forward. It involves accepting responsibility for our past and thus assuming responsibility for our future. Part of that means looking at our belief systems, examining where they came from and how they became so deeply ingrained in our culture. We can then decide whether they are useful to us.

THE OLD TESTAMENT

Chapter 28

A BRIEF HISTORY OF THE JEWISH PEOPLE

It can be tricky to make sense of the Old Testament because, unlike in other religions, when one refers to a Jew, one can be talking about either a member of a certain religion, or a member of an ethnic group. One does not have to be an ethnic Jew to belong to the Jewish faith, and vice-versa. To avoid some of this confusion and to get a better understanding of the identity of these people, let's take a quick look at some aspects of Jewish history as presented by the Bible. It should be noted that this account does not necessarily accord with the findings and views of modern archeology, which we'll talk about a bit later.

After the flood, one of Noah's sons, Shem, fathered the Semitic race. Almost all of the people descended from the Mesopotamian region, therefore, are Semitic. Of the patriarchs descended from Shem, Eber was the one from whom the name 'Hebrew' was derived, and several generations later, Abram (who became *Abraham*), left the Sumerian city of Ur with his tribe circa 1960 BC. One confusing aspect of the Bible is that it seems to be talking about individuals. It's important to realize that these individuals were patriarchs or kings of large numbers of people. So Abraham and his people settled in the land of Canaan, with a brief sojourn into Egypt.

Abraham's first-born son was *Ishmael*, born to him by his wife Sarah's Egyptian handmaid, Hagar. The second son, *Isaac*, was born to Sarah, who had come with Abraham from Ur. Isaac became the patriarch of the people that became the Jews and Ishmael became the patriarch of a people that became the Arabs. To Isaac came two sons, *Esau and Jacob*, who split the Hebrews into two factions. Esau's faction settled in Canaan and became known as the Edomites. Jacob's name was changed to Israel, which means 'soldier of El', one of the names of the Hebrew God.[51] He led his group into Egypt where they lived for hundreds of years.

A significant story is that of Jacob's son *Joseph* (Yusef), who was betrayed by his jealous brothers. He was taken to Egypt years before the arrival of the Israelites. He was an exceptional man and eventually rose to a very prominent position in the court of the Hyksos kings who ruled Egypt at that time. His descendants became, according to some researchers, a part of the Egyptian royal family.

By the time of *Moses*, there were three main factions of Hebrews, the Canaanites (Edomites), the Israelites and a faction that had settled and prospered in a land just beyond the Egyptian border, called the Midianites, also descended from Esau. Most of us are aware of the Exodus story, whereby Moses and Aaron lead the Israelites out of Egypt into the promised land, which is conquered by **Joshua**.

The **Twelve Tribes of Israel**, derived from twelve sons of Jacob/Israel from four different wives; Reuben, Simeon, Levi, Judah, Is'sachar, Zebulun, Benjamin, Dan, Naphtali, Gad, Asher and Joseph. There were also, amongst the Canaanites, twelve dukedoms of Edom, derived from Esau's heirs. (There is also said to have been twelve princedoms derived from Ishmael's heirs.) After the conquering of Canaan, the Israelites were led by various prophets, holy men and warriors known as the **Judges**. Eventually they felt the need for a king and, at the recommendation of God, a Benjamite named Saul became the first monarch. The tribe of Judah (from whence the name 'Jew') began to dominate after Saul was deposed by David.

After the collapse of the great empire led by **David and Solomon**, the Israelites split into two groups, Judah in the southern highlands, dominated by the tribe of Judah, and Israel or the Northern Kingdoms in the northern highlands, consisting of the other tribes. The two factions competed for control and quarreled with non-Israelite communities in the region. Beginning around the 8th century BC, they endured conquest by several groups, including the Assyrians, the Chaldeans, the Persians, the Syrians, Alexander the Great and Ptolemy I of Egypt. In 63 BC, they were conquered by the Romans. Expatriate Jews were by this time populating other parts of the Greco-Roman world and came to be known as the Diaspora.

By the time of Jesus the Israelites living in Palestine were divided into Judea in the south, Samaria and Galilee in the north. Not only was there a wide variety of tribes, there were **religio-political factions**, such as the Saducees, the Pharisees, the Essenes, the Zealots, etc. In 66 AD, the Romans crushed a Zealot uprising, resulting in the destruction of much of Jerusalem, the razing of the temple and the loss of 20,000 Jewish lives. Included in this are those that chose suicide rather than subjugation to Rome, during the famous **standoff at Masada**. There was another revolt in 132 AD which was also crushed. These two events caused a great outpouring of Jews from Palestine; a mass migration of Jews to all points of the civilized world. After the second uprising, the Romans under Hadrian passed a law expelling all Jews from Jerusalem, which became a Roman city called Aelia Capitolina.

Modern Jews consist of only about 40% of this Semitic lineage, called the **Sephardic** Jews. The other 60% are called the **Ashkenazim** Jews and derive from central and eastern Europe north of the Caspian Sea. They joined the Jewish faith in the 8th century AD. As mentioned previously, many people from different bloodlines and cultures have joined the faith and are referred to as Jews in the modern era.

It's clear that, even though the Bible tends to represent the Jews as being a tight, cohesive group, there are numerous factions, many of which the Bible largely ignores. There is much confusion around the entire 'Jewish' issue. For example, the term 'anti-Semite' has evolved to mean some one who is prejudiced against Jews. It seems ironical that modern Arabs are more purely Semitical, in terms of bloodline, than are most modern Jews. It seems a tragedy that such great animosity should exist between the two groups.

BIBLICAL CHRONOLOGY CHART

(Dates are approximate and do not necessarily agree with modern archeology.)

1960 BC: Destruction of Ur—Migration of **Abraham** into Canaan.

1750 BC: **Jacob/Israel** leads Hebrews into Egypt—Hebrews now known as Israelites (twelve tribes)

1350 BC: **Moses**—Exodus of Israelites from Egypt

1300 BC: **Joshua** conquers Canaan—tribes settle in various sectors of highlands

1025 BC: Monarchy of Israel established—King **Saul** of Benjamin

1000 BC: King **David** of Judah—beginning of Golden Era of Israel

950 BC: King **Solomon**—first temple built at Jerusalem

900 BC: Israel is split in two factions—Judah in southern highlands, Northern Kingdom in northern highlands

850 BC: Prosperous Omride Dynasty in Northern Kingdom—Omri, Ahab, Jezebel, etc.

725 BC: Shalmanezer V of **Assyria** invades Northern Kingdom—Hoshea, last king of Northern Kingdom

700 BC: Judah grows dramatically—Tribe of Judah rules both north and south—Jerusalem becomes centre

625 BC: King **Josiah** of Judah—strict religious reform, Deuteronomistic accounts written

600 BC: Chaldean King **Nebuchadnezzar of Babylon** conquers Israel— Jerusalem is razed, temple destroyed

550 BC: Old Testament compiled during Babylonian captivity

540 BC: **Persians** defeat Chaldeans—Jews allowed to rebuild temple—Judah becomes Persian Province of Yehud

330 BC: Conquered by **Alexander the Great**

60 BC: After occupation by Egypt and Syria, Israel is conquered by **Rome**— three sectors; Judea, Galilee, Samaria

0–30 AD: Time of **Jesus the Nazorene**

66 AD: Jewish revolt crushed by Rome—Jerusalem sacked, temple destroyed—standoff at **Masada**

132 AD: Rome crushes another Jewish revolt—massive outpouring of Jews—Jerusalem becomes **Aelia Capitolina**

315 AD: **Constantine** becomes first Christian Emperor of Rome—Edict of Milan, Council of Nicea

400 AD: New Testament books chosen, texts prepared—Council of Hippo, Council of Carthage

1209 AD: **Albigensian Crusade** ordered by Pope Innocent III—Cathars slaughtered

1500 AD: Start of the Reformation—**Luther, Calvin**

1600 AD: Bible is revised by **King James**, under direct supervision of Sir Francis Bacon

Chapter 29

GENESIS STORIES

At this point, let's look at some specific Genesis stories and compare aspects of them to their Sumerian/Mesopotamian counterparts. Several books citing this connection have been written from as far back as 1876, i.e. 'The Chaldean Genesis', by George Smith and 'The Babylonian Genesis', by Alexander Heidel. (It might be a good idea to review what was written in chapter four in the section dealing with Zecharia Sitchin's work.)[52]

The Biblical version of *the Creation Story,* with its six days of creation and one day of rest, is the same—in some cases word for word—as the one that comes from a Babylonian work called the Enuma Elish, which existed long before the time of the Old testament compilation. This work is, in turn, derived from older Sumerian works. The Biblical version is, however, far less detailed and appears to have been edited. It also differs in that it refers to the creator as God, in the singular, while the Sumerian account refers to a universal force that at one point creates the gods, as well as everything else.

The notion of the honoring of the sabbath as a day of rest comes from the Babylonian/Chaldean 'sabatu', which the Jews adopted while under Chaldean occupation during the period of the Old Testament compilation, circa 500 BC. The sabbath was always Saturday until changed to Sunday by Constantine in an effort to align the new Christian movement with the established Roman sabbath of the pagan Sol Invictus religion.[53] At the time of the exile, the Babylonians celebrated the new year by reciting the Enuma Elish and its creation story, something that would not have gone unnoticed by the Israelites.

One thing that I find interesting is that, in the Genesis account, God creates the light twice, on the first and fourth days. (see Genesis 1:3 and 1:14) Could it be that the light referred to on the first day is a misrepresentation of the original intent, which was to say that the universe comes from (is a manifestation of) light or energy?

The Genesis version of the *Adam and Eve* story has much in common with the Sumerian accounts, which mention the fertile region of Sumer known as E.Din. This is obviously the source for the Garden of Eden. The Sumerian accounts tell, in much more detail than the Adam and Eve story, of the creation of humanity. In their version, however, humanity is created by a group of gods who manipulate and upgrade the local, homegrown anthropoids. The Sumerian version seems to accord well with the anthropological view of a sudden development in human evolution, the radical change that occurred in the human lineage about 200,000 years ago.

Amongst the group of gods, there were those who felt that humanity should be given the tools by which to evolve toward enlightenment, and those who felt that humanity's usefulness as a slave nation would diminish if they were given such tools. In the Bible version, this conflict is represented by the idea of the two trees, the tree of the knowledge of good and evil, and the tree of life. The former represents free will and the ability to procreate, and the latter represents spiritual awareness and, thus, immortality.

A very interesting Biblical passage says;

"And the Lord God said, Look, the man has become as one of us, knowing good from evil: and now what if he puts forth his hand, and takes also of the tree of life, and eats, and lives forever?"
—*Genesis 3:22*

Adam and Eve are then driven from the garden and sentenced to endless toil. The way to the Tree of Life is then guarded by a flaming sword. It seems clear that a group of gods (note the use of plural in the quote), as represented by the 'Lord God', does not want humanity to evolve toward immortality.

According to Sitchin, Gardner and others, the Lord God referred to here, was known to the Sumerians as Enlil, who eventually became Jehovah, the angry God of the Hebrews. The Sumerian god, Enki, who is associated with Thoth/Hermes, is the one responsible for giving civilization to the humans. Gardner claims that he also gave us the tools and guidelines for achieving enlightenment. He is represented by the serpent and is said to have been the rival of Enlil. So they are saying that, contrary to what the Bible says, Enlil/Jehovah was the bad guy, and Enki/the serpent was the good guy! Expert interpreters of the Qabala, such as Carlos Suarez, seem to concur with this view.

There is no mention in the Sumerian account, of Eve having been made from the rib of Adam, or of her being the temptress who tricks Adam into eating the fruit. It is felt that these anti-feminine aspects were injected by the patriarchal ruling class at the time of compilation. In the Christian version of the Genesis account we can see the typical marginalization of the feminine role with the exclusion of any mention of Lilith. The Jewish Talmud mentions her as the consort of Adam before Eve, which is more in line with the Sumerian account. In the Sumerian version, Lilith was strong, proud and independent, mating with several males including Enki. The Hebrew religion vilifies her and refers to her as a temptress. There are many women, such as Nin-khursag, Ki, Erech-kigal and Inanna who play important roles in the Sumerian account.[54]

There is also no mention of Satan in the Sumerian account. In fact, there is no mention of him in the Genesis account. The notion that it was Satan who tempted Eve comes from non-Biblical books that were written by the Church circa 500 AD, the 'Book of Adam and Eve', the 'Book of the Bee' and the 'Book of the Cave of Treasures'. These simplistic books would be laughed at today, and yet the notions that they perpetuated, such as the concept of 'original sin' and Satan, persist to this day.[55] (See BOX 24—SATAN)

After a very strange passage in which, during the days of the Nephilim, 'the sons of God came in to the daughters of men, and they bore children to them', we come to the story of **Noah and the Flood**. Many cultures around the world have flood legends (approximately 500), often with a Noah-like character such as Nene in the Aztec version. From the Mesopotamian region there are several ancient texts with parallel storylines to the Biblical account, including the 'Atra-hasis Epic' from Akkad, and the Babylonian 'Epic of Gilgamesh', which has a character named 'Utna-pishtim' as the Noah figure. Other more ancient tablets were unearthed which contain poems that speak of the flood and a king 'Ziusudra' as the Noah figure.[56]

The main difference between these ancient accounts and the one in Genesis is that, in the case of the former, it is Enlil and the council of gods that plan to cull the growing human herd. In the Bible it is God, angry at the sins of mankind, who decides to eradicate all of humanity with a flood. In either case this seems a cruel and harsh action. In the Sumerian account, it is Nin-khursag and Enki who are opposed to the idea and provide the 'ark'. Rather than a floating zoo of animal couples, the ark carried the 'seeds' of many species to be preserved.

There is some disagreement about the date of the flood. There seems to be a good amount of evidence to suggest that a great flood, accompanied by other forms of cataclysm, took place about 10,000 BC, as noted previously in the book. Gardner, however, contends that there was also a local flood that occurred in Mesopotamia circa 4000 BC.

> **BOX 24—SATAN:** Virtually every member of western society is familiar with the image of 'Satan', the baddest of the bad, purveyor of all evil, the Prince of Darkness. It is a concept that has become a firmly embedded paradigm—an unquestioned, accepted part of religious dogma. However, modern research into the origins of this concept reveal that it was invented by the early Christian Church. The original Hebrew concept of a 'satan' had nothing to do with 'evil'. A satan was originally an obedient servant of God, an adversarial 'force' or 'entity' sent by God to challenge one's faith. The word then evolved to mean any kind of earthly adversary. King David is referred to in early editions of the Bible as a satan of the Philistines. The word was later appropriated by the early Christian patriarchs and made into a proper name. The goat-like imagery of Satan as a horned, cloven-hoofed demon was borrowed from the Greek god of sexual debauchery, Pan. The Church associated this image with 'evil' and wove it into its teachings. There is no mention of Satan in the Genesis stories, yet we've all grown to accept the idea that the serpent who tempted Adam and Eve was Satan in disguise. The symbol of the serpent (or dragon) appears as a positive force in many cultures. It represents the female 'kundalini' energy that resides at the base of the spine. Enlightenment occurs when this energy awakens and travels up the spine to unite with male energy. Judaism, Christianity and Islam have chosen to vilify the serpent.
>
> Some researchers, including Laurence Gardner, feel that the emerging Christian authority needed to invent Satan, to 'put a face' on evil and thus have a strong tool by which to rule the masses with fear.

One of the stranger and more interesting passages in Genesis is the story of *the Tower of Babel*. The gist of the story is that people came to the land of Shinar (the Biblical name for Sumer) and they said,

> "Now the whole earth had one language and few words…And they said, 'Come, let us build ourselves a city, and a tower with its top in the heavens, and let us make a name for ourselves'…" (The Lord sees this and says) "'Behold, they are one people, and they have all one language; and this is only the beginning of what they will do; and nothing that they propose to do will now be impossible for them. Come, let us go down and there confuse their language, that they may not understand one another's speech.' So the Lord scattered them abroad from there, over the face of all the earth…"
>
> —*Genesis 11:1-9*

There are three interesting points to be made here. Firstly, what is meant by 'make a name for ourselves'? The original Hebrew word here is 'shem', which has been replaced in the modern Bible by the word 'name'. According to Sitchin, a shem was an obelisk-like statue shaped like a rocket-ship. He is saying that the humans may have acquired the ability to build a rocket-ship and thus, to be more god-like. Gardner, on the other hand, says that 'shem' refers to a conical stone which was representative of the 'Philosopher's Stone', another name for the 'white gold powder' that was often pressed into such shapes. This would have been ingested to assist in the enlightenment process, rendering the humans more god-like.[57]

The second point is that, once again we have a situation where it seems that a group of gods, lead by the Lord, sabotage human endeavors and impair their ability to cooperate and progress. There seems to be a fear, amongst the gods, of human potential.

Thirdly, the gods decide to scatter humanity 'over the face of the earth'. As mentioned previously, there are many cultures that claim to have been brought to their land in strange flying machines. The Eskimos have legends of having been brought to the North by 'gods with metal wings'. Native Americans have their stories about being transported to their land by the 'thunderbird'. There are also many legends about the confusion of language. Conventional science claims that all languages derived from the same mother tongue. Many believe that tongue to be Sumerian. Others contend that the first universal language was from Atlantean times, a form of telepathy sometimes referred to as 'vril'.[58] (The word 'vril' has other meanings, including 'life-force' or 'prana'.) It is interesting that the first line in Genesis 11 says, 'Now the whole earth had one language and few words.' A telepathic language would certainly have few words.

We now come to the stories of **Abraham**. God (called El Shaddai at this point) guides him out of the Sumerian city of Ur and leads him to Haran and then to Canaan. This is backed up by ancient Sumerian texts, which report an attack leading to the devastation of Sumer and its cities circa 1960 BC. It is clear that the Sumerian account acknowledges the family of Abraham as a powerful dynasty. As mentioned earlier in the book, some feel that there is evidence of nuclear explosions related to this devastation.

El Shaddai appears often to Abraham, and it is at this point in the Bible that he begins to insist that he be the one and only God. He demands obedience, circumcision, sacrifices, etc. There is no mention of love, honesty or other virtues. In return, Abraham is promised prosperity in the land of Canaan (modern day Palestine) for him and his descendants. El Shaddai rules with fear. He seems to condone violence and slavery. (Genesis 17)

In his appearances to Abraham, El Shaddai is often accompanied by 'angels'. (The word 'angel' is derived from the Greek word, 'angelos', which means 'messenger'.) God and the angels are portrayed by the Bible as having flesh and blood bodies, accepting food and footbaths. (Genesis 18)

The Biblical account of the destruction of **Sodom and Gomorrah** is another strange tale. Lot, the nephew of Abraham, is spared while his wife is turned into a pillar of salt for the sin of taking a backward glance at the destruction. The Bible says that God destroyed the twin cities because of their wickedness, but according to a Coptic text called 'The Paraphrase of Shem', they were destroyed because of their wisdom and insight.[59]

The Biblical description sounds very much like some sort of bombing. (Genesis 19:24-28) Alan Alford talks about an ancient Sumerian text called the 'Erra Epic' which describes the destruction in detail, complete with the vaporizing of the entire population. A portion of the description reads, 'He who scorches with fire and he of the evil wind, together performed their evil.' Alford claims that the same Sumerian word for 'salt' can be interpreted as 'vapour'. Lot's wife turning into a 'pillar of vapour' makes more sense in this context. The two cities are said to have existed on land that is now under the waters of the Dead Sea. According to Alford, radioactivity is still measurable there.[60]

Shortly after this momentous event, Lot, who has just lost his wife, is set upon by his daughters who get him drunk and rape him!? (Genesis 19:30-36) There are several examples of less-than-noble behavior by Genesis characters; the patriarch Jacob cheating his brother Esau out of his birthright (Genesis 27); Reuben having sex with his father Jacob's concubine (Genesis 35:22); the sons of Jacob, jealous of their youngest brother Joseph, selling him into slavery and then lying to Jacob (Genesis 37:18-36). Many examples of this type of behavior, as well as some questionable behavior on the part of God himself, can be found in the ensuing books of the Old Testament.

Chapter 30

MOSES, JOSHUA AND THE ARK OF THE COVENANT

Some of the most puzzling and controversial of the Old Testament information, at least in my opinion, is that surrounding Moses, Joshua and the Ark of the Covenant. This is the story of how the Israelites, led out of Egyptian captivity by Moses, acquire the enigmatic Ark of the Covenant and then proceed to conquer everyone in their path, building a wealthy and powerful empire based in Jerusalem. The information in this story and the Mosaic law that it yielded is some of the most important in the Bible, as it forms the underpinning of the entire Judeao-Christian/Muslim tradition. This includes dangerous notions of 'promised lands' and 'chosen people'; concepts that continue to seriously threaten peace on this planet.

And yet, is any of this information being carefully examined or seriously challenged? The key questions that need to be addressed regarding this story are; who was Moses, what was the Ark of the Covenant, what was Joshua's mission and who was this mysterious entity called Jehovah? Furthermore, where does this information come from? Are these scriptures truly representative of 'the word of God'? Is it even accurate history?

Before taking a look at such questions, let me present a brief account of the story, in chronological order, *according to the Revised Standard Version of the Bible*, pausing now and then at passages that I find curious. After looking at the Biblical account, we'll check out some alternative sources.

It seems to me that, although many people have strong feelings about the Bible, very few have actually read it. It really is a strange set of writings. Even without referring to alternative information, there is much in the Bible to challenge the dominant religious paradigms of today.

A child born to a Levite couple was saved from the Pharaoh's pledge to kill the firstborn males of all Israelites by being set adrift in the Nile in a reed basket. The child was found by the Pharaoh's daughter who claimed it for her own, naming it **Moses**. She had it returned to its mother to be nursed, then, at an appropriate age, the child was taken by the princess. We hear nothing further about Moses' youth. As an adult, said to be forty years of age, he kills an Egyptian in the process of defending a Jew and is forced into exile amongst the Midianite Jews, living just outside of Egypt. He marries Zipporah, the daughter of the Midianite leader and priest, Jethro.

The Lord, the same God of Abraham, Isaac and Jacob, appears to Moses in a burning bush and recruits him as the man who will lead the Israelites to the promised land. When asked his name, the Lord says, "I am that I am", which in old Hebrew is YHWH, eventually coming to be known as Yahweh and/or Jehovah. After Moses pleads that he is "not eloquent" and "slow of speech", the Lord tells him to recruit his Levite brother **Aaron** who "can speak well", as a partner. God then instructs Moses to make sure he performs "all the miracles" for the Pharaoh, but makes the point that he will "harden his (the Pharaoh's) heart, so that he will not let the people go". (Exodus 4:21) In many subsequent passages, such as Exodus 10:1, it seems to be important to the Lord that the Pharaoh's heart be hardened, that he refuse to let the people go, so that he will be forced to witness the whole range of the power of the Hebrew god and thus conclude that he is more powerful than any other god.

Moses and Aaron go back and forth to the Pharaoh, demanding that he let the Israelites go or suffer the ever-worsening **plagues** conjured by Moses, acting on behalf of the Hebrew God. It is curious that Pharaoh and his "wise men and sorcerers" remain unimpressed by the first few 'plagues' because the Egyptian court magicians were equally capable of such magic feats. (Exodus 7:11, 7:22, and 8:7) Finally, at the urging of the terrified Egyptians who had had all their firstborn children killed, the Pharaoh succumbs and Moses leads the people out of Egypt. At that time Moses was eighty years old.

At the Lord's bidding Moses led them, not via the easy road, but into the wilderness towards the Red Sea. God did this so that he would "get glory over Pharaoh" and so that "the Egyptians shall know that I am the Lord". We all know about the parting of the Red Sea and the drowning of the Egyptian horde. (Many are unaware that there were other miraculous partings of the waters. At a later time, the Ark of the Covenant is used to part the Jordan River, allowing Joshua and the Israelites to cross.)

The subsequent meanderings in the Sinai Desert all occur under the watchful guidance of the Lord, whose presence is almost always accompanied by smoke, fire, ground tremors and loud noises. (Just a few examples—Exodus 13:21, 19:18, 20:18, 40:38, etc.) Moses is reportedly borne on eagle's wings to be shown things by God. These and many other references have led some researchers to contend that Jehovah was an ET, and it is easy to see how these depictions could be interpreted as a technologically advanced being in a flying machine.

The Lord makes it quite clear that he demands subservience and exclusive devotion from the Israelites, lest they suffer the same fate as the Egyptians. He professed to be *"a jealous God"* and promised to punish the offspring "to the third and fourth generation" of any man that would worship any god but him. (Exodus 20:4, 22:20) Rule by terror was clearly the order of the day, and the Israelites' *fear of the Lord* is often mentioned.

The Lord also provides them with quail, manna and water, as well as an enormous number of explicit, detailed instructions and regulations regarding their behavior. This included what and what not to eat, their laws, including the protocol around the buying and selling of slaves and the strange justice system based on the idea of "an eye for an eye, a tooth for a tooth". Amongst these ordinances are the 'shall nots', the commandments, although they are not called commandments at this point. (Exodus 20:2-17) This great volume of rules and ordinances called the book of the covenant (not capitalized as in Exodus 24:7) was given privately to Moses who then read it to the people.

He then went up into Mount Sinai again, for forty days, to be given another large volume of explicit, detailed instructions regarding various rituals, including the details of their animal sacrifices. He was also given specific directions and dimensions for the construction of their sacred objects, such as the seven branched lampstand, the altar and the Ark of the Covenant. Lengthy instructions were also given for the indoctrination into priesthood of Aaron and his sons. Then Moses descends the mountain carrying "the two tables of the testimony", covered on both sides with the "writing of God". There is no mention of the commandments. Were these lengthy instructions written on the stone tablets? What were these stone tablets? (That the commandments were written on stone tablets is mentioned briefly in Deuteronomy 5:6-22, although it is not made clear as to which set of tablets)

At this point Moses finds the Israelites worshipping a golden calf which, curiously, was built under the supervision of Aaron, Moses' right hand man. In a fit of rage he smashes the stone tables, an act which seems strange, given that these God-written objects would surely have been the most sacred things that Moses had ever held in his hands. He burns the golden idol into white powder and scatters it over the water which he makes the people drink.(Exodus

32:20) This is also very curious in light of the information on white powdered gold which was discussed in Part Three. At God's bidding, Moses then has 3,000 men killed by the Levite priests, but no mention is made of any retribution towards Aaron, the top Levite.

Moses then goes up the mountain to spend another forty days with the Lord, who gives him further instructions, ordering Moses to write down the words of God's covenant with the Israelites. Moses then "wrote upon the tables the words of the covenant, the ten commandments". This is the first mention of **the Ten Commandments** as such, and a footnote points out that the original Hebrew word used here was the word 'word'. Thus, it originally read 'the ten words'. As mentioned earlier in this book, the word 'word' was also used to represent 'sound', 'light' or 'vibration'. Curiously, the next section tells of Moses arriving at the foot of the mountain with the tablets, and "the skin of his face shone". (Exodus 34:29-34) Although I'm pointing these things out now, their significance will become clear later, when I'm talking in more detail about the Ark of the Covenant.

In accord with very explicit instructions, the Ark, its altars and tabernacle and various ceremonial trappings are constructed, Aaron and the Levites are consecrated as priests and the elaborate methods of worshipping the Lord are taught to the people. Detailed instruction on the sacrificial burning of livestock and crops, so as to provide "a pleasing odour to the Lord" is given to them, as recorded in the next Biblical book, Leviticus. The Lord outlines many laws, complete with the punishments that would accompany the breaking of such laws, many of them pertaining to acts that were deemed blasphemous or heretical. Even the slightest questioning of the authority of God was not tolerated. The punishments were very severe, the death sentence by public stoning used for a wide range of offences, including gathering firewood on the Sabbath.

Reported in the Book of Numbers are several examples of **insurrection**, situations where factions of the Israelites suggest returning to Egypt rather than face the continuing hardships of life in the desert. These challenges are always dealt with harshly and the numbers, quoted in the Bible, of Israelites said to have been put to death for such insurrection is in the tens of thousands. (All of the quantities of people cited in the Bible are quite large, leading some to believe they were errant or greatly exaggerated.) A plague sent by God in punishment kills 14,700 Israelites (Numbers 16:49); several influential families and the people affiliated with them were executed when God caused the earth to open up and swallow them; 250 were killed when "a fire came forth from the Lord" (Numbers 16:31). These types of incidents occur quite often.

One interesting insurrection occurs when God orders them to attack a settlement of Amorite 'giants' whom they called "Nephilim" or "men of great stature". (Numbers 13:32-33) In fear of these large warriors, the Israelites contemplate returning to Egypt. God becomes disgusted at their lack of faith in him and vows that they will never see the Holy Land but will die in the wilderness. In fact, the Israelites were made to wander in the desert for forty years because God wanted to test their faith in him. Most of the older generation failed this test and, along with Moses and Aaron, were forbidden to set foot in the Promised Land.

With God's help, they thump the Amorites and several other groups, whom they "**utterly destroyed**". This is an expression, often made clear in the Bible, meaning that every single person, including women and children, were put to death. They also warred against their kin, the Midianites, slaying every male. (Numbers 31:7-8) God continually reassures them that they will prevail in all the forthcoming wars and that they will enjoy the booty of such wars as long as they fear and serve the Lord. (Deuteronomy 6:10-15) God makes it clear that none of them are to marry or mingle with the conquered people or allow themselves to be exposed to their gods, ordering that they be 'utterly destroyed'. (Deuteronomy 7:1-5) He often makes it clear that the Israelites are his 'chosen people'. (Deuteronomy 7:6) The covenant between them would more or less read; 'If you make me your exclusive God and do whatever I say, I will make you my chosen people and make sure that you prosper. If you refuse, I will destroy you'. This sounds more like the classic notion of a 'deal with the devil'.

With the death of Moses (120 years old) and Aaron (123 years old), *Joshua* becomes the leader of the Israelites and the mayhem goes into high gear. On what seems to be a mission to exterminate the population of the entire area, Joshua goes from town to town killing every man woman and child, burning the city and leaving with the livestock, gold and silver. All this is done under the direct guidance of God who explicitly instructs Joshua. Jericho, Ai, Makke'dah, Libnah, Gezer, Eglon, Hebron and Debir are some of the settlements that were utterly destroyed. Some of the residents of towns such as Gibeon, Chephi'rah, Beer'oth, and Kir'iath-je'arim were spared total annihilation and were taken as slaves. This is all summarized in Joshua 10: 40-43.

God makes it clear that he will not tolerate the Israelites if they worship other gods. It is several times mentioned that they had served many gods in the past, including at the time of Abraham and during the time in Egypt. Joshua warns them to "fear the Lord" and to "put away the gods which your fathers served beyond the River, and in Egypt." (Joshua 24: 14, also 24: 2).

As pointed out in the next book, Judges, the Israelites often forgot this advice and slipped back into serving the *pagan gods*, especially Baal and the goddess Ashtaroth. This is often described as, "they played the harlot after other gods", a curious expression that is never explained in the Bible context.

The Book of Judges is almost totally concerned with the quelling of insurrection, always with a cruel and heavy hand, or with various internal struggles. In one curious story, 300 of them under the leadership of Gideon attack and subdue thousands of their kin, the Midianites, using some mysterious magic provided by God.

One of the stranger stories in the Bible is the one about **Samson**. (Judges 13 –17) He is a longhaired Nazirite, endowed with great 'strength'. We picture Samson as 'Arnold Schwarzeneggar with long hair'. Nowhere in this episode, however, is it made clear that this strength is merely physical, as we have come to believe. How likely is it that even the most incredibly powerful of physiques could slay a thousand Philistines using a donkey's rather small jawbone? The impressive feats of Samson, many of which are quite bizarre, seem to be implying some magical* ability which occurs when "the Spirit of the Lord came mightily upon him". It is also interesting to note that he is often in the company of harlots. (* The word 'magic' as used in this book, does not refer to the modern type of trickery used by an entertainer/illusionist, but rather the ancient body of knowledge by which an adept can learn to understand the various laws of energy and to control one's circumstances using a highly developed will.)

The Books of Samuel basically describe the fulfillment of the Israelites' wish to have a monarchy. Much of the action takes place in the context of the continuing struggle with the Philistines, and at one point the Ark of the Covenant is taken out of retirement in an attempt to defeat them. However, the Philistines capture the Ark and keep it for seven months. They then return the Ark, which has caused them nothing but grief in the form of tumors and other afflictions.

Saul, a Benjamite, is made king by God, only to be stripped of his title shortly thereafter for having "rejected the word of the Lord". David, a Judaite, is made king and is deemed "righteous in the eyes of the Lord". To make a long story short, he proceeds to conquer and pillage much of the region amidst a great deal of smiting in the name of God. Thus begins the Golden Age of Israel, an era of prosperity and victory that is the direct result of a renewed exclusive adherence to the laws of YHWH. The Bible continues to stress the righteousness of the tribe of Judah and the sinfulness of the other tribes. The center of the empire shifts to Jerusalem, in the heart of Judaite territory.

King David was greatly popular and united the Israelites as never before. The two Books of Kings continues the story, dealing mostly with the reign of **Solomon**, one of David's many children from many wives, and the kings that came after him. Solomon raises Israel to unprecedented glory, with the accumulation of great wealth and the implementation of many building projects. The greatest of these is the Temple of Jerusalem, which houses the Ark of the Covenant and is decreed as the exclusive location for sacrifices and rituals pertaining to the worship of YHWH.

Eventually, however, Solomon falls from grace because he "did what was evil in the sight of the Lord". Solomon must have had an incredible sexual appetite. According to the Bible, he had 700 wives and 300 concubines. Many of these wives, contrary to God's wishes, were from cultures foreign to Israel. What was worse, Solomon allowed them to influence his choice of gods and "did not wholly follow the Lord, as David his father had done". (1 Kings 11:1-9) God withdrew his support for Solomon, battles were no longer victorious and the Golden Age of Israel went into decline.

Shortly thereafter, the Israelites broke into *two factions*. The tribe of Judah lived in the southern highlands, which was named Judah, and the other tribes in the northern highlands, which became known as Israel. (Because it can be confusing to refer to this faction as 'Israel', which is also used to refer to the entire nation of the Israelites, I will use the term 'Northern Kingdom', which is also used in the Bible.) The two factions, with their own separate monarchies, develop an ongoing antagonism. The northern kings, including Omri, Ahab and his notorious wife Jezebel, and many others, are almost invariably portrayed as weak sinners, succumbing to idolatry and the worship of foreign gods. Finally, the Northern Kingdom is crushed by the Assyrians during the reign of its last king, Hoshea, circa 725 BC. Its residents are dispersed, some to Egypt and other countries, some to exile in Nineveh, the capital of Assyria.

The Judaite kings, by contrast, are usually portrayed as being loyal in the eyes of YHWH, the only hope of a united Israel nation. Although some of the Judaite kings, like Menasseh, are portrayed negatively, the Judaite monarchy is looked upon favorably by God. It peaks with the reign of *Josiah*, who introduces many strict reforms and conquers much of the land left vacant in the Northern Kingdom. The Israelites enjoy a brief mini-golden era under the rule of Josiah, but shortly thereafter, the Chaldeans of Babylon devastate Judah, razing the Temple and carrying the aristocracy and priesthood off to exile in Babylon. Many of the remaining people fled to Egypt.

One of the main reasons I have chosen to point out this Biblical narrative is because, when I read this section of the Bible, I couldn't help but notice that there is virtually no mention of love and compassion anywhere. It seems to me to be a story about terror, murder and thievery involving a people who are under the thumb of a very strange entity whom they are forced to call 'God'. I invite you to close your eyes and to get in touch with the image, residing in your heart of hearts, of the one Force, the Creator, the Source or, if you like, God. Then, read the Old Testament with its portrait of God and ask whether this character fits the image that resides in your heart.

I have no problem answering this question for myself. No amount of torture could make me willfully state that I believe this mysterious entity, as described in the Old

Testament, to be the one and only God. The image of the 'true God' that I have in my heart is not in accordance with one who rules with fear, who encourages genocide, slavery and theft, and who would try to trick and manipulate a people into thinking they were the 'chosen race'. We recently had such an entity living amongst us; his name was Adolph Hitler. He was, in my opinion, a very confused individual, a player of the Game making strange decisions for strange reasons, who came to wield great power. If this Old Testament account is accurate, then the above description could also be applied to the Biblical 'God'.

One big difference between this 'God' and Hitler is that the biggest religious movements on the planet, that have had a huge hand in shaping life as we know it, are not based on the actions of Hitler. They are, however, based on those of this strange Biblical character who has become known as YHWH or Jehovah. The 'God' outlined in the first part of the Bible is the one on which the entire Old Testament is built upon, the same entity known to Muslims as Allah and the same entity known to Christians as God the Father of Jesus. How can this be?

How can we have been led to believe that this Jehovah dude, as described in the Bible, is the one and only God? How can we believe that this book is the 'word of God'? Have humans altered the book beyond recognition? Maybe the Biblical God was not as nasty as portrayed by the authors. Have they misrepresented this God to achieve their own selfish ends? Is this entity, who insists on being called God, actually just a confused player of the Game like you or I, with his own imbalanced agenda? If the Old Testament depiction of the one and only God is accurate, I'd say we're all in big, big trouble.

Chapter 31

TRYING TO MAKE SENSE OF A NASTY GOD

It is not easy to make sense of this angry, vengeful, jealous version of God. How did this portrait come about? Did he really name the Israelites as the chosen people with sole entitlement to the Promised Land? Did he actually terrorize his subjects as depicted in the Bible? Did he name the tribe of Judah as the only ones fit to rule the Israelites? In an effort to answer some of the many questions regarding this quandary, let us take a look at some possibilities that may shed some light and perhaps offer some explanations.

Possibility # 1. This image of Jehovah originates with Moses. Was he a very clever magician (possibly the same person as the pharaoh Akhenaten) who either—a) tried to get the message of 'one universal god' to the people, or—

b) manipulated the people into subservience. He may have been a volunteer soul come to help humanity, or the servant of some less noble intent. Mosaic Law is the very foundation of the entire Judeo-Christian heritage. Who was Moses?

Possibility # 2. Jehovah was some alien entity with his own agenda who had at his disposal advanced technology, which he used to bend Moses and the Israelites to his will. Perhaps the Ark of the Covenant, flying machines and sophisticated weaponry are some examples of this high technology.

Possibility # 3. The compilers of the Old Testament distorted the ancient writings and oral traditions, misrepresenting Jehovah as an angry, jealous and vengeful God who would severely punish whomever disobeyed the law. This was done largely for political motives, to unite the Jewish people under one belief system so that they could be controlled and manipulated.

Possibility # 4. None of the above.

Possibility # 5. All of the above.

Possibility # 1. This image of Jehovah was introduced to the people through Moses.

Without denying the importance of the Genesis stories, probably the section of the Bible most basic and central to the subsequent development of the entire Judeo-Christian tradition is the one dealing with the adventures of Moses. He is credited with having written the first five books of the Bible. He is cited as the key intermediary between God and the people, the vehicle through whom God's will was made known. The events surrounding Moses can be said to represent the very foundation of the entire Bible. Not before this time does God come into direct contact with the people. It's time to ponder the question, ***who was Moses?***

The Bible's sketchy account of the dubious notion that Moses was rescued from a reed basket floating in the river is almost certainly borrowed from other stories such as those surrounding Osiris. Babylonian legends of Sargon the Great of Sumer also have him being rescued from a floating basket. However, the idea that he was adopted as a youth by the Pharaoh's daughter, Thermuthis, was acknowledged by Josephus, who suggests that she was drawn to the youth's "beauty, strength and understanding". Flavius Josephus was a historian who lived around the time of Jesus, many hundreds of years after the time of Moses. The sources of his information are uncertain.[61]

There are different explanations for the name 'Moses'. Josephus says that the name means 'one who is saved from the water', but also suggests that Moses was a high-grade priest with the name Osarsis, which means 'Child of Osiris'. Laurence Gardner claims that 'Moses' is not an actual name, but comes from a word that means 'born of', used in conjunction with a name. The pharaoh, Thutmoses, for example, means 'born of Thoth'. There are several names of pharaohs that include the word 'moses'.[62]

The Bible says nothing about Moses after his adoption by the princess, until he is well into adulthood. Certainly he must have had a very interesting youth and upbringing. According to Philo Judaeus, a Jewish philosopher/theologian living in Alexandria at the time of Christ, he was taught mathematics, geometry, rhythm and harmony, astrology, necromancy, the occult sciences, etc. The great scholar, Sir E.A. Wallis Budge claims that he was trained in the various branches of Egyptian magic, and that Moses was a 'Kher Heb', a high priest of the Egyptian Temple. As such, he would have had access to secret writings and esoteric knowledge.[63] The Bible says that he was instructed "in all the wisdom of the Egyptians", and that he was "mighty in words and deeds". It was already pointed out that he was a weak orator, so was this statement referring to magic which is often associated with special words, sounds and incantations?

An enigmatic character in the Moses story is that of Miriam, said by the Bible to be Moses' sister. In the Book of Jasher, one of the most important of the ancient books which was not chosen to be part of the Old Testament canon, there is much information on this woman. However, the Bible completely marginalizes her. According to Jasher she was a powerful woman, a leader in her own right and an ongoing guide and advisor to Moses and Aaron. She was very much beloved by the Israelites and the Book of Jasher implies that she was more popular than Moses himself. This important part of the equation was completely ignored by the Bible, as were all women who played important roles.[64]

Several opinions have contended that Moses was the same man as *Akhenaten*, the one called the 'heretic pharaoh'. Interestingly, this opinion is held by the famous purveyor of psychoanalysis, Sigmund Freud, who was obsessed with Moses and wrote the book, 'Moses and Monotheism'.

Laurence Gardner also feels this way and goes to great lengths explaining it in terms of bloodlines and 'who begat whom' at that time. He says that Akhenaten/Moses was the offspring of the pharaoh Amenhotep III and his second wife, Tiya, daughter of Yusef-Yuya, Vizier to the pharaoh who was a Hyksos. Some claim that he was the same Yusef/Joseph, son of Jacob that had risen to prominence in the Biblical account. Gardner claims otherwise. There is much confusion and controversy about this point amongst various sources.

Gardner claims that Nefertiti was half sister to Akhenaten/Moses, the offspring of the pharaoh and his first queen. She was a full-blooded heir of Egyptian royalty. Another half sister from yet another marriage of the pharaoh and an Egyptian was Merry-Amon, who joined the Exodus, becoming the Biblical Miriam. One of Akhenaten's first cousins was named Smenkh-ka-ra, or

Smenkh-ka-ra-on. He was actually pharaoh for a very short while after Akhenaten's abdication, while Akhenaten's son Tutenkhamen was too young. Gardner says that he was the Biblical Aaron, a name derived from the last few syllables of the full name. Strangely, both he and Akhenaten seem to have disappeared, no tomb ever having been discovered. Gardner says that Akhenaten/Moses was married to both his half-sisters, Nefertiti and Mery-Amon as well as Zipporah, the daughter of the Midian leader, Jethro.[65]

Other opinions contend that Moses' ideas of monotheism influenced Akhenaten's or vice versa. Scholars, in trying to reconcile historical dates with Biblical dates admit that there is a great deal of confusion regarding the time of the Exodus from Egypt. Thrown into the mix of confusion is the eruption and destruction of the Santorini volcano, which occurred right around the same time. It would have been an enormous event, occurring over a span of thirty years, that would have effected the entire region with huge tidal waves, smoke, debris, etc.

It is possible that Moses and Akhenaten were contemporaries or that they were in fact the same person. Much of this speculation is based on the writings of the ancient historian, Manetho. As previously mentioned, the Semitic people known as the Hyksos were in power in Egypt up until shortly before the Exodus. The defeat of the Hyksos and takeover of power by the 18th dynasty, the forebears of Akhenaten, happened during a time of schism within Egypt. There is no reason to believe that all Semites were immediately expelled. There was almost certainly a period of overlap between the two dynasties. Both Moses and Akhenaten, it would appear, are half Semite and half Egyptian. (In Moses' case, the Egyptian half comes from his adoption, according to the Bible, although other sources hint strongly that it was also genetic.) In fact, there are some very interesting co-relationships between Moses and Akhenaten.

Let's review for a moment, the relevant information about the life of this enigmatic pharaoh. Akhenaten was a devout mystic, some say a religious fanatic, who ruled for thirteen years (some say seventeen years). In that short time he turned Egypt upside down, disbanding the army and proclaiming the virtues of peace. He dismantled the priesthood and abolished the polytheistic system that had dominated Egypt for centuries, in favour of monotheism. He legislated worship of one universal energy source, which was symbolized by the solar disc called the 'Aten', changing his name from Amenhotep IV to Akhenaten. (Most pharaohs had the name of a god incorporated into their own name. Thus 'Amen' was changed to 'Aten'.) He then moved the Egyptian capital from Thebes to Akhetaten, which means 'city of the sun's disc'. There he built new temples in accordance with sacred geometric proportions.

He and his wife *Nefertiti* are depicted with strange, bulbous heads, elon-

gated bodies and androgenous shapes. No Egyptians before or after are depicted in this way. Some sources have said that they were ET's or 'volunteers' who
came to try to get Egypt back on track as a theocracy intent on facilitating the
enlightenment process of any or all of the people. Other sources, such as
Alford and Icke, say that it was Akhenaten who distorted the notion of one
central 'source', assigning the idea of 'one God' to an individual entity—
YHWH. This distortion was then used as a way to oppress the masses, and was
transferred to the Israelites via Moses.

Sources other than Gardner say that there is controversy about the way in
which Akhenaten came to power. His mother, Tyi (or Tiya) was said to have
been an exceptional woman, not of royal blood, who was married by
Amenhotep III, Akhenaten's father. She is said by some sources to have been
Hebrew, a descendant of Yusuf, the Vizier. Thus he was not of royal lineage by
both parents and his right to the throne was said to be dependant upon his
marriage to Nefertiti, who was of pure royal blood. Some say that she was his
half sister. Royal marriages to a half-sister were very common, a way of keeping bloodlines as pure as possible.

Akhenaten was not popular. The people looked forward to the wealth that
an aggressive army could bring home and were fond of their old polytheistic
religious customs. They wanted their army and priest-hood back, so
Akhenaten's reign was cut short. He is said to have gone into exile. It is strange
that, despite the fact that so many of his works and information about him
was found, the whereabouts of his tomb remains a mystery. The tombs of
almost all of the pharaohs from this period have been found, yet Akhenaten
seems to have just disappeared. Is it possible that his tomb, as well as that of
Smenkh-ka-ra, were not found because they left with the Israelites, to become
known eventually as Moses and Aaron?

Were the Israelites in the Bible the same people as the Hyksos Semites? This
is the view held by Manetho, according to Joy Collier in her book, 'The Heretic
Pharaoh'. Archeologists have also suggested this based on the complete
absence in the extensive Egyptian records of any reference to a group called
'Israelites'. (more on this later) Is it possible, then, that having failed to convey his message of one god to the Egyptians, he became leader of the Hyksos,
to whom he was kin? Were his efforts to teach monotheism transferred to
them? Was it the Hyksos Semites that Moses/Akhenaten led out of Egypt?

All of this information about Moses is very confusing, yet much of it seems
quite convincing. Without arriving at any definite conclusions, it seems clear
that there is much more to the Moses story than what is given in the Bible.
Were the Bible writers trying to hide something or put forward a false picture?
Modern writing analysts have identified several different sources responsible
for the authoring of the hodge-podge of conflicting and differing accounts

that became the Biblical Moses story. It differs significantly from the information from other sources. Along with the many questions about his identity and his motives, this important question remains; Was Moses responsible for the picture we have of this nasty God?

Perhaps he was an incredibly skilled magician whose feats came from a special awareness and facility with the 'laws of energy', or in other words, someone who was in touch with the 'one source'. Were these 'supernatural' feats thus assigned to the idea of one universal God? Was the Ark of the Covenant some sort of magical device?

Given the volumes of scholarly evidence, I believe it is safe to say that Moses himself did not write the first five books of the Old Testament. Possibly whoever did write them chose to distort the story by assigning the idea of the 'one source' to an entity that they called Jehovah, and by portraying this entity as being angry, jealous, vengeful, etc. Maybe this happened deliberately, for political reasons, or maybe it was due to a genuine misunderstanding, or maybe a little of both.

According to the Bible, Moses did not make contact with this entity who insisted on being called YHWH/Jehovah until the burning bush incident in Midian when he was forty years old. The Book of Jasher, in which there is no mention of Jehovah, tells of Moses' attempts to consolidate his views with those of the Midianite leader, Jethro. The Midianites, who lived just outside of Egypt, were also Hebrews descended from Esau and worshipped an entity they still called El Shaddai. Did Moses compromise the idea of a single, universal force (Aten) with the Midian devotion to their god in an attempt to unite the two Hebrew factions? Jasher suggests this and says that it caused Moses to have a big falling out with Miriam, who was dead against such a compromise.

Was Moses an ambitious man, hungry for power? Maybe it was Moses himself who was distorting the truth and manipulating the people. Or maybe it was Moses being manipulated. Was he under the control of some nasty entity who called himself Jehovah? This leads us to our next scenario in an attempt to address the question; who or what was Jehovah?

Possibility # 2. Was Jehovah an Extraterrestrial?

Modern Bibles refer to the Hebrew god as either 'the Lord' or as 'God'. This however, is the result of fairly recent translations. In the original texts, up until the scene with Moses and the burning bush, the Hebrew God was referred to as *El Shaddai* (god of the mountain) or the *Elohim*. ('Elohim' is a plural, feminine word meaning 'gods', the singular being 'El'. Thus 'Israel' means 'soldier of El'. All the archangels' names end with 'el'.)

It is the contention of Sitchin, Gardiner and others, that the Elohim refers to the Sumerian gods, ETs known as the Annunaki, and that El Shaddai was the leader of that group, known as *Enlil*. He was known to the early Mesopotamians as Ilu Kurgal, which also means 'god of the mountain'. Enlil's sister/consort was Ashtoreth (the Biblical Ashteroth or Asherah), and his son was Baal. Both of these deities are mentioned often in the Old Testament as the evil Canaanite gods whom the Israelites worshipped when they went astray from the righteous worship of God alone.

Moses, however is instructed to refer to El Shaddai as *YHWH*. Traditionally, Hebrew was written with no vowels or punctuation and the original YHWH eventually became Yahweh (pronounced yahveh) and then Jehovah (pronounced 'yehoveh'). According to the Bible, YHWH means 'I am that I am'. To the occult, mystical traditions of Judaism, known as The QBLH or Qabala, YHWH is known as the *Tetragrammaton.* It is said to have been a powerful mantra, capable of invoking 'magic', and the Jews were forbidden to say the word aloud. The correct pronunciation of this word, instrumental in unleashing its power, is a well kept secret. This is what led to the use of 'Jehovah'.

The Qabala also cites the four letters of the Tetragrammaton as representing father, mother, son and daughter. Some researchers feel that the compilers of the Bible during the exile in Babylon (c. 580 BC) deleted all reference to the mother/goddess. They say that the true power of the Tetragrammaton, YHWH, will not return until the female component is reintroduced and becomes, once again, entrenched in the human psyche as equal to the male component. (Another powerful Tetragrammaton is said to be MRYM, [some say MRAM] the source of names such as Miriam and possibly Mary M. 'Mary' is thought to have originally been a title rather than a name. It was given to a woman who was considered a priestess or prophetess.[66]

What was the *Ark of the Covenant*? In the Bible it is often referred to as the embodiment of God himself, imbued with various supernatural powers which were often deadly. It has been described as emitting strange lights and fire, being surrounded by smoke or 'cloud', and even dispensing advice like some sort of oracle. Its powers include the infliction of cancerous tumors and burns, leveling whole cities, including the walls of Jericho, subduing vast armies and parting the waters of the Jordan so that Joshua and his men could cross at flood time. It was dangerous to be anywhere near the Ark and many died just by looking at it or touching it. Even King David was afraid of it. (2 Samuel 6: 6-12)

According to Louis Ginzberg writing in 'Legends of the Jews', and to Midrashic accounts, the Ark also displayed some strange anti-gravitational qualities. There are several stories of it levitating or throwing its bearers into the air.[67]

One of the great mysteries is that such an important object actually *disappeared* without explanation in the Bible. There have been many attempts to locate the Ark, including those made by researcher Graham Hancock in his book, 'The Sign and the Seal'. He makes a case that the Ark is hidden somewhere in Ethiopia, having been brought there by Menelik, the son of Solomon and Makeda, the Queen of Sheba.

The instructions for the construction of the Ark were very specific and its handlers were specifically trained and clothed. A ***description of the Ark*** is given in Exodus, where the dimensions are in cubits, a cubit being equal to eighteen inches. It was a wooden chest measuring three feet nine inches long by two feet three inches high and wide. It was lined inside and out with pure gold. On its heavy golden lid there were two figures of winged cherubim facing each other. The Ark was carried by four bearers holding two poles that passed through rings under the bottom of the Ark.

In Joshua 3:34 the people are instructed to "come not near unto it", and to stay at least 2000 cubits from it, which is equivalent to about a half-mile. Its use in the conquest of ***Jericho***, as reported in chapter six of the Book of Joshua, is puzzling. With the main mass of Israelites well back, the Ark was carried around the walls of Jericho for seven days, accompanied by seven priests blowing trumpets. On the last day, assisted by the loud shouting of the masses, this process brought the walls tumbling down.

So, does the Ark use some kind of radioactive force? Is it a sonic device that somehow generates or amplifies sound vibration? Does the Ark itself emit these forces, or is it the tablets contained by the Ark that make up the power source? Here are some points to consider:

1. The Ark was made with a large amount of gold, which sealed it completely. Gold is a dense, chemically non-reactive element, which like lead, can contain radioactivity. The Ark is very similar in appearance to other Egyptian containers used to transport important items, such as those found in King Tut's tomb with the sarcophagus. The Ark had to be draped in its protective covering of heavy cloth and leather, possibly to protect from electric shock. All this suggests that it was a container for the real power source.

2. When Moses came down the mountain with the second set of tablets, his face shone as though it had been exposed to some strong light. There is no such report regarding the first set, which he discarded, throwing them to the ground. As I mentioned previously, in the Exodus account the tablets are inscribed with the ancient Hebrew word for 'word', which also means 'sound'. (Exodus 34:28) Were these strange tablets capable of emitting sound? Were they radioactive? Were they made from some meteorite?

3. According to the combined descriptions in the Old Testament, and Jewish texts such as the Mishnah, the Midrash and the Talmud, the tablets were made from a very heavy, sapphire-like stone which was transparent and hard, yet flexible!?[68]

The Ark of the Covenant is surely one of the greatest mysteries. Did it really exist, or was it purely a product of fiction? If it was real, it certainly sounds like it could have been some sort of advanced technology, possibly of other-worldly origins.

So how do we make sense of all this as it relates to the angry God of the Old Testament. Was he an ET with his own agenda, named Enlil, who appropriated the magical mantra YHWH, bullying the Hebrews into calling him by that name? Was this mantra actually his 'calling card', a tool by which people could summon him and his powers? Was he really as nasty a fellow as the Bible makes him out to be, or was his identity blurred by the manipulations and political motives of the Old Testament compilers?

Possibility # 3. The image of Jehovah was a man-made distortion.

The notion that YHWH and his message, via Moses, was misrepresented by 'the compilers', as well as many aspects of history, is not hard to imagine. It is certainly no secret that many pertinent texts such as the Book of Jasher, the Book of Jubilees, the Book of Enoch, and many others were consciously excluded from the collection. That the chosen texts were manipulated and highly edited is also no big secret. What is surprising, however, is the degree to which this was done.

Although we'll probably never know with accuracy the degree to which the 'truth' was altered, one good measuring device is to compare Biblical information with the findings of **modern archeology**. A very useful book for such an endeavor is 'The Bible Unearthed', by two Jewish scholars, Israel Finkelstein and Neil Asher Silberman. This book is a synopsis of the latest developments and opinions held by a large number of archeologists around the world. Much of the information in this next section comes from this source.

One of the first issues addressed by the book is the contention that Moses wrote the Torah or Pentateuch (the crucial first five books of the Bible). Most modern scholars feel that, based on expert analysis of the writing styles, among other factors, Moses could not have been the writer. They have identified two main styles or sources among several lesser sources. The first source refers to God as YHWH and focuses on the tribe of Judah and is thus called 'source J'. The second one, referring to God as El and focusing on the northern tribes, is called 'source E'. The Book of Deuteronomy is said to come from a third source, an independent document that was labeled 'source D'. Several others are known collectively as the priestly source—'source P'.

The Pentateuch, therefore, is a collection of a variety of circumstances and perspectives. Differing to a greater degree from the other sources, Deuteronomy is said to derive from a mysterious 'Book of the Law', which was reputedly 'found' by the high priest, Hilkiah, during the reign of the Judaite king, Josiah (c. 622 BC) during a renovation of the Temple. This led to a strict puritan reform. The books following Dueteronomy are similar in tone, and are referred to as ***Deuteronomistic history***. Scholars feel sure that these books were written during the time of Josiah and were edited and compiled, together with other writings, during the Babylonian exile a few decades later.

These books heavily favor the tribe of Judah, almost always extolling their acts as being favorable to God. The other tribes of the Northern Kingdom are depicted as weak, idolatrous sinners who are not viewed favorably by God. The authors make no bones about their contention that much of the Old Testament was doctored by the priests and aristocrats surrounding Josiah of Judah. The reasons for this propaganda will become clear shortly.

Without going through all the archeological evidence, which would require a fair bit of space, but which is outlined very comprehensively in 'The Bible Unearthed', I will attempt to put forth the main observations, which are quite shocking.

Many of the places and peoples that are mentioned in the Genesis accounts of the patriarchs, Abraham, Isaac, Jacob, etc, are said by archeology to have been non-existent at the time of the patriarchs, which was from about 1960 to 1500 BC. They are much more indicative of the way the world looked at the time of Josiah, about 625 BC. Most of the villains and enemies throughout the Old Testament turn out to be representative of the enemies of Josiah. The state of Edom, for example, said to consist of the descendants of Esau, the disinherited brother of Jacob, inhabited the same region of Palestine as did the Israelites at the time of Josiah. They often appear as adversaries, going as far back as the Moses stories, yet archeology says there was no Edom until the late 8th century BC. Mentioned in the Books of Exodus, Numbers and Joshua, the Aradites, Moabites, Amorites and many others did not exist at the time of Moses and Joshua.

In Genesis 25:23, God says that Esau's bloodline will be weaker than Jacob's, and that they are meant to serve Jacob's offspring. Similarly, Ishmael the brother of Isaac and the patriarch of the Arab lineage is described unflatteringly as a "wild ass of a man" who could get along with no one. (Gen. 16:12) The Old Testament makes no bones about it; the Israelites are the good guys, especially the Judaites. But what does archeology have to say about the Israelites?

In the extensive official records kept by the Egyptians during the time that the Jews were said to be captive in Egypt, no mention is made of a people known as Israelites. They are said to have wandered in the desert for forty years, rather than the four weeks it would have taken them to march directly into Canaan. Despite this long time, archeology can find not a shred of evidence to support this exodus, nor the subsequent conquest of Canaan by Joshua. Extensive Egyptian records were kept at the time of Rameses, yet nothing is mentioned of a large body moving through the desert, or of any of the other key events in Exodus.

The coastal Canaan settlements and many of the citystates mentioned in Exodus were important vassals in the Egyptian Empire and are mentioned often in Egyptian records. How can there be no mention of wandering Israelites and their attacks on many of these towns? During the rule of Rameses II, Egypt was at the height of its power and the empire extended through Canaan into Syria where it bumped into the southern border of the powerful Hittite Empire. It is inconceivable that there would be no record of settlements being 'utterly destroyed' by a band of upstarts.

In the Bible, the reigns of David and Solomon are depicted as a golden era, a time when all the tribes of Israel were united in what was virtually an empire. It was a time of great prosperity when David, with the assistance of an approving God, conquered many peoples and Solomon erected great buildings. Unfortunately, despite extensive efforts at excavation spanning two centuries, no archeological evidence can support this. There is no trace of the infrastructure needed to support the large armies cited in the Bible. There is no mention of David or Solomon in any records outside of the Bible. There has never been evidence of the original Temple of Solomon. The other building projects found by early excavations and originally credited to Solomon have now been shown to come from a more recent time, probably during the reign of the Omride kings. (As shocking as all of this sounds, it is actually beginning to be accepted even by Jewish rabbis. See **BOX 25—RABBIS FACE ARCHEOLOGICAL RESEARCH**.)

I'll now attempt to paint the picture of the ***archeological history of Israel*** according to the current body of information. Evidence suggests that a small body of people who became known as Israelites began to emerge from within Canaan circa 1200 BC. (According to the Bible, they came into existence circa 1800 BC.) They were pastoral nomads moving their herds through the arid highlands of the interior. The more substantial and prosperous coastal and lowland settlements were never a part of Israel, even in its heyday. Scholars believe that there were always two distinct highland cultures. The more arid south was sparsely populated, less prosperous, more nomadic and came to be called Judah. The more fertile northern highlands were more populated, prosperous and less nomadic, and came to be called Israel or the Northern Kingdoms.

There is some evidence that a leader named David did exist, but evidence suggests that he led a small band of raiders who pillaged the odd village and achieved a certain amount of notoriety. There is no evidence of a bonafide monarchy, no evidence of literacy among the Israelites at this time. Around 1000 BC Jerusalem was a small village of a few hundred people and the entire population of Judah may have been three to four thousand people. Archeology suggests that the story of David was embellished by the Judaites and used as a propaganda tool. It was used to show God's endorsement of the tribe of Judah as the rightful leaders of all the people of Israel. (see 2 Samuel 7:8-16)

During the time from 930 to 720 BC, the Northern Kingdom began to prosper while Judah remained much the same. Compared to other states at the time, it was still insignificant, although compared to Judah, it was booming. Both north and south had things in common; they both worshipped YHWH, but definitely not exclusively, they both spoke a similar brand of Hebrew, and they both shared legends and traditions. Their main differences were mainly to do with the economy and their relationships with neighbors.

According to archeology, the first great kingdom of Israel occurred in the Northern Kingdom between 884 and 842 BC. Known as the Omride dynasty, it included the infamous King Ahab and his queen, Jezebel. This dynasty far surpassed other Judaic or Israelite monarchs in terms of building projects, size of army, wealth, etc, yet it is vilified and given very sketchy coverage in the Bible. This growing prosperity inevitably attracted the attention of the growing Assyrian empire who conquered the Northern Kingdom circa 735 BC. Many Israelites were taken into exile, and many fled to Judah and Egypt. Judah, not being worth the effort, was ignored by Assyria.

What happens next is very significant. Judah, its population swelled, begins to grow. In one generation Jerusalem's population increased fifteen-fold to 15,000 people, going from twelve acres to 150 acres in size. A new opportunity presents itself to the Judaites, a chance to unite with the remnants of the Northern Kingdom under Judaite rule. It then becomes a vassal of the Assyrian Empire and begins to accumulate some wealth.

Up until this era, it is clear that both factions worship an assortment of pagan gods, most notably Asherah and Baal. In accord with archeology, Biblical scholar Baruch Halpern cites this time in the early seventh century as the beginning of the monotheistic tradition.[69] This happened because of a big push to unite Israel under a common God, culminating with the ***strict puritan reforms*** imposed by the court of King Josiah, who came to power when he was eight years old in 639 BC. Excavations of private homes from this time show, however, that the people still retained their statuettes of naked fertility goddesses, despite the impositions of reform.

The authors strongly imply that the priests told the people that they had found the mysterious Book of the Law, which became the Book of Deuteronomy and the subsequent books. The priests claim to have found it tucked away in some corner of the temple, when in actuality, it was written by them to justify the reforms and to endorse the rule of the tribe of Judah. There are many such endorsements of Judah in the Deuteronomistic accounts, as well as endorsements of Josiah. In 1Kings 13:1-2, there is a prophecy of the coming of a great leader, Josiah, who will set things right and bring prosperity to the nation.

With the unexplained decline of the Assyrian empire, Judah under King Josiah experienced a short-lived period of glory. Many of the city-states said to have been conquered by Joshua, were conquered at this time by Josiah. The authors suggest that the stories of Joshua were invented to pave the way for Josiah, the rightful inheritor of the Promised Land.

For no apparent reason, Josiah was killed by the Egyptian pharaoh, Necho II. Shortly thereafter, the newly emerging power known as the Chaldeans out of Babylon, led by King Nebuchadnezzar crush the Israelite state, thoroughly destroying Jerusalem. (According to the Bible they also razed the temple of Solomon, but archeology has no evidence of a temple.) The aristocracy and priesthood are taken into exile in Babylon, while many Israelites seek refuge in Egypt.

After this point in the Bible, which represents the end of the Deuteronomistic history, other authors take over. The Persians defeat the Chaldeans in 539 BC and allow the Jews to build their temple and to follow their own customs. For the next two centuries, Judah becomes a province of Persia known as Yehud. Alexander the Great conquers the land in 332 BC and it becomes known as Judea. It passes through the hands of the Ptolemies of Egypt and then the Seleucids of Syria, being conquered by the Romans in 63 BC.

After the Babylonian exile, there is no further monarchy of consequence and affairs are managed by the priesthood. The foundations of Second Temple Judaism are laid by Ezra and Nehemia. Sections of the Old Testament are added by Jeremiah, Ezekiel, Zecharia and others until, by approximately 70 BC, it reached its final form.

In summary, then, the archeologists largely feel that the history and circumstances described in the Old Testament have been greatly exaggerated and distorted. Allow me to quote Silberman and Finkelstein:

"...the historical core of the Bible arose from clear political, social and spiritual conditions...Much of what is commonly taken for granted as accurate history—the stories of the patriarchs, the Exodus, the conquest of Canaan, and even the saga of the glorious united monarchy of David and Solomon—are, rather, the creative expressions of a powerful religious reform movement that flourished in the kingdom of Judah in the Late Iron Age. Although these stories may have been based on certain historical kernels, they primarily reflect the ideology and the worldview of the writers...the narrative of the Bible was uniquely suited to further the religious reforms and political ambitions of Judah during the momentous concluding decades of the seventh century BCE."[70]

The ***propaganda of the Old Testament*** seems to be saying, " See what happens when you don't obey God, like those sinners in the Northern Kingdom? When bad times befall you, throughout history, it is because you are worshipping other gods. See what happens when you are faithful to the Lord our God exclusively, like the good kings of Judah? Only then can we utterly destroy the enemy and prosper as a nation. Come to your senses, people, and follow the righteous king of Judah. We are the priestly authorities who have the ability to interpret God's will. Do as we say." The idea of one exclusive God, the concepts of a 'chosen people' and a 'promised land'; these were useful ways to unite the people to a common task, under Judaic rule.

We'll now take a look at possibilities 4 and 5 in an attempt to make sense of the Old Testament. As this process mostly involves my own interpretations of the information previously presented, I will put these next two sections in italics.

BOX 25—RABBIS FACE ARCHAEOLOGICAL RESEARCH: While Orthodox Jews still insist that the Torah (first five books of the Old Testament) is the immutable word of God, many Conservative Jews are now admitting that it may in fact be the work of mere mortals. The United Synagogue of Conservative Judaism has issued a new Torah with commentary, called 'Etz Hayim', compiled by David Lieber of the University of Judaism in Los Angeles. It is expected to become the standard in America's 760 Conservative synagogues. The book contains 41 essays by prominent rabbis, some of which admit that many Old Testament stories are probably fictional. For example, Robert Wexler, president of the University of Judaism, wrote that the Genesis stories come from Mesapotamia. Lee I. Levine of the Hebrew University in Jerusalem wrote an essay called 'Biblical Archaeology' that questions the historical authenticity of the Moses, Joshua, David and Solomon stories. This movement to accept the findings of scholarly investigation has been largely spearheaded by Rabbi David Wolpe of Sinai Temple in Los Angeles. He claims that most Conservative rabbis agree with him and have told him so. He also says that most rabbis are reluctant to share these views with the public. (From an article by Michael Massing, the New York Times, March 9, 2003)

Possibility # 4. None of the above.

Is it possible that the Old Testament, as it stands today, is not a product of deliberate manipulation and misinterpretation, as suggested in possibility # 3? Are the factors mentioned in possibilities # 1 and 2 completely off the mark? It could be. There may be better explanations out there, to which I'll always remain open.

Although there may be more to the picture than the factors outlined in the previous sections, I must admit that I am pretty much convinced that these factors are very relevant. Although my beliefs are not written in stone, I believe that a combination of these explanations, as well as others, are valid in attempting to understand how the Old Testament came about. That leads us to the next section.

Possibility # 5. All of the above.

Is the information in the Old Testament a result of a combination of the factors pointed out in the preceding 'possibilities'? As with most enigmas and mysteries, I believe the solution is neither black nor white, but somewhere in between. It seems completely feasible to me that the compilers of the Old Testament were using texts they found in Babylon, as well as the historical legends, heroes and oral traditions that belonged to the Semitic peoples, as a basis for a new and powerful religion. This vast body of information, even before the compilers began to doctor it, had probably undergone a great deal of embellishment and distortion over the years.

In some cultures the passing on of oral traditions is taken very seriously and much attention is paid to the accuracy of stories as they are passed from generation to generation. In such cultures there are usually strict rituals and special positions for whoever is chosen to carry on the stories. The degree to which importance was placed on this process in a given society would determine the purity of any information that was passed down through the centuries. We'll probably never know the actual degree of purity of the hereditary information used by the compilers as a basis for the stories as they appear in the Bible.

I do believe that the pre-Abraham Genesis stories come from very ancient texts and knowledge, which originated in the Sumerian or Mesopitamian cultures. It isn't difficult to see how these stories have been tailored to accord with the religio-political positions held at the time of compilation. I feel confident that some of these stories were further tailored by the Christian movement later on.

As for the stories surrounding the patriarchs and Moses, these would seem likely to have derived from oral traditions and legends that survived until the time of the compiling. How closely they resembled the original events that they describe, is anybody's guess. Again, it's not hard to see how such information could have then been distorted to assist with the political ambitions of certain groups of people. It's easy to put words in the mouth of some 'god'-entity in order to justify the notion of a chosen people who were given a promised land. It's very hard for me to imagine the Source, the Oneness, the Universal Force of Love saying such things.

It's puzzling, however, that there are some passages which seem as though they should have been doctored for political reasons, and yet they were not. There is much about the behavior of the patriarchs, condoned by God, that seems rather unflattering, to say the least. Tales of incest, rape and underhandedness notwithstanding, why did the compilers neglect to delete the part about Jacob and his mother, Rebekah, cheating Esau out of his rightful inheritance? (Gen 27) Such an oversight seems to be saying that the entire lineage of what was to become the 'chosen people', the Israelites at the time of compilation, was illegitimate; that all the promises God made to Abraham and Isaac rightfully belonged to the descendants of Esau, the enemy of the Israelites. This type of information does not fit the bill as propaganda to glorify the tribe of Judah.

I do feel that there must be a degree of truth to most of the Bible stories. Even those that were obviously doctored probably had a certain amount of underlying truth. For example, in light of the archeological evidence and the information from various sources, it seems very feasible to me that the Exodus refers to the end of the Hyksos rule in Egypt and that this story was later exaggerated and manipulated. Thus a story that probably belongs to a large segment of the Semite population, may have been made larger than life and then appropriated by the Judaite tribe of Israel to further their own cause.

Moses could well have been the same person as Akhenaten. It is equally feasible that, if they were separate people, one could have influenced the other with the notion of monotheism. There seems little doubt that this notion of one God was exploited by the compilers, as suggested in the previous section. It could be that the compilers portrayed God as such a fearsome threat because they believed it to be easier to control the people with fear. The Biblical portrait of God could easily be a combination of this tactic, and legendary information about some ancient god.

According to some sources, the one-god concept became distorted long before the time of compilation in the years subsequent to Moses/Akhenaten, as the people sought to incorporate it into more ancient belief systems. In other words, the people couldn't grasp the idea of a single source/force/creative entity without personifying it with a 'god'. They looked toward the ancient traditions for a good candidate. These ancient traditions included many deities, but the one deity that seemed to have played a great role with the patriarchs, was El Shaddai. This god, also known as El Elyon, goes back a long way to a time when a group of 'gods', known in the Bible as the Elohim, had a large role to play in the affairs of humanity. According to Sumerian accounts, he was the leader of a council of gods that made collective decisions, some of which helped mankind, and some of which hindered. They were imperfect beings making imperfect choices. The Sumerian pantheon was depicted this way, with imperfection, as were the Greek gods and many others.

At the time following Moses, then, the idea of one universal energy source, symbolized by the solar disc called the 'Aten', was supplanted by that of El Shaddai who became known as YHWH/Jehovah. The seemingly schizoid nature of this god resulted from the assigning of the actions of a group of entities to this singular entity. The fearsomeness of Jehovah was further exaggerated and emphasized by the compilers who tried to use fear to control the people and forward their own agenda. This scenario, or some variation thereof, seems very feasible to me, much more so than the Biblical account.

It seems likely that the powerful mantra, YHWH, which is representative of divine power, became the new name of El Shaddai, due to some form of confusion. To make proper use of the power of mantra, one must be acquainted with the 'law', that is, with the ways that energy likes to behave. At some point that acquaintance, that knowledge, became lost to the general populace, while some memory of it remained. Thus, this universal power of energy became assigned to El Shaddai.

Possibly this power became assigned to the legend or memory of an ancient god-entity from a distant past. Or maybe that god-entity was very real in the Moses era, using technology to convince a people that he was the one and only God. Thus he appropriated the people's memory of the powerful mantra, YHWH, claiming it as his name. On the other hand, perhaps some skilled magician, familiar with the use of this power, used it to manipulate a people by convincing them that the magical feats they witnessed were the work of a fearful and jealous God. There are many possible takes on the way in which things became confused or distorted. **Who distorted the message, or how and why it changed, is less important to me than**

the acknowledgement that it did indeed get distorted. This distortion, in my opinion, has been one of the key factors that has held humanity back from progressing along the path to enlightenment.

The idea that El Shaddai/Enlil was an ET with his own agenda is also feasible in my mind. Certainly, when I read the Old Testament after having looked at much of the information supporting such a view, I could see this idea fitting well with the Biblical accounts, even shedding light on some of the more puzzling passages. As I've said, there is a great deal of convincing information regarding this point of view.

The difficult question for me is why; what was in it for Enlil? Why would he want to enter into an exclusive relationship with one particular people? It seems more likely that such exclusivity was the invention of the compilers. Some would say (as discussed in Part Three) that Enlil was a leader of a strange 'reptilian' root race that feeds on fear or negative energy, and was thus invested in creating as much fear as possible. Although there may be a good deal of truth to that, it seems too black and white an explanation to me.

To blame all of mankind's problems on an external source, on foreign exploiters, seems a cop-out to me. If one embraces the idea of Jehovah as ET, then it seems closer to the truth to say that the Annunaki overlords were imperfect beings (but not totally evil), making imperfect decisions at various levels of the Game, just like humanity or any other group of Game players. Ancient stories of these imperfect gods were very likely manipulated by certain factions of humanity for less than noble reasons, as well as being inaccurately interpreted by a people who had great difficulty understanding their true nature.

Furthermore, this 'foreign entity' has likely become a part of our collective genepool, so that the boundary between us and them has become very blurred. Much of the conflict and fear-generating attitudes in our history, which continue today, have come from various notions of superior races and inferior races, chosen people and questionable concepts of land ownership. There seems to be a new line of thought these days suggesting that certain bloodlines contain greater degrees of Anunnaki genes and are thus more 'pure'. That seems a dangerous and foolish tactic.

Pointing fingers at bloodlines or foreign influences is missing the point. The point is, we are all in this together, hurtling along in the same spaceship, headed toward the same set of circumstances. Our best chance of benefiting from the opportunity that those circumstances provide would come by accepting responsibility, forgiving ourselves and others, and moving on. Hopefully we'll not make the same mistakes and will learn to treat each other compassionately. If we succeed in raising the vibrations on this planet, then those entities that may be feeding on lower vibrations will just have to change their diet.

There is so much fear and hatred today in the Middle East, which has the potential to threaten the welfare of the entire planet; so much negativity holding back the spiritual progress of humanity. It seems clear to me that much of this negativity is the direct *result of the dubious information and history in the Old Testament. How long will we go on calling this the 'irrefutable word of God'? How long will we continue to allow power groups to manipulate this ancient 'holy' book for their own selfish interests?*

Before we leave this section and go on to the New Testament, I'd like to make one more point. The Old Testament seems to accord with a lot of other information which recognizes that, up until about two or three millennia ago, there was much more awareness of a set of phenomena that has come to be called 'magic'. It seems that many cultures maintained a great respect for this knowledge and certain members of their population were entrusted to protect and carry on these traditions. It seems likely that the Nazirites or Nazorenes were one such group, at least initially.

There were many groups involved in pursuing and preserving this knowledge in Egypt, including the White Brotherhood, the Dragon Court, etc. In Greece it was the Therapeutae, amongst others. The Gnostics, the Rosicrucians and various Mason-like secret societies also sought to preserve this knowledge which was also referred to as alchemy. (To oversimplify, magic often creates results using sound, ie, mantras and incantations, while alchemy tends to use the manipulation of substances, ie white gold powder and possibly psychotropic drugs. Both involve the acquired skill of controlling one's actions while in altered states of consciousness.)

What we think of as magical or 'miraculous' ability is actually just a capacity to create results based on a better understanding of the laws of energy. A skilled adept is able to see through the illusive fabric of Maya and manipulate circumstances to create desired results. Of course there are many pitfalls associated with such endeavors and purity of intent is a big factor.

In any case, the point I want to make here is that the ancients were much more aware of these things, which are more conducive to a right-brained consciousness, than are we. In our left-brained arrogance, we often scoff at such ideas, but I believe that we will become more and more aware in the near future.

I believe that the secret governments, string pullers and elite power groups have always been, and still are, aware of these 'magical' phenomena. They have conducted extensive research in these areas in endeavors such as the Rainbow, Phoenix and Montauk projects, the H.A.A.R.P. in Alaska and others. Much of this research is an extension of that done by the Nazis, (which was inherited by the CIA) in conjunction with information that had been kept secret over the ages.

THE NEW TESTAMENT

Chapter 32

LIFE IN PALESTINE AT THE TIME OF JESUS

Most people have a very distorted view of the way things were, 2000 years ago in Palestine. The typical mental image of life at that time owes more to Hollywood than it does to any historical or archeological account. We tend to view the Jews as a homogenous, close-knit group who believed the same things and behaved in the same way. Maybe that's because we take for granted the transportation and communication technology that we enjoy today. In those days, however, Jewish communities, like those of most nations, were relatively isolated and the closest neighboring town would have been a long donkey ride away. In the same way that neighboring towns could develop completely different dialects of the same language, they also often had differing cultures and belief systems, *differing versions of Jewish faith.*

At that time there were many Jews, often the more prosperous and worldly, who lived outside of Palestine and are known collectively as the *Diaspora Jews*. There were many in the major cities such as Rome, Alexandria, Ephesus, etc, and in regions such as Babylon, Egypt, Asia Minor and the South of France. They were exposed to a wide range of religio-cultural influences and practiced many diverse, less strict forms of the Hebrew religion. Some worshipped non-Hebrew deities.

Within Palestine, there were three main geo-political sections, Judea to the south with Jerusalem as its capital, Samaria and Galilee to the north. There were many factions, bickering and squabbling and competing for control. Galilee, which was located at a crossroads of several trade routes, was particularly varied and more sophisticated, being influenced by a diversity of cultures and beliefs. The province of Galilee, which included Samaria, was ruled by an Arab family of *puppet kings* appointed by Rome, known as *the Herods*. There were several kings named Herod, and many family members were busy plotting behind each others' backs, manipulating and jockeying for position. Generally, they were despised by the Jewish people, although they had many Jewish allies.

The province of Judea was ruled by a *Roman procurator*, such as Pontius Pilate, who ruled for about ten years at the time of Jesus' death. These procurators, Pilate included, ruled with brutality and intolerance, showing no respect for Jewish culture and tradition. At the point when this procurate took power in Judea, 3,000 Jewish dissidents were crucified.

In Judea, the home of Temple Judaism, there were **many sects**:

- the Saducees, led by priests who co-operated with Rome
- the Pharisees, led by priests who were passively resistant to Rome
- the Essenes, who were more austere, strict and mystically oriented, and were hostile to Rome, even though they were typically more apolitical
- the Zealots, a non-religious group that could contain both Pharisees and Essenes, who were violently opposed to Rome
- numerous other groups and sub-sects, including the Nazorenes, Zadokites, Ebionites and Maccabees.

Religion, in those days, was big business and in order to officially belong to a particular faith, one invariably had to pay money. People were shopping for the best ticket to salvation. Religions from within and from beyond the Roman Empire were constantly competing with each other and were highly political. Whoever controlled a particular religion and its priesthood controlled the wealth. Thus, there was much infighting, with different groups vying for control, trying to 'get their guy in' using different claims to the 'throne'.

Amongst the many religions, Judaism was quite popular. This was probably due to its great book, which contained fascinating tales of intrigue, history and adventure as well as guidelines and advice on how to lead a good life. Most religions had no such book. A book in those days would have been the object of great awe and wonderment, even though the vast majority could not read. Whoever controlled this popular religion and its great book had access to a formidable source of wealth and power.

The Jewish religion, like any other, was subject to these conditions of constant squabbling. Temple Judaism, itself factionalised, tended to be stricter, to adhere more closely to traditional law. King Herod was a great exporter of Judaism and the royal coffers fattened considerably under his reign, a good portion going on to Rome. Much of the accounting of this was recorded in the Copper Scroll, one of the many recently discovered near the Dead Sea. Herod sold a watered down version of Judaism, less strict, with no need for circumcision. This milder form of Judaism was much more palatable to the general public, which is understandable, considering the painful process of parting with a piece of one's penis. Many diaspora Jews and many non-Jews subscribed to this form of Judaism. This caused a great deal of distress amongst the various factions of traditionalists and liberals, who rarely agreed on the definition and/or interpretation of Hebraic and Judaic law.

Into this turbulent milieu came Jesus the Nazorene and his assortment of associates.

Chapter 33

ISSUA BAR YUSEF, aka JESUS CHRIST

You could probably read a different book about Jesus every day for the rest of your life. These books range from the absurdly fanatical, to the conventionally devout, to the purely historical. In this book we're only concerned with those that challenge the conventional views as purveyed by Rome, based on the large body of information that has come to light in the past century or so. Although this will constitute the main source of our reporting, we will also consider some channeled sources.

From this new wave of books trying to discover the 'real Jesus', comes a wide range of opinions and theories. Some of them claim that Jesus was: a divorced father of three, a Freemason, a Buddhist, a master of Egyptian magic, a shaman, a political opportunist, the leader of a magic mushroom cult, a hypnotist, an invention of the Church, a woman, a committee, etc. Here is *a short list of respected books* that caused a good deal of controversy over the years:

- In 1863, Ernest Renan published 'The Life of Jesus', which presented Jesus as an amazing man, but not as God. This caused some shock waves, even though it was mild compared to work being done by an emerging group working within the Church who became known as the 'Modernists'. In 1907 this group was condemned by Pope Pius X.
- In 1916, George Moore published 'The Brook Kerith', a fictionalized, but well researched account of Jesus having survived the Crucifixion, having been nursed back to health by Joseph of Arimithea. Other fictional accounts such as 'King Jesus', by Robert Graves and 'The Last Temptation of Christ', by Nikos Kazantzakis also caused a stir. The latter was recently made into a movie by Martin Scorcese, which also caused quite an uproar, even though it too is mild, compared to the information being revealed by serious research.
- In 1963, Dr. Hugh Schonfield released 'The Passover Plot', in which he contends, based on information in the Gnostic gospels, that Jesus and his associates staged the Crucifixion. This book sold over 3 million copies.
- 'Jesus the Magician', by Dr. Morton Smith, claims that Jesus was one of many 'messiah-styled' preachers who went about performing miracles and healings. He is said to have been a practitioner of Egyptian magic. This viewpoint is also backed up by some of the Gnostic writings.
- In 1979, Elaine Pagels wrote 'The Gnostic Gospels', which presented many unconventional interpretations of the Jesus message.
- In 1994, Burton Mack released 'The Lost Gospel', based on the Gospel of Q. It contains many sayings and teachings of Jesus and concludes that he was not preaching traditional Judaic material.

- Other significant works are 'Jesus the Jew', by Giza Vermes, 'Revolution in Judea', by Haim Maccoby, and a book about Paul by a former nun, Karen Armstrong, 'The First Christian'.[71]

Some researchers say that Jesus didn't approve of the 'messiah' label, while others claim that he used and manipulated it for political gain. Some opinions state that he never actually existed, or that he was such a far cry from the image presented by the Church, that he might as well have not existed. Josephus, the main historical documenter of the Jews at that time, never mentions Jesus at all, although other characters from the Jesus story are talked about. This seems strange, although Flavius Josephus was a wealthy ex-Jew who became a Roman and it is entirely conceivable that his work was subsequently edited to omit mention of Jesus.

There are many differing opinions amongst Bible scholars regarding the identity and mission of Jesus, and though we can't look at all of them here, we'll try to discuss some of the main points. Much of the 'alternative' information about him, however, is in accord, and I will attempt to provide a portrayal of Jesus and to undo some of the misconceptions associated with him, based on this variety of material. Before we look specifically at his life, we'll take a look at some of the *key persons in his life* and the circumstances of his youth.

The characters surrounding Jesus also played important roles in the 'Jesus movement', and in order to understand the events in Jesus' life, we should look at some of them. Many of the key players have been totally marginalized by the Bible, including Mary Magdalene, Joseph of Arimithea, Nicodemus, Simon Magus and his wife Helen, Judas, John the Baptist, Mary the mother of Jesus and her sister, and Jesus' brother, James. Many of these characters had several names and/or titles and keeping track of who's who can be confusing. Let's first talk about *the Apostles*.

It is highly unlikely that the Apostles were humble fishermen and shepherds, although it's possible that some of them were. Most of them were important men in the Jewish community. Some may not have been Jewish at all; Philip is a Greek name. They definitely didn't follow Jesus around, blindly agreeing with everything he said. Different Apostles had different agendas and allegiances; some were more liberal while others adhered more strictly to tradition. Jesus is considered to have been a liberal, more concerned with 'spreading the word' to as many as possible, rather than the enforcement of laws and regulations.

At least two of the Apostles, *James and Thomas*, are now believed to have been Jesus' brothers, and thus, also royal descendants of the King David lineage. According to Matthew and Mark, there were four brothers, Joseph, Simon, James and Jude, and two sisters. Information from the Dead Sea Scrolls suggests that there was a competition between Jesus and James as to who was the rightful heir, with each of them having their own allies and enemies. James was stricter and more conservative. In the years after Jesus his role became even greater, as the new leader and heir apparent. He disagreed violently with Paul, sending missionaries after him to try to undo the damage of Paul's teachings. Even though his official position was stricter than Jesus', he expended a great deal of energy defending Jesus' teachings, protecting them from distortions. He was put to death in 64 AD.

The word 'Thomas' actually means 'twin' in Hebrew, and it is thought that his real name was Jude and that he was Jesus' twin brother. There are several references to this in some of the Gnostic Gospels and researchers seem quite confident that this startling statement is true. In the years after the Crucifixion, Thomas is said to have carried 'the message' into what is now Iraq and Iran, dying in India somewhere near Madras. To Christians living in that part of the world, Thomas is a major saint.[72]

(Two interesting excerpts from the Gnostic Gospel of Thomas quote Jesus as having said, "We have come from the light, from the place where light is produced."—and—"When you make the two one, and when you make the inner as the outer and the outer as the inner and the above as the below, and when you make the male and the female into a single one, so that the male will not be male and the female not be female, then shall you enter the kingdom of Heaven.")[73]

A major player barely mentioned in the Bible is **Simon Magus**, who is also thought to have been one of the Apostles and is known to have had several pseudonyms. Most of the information about this controversial figure is available in the Apocryphal texts known as the Clementine Books. He was the leader of a Gnostic sect and a powerful, charismatic speaker and performer of magic or 'miracles'. He also presented himself as a messiah and an incarnation of God and had a large following. His teachings were a mixture of Greek philosophy, liberal Judaism and science and were in accord with much of Jesus' teachings. He taught that God's first thought was female which then gave birth to the universe.

He and Jesus were close friends and allies, their main difference being that Simon was more a Zealot than Jesus. Some say that his following was large enough that the Roman Church could just as easily have been built around him, if he wasn't so blatantly anti-Roman. His wife/mistress Helena was also a powerful teacher, a sacred prostitute and a priestess. She and Simon are said to have regularly partaken in sex rites and magic, involving menstrual blood and semen. (We'll talk more about these things in Part Seven.)

Jonathan Anas, aka the Apostle Jacob of Alphaeus, was a Levite priest who was Simon's chief rival. Many in the movement claimed that Jesus embodied both high priest and king, but Anas maintained that only a Levite could be high priest. He thus opposed Jesus, yet in the sense that he was also pro-peace, he was an ally.

Judas Iscariot was an important and powerful man, leader of the Zealot movement and a chief scribe. He was a rival of Anas and wanted Jesus to appoint him as high priest. He was also a 'satan', whose job it was to act as foil to Jesus in debates. (See **BOX 24—SATAN**)

Simon Peter, the rock, was a simple man who acted as Jesus' bodyguard. The Bible has probably assigned him a greater role than he actually played. In the post-Jesus years, he was aligned with James, but gradually went over to Paul's side.

John the Beloved, supposedly Jesus' favorite, is another enigmatic figure. He is now thought to be an uncircumcised proselyte, possibly not Jewish, who was more interested in the mystical nature of Jesus' teachings. It is said that he was taught Egyptian mystery school magic by Jesus, and that he was the same person as Lazarus. As mentioned earlier, the 'raising Lazarus from the dead' story was originally about an initiation ceremony during which he figuratively dies and is reborn.

As important as the Apostles were, they were not a part of *Jesus' inner circle*, something they always resented. Interestingly, the inner circle of advisors and confidants consisted mostly of women; Mary Magdalene, Jesus' mother and her sister. Lazarus/John the Beloved, who is thought to be the brother of Mary Magdalene, aka Mary of Bethany, may also have been part of the circle. Some people feel that they were privy to Jesus' true mission and message. Mary Magdalene played a very important role and I have devoted the next chapter entirely to her.

Jesus' mother, who has come to be called the Virgin Mary, is an enigmatic figure who is given very little press in the Bible. There is some controversy around the word 'virgin'. Some scholars say that this word had a very different meaning back then than it does today. They say that back then it was used to refer to a strong, independent woman of means who was not attached to a man. (The first syllable of 'virgin' comes from the same root as the first syllable of 'virile' and 'virtue'—it connotates strength.)[74] There are several applications of this word in the Bible and elsewhere, in which such a meaning makes more sense. It's been suggested that it was the Roman Church that changed this word to refer to a woman who has never had sexual intercourse. Jesus' mother was called a virgin before the idea of an 'immaculate conception' was introduced by the Church. As a direct descendant of King David she would have enjoyed privileges not available to other women, such as being allowed to travel without the company of a husband, as depicted in the Gospels. At the time, Jewish law strictly forbade such behavior for most women.

Joseph of Arimithea is also thought to have been part of this inner circle. He was a wealthy and powerful member of the Jewish community and, along with Nicodemus, a member of the Sanhedrin, the supreme Jewish legislative council. As part of the Jewish ruling party, he would have been overseen by, and interacted often with Pontius Pilate. He was definitely close to Jesus. Some scholars suggest that he is the same as Joseph the father of Jesus, about whom very little is written in the Bible. According to Gardner, he was a 'naggar', a master of 'the craft', named Joseph ab Heli.[75] The word 'Arimithea' derives from 'ha-Rama-Theo', which translates roughly as 'the Divine Highness'. He (and others) taught this 'divine highness', this knowledge of the 'craft', to Jesus.[76]

An important and controversial figure was *John the Baptist*, a very popular saint who has probably had more churches built in his name, throughout the centuries, than any other saint. Most Bible scholars agree that he was Jesus' cousin, that he was a devout Essene, and that, before his death at the hands of King Herod Antipas, he was more popular than Jesus. He was a man of the people, denouncing the temple priests and their thirst for money, claiming that all were entitled to be baptized, free of charge. John was stricter and less tolerant of non-Judaic ways. His mission was to destroy paganism, bringing former pagans into the fold through baptism. He was also, according to Picknett and Prince, a true gnostic—someone who advocated direct, experiential knowledge of divinity.

Herod Antipas had him killed for several reasons. John openly criticized Antipas for having married his brother's ex-wife, which was against Judaic law. Herod was in the business of selling a milder form of Judaism while John was insisting on a stricter, Essene flavored version that was available free of charge. The other factor was that John had a large, devoted following, which was a threat to Herod's position.

The controversy about John is in regard to his relationship with Jesus. Some say they were allies who differed slightly in their beliefs, or that they were rivals, while some claim they were bitter enemies. John's followers referred to him as the Messiah, and after his death, many of them began to follow Jesus. Yet his cult continued for another fifty years. There has been somewhat of an obsession with John throughout the centuries, especially in France.

In their book, 'The Templar Revelation', Lynn Picknett and Clive Prince point out that Leonardo DaVinci, the great artist and scientist, was obsessed with John and that he appears in many paintings. They contend that he, like many, felt that John was the true Christ, but that to say so at the time would have meant heresy and death at the hands of the Church. They claim that it was Da Vinci that forged the Shroud of Turin, using an early knowledge of the photographic process and artistic wizardry. The image on the Shroud clearly shows that the head had been severed from the body, thus representing John who was beheaded. The authors contend that, with the Shroud as well as other paintings, Leonardo was secretly expressing his belief that John was the true Messiah. They feel that this, as well as information about Mary Magdalene, was one of the secrets protected by the Knights Templar and other secret societies.[77] (The best-seller, 'Holy Blood, Holy Grail', by Baigent, Leigh and Lincoln, claims that Leonardo, along with many other well-known individuals throughout history, served as Grand Master of the Priory of Sion. This was a very powerful underground group or secret society with Masonic roots that had a great deal of influence over key events throughout history. It is well known that Da Vinci had a great interest in the occult, including Hermetic magic and alchemy.)[78]

Jesus was many things—wore many hats. Amongst other things, he was a king, high priest, rabbi, Essene and Nazorene. Most scholars agree that Jesus was not a poor carpenter, but rather, as a direct descendant of King David, an aristocrat who would have enjoyed a more privileged lifestyle. Some say that the wedding at Cana was Jesus' own wedding, but even if it wasn't, it is evidence that he moved in wealthy circles. No poor carpenter would have been a guest at such a lavish feast, as described in the Bible. He was definitely well educated and could hold his own with the temple priests. He is said to have traveled widely, often with Joseph of Arimithea. He is reputed to have received a good part of his education in the East and was well-versed in Buddhist, Zoroastrian, Greek and Egyptian mysticism. (See **BOX 26—THE LEGEND OF ISSA**)

> **BOX 26—THE LEGEND OF ISSA;** In 1887, an old Buddhist document was found in a Himalayan monastery by Nicolas Notovich. In this document was an old story of a Palestinian named Issa, who had come East to study with the Brahmins. Much to the dismay of the Brahmins, however, Issa spent as much time with the lower castes as he did learning the Hindu scriptures. He spoke out often against the caste system, insisting that all were equal in the eyes of God. He often challenged the Vedas and Puranas and his constant questioning and debating soon angered the Brahmins. He eventually left for Persia, Greece and Egypt, continuing his studies until he returned to Palestine. Although there is no concrete proof that Issa was the same person as Issua Bar Yusef, many feel that there are too many similarities for it to be a coincidence.[79]

Jesus and many of the characters in his life are said to have been raised within the Essene tradition. It would be a good idea to take a look at some of the controversy surrounding **the Essenes**. There are many varied opinions about this enigmatic faction of Jews, probably due to the tendency to view them as a cohesive group whose members lived similar lifestyles and obeyed similar rules. The most recent research suggests that this was not true. There were the more monastic Essenes, like the ones who lived at Qumran, as well as city Essenes living in 'houses' in many cities, including those outside of the Palestine region. There was also an Essene center in Egypt.

Despite varying opinions, most say that the Essenes were more removed from temple Judaism with its hierarchy of priests and political agenda, and more involved in the esoteric, mystical aspects of the faith. They are said to have been vegetarians who valued honesty and justice, to have opposed animal sacrifice, and to have had a great deal of knowledge about the healing arts and the use of herbs. Qumran was run by celibate monks who lived a life of strict austerity, although the remains of women and children have been excavated there. They are also said to have been very dogmatic and rule-oriented and were especially fanatical about cleanliness. It is said that they imported the ritual of baptism from the Egyptians and then brought it to the Jewish people via John the Baptist.

Some opinions contend that the Essenes were an Aryan group and that Jesus was a redheaded, white-skinned Aryan. Some of the information about the Essenes comes from the Dead Sea Scrolls found near Qumran, which are said to have been written by the Essenes. One of the scholars assigned to work on the scrolls, author of the book, 'The People of the Dead Sea Scrolls', was John Allegro. He, along with Albert MacKey who wrote, 'The History of Freemasonry', claim that the Essenes operated much like a secret society in the Freemason tradition, using typical masonic symbols and iconography.[80]

There is a lot of evidence to suggest that, even though Jesus was raised an Essene and believed in some of their ways, there was much that he rebelled against, particularly their strictness about who could be this and who could do that. He tended to teach that all people were equals who could partake in any ritual and hold any position. In some of the Dead Sea Scroll information he is referred to as the 'Wicked Priest' or the 'Man of a Lie', and it is clear that they felt he broke too readily with tradition and taught non-Essene messages. John the Baptist, on the other hand, was called the 'Teacher of Righteousness' and was considered a true representative of Essene ways. Jesus' brother James is also thought to have been one who adhered more closely to their ways.

Another group to which Jesus belonged was **the Nazorenes**, thought to have been a subsect of the Essenes. This name comes from the Hebrew word 'notsrim', which means 'keepers or preservers of true teachings'. A Nazorene (often spelled 'Nazarene') is not someone who comes from Nazareth, which we have been led to believe. Scholars have now established that there was no town of Nazareth during Christ's time, and that it did not exist until the 3rd century AD.[81] We even run across this term in the Old Testament, where it is spelled, 'Nazirite', defined there in the footnotes as 'one that is separated or consecrated'. (Numbers 6:2-22) We run across it again in the story of Samson, (Judges 13-17), who was a long-haired Nazirite who was often in the company of harlots, and who was endowed with magical 'strength' or power.

Until recently, very little was known about the Nazorenes. There is some suggestion that their mission to preserve ancient knowledge included a strong association with magic. Whatever they were in their original conception, it is now believed that they eventually became an elite group of Jews whose job was to keep the essence of Judaism intact. They traditionally wore long hair and beards, which is the way Jesus (and Samson) is typically portrayed. After Jesus, James became the head of the Nazorene authority, which was the same as the early Christian Church, the ones we picture hiding out in catacombs. They were persecuted by Rome and by Saul, acting on behalf of the Saducees, who, in cooperation with Rome, were trying to keep Judaism under their control. When Saul became Paul, it was this Nazorene movement that he infiltrated and eventually split from. Descendants of Jesus' family, collectively called the Desposyni, met with the Bishop of Rome, Pope Sylvester in 318 AD in a futile effort to regain control of the assigning of bishops and of Christian church money. That represented the final contact between the Roman Church and the Nazorene tradition.[82]

In the 1960s, Professor Schlomo Pines found some old Arabic writings that dated back to the 5th or 6th centuries. They contained records of a group referred to by the Arab name, 'Al-Nasari', which talk about the Nazorene tradition going back to the Jewish revolt of 66 AD. These writings express displeasure at the notion of Jesus being called the Son of God. Paul's teachings are renounced and his followers are said to have "abandoned the religion of Christ and turned towards the religious doctrines of the Romans."[83]

Picknett and Prince talk about a sect living today in southern Iran called the Mandaeans. They have retained their own language, which is derived from Aramaic, and they are said to have been non-Jews who came from the Palestine region by way of Egypt circa 100 AD. Their priests are called Nasoreans and they revere John the Baptist as their greatest teacher, a Nasurai. Jesus is also said to be a Nasurai, but one who became a rebel and led people astray. There are other similar sects living in parts of Syria and Iraq who have taken on Islamic trappings to avoid persecution, but who practise a different religion. They are called the Nosairi. All these names; Nazirite, Nazorene, Nasurai and Nosairi, are all very likely derived from the same root and have, or have had, similar meanings.[84]

Jesus is often referred to as *the Messiah*. Some researchers claim that he was not comfortable with this label, while others say that he exploited it to further his cause. But what is a messiah? The word comes from 'Messeh', the sacred Egyptian crocodile whose fat was used to anoint the pharaoh. 'Messiah' means 'anointed one'. It probably had its roots in Egyptian magic; an initiate was annointed after s/he had reached a certain level of expertise. Jesus became a messiah after he was annoited by Mary Magdalene.[85]

Nowadays we have come to interpret the word to mean 'the one and only dude, the God made man who is coming to save the world'. In those days, however, it probably had more of a political application than spiritual. Rather than referring to the 'one and only', it was used to refer to any leader, especially one who could lead his people out of bondage. Virtually all the Jewish kings since David were called messiahs.[86] In Palestine at the time, there were several 'messiahs'. There was an obsession with the notion of a great messiah who would free the Jews from Roman subjugation. It's not hard to imagine such an obsession coming from a people who were subject to such brutal overlords. The civilized world at that time was full of itinerant preachers calling themselves messiahs.

Another aspect of the Jesus story that's rife with controversy is **the Crucifixion**. Some scholars say he died but was brought back to life, some that he didn't die and was nursed back to health, and some say that the whole affair was staged and that a stand in, usually cited as Simon of Cyrene, was crucified in his place. Some even contend that the event never took place at all, that it was a story invented by the Church. There definitely are some interesting questions that have been asked. For example, why was Jesus taken down from the cross after less than twenty-four hours? Typically, victims were left on the cross for at least three days, while some were left till the birds had picked the bones clean. How is it that Jesus was crucified in proximity to the Garden of Gethsemane, which was owned by Joseph of Arimithea? Most crucifixions took place at the location designated for crucifixions.

The description, derived largely from the Gnostic gospels, of what actually happened at the Crucifixion goes something like this. The event was planned by the 'inner circle'. Jesus' entry into Jerusalem and the subsequent agitation and tirade against the vendors at the Temple, etc, was planned to occur at a specific time. Joseph of Arimithea and Nicodemus made some sort of arrangement with Pilate whereby the crucifixion could occur near Gethsemane on Friday, so that Jesus would die and be taken down before Saturday, the Jewish sabbath. It could have been a bribe or it could have been a way for Pilate to rid himself of Jesus, but still appease the Jewish people by respecting their sabbath.

In any case, it is thought that when Jesus was on the cross and offered the soaked sponge, it was laced with a prepared toxin called 'toska', a mixture of wine-vinegar and wormwood. The other two 'thieves' on the cross, (probably Zealot dissidents) had their legs broken. While this may seem extraordinarily savage, it was somewhat of an act of kindness, since the inability of the broken legs to support the body weight would cause death by asphyxiation to occur sooner. In other words, the cruelty involved in smashing someone's legs pales by comparison with the cruelty of crucifixion, the preferred method of execution by the most 'civilized' empire in the world at the time.

Jesus' body, because of the toxin, appeared to be dead. The piercing of his side with a lance was not part of the plan. His body was taken down and placed in the tomb/cave in Joseph's garden, where he was tended to by Essene herbalist healers who restored him to life. The 'angels in white' who were reportedly by Jesus' side in the tomb, were Essenes who typically wore long white robes.

Some might question why the Crucifixion was planned and staged by the inner circle. Possibly it was because they knew that, if they hadn't planned it, it was probably inevitable anyway. This way they controlled things. The entire population of Jerusalem would have been aware of these events, especially after the 'Palm Sunday' entrance on a donkey, which was also carefully planned to accord with prophecies. Jesus' message of love would be heeded to a much greater degree after such an event, especially if he was seen to be alive afterwards.

Some have claimed that it was staged as a way of gaining some kind of political control, or for motives that were less than noble. It's hard for me to imagine anyone of ignoble intent allowing themselves to be whipped, beaten and crucified, even if they knew they would emerge from the ordeal alive. This is surely the act of a sincere and passionate man, unless the one who was crucified was a substitute. This contention is made in several of the Gnostic writings and in the Koran. Most commonly, the 'substitution theorists' claim that it was a man named Simon who took Jesus' place, possibly Simon Magus, a.k.a. Simon of Cyrene or Simon Zelotes.[87]

After the Crucifixion, Jesus, Mary Magdalene, her sister Martha, Lazarus and Joseph of Arimithea were taken by boat to the south of France. There was a large number of Jews living in this region at the time. Jesus had children with Mary and continued to work in a low-profile way. In her book, 'Jesus the Man', Barbara Thiering says that he later divorced Mary in 50 AD and married a woman named Lydia, a bishop of a Hellenist woman's order called the Thyatira Virgins. She also claims that there is evidence that Jesus was in Rome as late as 64 AD, at the age of seventy. There are differing views about where he died, such as; Kashmir, Egypt, Masada or Rome.

According to several writers including Laurence Gardner and Baigent, Leigh and Lincoln, *the lineage of Jesus* continued from the southern France region, spawning many of the Grail legends. The Merovingian dynasty of French kings is said to have been associated, if not actually descended from this lineage. This mysterious dynasty was reputed to have been involved heavily in magic, alchemy and the supernatural, wearing beards and long hair like the Nazorenes. They were referred to as the Sorcerer Kings. They are said to have been great healers and psychics, were very learned and sophisticated, and that they ruled but did not govern. They left the nitty gritty of the running of affairs to chancellors and other officials. Interestingly, they were polygamous. They were eventually betrayed by the Roman Church and over-thrown by the

Carolingians led by Charlemagne. The alliance between the Church and Charlemagne, the first Holy Roman Emperor, was a major step, and together they ruled all of Western Europe.

So who was this man, Jesus the Nazorene? Most of the writings portray a man who, although not completely apolitical, was less concerned with such matters as were many of the other leaders around him. The one image that seems to be prevalent in most writings is that he was a rebel, someone who questioned and challenged tradition and dogma. It seems that, though he tried to work within the Judaic tradition to a certain degree, he was well versed in the mystical traditions of many cultures. He was more concerned with teaching the underlying wisdom common to all these traditions, rather than the finer points of Jewish laws and regulations.

Jesus is consistently portrayed as a champion of the poor and underprivileged. It is known that he was very much against the selling of salvation, feeling that anyone and everyone was entitled to the pursuit of the spiritual path. Even the Bible portrays him in this way. However, in this book we are more concerned with the aspects of Jesus that the Bible ignores and downplays. For example, although he was a pacifist, he almost certainly was not as apolitical as the Bible deems him. How could such a spiritual rebel be unconcerned with the oppressive, brutal rule of the Romans? There are several sayings attributed to Jesus that seem to be saying, "Don't worry about paying taxes to Rome or any of the difficulties of life on Earth, you'll get your reward in good time". *Such quips are highly suspect and seem to be tailor made by an oppressive regime trying to avoid dissent. Jesus may have been a pacifist, but was he a 'passivist'? I doubt it.*

There are other aspects of Jesus that have been downplayed, ignored and suppressed. Before we continue to attempt to portray him and define his mission, let's take a look at another character whose role was critical, if not equal in importance to that of Jesus. Let's take a look at the one who, according to many writings, was Jesus' wife.

Chapter 34

MARY MAGDALENE

It's amazing how information can be manipulated and become distorted as it filters down into common knowledge. Most of us think of Mary Magdalene as *a street prostitute* that begs Jesus for forgiveness and is taken underwing, much like one might care for a stray dog. And yet nowhere in the Gospels of the New Testament is she referred to as a prostitute. The Bible calls her a 'sinner', which meant at the time, one who lives outside of Jewish law. Of all of the characters whose name was slandered or whose role was marginalized by the editing and doctoring of the Bible, hers was probably the most blatant example.

Even though it acknowledges her presence on several important occasions, such as the Crucifixion and as the first witness to his resurrection, the Bible has very little to say about her. We are introduced to her briefly as Mary of Bethany who, along with her sister, Martha, asks Jesus to raise their brother Lazarus from the dead. The Bible does not make it clear that the two Marys are the same person, but most modern scholars now believe this to be the case.

Thanks mainly to the Nag Hamadi discovery and many of the Gnostic writings including the Gospel of Mary, many scholars now feel that the Magdalene played a crucial part in the 'Jesus movement', both in and behind the scenes. Far from being a destitute hooker, she is now thought to have been a very active member of a wealthy and powerful family, and to have provided the bulk of the financial backing of the movement. Jesus and his entourage were often sheltered at their house in **Bethany**, as they were just before the Palm Sunday entrance into Jerusalem. This attests to the size of the house, far grander than the typical huts of the poor. Bethany, the place where Jesus first started his ministry, was an upscale suburb just outside of Jerusalem.

Mary was not, however, merely a silent financial partner. In various Gnostic gospels Jesus refers to her as 'the Apostle of Apostles', 'she who knows all' and the 'illuminatrix'. She was a priestess in her own right, very knowledgeable in magic and the occult arts, a great healer and a **sacred prostitute**. (We'll speak further on the relationship between sex and spirituality in the next chapter.)

She is said to have spent most of her early life in Egypt where she studied the Hermetic sciences and the mystical traditions. The contention that she comes from the Galilean town of El Mejdel is now thought to be mistaken. She probably came from the Egyptian town of Magdolum, close to the Palestinian border, which in the Old Testament is referred to as Migdol. In a church in Marseilles there is a statue of 'Sarah the Egyptian', said to have been the servant of Mary Magdalene. (Interestingly, Sarah has become the patron saint of that enigmatic group of people called the Gypsies.)

Another possible source for the name or title, 'Magdalene', comes from Margaret Starbird's book about the Magdalene cult, 'The Woman with the Alabaster Jar'. She claims the word Magdala derives from a Hebrew word meaning 'elevated, great, magnificent'.[88]

The downplaying of the role of Mary, as well as all women in the Jesus story, is now thought to have started with Paul and then Peter, who was very uncomfortable with females and is said to have feared and hated Mary. In the Gospel of Thomas, Peter says, "Women are not worthy of life". In the Pistis

Sophia it states that he "hates the female race". At that time most women were held in about the same esteem as livestock and it must have been very disconcerting for the Apostles and other authorities that Mary held such sway over Jesus. The fact that she was probably not of the Judaic faith, combined with her strange practices, was enough to make them fear and mistrust her.[89]

It is clear though, that such was not the case with Jesus. According to the Gospel of Philip, "Jesus loved her more than all the disciples and used to kiss her often on the mouth".[90] Most scholars now feel certain that **Mary was married to Jesus** and that the wedding at Cana was probably their wedding. Jesus was a rabbi and, in those days, it was against Judaic law for a rabbi to be unmarried. For a man of his import, it would have caused a huge outcry to be single and without children, and even though Jesus was a rebel and not afraid to stir the pot, such an outcry would certainly have been reported somewhere in the Gospels.

Some scholars believe that Mary was a Benjamite. Since the days when King Saul, a Benjamite, was overthrown by David, a Judaite, there had been tension between these two tribal factions. If this idea about Mary is true, then her marriage to Jesus would have been seen as a strategic, if not an ideal union. Her eccentricities are more likely to have been tolerated.

Some scholars feel that, further to being his wife, Mary was a sacred consort to Jesus, initiating him in various mysteries, many of which involved **sexual rituals**. The Bible downplays the scene, just before the Crucifixion, when Jesus is anointed by Mary during what must have been a very important ceremony. A quantity of spikenard, a very expensive scented oil, said to be worth 300 denarii (about 10,000 dollars by today's standards), was used to 'christen' him in the tradition of the 'Hieros Gamos', a sacred union of priest and priestess.[91] The christening by water at the hands of John the Baptist is given much more coverage than the occasion of the anointing with oil. This seems strange for someone thought of as the Messiah, which means 'the anointed one'. It is interesting that the annointing with water represents initiation into the male aspect of the religion, while annointing with oil represents the feminine aspect.[92]

The region known as Provence in southern France was highly civilized at that time, with Greek, Roman and Jewish communities. The Herods owned large estates there, as did many wealthy Jews. It is to this region that Mary Magdalene is said to have moved after the events surrounding the Crucifixion.

In southern France, Arles was a major center of the **Isis cult**, as well as many other 'goddess' groups. The Isians were a large group, extending as far north as Paris for hundreds of years after Christ. In fact the worship of goddesses was widespread and popular at the time, until, over the ensuing centuries, these groups were systematically crushed by the Roman Church. Their organizations outlawed and their temples destroyed, the goddess cults were forced to 'go underground'.

Originating in Egypt, Isis was a multi-faceted deity, a healer and magician associated with the moon and the sea. Isians worshipped three essential facets of femininity corresponding to different ages; the virgin, symbolized by the new moon, the mother, symbolized by the full moon, and the crone, by the dark moon. The virgin represented the sexual seductress, the nubile potential of youth. The mother embodied the middle-aged qualities of nurturing and the crone is associated with the feminine wisdom of old age.

Isis was also traditionally known as a 'virgin mother', but because the Isians, like most pagans, were not invested in proving that she was a real, historical person, this did not register as a contradiction. Even though Isis may well have walked the Earth at some point in the distant past, she was considered to be an 'archetype' by most pagans, or at least the ones that had a more balanced view of things. (An archetype is like a sub-set of human qualities embodied by a particular god, so that an entire pantheon of gods would represent the entire spectrum of human characteristics. Thus, gods and goddesses often had a dark side which enabled worshippers to acknowledge, and thus deal with, their own dark sides.)

It had once been commonplace for early Christians, fond of their goddess traditions, to attend church services on a Sunday morning and then head over to some secret goddess meeting in the afternoon. It was necessary for the Roman Church to appease this yearning for feminine archetypes, while maintaining an anti-feminist attitude. They did this with the image of *the Virgin Mary*. Much of the Isian iconography was appropriated, including the common depiction of Isis with stars in her hair, holding the baby Horus. Although Jesus' mother is barely mentioned in the Gospels, this image of the Holy Mother was made and promoted by the Church into the second most important figure after Jesus.

The big difference between this virgin icon and the old goddesses was the fact that it had been made completely asexual. With the Virgin Mary, the sexual, nubile aspect of the feminine archetype was completely overlooked. Since we have no words of wisdom from the Virgin Mary, it is safe to say that the crone aspect was also overlooked. The people were left with less than half a goddess, the one associated with motherhood.

It is not an accident that there are far more churches named after Mary Magdalene, especially in southern France, than there are for the Virgin Mom. In many of these churches, usually tucked away in a corner, or completely hidden, one can still find curious little statues called *Black Madonnas*. These statues, reminiscent of the pagan goddesses such as Isis, Diana and Cybelle who were often depicted as black, were mistrusted but tolerated by the Church because they were held precious by the people. Over the years they became associated with the Magdalene—the people recognized, silently, that she was a goddess that had all her sexual aspects intact.

I've run across several well-argued opinions, including those of Picknell and Prince, Jean Markale[93] and others who contend that Mary Magdalene was a powerful sacred prostitute who supervised other sacred prostitutes called 'hierodulai' (from the same root as 'harlot'[94]). They say that she was as vital to the 'Jesus movement' as was Jesus himself, and that a big part of that movement was to reintroduce the feminine principal to its rightful place, to pave the way for the 'return of the goddess'. When the consciousness of humanity is too left-brained or masculine, there can be an absense of love and compassion. The return of the goddess implies the return of right-brained/feminine softness, kindness, compassion, etc. The 'Jesus movement' advocated a 'love thy neighbour' attitude and recognized the sex act as a means by which to do so, as a powerful healing tool.

According to Picknell and Prince, these secrets surrounding Mary Magdalene were among several kept by the Knights Templar and other secret societies. They also kept secret the knowledge of the alchemical-magical potential of the sex act, which was well known to many ancient cultures and was well documented in the Tantric writings. It is believed that, throughout the ages, ceremonies that included sacred sexual rituals were practiced in secret by these societies. To the Roman Church, of course, such things were heresy, and to speak of them was to be put to death.

Mary Magdelene may well be the most controversial figure in the New Testament. Whether the role she played was equivalent to that of Jesus, as some have claimed, it seems certain that it was much greater than the legacy given to her by the Church establishment.

So again we address the questions; *who was Jesus?* What was his mission? As previously mentioned, he was a rebel, a champion of the poor, a king, a priest, a rabbi (a scholar of Judaic law) and a political leader who was expected to lead his people out of bondage. These characteristics are not so hard to imagine, not so different from the typical Hollywood/Bible image that is imprinted on our minds. The picture emerging from the work of recent Biblical scholarship, however, suggests that there are many more things to consider. The evidence increasingly points to a man with two parallel agendas, one more public, fed to and fuelled by the outer circle, and one covert, administered by a knowledgeable and dedicated inner circle.

Jesus appears to be a man concerned greatly with mystical truths, the kind that underlie most of the religious movements. He seems to have been well versed in the occult sciences, a skilled magician in the Hermetic traditions. In 'Jesus the Magician', Dr. Morton Smith claims that Jesus was raised in Egypt, where he was initiated into Egyptian magic. He became the most accomplished of a slew of itinerant healers and exorcists who were common at the time. The Gnostic writings as well as the Jewish Talmud back up these claims.

Desmond Stewart, author of 'The Foreigner' also argues that Jesus came from Egypt, pointing out that there were many Jews living in Egypt at the time. There is no question that he was more than familiar with Egyptian writings and many of his sayings and teachings come directly from them. The saying, "In my Father's house are many mansions", comes directly from the Egyptian Book of the Dead.[95] The Lord's Prayer is also from the Book of the Dead, with the opening line translating as "Amon, Amon who art in heaven...",[96] The saying associated with Jesus, "Come to me all you who are heavy laden and I will refresh you", was lifted word for word from the sayings of Isis.[97]

Many feel that part of the Jesus mission was to restore gender equality, to bring the feminine principles back into the equation. In the Egyptian traditions, Isis was not seen as a subordinate, but rather as an equal, a creator. One Egyptian scripture reads, "In the beginning there was Isis, oldest of the old".[98] The Jews had once worshipped a feminine deity, the Hebrew goddess Raphael Patai, a pseudonym for Asherah. It was once an accepted part of ancient wisdom to use the practice of sex as a way of recognizing the union of the sexes, and thus, the underlying unity of all things. This awareness is an essential step on the path to enlightenment. Was the Jesus movement attempting to bring that consciousness back to humanity?

Much of the channeled information speaks of Jesus in a different way. His essence is described as a 'volunteer soul' who has come to Earth many times in an effort to help us to help ourselves. Some say that this entity came as the Buddha, Thoth, Quetzelcoatl, and others. Some say he is the same entity as the archangel Michael. It's been said that, in the Jesus incarnation, he, the Mary Magdalene soul and a few others, volunteered to come with a common mission. Some have described Jesus Christ as a 'committee' rather than an individual.

As I mentioned earlier, the process of writing this book is a strong healing tool for me. That was very evident to me as I went about putting together this section about the Bible and the Christian Church. I often felt overwhelmed and was unsure that I could go on. It was not only the incredible volume of information that exists regarding this topic, but also the feelings and emotions that welled up inside of me. An emotion is like a knock on the door, an opportunity to open the door and come face to face with one's soul.

Many aspects of this chapter have an emotional effect on me. For example, I have some strange connection to Mary Magdalene and find it difficult to talk about her without becoming choked up with some form of sadness. It must be tied in with the feelings I've had for all of womanhood, who have suffered so much at the hands of the patriarchy. Part of this feeling is a deep-rooted sense of guilt that I've inherited and that I know must be set free. The sadness extends to all of humanity who have endured all these centuries of human bondage, chained by oppressive regulation and crippling belief systems.

I've had to deal with the great trepidation I've felt in actually questioning and criticizing the Bible. This involves dealing with my own indoctrination, my own deeply ingrained beliefs surrounding Jesus, the various Bible stories and the many behaviors that have been deemed 'sinful' by the Church. Having been brought up in the Catholic tradition, I still find myself in the grip of some very questionable doctrine.

Much more difficult to deal with has been the rage and disgust I've felt toward organized religion; knowing that Muslim youths are sent on suicide missions to kill innocent civilians based on the indoctrination that they will go immediately to heaven; knowing that the state of Israel justifies its oppressive actions by using the belief that the Jews are entitled to Palestine, based on the promises of some bogus 'god' in the Old Testament. Especially infuriating is the shameful history of the Christian Church. Twenty-five million people put to death in the western world, whole cultures and civilizations of natives devastated and 'converted', libraries burned, knowledge suppressed—all by a mindless, soulless machine, blinded by its quest for power! It's not easy to digest.

It's not easy to forgive. It can be difficult to understand that the individuals making decisions on behalf of the Church were simply making mistakes, acting in ways that they believed, in their imbalance, were of benefit to mankind. It's easy to forget that, within the mindless, soulless machine are countless good-hearted, well-meaning individuals who wouldn't hurt a flea. To extend this further, it can be difficult to accept the incredible stupidity and cruelty with which humanity has gone about its business in most of its endeavours throughout history.

In short, it's not easy to see through the Maya, to peer through the elaborate veils of illusion and catch a glimpse of the truth that lies beyond. My own personal attempts to do so have involved a long process of change, of healing. I've come to the belief that ultimately, nothing is wrong, that we have proceeded and are proceeding as we should be. The pendulum is swinging. The collective consciousness is always learning and, like in all learning processes, there are peaks and valleys. We've made mistakes in the past, but we are becoming ever more vigilant, ever more compassionate, ever more awakened. We are moving forward.

To those who form their opinions based on what they read in the news or see on the television, this may seem very idealistic and naive. Thousands die daily of starvation. Wars that have the capacity to devastate vast numbers of people are a constant threat. By standing back a little further, however, I believe one would see that human consciousness has steadily evolved over the centuries. Generally speaking, we are less tolerant today of cruelty and oppressive injustice than we were hundreds of years ago. In the past the oppressors imposed their will with a purer form of brute force. Today they must use a greater degree of brainwashing and manipulating, using deceptive notions of democracy, free enterprise and globalization.

The modern oppressors are much more aware of the power of human conscious-ness than most of the general public. They know that as long as we believe that they are acting nobly, defending the world from terrorism, for example, they will be allowed to continue in their ceaseless quest for power. They employ ever more sophis-ticated mechanisms by which to impose their brainwashing, ie; television, Hollywood, news-media, etc, because they know that as soon as a sufficient number of people become aware of what is really going on, the collective will of humanity will totally overpower them.

I'm sorry, am I digressing? I'm supposed to be talking about my beliefs regarding the Bible. Any discussion of the ways in which the power elite seek to disempower and oppress the masses, however, must surely include mention of the Bible and the organ-izations promoting it. If one accepts the Machiavellian concept of 'divide and con-quer', then it's plain to see that religion has been something that has always kept the people fighting amongst themselves. Today there are many religious factions fighting amongst themselves throughout the globe. Some of them are directly caused by or involve the animosity between religions. With others the religious connection is more indirect. One huge division is currently occurring between two fanatical mindsets—religious fundamentalism with its stifling repression of human joy on the one hand, and consumerism, with its profit-worshipping, 'globalization' agenda on the other. Both 'jihad' and 'free trade' seem to me to be totally devoid of love and compassion.

It must be obvious by now that I believe that, even though there are many valu-able nuggets hidden in it, the modern day Bible has been edited, manipulated and misinterpreted to the point where it probably bears very little resemblance to the Bible that could have been. Some of this misinformation has had dire consequences in the past and still continues to threaten. Absurd notions of a chosen people and a prom-ised land still underlie the current problems in the middle east. These notions are used by the power elite to manipulate the people and thus justify actions that further their own ends. A great many people feel that Armageddon and the conflict between Gog and Magog is an inevitability. The fear and hatred surrounding these beliefs are big obstacles to our collective quest for enlightenment.

It seems clear to me that the scars and wounds resulting from Bible beliefs run very deep. The Jews have been wrongfully persecuted over the years because the Bible has portrayed them as the killers of Christ and because they have not recognized him as the Messiah. After encountering all the information I've encountered, this seems just as ridiculous as the idea that the Jews are the chosen people and that Palestine was given to them by God.

Regardless of what one chooses to believe regarding the Crucifixion, Moses or any of the contentious issues mentioned in this part of the book, it is hard not to arrive at the conclusion that the information in the Bible is just not reliable. How can we possibly see it as the indisputable word of God? There are important questions that must be asked. Is this book a useful tool? Does it help us to know who we are, where we came from and where we're going? Do the good points of the Bible outweigh the bad? Maybe it would be useful to ask oneself whether; a) all of the information in the Bible is useful, b) none of it is useful, c) some of it is and some of it isn't d) even the good information is useless because it's all a hopeless mish-mash of contradictions, impossible to sort out.

I believe that the mission of the Jesus entity/committee was to attempt to steer humanity toward enlightenment, just as many volunteers have done in the past and continue to do. I believe that there are many volunteers on the planet at this time, some of them working silently and maintaining a low profile, some working more in the public eye.

The Jesus mission sought to give humanity the opportunity to embrace the concepts of love and compassion, and of unity and the power of human consciousness to affect change in our universe. These concepts can be learned and developed in many ways, using many different methods, such as prayer, meditation, etc. Included in this list of methods is the mindful use of the sex act. I believe that the Jesus committee was well aware of this potential and used and taught some of these empowering sacred sexual techniques. The last thing that a 'power-elite control group' wants, however, is for the masses to become empowered. Thus the sex act, possibly the most beautiful, joyful gift ever given to mankind as a means of experiencing the divine, was vilified—made into something dirty.

They say that the darkest hour is just before dawn. Regarding our attitudes toward sexuality, the Christian era has been a very dark hour indeed. I believe that, even though the human psyche is deeply scarred by the indoctrination of nonsense that surrounds sexuality, we are on the verge of a great and joyous awakening. We will soon remember that the sex act is a powerful healing tool, an expression of joy and an incredibly beautiful celebration of love and life.

ENDNOTES—PART SIX

1. Baigent, Leigh and Lincoln—*The Messianic Legacy*, Dell, 1986, New York, p. 2
2. Cerminara, Gina—*Insights for the Age of Aquarius*, Quest Books, 1973, London, p.125–126
3. ibid. p. 135–136
4. ibid. p. 144–154
5. ibid. p. 212
6. ibid. p. 237–246
7. Gardner, Laurence—*Genesis of the Grail Kings*, Bantam Press, 1999, London, p. 189
8. Picknett, Lynn and Prince, Clive—*The Templar Revelation*, Bantam Press, 1997, London, p.254
9. Cerminara, Gina—*Insights for the Age of Aquarius*, Quest Books, 1973, London, p. 214 223
10. Finkelstein, I. And Silberman, N. A.—*The Bible Unearthed*, Simon & Schuster, 2002, New York, p. 11
11. Gardner, Laurence—*Genesis of the Grail Kings*, Bantam Press, 1999, London, p. 45–50
10. ibid. p. 99–109
13. ibid. p. 97–98

14. ibid. p. 306–308

15. ibid. p. 299

16. Cerminara, Gina—*Insights for the Age of Aquarius*, Quest Books, 1973, London, p. 163

17. Icke, David—*The Robot's Rebellion*, Gateway Books, 1994, Bath U.K., p. 74

18. Baigent, Leigh and Lincoln—*The Messianic Legacy*, Dell, 1986, New York, p. 107

19. Icke, David—*The Robot's Rebellion*, Gateway Books, 1994, Bath U.K., p. 85

20. ibid. p. 71

21. Thiering, Barbara—*Jesus the Man*, Corgi Books, 1992, London, p. 187–214

22. Cerminara, Gina—*Insights for the Age of Aquarius*, Quest Books, 1973, London, p. 155

23. Icke, David—*The Robot's Rebellion*, Gateway Books, 1994, Bath U.K., p. 73

24. Baigent, Leigh and Lincoln—*The Messianic Legacy*, Dell, 1986, New York, p. 39–45, and Baigent, Leigh and Lincoln—*The Holy Blood and the Holy Grail*, Corgi, 1982, London, 385–389

25. Baigent, Leigh and Lincoln—*The Messianic Legacy*, Dell, 1986, New York, p. 52 and Baigent, Leigh and Lincoln—*The Holy Blood and the Holy Grail*, Corgi, 1982, London, 367–368

26. Icke, David—*The Robot's Rebellion*, Gateway Books, 1994, Bath U.K., p. 75–76

27. Bramley, William—*The Gods of Eden* , Avon Books, 1990, New York, p. 146–147

28. Icke, David—*The Robot's Rebellion*, Gateway Books, 1994, Bath U.K., p. 81

29. Bramley, William—*The Gods of Eden* , Avon Books, 1990, New York, p. 147–148

30. Hancock, Graham—*The Sign and the Seal*, Doubleday Canada, Ltd., 1993, Toronto, p. 303

31. Cerminara, Gina—*Insights for the Age of Aquarius*, Quest Books, 1973, London, p. 275

32. Baigent, Leigh and Lincoln—*The Messianic Legacy*, Dell, 1986, New York, p. 110–111, and Icke, David—*The Robot's Rebellion*, Gateway Books, 1994, Bath U.K., p. 82

33. Icke, David—*The Robot's Rebellion*, Gateway Books, 1994, Bath U.K., p. 82

34. ibid. p. 117

35. Bushby, Tony—*The Bible Fraud*—**www.thebiblefraud.com**

36. Icke, David—*The Robot's Rebellion*, Gateway Books, 1994, Bath U.K., p. 77–79

37. Bushby, Tony—*The Bible Fraud*—**www.thebiblefraud.com**

38. Icke, David—*The Robot's Rebellion*, Gateway Books, 1994, Bath U.K., p. 82

39. Bramley, William—*The Gods of Eden* , Avon Books, 1990, New York, p. 148

40. Picknett, Lynn and Prince, Clive—*The Templar Revelation*, Bantam Press, 1997, London, p. 241–244, and Baigent, Leigh and Lincoln—*The Holy Blood and the Holy Grail*, Corgi, 1982, London, p. 343—346

41. Baigent, Leigh and Lincoln—*The Holy Blood and the Holy Grail*, Corgi, 1982, London, p. 332

42. ibid. p. 343–346

43. ibid. p. 400–401

44. Baigent, Leigh and Lincoln—*The Messianic Legacy*, Dell, 1986, New York, p. 107–108

45. ibid. p. 115–123

46. Baigent, Leigh and Lincoln—*The Holy Blood and the Holy Grail*, Corgi, 1982, London, p. 50

47. Bramley, William—*The Gods of Eden* , Avon Books, 1990, New York, p. 201–206

48. ibid. p. 221–224

49. Capra, Fritzof—*The Tao of Physics*, Harper Collins, 1976, London, 368

50. Bramley, William—*The Gods of Eden* , Avon Books, 1990, New York, p. 307–320

51. Gardner, Laurence—*Genesis of the Grail Kings*, Bantam Press, 1999, London, p. 35

52. Sitchin, Zecharia—*Genesis Revisited*, Avon Books, 1990, New York, 41–47

53. Baigent, Leigh and Lincoln—*The Messianic Legacy*, Dell, 1986, New York, p. 42

54. Gardner, Laurence—*Genesis of the Grail Kings*, Bantam Press, 1999, London, p. 329

55. ibid. p. 134–135

56. Alford, Alan—*Gods of the New Millennium*, Hodder and Stoughton, 1997, London, p. 216–217

57. Gardner, Laurence—*Genesis of the Grail Kings*, Bantam Press, 1999, London, p. 119 —120

58. Moon, Peter—*The Black Sun, Montauk's Nazi-Tibetan Connection*, Sky Books, 1997 New York, p. 103

59. Gardner, Laurence—*Genesis of the Grail Kings*, Bantam Press, 1999, London, p. 164

60. Alford, Alan—*Gods of the New Millennium*, Hodder and Stoughton, 1997, London, p. 321–328
61. Hancock, Graham—*The Sign and the Seal*, Doubleday Canada, Ltd., 1993, Toronto, p. 325
62. Gardner, Laurence—*Genesis of the Grail Kings*, Bantam Press, 1999, London, p. 358
63. Hancock, Graham—*The Sign and the Seal*, Doubleday Canada, Ltd., 1993, Toronto, p. 297–303
64. Gardner, Laurence—*Genesis of the Grail Kings*, Bantam Press, 1999, London, p. 288–294
65. ibid. p. 259–270
66. Thiering, Barbara—*Jesus the Man*, Corgi Books, 1992, London, p. 119–120
67. Hancock, Graham—*The Sign and the Seal*, Doubleday Canada, Ltd., 1993, Toronto, p. 276
68. ibid. p. 350
69. Finkelstein, I. And Silberman, N. A.—*The Bible Unearthed*, Simon & Schuster, 2002, New York, p. 247
70. ibid. p. 23
71. Baigent, Leigh and Lincoln—*The Messianic Legacy*, Dell, 1986, New York, p. 3–5
72. ibid. p. 94–97
73. Cerminara, Gina—*Insights for the Age of Aquarius*, Quest Books, 1973, London, p. 145
74. Markale, Jean—*The Great Goddess*, Inner Traditions, 1997, Rochester VT, p. 19–20
75. Gardner, Laurence—*Genesis of the Grail Kings*, Bantam Press, 1999, London, p. 189
76. ibid. 295–296
77. Picknett, Lynn and Prince, Clive—*The Templar Revelation*, Bantam Press, 1997, London, A summary of the book's main viewpoint.
78. Baigent, Leigh and Lincoln—*The Holy Blood and the Holy Grail*, Corgi, 1982, London. A summary of one of the book's contentions.
79. Bramley, William—*The Gods of Eden* , Avon Books, 1990, New York, p. 130–131
80. ibid. p. 127–128
81. Baigent, Leigh and Lincoln—*The Messianic Legacy*, Dell, 1986, New York, p. 276
Baigent, Leigh and Lincoln—*The Messianic Legacy*, Dell, 1986, New York, p. 100–101
83. ibid. p. 107
84. Baigent, Leigh and Lincoln—*The Messianic Legacy*, Dell, 1986, New York, p. 332–334
85. Gardner, Laurence—*Genesis of the Grail Kings*, Bantam Press, 1999, London, p.172
86. Baigent, Leigh and Lincoln—*The Messianic Legacy*, Dell, 1986, New York, p. 26
87. Icke, David—*The Robot's Rebellion*, Gateway Books, 1994, Bath U.K., p.66–68, and Thiering, Barbara—*Jesus the Man*, Corgi Books, 1992, London, p. 154–160, and Baigent, Leigh and Lincoln—*The Messianic Legacy*, Dell, 1986, New York, p. 401, 366–378
88. Picknett, Lynn and Prince, Clive—*The Templar Revelation*, Bantam Press, 1997, London, p. 248
89. ibid. p. 261–262
90. Baigent, Leigh and Lincoln—*The Holy Blood and the Holy Grail*, Corgi, 1982, London, p. 404
91. Picknett, Lynn and Prince, Clive—*The Templar Revelation*, Bantam Press, 1997, London, p. 251–260
92. Markale, Jean—*The Great Goddess*, Inner Traditions, 1997, Rochester VT, p. 23
93. ibid. p. 19–27
94. Gardner, Laurence—*Genesis of the Grail Kings*, Bantam Press, 1999, London, p. 181
95. Picknett, Lynn and Prince, Clive—*The Templar Revelation*, Bantam Press, 1997, London, p. 288
96. ibid. p. 288
97. ibid. p. 293
98. ibid. p. 292

Part Seven

Sex and the Return of the Goddess

"Understand what great power
undefiled intercourse possesses"
—*Gnostic Gospel of Philip*[1]

It seems obvious to me that collective humanity could definitely use a good orgasm. Imagine that! The entire human population simultaneously enjoying an enormous collective orgasm, moaning together in ecstasy! The world would never be the same. I'm sure that many of the wounds deep within the human psyche would spontaneously heal. For a while, at least, there would be no thought of war, politics, crime, starvation, the rat race, etc. There would only be a basking in the glow of joy and bliss.

Soon afterwards, however, many of us would be brought back to 'reality' by familiar feelings of guilt and shame. Some of us would feel dirty. Some would even feel that we'd been attacked by Satan himself, while others who would definitely number in the minority, would actually feel as though we'd been blessed by something truly divine.

Many people, including myself, feel that our attitudes toward sex are some of the greatest impediments to our ability to move towards self-actualization and enlightenment. These attitudes are directly related to those attitudes that govern the way we view our own bodies and the way we think of life itself. It seems to me that the healing of this enormous 'sexual wound', both in the individual as well as the collective, would represent a huge step forward toward liberty, light and the realization of human potential.

The human animal is very different from other mammals regarding its sexual characteristics. More so than most other mammals, the difference in outward appearance between the male and female is pronounced. Human females are the only female mammals that are receptive to sex all year round, the only ones to experience orgasm, the only ones with breasts that are disproportionately large, even when not involved in the feeding of young. In fact, human sex organs of both genders are disproportionately large. Human skin is relatively hairless and very sensitive to the touch. Human lips are relatively large and fleshy. Unlike other mammals, humans have 'erogenous zones'; regions of the body that stimulate the sex drive when caressed. Humans are the only mammals that mate face to face, and the vaginal angle seems to encourage this. Relative to other mammals, a human coupling lasts much longer. We are the only ones who include a wide variety of caresses and kisses in our mating behavior.

356   WHY IS LIFE?

The list goes on and on. Clearly, sex means much more to humans than to other animals. It goes well beyond the purely procreative function.

For the longest time the Church was embarrassed by, and denied the existence of the clitoris. It is the only human organ whose sole function is to give pleasure. Many people are so conditioned that they have a difficult time even saying the word 'clitoris'. Clitoris, clitoris, clitoris, clitoris, clitoris, clitoris!

Humanity is clearly obsessed with sex. It dominates our consciousness. This obsession is exploited, ad nauseam, and scantily clad women, wiggling and smiling seductively, are used to sell just about anything. This obsession underlies prostitution, pornography and rape. Is this exaggerated fascination a product of our natural, extraordinary attraction to sex, or is it the result of confusion and twisted attitudes toward it in reaction to all the imposed taboos, dogma and indoctrination? Or is it a combination of both of these perspectives?

At this point, I'd like to make some statements about some of my beliefs regarding sex. I believe that sex heals. Under the right circumstances, the sex act has the power to awaken dormant memories, along with the emotions that surround them. It has the potential to open our hearts and to help us to understand that:

- *we are not really separate entities, but a part of a greater whole*
- *the duality of male-female is an illusion*
- *our consciousness literally creates our reality.*

The sex act is a powerful opportunity to confront fear and replace it with love. It can be a window into other realms and a means by which to assert greater control over our lives. I believe that the human body, with its sensitive skin and face to face vaginal angle, is a 'special design', meant to foster feelings of love during sex; the linking of sex with the highest form of human expression. In short, I believe that the sex act is a powerful and beautiful tool for achieving enlightenment.

I believe that the ancients were far more consciously aware of this potential than we are today. Buried in our subconscious, however, is the memory of this awareness. We yearn for sexual freedom. We all know that, stripped of its negative baggage, the sex act is divine, the orgasm is bliss, sexuality is amongst the greatest gifts bestowed upon humanity.

I believe that the 'power elite' or the 'negative forces' throughout the ages have also been more aware of this sexual potential than were the masses, and have tried to keep this knowledge hidden. Whether wittingly or unwittingly, they have perpetrated the idea that sex is dirty and evil, and have suppressed the feminine aspects of humanity. With the feminine side disempowered, we are only half-human. Without the empowering potential of the sex act, we are weak. When we are weak, we can be easily dominated and controlled.

I believe we are on the mend. Our attitudes toward sex have taken great leaps forward in recent history and will continue to do so. With this mending will come greater freedom, greater power, greater love.

Chapter 35

FROM MATRIARCHY TO PATRIARCHY

According to most scholars, at one time in the distant past the world was predominantly gynaecocratic with a culture that was more telluric, and that it eventually became androcratic with a culture that looked increasingly toward the heavens. This is a fancy way of saying that the world was once dominated by women who were largely concerned with earthy, inward matters, until it changed to a male-dominated culture concerned largely with more cosmic, outward matters. This is the same as saying that humanity moved from a predominantly right-brained consciousness to a predominantly left-brained consciousness.

Simply stated, *a right-brained, matriarchal society* would typically be more of a shamanic, hunter-gatherer society seeking to live in harmony with nature. Intelligence would be more intuitive by nature, and psychic abilities, especially the capacity to willfully enter into trance states of altered consciousness, would be highly valued. This could be thought of as internal technology. Because lineage was based on the offspring of the females, the identity of the father was not as important and polygamy was probably the order of the day. (I am not referring here to the patriarchal type of polygamy whereby a wealthy man might have several wives. In such a patriarchal society it would be unheard of for a woman to have many husbands.) With a matriarchal society the whole concept of blood lineage was less important. The worshipping of deities tended toward the qualities of fertility and the ability to find prey. Such deities were predominantly female goddesses.

A left-brained, patriarchal society was usually an agricultural society and was thus concerned with land ownership and the notion of storing food and other goods. This led to an aggressive attitude of land acquisition, including the acquisition of slaves to work the land, so that the strategies and tools of war became highly valued. The ability to conquer others or to avoid being conquered by others was prized. A logical, deductive type of intelligence leading to external technology was more conducive to such circumstances. The determination of lineage and rightful inheritance became more important because of the idea of ownership. It became very important for a man to be sure that his woman was giving birth to children that were from his seed. Thus monogamy and the various taboos regarding sex became prominent, contributing further to bellicose attitudes. The worship of deities tended toward the qualities of ferocity and the ability to win wars and raise crops. Such deities were predominantly male gods.

It is difficult to know exactly when the transition from masculine to feminine consciousness occurred. It does not happen abruptly. Some opinions hold that it happens in conjunction with exposure to different types or 'flavors' of cosmic energy. In other words, when the Earth is in a position, relative to the rest of the cosmos, that exposes it to greater amounts of masculine energy, then this affects the collective consciousness on the planet, causing masculinity to dominate. According to the Mayans, each precessional cycle of 25,920 years breaks down into five periods called 'ajars', each lasting 5,184 years. Each of the first four ajars alternates between masculine or feminine energy. The current ajar, the fourth which is masculine, is said to have started about 3114 BC and will end on the winter solstice of 2012. We will then enter the fifth ajar, a period of harmony during which we will be exposed to an equal amount of masculine and feminine cosmic energy.

Some scholars suggest that, during the time of the matriarchy, people were not aware of the male's contribution to procreation; that people did not make the connection between childbirth and sex. Thus the female ability to bring forth life was considered 'magic'. Also considered magic was their ability to cause arousal in the males.[2] This magical female power was intimidating to the males, until that point in time when they began to realize that their sperm was essential to the procreative process. At this point they used their superior physical strength to take control from the females, ushering in the dawn of the patriarchal take-over.[3] *While this explanation seems to make sense, I believe there is more to the story. I will elaborate at the end of the chapter.*

How do scholars know this about our ancient past? What evidence is there to suggest that we were once a matriarchal society? Historian Jean Markale, in his book 'The Great Goddess', gives a thorough account of such evidence. The earliest forms of art dating as far back as the Upper Palaeolithic Age (25,000 to 20,000 BC) such as cave paintings and statuettes, were of animals of prey and of the female form. Many ancient statuettes have been found, often with exaggerated maternal body parts like breasts and buttocks, suggesting an honoring of the female form. Some of these statuettes are faceless, possibly corresponding to the anonymity of the female aspect of humanity. Others had ferocious faces, possibly corresponding to the female principle of the cycle of destruction and creation.

Strange sculptural depictions of gargoyle-like females with wide-open genitals, called **shela-na-gigs** have been found throughout the Celtic areas, especially Ireland.[4] Usually found in old churches or temples, they are similar, in terms of the body-posture, to that of a Tantric ritual called the 'stri puja', a ceremony during which a congregation of people pay homage to a woman who has her legs wide open with her genitals exposed.[5] They are also reminiscent of some depictions of the Hindu goddess, Kali. The open genitals, a common motif in prehistoric art, symbolize an initiatress inviting penetration and entrance into the cave of knowledge and wisdom, the divine womb. The oldest temples and sanctuaries are very womb-like and the many sacred mounds found throughout the world seem to be a tribute to the female form. According to John Allegro, ancient sacred prostiutes also had ceremonies where they squated with their open genitals exposed to the ground, inducing psychedelic mushrooms to grow on that spot.[6]

There are many myths and legends from various traditions that are indicative of this switch from matriarchy to patriarchy. An example of this is the **Greek legend of Delphi**. In this story, Apollo is a patriarch who comes from the north. Pythia, the great serpent and matriarch of Delphi is slain by Apollo. She fools Apollo, however and is not really dead, hiding in a deep pit below the temple and becoming the Oracle of Delphi. In other words, the wise goddess 'goes underground', hiding from and taking a back seat to the new patriarchy.[7]

The serpent is traditionally viewed in most cultures as a female symbol, something that is close to the earth. In Hindu traditions the snake represents the female Kundalini energy that lies dormant at the base of the spine. When activated, this energy rises through the chakras until it achieves unity with male energy. In the mythology of many cultures, some serpent-like creature is often credited with 'bringing knowledge and civilization'. In Judeo-Christian traditions, however, this is often reversed. Legends, such as the story of St. George, tell of heroes who slay serpents or dragons and bring 'civilization' to the people. In Christian iconography, the serpent is trampled underfoot by the Virgin Mary. Generally speaking, Christianity has vilified the serpent.

As mentioned earlier, **Roman Church attitudes** toward sex and females have been major components in the suppression of feminine principals and the marginalization of female contributions throughout history. The Christian Trinity of Father, Son and Holy Spirit, is the only one of several trinities from various traditions that does not include a female component. According to David Icke, the Roman Church didn't acknowledge that females even had a soul until a decree was passed in 1545. It only passed by a majority of three votes.

Many Biblical stories, most notably Adam and Eve, portray woman as being the source of all of our problems; the temptress that manipulates Adam. (This is also evident in the Greek myth of Pandora, who releases from her box all the evils of the world.) God curses Eve, saying, "In pain shall you bring forth children, yet your desire will be for your husband and he shall rule over you."—Genesis 3:16

Church doctrine, both official and unofficial, has done much to put down the feminine and to promote the idea that the human body and the sex act are dirty and immoral. During the first centuries of Christianity, the goddess based cults were very tenacious and people still attended goddess services which often included sexual rituals. The cult of Mary Magdalene was very strong until about 400 BC, as were the cults of Isis and other goddesses. This represented a serious threat to the new Roman Church, who soon began to persecute such groups, driving them underground.

Aware that the people required a female deity, the Church attempted to fill this need by proclaiming *the sexless Virgin Mary* as being the 'mother of God', and thus a deity in her own right. This took place at the Council of Ephesus in 431 AD. In 1854, Pope Pius XII decreed the idea of Mary's Immaculate Conception and the notion that her living body was taken up into heaven, which is called the Assumption.[8] Much of the 'mother' iconography of Isis, depictions of her with stars in her hair, holding a baby, were appropriated and assigned to the Virgin Mary. As mentioned previously, the mother of Jesus is given very little coverage in the gospels. Modern scholars, however, acknowledge that she was a socially prominent, relatively wealthy and powerful woman—a descendant of King David. She was a part of Jesus' inner circle and played a bigger role than we've been led to believe.

It is important to note that other organized religions have also done a great deal to suppress and oppress women and the feminine components of humanity. An old saying amongst Jewish rabbis shows their contempt for women—"Better to burn the Law than to teach it to a woman". To this day orthodox Jews begin their day with a prayer that includes the statement: "I thank God I was born a man and not a woman".[9]

It is no secret that life under the rule of various Islamic regimes has become extremely difficult for many women, who are often treated worse than livestock. Paranoia over sexuality has reached ridiculous extremes so that even the exposing of a bare female forearm could result in a vicious beating, which is condoned by the authorities. Women in many Hindu societies often don't fare much better. A Hindu law-giver named Manu wrote, "Women are as impure as falsehood itself. A woman is never fit for independence. Day and night women must be kept in dependence by the males of their families".[10]

Chapter 36

GODDESSES

Archeology tells us that goddesses were worshipped in a wide variety of cultures and civilizations before, during and after the take-over of the patriarchy. Many of these goddesses embody the concepts of nubile seductress, nurturing mother and wise crone, as well as skilled huntress and warrior.

In Greek/Roman mythology, Athena/Minerva is a warrior goddess who is often pictured with an owl, symbolizing wisdom. Aphrodite/Venus is a sex goddess radiating beauty and strength. Hera/Juno is a maternal goddess, both sister and wife of Zeus/Jupiter. Diana/Artemis is a huntress, usually depicted with a bow and arrow.

Ishtar (Babylon) and Isis (Egypt) were sex goddesses who were very popular at the time of Christ, and remained so for hundreds of years after. Ishtar, the goddess of 1,000 aspects and often depicted with winged arms, is the same entity represented in many cultures, such as Astarte (Phoenician), Ashtoreth(Hebrew), Aphrodite/Venus(Greco-Roman), Cybelle(Turkish) and others. The Egyptian goddess, Hathor, embodies beauty and eroticism, and is associated with the cow, representing motherhood, and the lion, representing the wild, untamable feminine spirit. Isis, both sister and wife to Osiris, embodies the three aspects of womanhood, seductress, mother and sage.

In Egypt, the primordial couple is Maat (female) and Shu (male). Maat is considered to be the source of all life and the material world. Demeter is the Greek counterpart. Note that the word 'Maat' and the last two syllables of 'Demeter' is very similar to 'mater', which is the root of such words as 'maternal', 'matter', matrix', etc. The idea that the universe was created from the feminine aspect is widespread.

In Indian mythology, female energy is represented by Shakti, who has several aspects. Parvati represents the sexual, while Kali and Durga represent the destroyer and creator. The idea that there must be destruction before there can be creation, in an endless cycle, is a concept ascribed to the feminine. Lakshmi is the aspect representing abundance.

Some other goddesses are; Rhiannon, Epona and Dana (Celtic); Freya, He and Erda (Germanic); Tanit (Carthage); Kuan Yin, Benzai-Ten, Chang O, Hsi Wang Mu and Ukemochi (Far East); Estanatlehi, Wawalak, and Xochiquetzal (Native American); Maia, Persephone and Demeter (Greek); Sarasvati (Indian); Pele (Hawaiian); Ochun (African); Tara (Tibet); Inanna, Ninkhursag, Lillith (Sumerian).

Chapter 37

STRANGE SEX

In many indigenous, shamanic cultures, some of which still exist today, some of the sexual practices would seem shockingly immoral to most westerners. Such shocking practices were common and widespread in societies all over the globe. Some had various forms of *sexual hospitality*, where a guest was invited to have sex with the woman of the house.[11] Some cultures practiced forms of *bridal prostitution*, whereby a new bride would have sex with other members of the tribe, sometimes the entire tribe, sometimes just members of the groom's family.[12]

In some cultures it was common for wandering priests, holy men or shamans to have sex with whomever they chose. This practice is sometimes referred to as *carte blanche*. It was often considered an honor to be chosen and sometimes such holy men were actually paid by a man to have sex with his wife. In some indigenous cultures, the shaman would have slept at least once with every female in the tribe.[13] Some cultures partook of *ritual promiscuity* during key festivals or special occasions. During such events marriage vows were often suspended and participants were encouraged to couple with whomever they chose.[14] (For more detailed descriptions of such rituals in cultures around the globe, I recommend a book called 'The Encyclopedia of Sacred Sexuality', by Rufus C. Camphausen.)

The practicing of sexual rituals was prominent in many cultures in ancient times. In Sumeria there were sex cults centered around the goddess, Inanna/Ishtar/Astarte. The Chaldeans practiced temple prostitution—the Egyptians had the Isis cult and worshipped the phallus—India and Tibet had Tantrism, with a wide range of sexual rituals—the Greeks had their sacred Eros and the Demeter mysteries—China had its 'inner alchemy of Tao', sometimes called Taoist Tantra—within the Qabalistic traditions of Judaism, the Sabbatarian sects had sexual rituals—the late Hellenistic Gnostic sects such as the Ophites, Simonites and Barbello Gnostics had sex rites such as the Hieros Gamos.[15] Some of these Gnostic practices are similar to the 'sex magic' that has evolved into more recent times.

The word 'prostitute' had different meanings back then, usually referring to one who had non-procreative sex.[16] A *'sacred prostitute'* was someone who had sex for some divine purpose. The word 'orgy' originally meant a ritual religious ceremony, which was imbued with divine power.[17] In the Babylonian temples of Ishtar (Astarte/Ashtoreth), ritual prostitution, or *temple prostitution*, was practiced whereby a man would have sex with a priestess for money, which went to the temple. This was a religious ceremony, the idea being that the man could 'taste divinity'. In addition to the resident prostitute/priestess, all women in the congregation were required to offer these services at least once.

Interestingly, at the ancient temple at Erech in Mesopotamia, the sacred prostitute was called the 'nu-gug', which means 'the pure and immaculate ones'.[18] This word is very similar to the name of the strange sculptures previously mentioned, the sheela-na-gigs. The origin of this name has always been a mystery, as it has no roots in the Celtic cultures to which it belongs. This suggests that the two words may have a common source.

Sex with priestesses, called 'horae', was also practiced by the Gnostics in the hopes of receiving 'gnosis', defined as intuitively revealed divine knowledge on the physical, mental and spiritual levels. The practice of achieving a prolonged, full-body orgasm called 'horasis' was seen as the best way of receiving gnosis, which would then lead to transformation. It is likely that the root of such words as horae and horasis also spawned the word 'whore', which eventually came to have a negative stigma.[19]

In certain Indian and pre-Zoroastrian Persian ceremonies, a virgin (a strong independent woman) was 'ordained' a goddess and the men of the village had sex with her. In a different Persian ritual, a selected couple had sex in full view of the temple gathering, after which a five-day orgy ensued. During this ceremony all marital vows were suspended. (A swinger's dream come true!)

Another strange practice among the ancients was the ritual ingestion of sexual body fluids, especially after they had been united in intercourse. This line of thought existed more recently as well, amongst the European alchemists. **Semen** was thought to be a powerful elixir both in a bio-chemical, physical sense (referred to as 'liquor vitae'), as well as in a subtle, metaphysical sense (known as the 'aura seminalis'). **Menstrual blood** in particular was seen as very powerful medicine and was mixed with food, used as an ointment or diluted and fed to crops.[20] It was considered to be 'fluid intelligence' and was thought of as a tool for longevity and enlightenment.

To the ancients of the pre-patriarchal era, it made sense to have intercourse during menstruation because this was seen as a great opportunity to utilize vital and magical energies that are at their peak at this time. Until very recently, however, western cultures took a very dim view of this practice. It is interesting to note that recent tests have shown that women experience a heightened sense of sexual desire during menstruation. As this heightened urge has nothing to do with procreation, could this be another aspect of the 'special design' of human sexuality?

The menses may have been honored in matriarchal societies and even in some patriarchal societies that still valued the more ancient wisdom, but as time went on the mainstream patriarchies such as that of the Old Testament Hebrews viewed menstruating women as unclean. They were often temporarily segregated from the rest of the tribe. Mostly due to the teachings of various organized religions, this attitude was/is prevalent in many cultures, including that of India, despite what the Tantras have to say about it.

Although the ingesting of body fluids may seem bizarre and even disgusting to us, without the baggage of programming to which we've been subjected, we would realize that menstrual blood is rich in melatonin, serotonin and other hormone-like substances such as prostaglandins. Menstrual discharge contains substances including some 'toxins' such as iron, lecithin and traces of arsenic. Sometimes known as the 'elixir rubeus', it is considered to have great magical, alchemical qualities.[21] From an 'energy' point of view, one could say that it contains chemical information harboring the secrets of life itself.

'Blood rituals' were widespread amongst many pagan groups. Many organizations such as the Great White Brotherhood, the Therapeutae, the Essenes, and the Rosicrucians also had similar rituals, which were usually carried out in a more private way. This type of knowledge was preserved by many of the secret societies concerned with alchemy, but represented a threat to the organized religions such as the Roman Church. The establishment of the sacrament of the Eucharist, the symbolic ingestion of body and blood, was meant in part as a replacement for these rituals.

Legends of **the Holy Grail** were widespread and ancient, existing long before they were interpreted and written into stories. The Church feared these legends and tried to Christianize them, claiming that the Grail was the cup used in the Last Supper by Jesus and the Apostles. The chalice, however, has long been a symbol for the womb, containing the blood of life. The word 'grail' comes from 'sangre réal', which means 'royal blood'. Although Laurence Gardner claims that this royal blood refers to the royal lineage of Jesus and his predecessors going back to Cain, many feel that it is referring to menstrual blood, symbolizing life, wisdom and the feminine principles. The quest for the Grail is symbolic of the return of the goddess and the quest for enlightenment. In all grail stories, the Grail is kept by women.

I believe that many of these sex rituals, including those mentioned above, were based on an awareness of the natural divine healing properties inherent in the sex act. Such knowledge was probably purer during the time of the matriarchy, and was deteriorating and distorting by the time of the above-mentioned rituals. I believe that in many cases this sacred knowledge became dogma and many of the rituals degenerated into meaningless (and sometimes cruel) gestures. I believe it was also exploited for less-than-noble motives. The purer knowledge was often kept by the select few who, for various reasons, chose not to share it with the masses. Even this information became distorted, however, often lacking the essential ingredients of love and compassion.

Chapter 38

TANTRA AND SACRED SEXUALITY

'Tantric sex' is a phrase that has been bantered about and gained a degree of popularity in the past several decades. The entire concept of sacred sex is becoming more familiar and a search on the Internet will yield over 50,000 sites offering information about it. Nowadays, almost anything to do with sacred sex or sex magic is wrongly referred to as Tantric sex. It can run the gamut from genuine Tantra to what is tantamount to a 'swingers' club.

There is a growing movement of what might be called 'neo-Tantra', which incorporates methodology and philosophy from several different disciplines. Elements of the traditions of Tantra, Taoism, Buddhism, Native American Quodoshka, Wicca and Gnosticism have been combined in a way that is less blatantly religious. We'll address some of these other traditions later, but first let's take a look at the body of knowledge that most consider to be the source from which many other traditions grew.

Sex is only one of the many aspects of the body of knowledge that has come to be called *Tantra*. As previously mentioned in Part One, it covers a wide range of topics and has much to say regarding the nature of reality. Its views on the origins and workings of the universe, both at 'macro' and 'micro' levels, seem to accord with the findings of modern science. Before we can look specifically at the sexual aspects of Tantra, it is important to come to a basic understanding of its entire philosophy, which is very relevant to everything that has been said in this book. (It might be helpful to review what was written about Tantra in Chapter 3.)

As well as being a type of 'science', Tantra is a mystical methodology of rituals designed to aid in the process of enlightenment. It is a practical yogic discipline based on ancient principles, which involve a wide variety of viewpoints. These practical methods of healing are based on an understanding of the way that we interact and relate to the rest of creation. Before we can understand the healing potential of the sex act, it is important to have an awareness of Tantric concepts such as the chakra system with its web of pathways or 'nadis', the flow of 'vital energy' (prana, chi, etc.) and the way that these things relate to health. (It may be a good idea to quickly review the information on chakras in Chapter Seven.)

One of the concepts central to Tantra is the idea that all manifestations in the physical realm are the result of **male/female dualism**, giving rise to all the illusions of duality or polarity, i.e., good/bad, light/dark, yin/yang, right/wrong, etc. All healing involves seeing through these illusions and ultimately overcoming all fears. Beyond this illusion of duality is **unity**, an indefinable, omni-present oneness of which we and all things are a part. Sexual union is a bringing together of the two components of duality. In Tantra it is symbolized by the union of Shiva/Shakti. In Gnostic terms it is called 'syzygie', and one of its symbols is the union of Simon Magus and Helena.[22] It is one of the ways to see beyond the illusions to the underlying unity, leading to the knowledge of one's connection to all parts of the universe, resulting in a state of bliss called 'Ananda'.

There are many methods by which to arrive at this state of unity awareness. In Tantra, most of these methods involve a way of causing the Kundalini energy (female) residing at the base chakra to rise up along the Sushumna, through the other chakras, till it meets the cosmic conscious-ness (male) that resides at the crown chakra. Along with the willful and mindful use of the sex act, there are other **healing methods** that facilitate this process. We'll now take a brief look at some of these tools.

Tantra says that everything in our reality is the product of energy vibrating at different frequencies. This vibration, or 'sound' is said to precede the manifestation of matter in the process of creation. According to Tantra, all objects including non-material objects, have their own innate sound. One of the healing methods associated with sound is the use of **mantra**. The word 'mantra' roughly translates as 'that which when reflected upon gives liberation'. A mantra is a word or a sound that has inherent power and when repeated many times (an activity called 'japa'), creates a wave pattern.

A mantra is similar to an affirmation, but it has much more power because the message is not just in the words, but in the actual sound vibration. If a mantra has been repeated often enough, its vibrational power reverberates in the brain for a long time afterwards. Each sound has a 'charge', which affects the superconscious mind. Thus, mantras can be used to 'magically' affect one's circumstances. Each 'divinity' or aspect of humanity has a seed mantra, called a 'bija', which usually ends with a nasal sound. Some examples of bijas are hrim, srim, krim, klim, etc. The most powerful of mantras is 'aum', which is actually three sounds in one—ah, oh, um. These three sounds represent the three phases of the cosmic cycles; creation, preservation and dissolution. (See **BOX 27—CHANTS AND MANTRAS**)

As attested by the branch of science called 'cymatics', pioneered by Hans Jenny, form and sound are interrelated. This is also a contention of Tantra, which claims that every mantra has a corresponding **yantra**, a geometrical, linear representation of sound. This hints at the underlying mathematical order of all of creation and Tantra suggests that prolonged staring at a yantra can trigger deep memories and stimulate awareness.

Another geometrical aspect of the Tantra traditions is the **mandala**, a design or artistic expression consisting mostly of circles, triangles and squares.

Circles signify completeness, with no beginning and no end. Within the main circle of a mandala, the squares and triangles represent the absolute and paradoxical elements of totality. Triangles, used in both yantras and mandalas, represent the three gunas. A downward pointing triangle also symbolizes the female genitalia, called the 'yoni'. The upward pointing triangle represents the male genitalia, called the 'lingham'. The union of these two triangles forms a six-pointed star (like the Jewish star of David), symbolizing the union of Shiva/Shakti. A five-pointed star represents the five elements; earth, water, fire, air and ether. A mandala, then, uses symbols and iconographic images to allude to creation and the nature of reality.

> **BOX 27—CHANTS AND MANTRAS;** There are male, female and neutral mantras; the males usually end with 'hum', the females with 'svaha' and the neutral with 'nama-ha'. Root or seed mantras representing different aspects of divinity are called 'bijas'. Here are some bijas and their meanings;—krim; (called the Kali Bija) = power over creation and dissolution, recited for conquest of limitations.—srim; = feminine energy of abundance, recited to acquire earthly joys and gains.—klim; = procreative desire, recited for joy, bliss and pleasure. Chanting is the repeated singing of mantras and devotional affirmations, which have been put to music. The repetition, the beauty of the melody, the rhythm—they all help bring the participant into a state of trance. This joyful activity has great power potential and is one of my personal favorites as a healing tool. The reciting of mantras and the act of chanting leads to more coherent and harmonic brain patterns and to better communication between left and right hemispheres of the brain. There are chants from different cultures around the globe. Some well-known chants are; 'Om Mani Padme Hum', Sanskrit/Tibetan; 'the Mahamantra—Hare Krishna, Hare Rama', Sanskrit/Hindu; 'Gloria, In Excelsis Deio', Latin/Christian; 'Kyrie Eleison ', Greek/Christian. There are many excellent teachers and musicians who have done much to bring chanting to the west; Robert Gass, Krishna Das, Jai Uttal, Wah, Deva Premal and many more.

One of the best ways to arouse the Kundalini energy or in other words, one of the best tools for enlightenment is *meditation*. There are countless variations and methods of meditating, most of which are designed to still the inner chatter of the mind and to focus inward. This results in a diminished connection to the outside, material world, a reduction in the processing of sensory information. This allows the consciousness to access information from 'the silence within', which eventually leads to a heightened state of awareness. The benefits of meditation are scientifically measurable in terms of brainwave frequencies and the meditative phenomenon has been proven in labs using electroencephalographs. (See **BOX 28—THE SCIENCE OF MEDITATION**)

Tantra recommends several different devices to facilitate the meditation process, or as tools in their own right. Amongst the most important of these is control of the breath, called *pranayama*. Breathing is not only a way of bringing in oxygen for combustion in the cells, but also brings the life force, called 'prana', into the body. Breathing and psychic well being are deeply linked—the Greek word, 'psyche', also means 'wind' or 'breath'.[23] There are many different breathing techniques, some designed to relax, others to invigorate. Pranayama purifies nerve circuits, amplifies consciousness and revitalizes the chakras.

Mudras are different hand positions that are used often in conjunction with meditation. The different hand positions cause certain energy circuits to stay closed and thus prana is retained more effectively. *Nyasa* is the placing of fingertips and palms of the hands on various body parts considered to be sensory zones, usually while chanting or reciting mantras. Various yoga postures called *asanas* are used to teach the body to relax, to open energy pathways and to prepare the body to sit for long periods in meditation.

> **BOX 28—THE SCIENCE OF MEDITATION:** Thanks to the work of researchers like Dr. Herbert Benson, Dr. Gregg Jacobs, Dr. Andrew Newberg, Dr. Richard Davidson, Dr. Dean Ornish and Jon Kabat-Zinn, we have a much better understanding of the effects of meditation on brain activity. Lab experiments have shown that activity in the frontal lobe (responsible for reasoning, self-awareness) and the parietal lobe (responsible for processing sensory information) slows down. Beta waves are reduced, indicating that the brain is not processing as much information. Meditation also affects the thalamus and reticular formation so that flow of outside data is greatly reduced. Studies have suggested that regular meditation boosts the immune system, prolongs life and reduces stress. In terms of observable medical benefits, it can be an effective treatment of some diseases such as heart disease, aids, and cancer, as well as psychiatric conditions like depression, attention deficit disorder, etc. There are many methods of meditation, including those from all of the mystical traditions. There are also many modern methods that have been recently developed.[24]

All of the above-mentioned techniques have multiple benefits, which include heightening the intuition and awakening dormant memories of one's own divinity. *In my opinion, however, these and all techniques are of limited use unless they are accompanied by a genuine effort to examine one's own behavior. A synonym for 'enlightenment' is 'self-realization'. Enlightenment cannot happen unless one thoroughly knows oneself. Healing is a process of owning up to one's 'dark side', of digging up the fears that underlie one's behaviour, both past and present. Facing such underlying motives can be very uncomfortable, but it is necessary to look one's fears in the eye in order to forgive oneself and others. Eventually one overcomes such fears and learns to react to all circumstances with love and compassion. It sometimes happens that the above-mentioned techniques become ends in themselves, rather than the means to an end.*

Of all the healing techniques recommended by Tantra, some of the most powerful, and the ones in which this chapter is most interested, are those that involve **the sex act**. There are differing views about this and over the years Tantra has split into several branches. The Shiva branch condones sex accompanied by love and sees the body as a microcosm of the universe. The union of male and female is viewed as a way of achieving unity consciousness. The more ascetic branch is male oriented and very technical. It discourages love in sexual rituals and tends to see emotion as a distraction. In the Tibetan version, which is a combination of Buddhism and the older shamanic religion called 'Bon', there is more of a focus on meditations designed to transcend death. In the branch that ended up as Taoist Tantra in China, there was more emphasis on health and longevity. Sex is seen as a medicine to stimulate the 'chi' energy, balance the yin and yang and thus achieve both physical and spiritual benefits.[25]

For the most part, aside from the more ascetic branch, the Tantric path is not about renunciation or detachment from worldly affairs. Rather, it embraces and accepts the gamut of human desires, emotions and circumstances, recognizing them as opportunities for growth. Within this context sex is seen as something basic and essential to the human condition and to neglect or deny our connection to these basic instincts is to remain subservient to them, to be imprisoned by them. The body is revered and viewed as a link between the Earth and the cosmos. Knowledge of the body leads to knowledge of the universal truth.

Sex is not viewed in a moral context, not judged as right or wrong, as indulgent or hedonistic. Tantra is not interested in the 'correctness' of monogamy versus polygamy or any of the stigma and taboos regarding promiscuity. Sex is not judged in these terms. It is only seen as an important method by which to stimulate feelings of love, to awaken memories and thus deal with fears, and to increase the awareness of unity by integrating the opposite polarities. This is enhanced by rituals that involve worshipping the partner's divinity, deep eye gazing, toning and chanting, etc. It provides the opportunity to experience bliss, even if it is only temporary, hinting at what is to become permanent ananda (joy) once enlightenment is achieved.

The energy exchange between two lovers in sexual embrace causes a powerful flow, which can kickstart the rising of Kundalini. During **maithuna**, the Sanskrit word for sexual union in a ritual context, a great energy loop is established which, with correct intent, has great healing and transformative power.[26] Sexual union is like the completion of an electrical circuit that results in a much more powerful flow of energy. In other words, it is a great opportunity to experience love, with all of its transformative potential.

A prolonged sexual union can bring about a feeling of detachment from the rest of the world, becoming a type of meditation. Each individual begins to 'melt' into the other, so that the boundaries between individuals dissolve. A couple becomes one entity, enjoying a trance-like bliss. This leads to 'samsara', an experiential awareness of the unity of all things.

The sex act brings with it a great opportunity to learn to control one's circumstances using the will, and this particular aspect will be discussed later in the section on 'sex magic'. By partaking in sex with the proper intent, we can learn to see the body as a beautiful instrument, which no set of ethics can imprison. We can willfully and consciously transform and transcend.

One aspect of Tantric sex is the ability, developed over time with much practice, of controlling breath, thoughts and ejaculation. One of the great debates amongst the many factions of Tantra is the question of whether the male should ejaculate. Some schools of thought say that **semen retention** is a way to enhance sexual potency, seeing ejaculation as a waste of energy. On the other hand, some sex magicians claim that one can learn to retain the subtle, metaphysical energy of the semen, thus rendering ejaculation irrelevant. With practice, an initiate can learn to experience orgasm without ejaculation, and to prolong the orgasm. One can also learn to have **whole body orgasms**, rather than those that are merely localized and groin-centered. Such extended orgasms have a much greater magical potential.

Using various techniques and sacred rituals sometimes called 'pujas', a couple engaged in Tantric sex would be attempting to be free from the fears, anxieties and insecurities that often accompany the sex act. They would seek to encounter themselves in each other, working towards dissolving the ego and living completely in the moment.

Although there are many variations, here is an example of *a typical sexual ritual*. Both parties would bathe. The male then massages the female with scented oils, caressing each body part while reciting purifying mantras. There are various rituals, such as sprinkling wine on the body, special cloths and dramas that are meant to transform the female into a goddess. The female's yoni is then worshipped with loving caresses and special words. The man worships at the feet of the woman, offering to give up certain ego-based feelings such as; pride, greed, illusion, envy, lust, etc. The man's lingum is also worshipped by the female. At the female's bidding, union occurs. Using breath control, thought control, mantra and the willful setting of intention, union is prolonged.

A concept that is shocking to most people in the west is the idea of *collective sex*. In Tantra, however, group sex accompanied by correct intention is seen as yet another powerful tool or opportunity for spiritual growth. Again, there are many variations, but here is a sample of a group sex ritual sometimes called 'chakra puja'. In this context, the word 'chakra' refers to a circle, in which position eight couples are arranged. After going through similar procedures as outlined above, they have sex with their partner in the company of the other partners. (Groups involving sex with multiple partners, sometimes called orgies, have a different place and we will speak of this in the section on sex magic.)

These sixteen tantrikas (students) are carefully screened by a guru against eight negative criteria; hatred, doubt, fear, shame, backbiting, conformity, arrogance and status-consciousness. There is great emphasis placed on the quest for unity and knowledge and for the overcoming of fears and obstacles. If the participants are sincere, harmonious and aware of their innate divinity, the experience can be very rewarding. If, on the other hand, they succumb to insecurities and 'ego games', this will lead to feelings of fear and alienation from each other, making it very difficult for them to achieve an awareness of unity. The experience could become self-defeating and possibly harmful.

Many Tantric rituals have built-in mechanisms designed to cause conflict and stress. In other words, they are designed to challenge the ego-issues and the insecurities that often relate to the sex act. Such fear-based feelings would be even more evident in a group setting. It is the aim of Tantra to outgrow ego games and to see the greater truths that lie beyond the illusions of duality. This almost always involves being willing to face up to one's shadow side and to confront one's personal demons, rather than being bound by conventional taboos and value systems. Tantra holds that spiritual progress is very difficult, if not impossible, if one chooses to hide from oneself.

(Much of the specific information in this section on Tantra comes from the following books; 'The Tantric Way', by Ajit Mookerjee and Madhu Khanna; 'Tantric Love', by Ma Ananda Sarita and Swami Anand Geho; 'The Encyclopedia of Sacred Sexuality', by Rufus Camphausen.)

There are other schools of sacred sexuality that are different, although derivative, of Tantra. One of these is named ***Karezza***, which comes from the Italian word for caress, and was introduced by an incredible American woman named Alice Bunker Stockham in the 19th century. Her name should be much better known than it is. The fifth woman to achieve the status of medical doctor, she was a fearless fighter for women's rights. She made public declarations against corsets, alcohol and tobacco, was sympathetic to the plight of prostitutes and divorcees, and advocated masturbation for both sexes.

After returning from India where she became familiar with the Tantric principles, she founded Karezza, which retains many of the same principles without the 'Hinduisms' and religious undertones. Stockham saw the Indian version as being sexist, in that it focused more on the male's benefit, with the female's role being more supportive. She advocates abstinence from orgasm for both sexes. Karezza places less emphasis on breath control, yogic postures and visualizations, and is generally more eclectic and less dogmatic.

As outlined in her book, 'Karezza, An Ethics of Marriage', Stockham's methods were designed to spiritually enhance the sex lives of married couples. They entail long sessions of penile penetration with little movement, thus accommodating a lengthy co-mingling of energy currents and 'spiritual fluids'. Stockham's concern with the health benefits of such unions suggests that she was also aware of Taoist philosophies about sex.

Another American who has developed a philosophy about sex and its ability to enhance one's spiritual growth was John Humphrey Noyes. A strong advocate of non-ejaculation in males, Noyes felt that the benefits of sexual union need not be confined to marriage. In 1841 he founded the controversial **Oneida Community** in New York State, a setting where the residents lived in a polygamous, free-sex 'marriage'.

Chapter 39

SEX MAGIC

The term 'sex magic' is sometimes used to refer to the many ways in which the sex act can be used to move one towards enlightenment, as in Tantric, Taoist, Gnostic, Hermetic and some Islamic Sufi traditions. Sometimes, however, it is used to refer to the magical potential of controlling one's circumstances without necessarily having a spiritual or religious component. This latter use of the term applies mostly to the more recent 'occult' forms from the western world. In this section we will look at both versions, focussing a bit more on the latter version, since much of the spiritual components have already been covered.

Let's take a quick look at the *history of sex magic*. As we know, the practice of sex magic goes way back in our history and exists in many cultures, especially those that are shamanic in nature. As time progressed this knowledge became distorted in the mainstream and was eventually vilified and forbidden by the establishment, especially in the Judeo-Christian and Islamic cultures. Throughout the years sex magic has been persecuted and even today it is referred to negatively as Satanism, Black Magic or some sort of perversion. Most people still have a dual reaction to it, with fascination and attraction on the one hand, and condemnation and revulsion on the other. The knowledge of sex magic was not completely lost, however, but was kept secret by many groups, including the 'secret societies' such as the Knights Templar, the Rosicrucians and various Masonic-based organizations like the Order of the Priory of Sion.

In more modern times, like other bodies of knowledge, sex magic is making a comeback and this information is becoming available to the common people. Such movements as Wicca and Neo-shamanism, which recognize some forms of sex magic, came about after World War II and have been growing steadily.

Sex magic, in its more focussed forms, started taking a foothold in the late 1800s, due to the efforts of men such as Pascal Beverly Randall (USA) and Edward Sellon (England). Circa 1900, an organization dedicated to the principles and methodology of sex magic was formed, called the Ordo Templi Orientis (OTO). Two very colorful figures were instrumental to its conception. The great spiritualist and educator (and one of my personal heroes), Rudolph

Steiner was head of the German branch for nine years until he dissociated himself from it just before the outbreak of World War I. It is said that, according to his wishes, Steiner was buried in his OTO regalia.[27]

The leader of the English branch was a very controversial man named Aleister Crowley. Probably the most well known sex-magician, he is referred to by some people as the most evil man that has ever lived, and to others as a genius. He and a man named Austin Osman Spare did much to develop the OTO, including extensive writing on the subject of sex magic. After Crowley's death in 1947, the OTO broke up into several factions.

How would one *define sex magic*? First it might be helpful to define 'magic'. This is Crowley's definition of magic; "Magic is the science and art of causing change, on a material as well as a spiritual level, to occur in conformity to will by altered states of consciousness." This is the notion, talked about near the beginning of the book, that consciousness has the power to shape our reality. The knowledge of this primordial power is said to be programmed into our DNA, but it is something that must be remembered. Knowledge of magic requires a deeper awareness of how the universe works, especially in terms of cause and effect.

There are many methodologies associated with magic, including the use of sound, the use of ingested substances and the use of the sex act. Sometimes a number of methods may be used in conjunction with each other. These techniques affect three essential components of effective magic—*control of the will*,—*visualization*, which is the ability to imagine vividly,—and the *ability to remain lucid while in a trance state*. The first two components have power even without the use of trance, but that power becomes greatly magnified in relation to the depth of the trance state. The barriers between the conscious and unconscious minds break down in trance. Put another way, the internal shields are lowered, allowing the entranced consciousness access to a larger degree of 'truth' or reality. Put yet another way, the magnetic aspect of our electro-magnetic essence is relaxed, allowing access to a greater portion of the electric aspect, which is the 'totality of information' or the 'truth'. Achieving trance states is an important aspect of most shamanic traditions, including; Vodun (Voodoo), Macumba, Canomble and Santoria.

There are many ways to achieve a trance state, including; exhaustion, dance, music, spinning, psychotropic drugs, meditation, dreaming, etc. Some of these methods provide relatively easy access to trance. Today's youth dance culture, with its raves and house music, is reminiscent of some shamanic practices. Trance-like states can be achieved when a gathering moves to the same hypnotic rhythms for a prolonged time. Although these raves are often accompanied by drug use, there is a growing movement that recognizes the benefits of drug-free trance.

One of the easiest ways to enter a deep trance is to fall asleep and dream. The trick, the difficult part, is to retain lucidity and control of one's thoughts and actions while in trance. One who has a good ability to remain in control while dreaming would be a very powerful shaman. This is very rare, however, and it is usually wiser to develop these skills by starting with shallower trance states in which it is easier to maintain control. To plunge deep into trance using drugs, for example, may be useful in allowing one a 'glimpse of divinity', or to open the mind to the idea of other realities. However, it is very difficult to maintain a good grasp on this altered reality, to retain control and to negotiate one's way to a desired end while in such a deep trance.

A key to magic, and all endeavors, is *clarity of intent*. It is very difficult to control the outcome of any action without a clear awareness of one's intentions. For any endeavor to be successful, we must be aware of what it is we are trying to achieve. Where are we going? Why do we desire this? This is especially true of any magical practice. Good magic requires an awareness of the power of will. A clear intent combined with a strong will equals great power.

Without proper intent and the willful discipline required to see the intent through, there are some dangers. *Addiction* is one of them. It is easy to become addicted to artificially induced glimpses of divinity or bliss. We all know of the addictive potential of mind-altering drugs, but even sex can become addictive. When we clearly intend to learn how to achieve such bliss without any external agent, then the risks of addiction are minimalized. Another danger is the risk of losing personal power or confidence while in trance. There are other less common risks as well, such as becoming prey to the less noble intentions of other magicians. These risks are mininmalized when one is aware of the power of one's own will, and thus willfully blocks the intentions of others. In other words, no one can subject you to his or her will unless you somehow allow it. The deeper the trance, the greater the risk. That is because it is more difficult to be in control of will and intent while in a deeper trance.

During the sex act, depending on the degree of relaxation and other factors, one can achieve a mild form of trance, especially at the point of orgasm. Crowley has named this sexually induced trance 'erotocomatose lucidity'.[28] A strong intention or desired outcome, if held in the mind and visualized throughout the sex act and especially at orgasm, has an increased likelihood of realizing. Again, a deeper trance, a clearer visualization and a stronger will results in greater magic potential.

There are exercises to strengthen the will and to improve one's ability to visualize. There are also methods to deepen and lengthen the trance state. Breathing techniques, mantras and intonations, exhaustion, music and the use of mild drugs are all ways of increasing the trance potential. Although some sex magicians decry feelings of love as a distraction to the more practical intentions, deep eye gazing and various ways of expressing affection can also deepen the trance.

Perhaps the best way of intensifying the trance is to develop the ability to have *extended, full-body orgasms*. With much practice, one can learn to come to the very brink of orgasm and to prolong that state indefinitely, without going over the edge and ejaculating. One can also learn to spread the sensation of the orgasm throughout the body, rather than confining it to the groin region. As well as considerably heightening the level of bliss, it is easy to see that this would greatly increase the depth of the trance and thus greatly increase the magical potential. (A much more complete discussion of this type of orgasm, sometimes called a 'valley orgasm', can be found in the works of Mantak Chia—'Tao Yoga' and 'Tao Yoga of Love'.)

An awareness of the potential of sex magic can benefit one's life to varying degrees, but like anything else, serious mastery of this art requires dedication and practice. It involves confronting and conquering various fears, such as; performance anxiety, fear of sex, fear of losing control, oversensitivity to body-image, fear of rejection, of intimacy, of the opinions of others, etc. Such a process, followed through to a significant degree, requires time, devotion and a good amount of courage.

Being an effective magician involves learning to control one's actions in a wide variety of circumstances. This control is not an 'anal', suppressive type of control, but one that comes from an inner confidence achieved by the overcoming of fears and doubts. This process involves a willingness to break social taboos and mores, leading to freedom from the confines of social conditioning and an attitude of open-minded respect for the mysteries of life.

There are three main schools of techniques identified by sex magicians. *Autoerotic* practices involve masturbation and self-sex; *heteroerotic* practices are with two partners of different sexes and *homoerotic* practices involve a same-sex couple. If one person can harness magical potential by achieving a trance state with a focussed intent, then it's clear that two people in trance with the same intent can harness an exponentially increased potential. This potential is further amplified by the looping of energy that occurs during sexual union. Masturbation, though not as powerful as partner sex, is also very useful as a way to practice and develop certain techniques.

Following this line of logic, group sex has an even greater potential. This is particularly true if all participants can arrive at orgasm at the same time while visualizing the same intent. The obstacles to this, however, come in the form of the increased fear and anxiety that would arise under such conditions. For most people it would be very difficult to overcome ego-based hang-ups and social conditioning to a sufficient degree to make such a ceremony function efficiently.

For the adventurous and courageous sex magicians, there are some specific **group sex rituals** belonging to various traditions. In the practice of Wicca there is one called the Great Rite, which is an approval and celebration of life. The Night of Pan is a feast and celebration dedicated to the Greek/Arcadian god of sexuality and fertility, Pan. The Night of Hecate is a 'darker' ritual celebrating the principal of creation and destruction.[29] Many of these rituals involve food, dance and music and, although still involving sex magic, they also have a strong devotional, mystical aspect.

Some of the information in this chapter may seem somewhat risqué; some might find it downright shocking. In my opinion, stripped of the stigma attached to it as a result of social indoctrination, it makes a lot of sense. With the proper intention, the sex act becomes more than just a physiological release or a hedonistic pleasure, although even in that context it is still a beautiful, divine gift. Its most sacred aspect, however, is evident when the sex act becomes a way to 'make love'. What better thing can one possibly make?

Making love, like all true forms of communication, is an exchange of energy. The presence of dishonesty or deceit blocks this exchange. True, honest communication involves an openness, a vulnerability, an intimacy that requires a certain degree of risk. Making love, as opposed to just having sex, is probably the greatest form of communication there is at this level of the Game.

I would say that it is probably rare that, even in long term relationships, the sex act happens without the presence of some sort of fear or ego-based anxiety on the part of at least one partner. Insecurities about physical appearance or the ability to perform are widespread and can be difficult for two partners to discuss. Such fears are often based on the fear of not being accepted, or the fear of inadequacy. It is easy to see a sexual relationship as an opportunity for deep healing, an opportunity to confront and overcome fears and to express love as purely as possible. It requires courage and a strong intention to grow. It's not hard to see sex as a great tool on the path to enlightenment.

As difficult as it is to have fearless and loving sex with a single partner, it is considerably harder to do in a group setting, more difficult yet with multiple partners. Even if one succeeds in getting past the social stigma of such actions, the potential for anxieties and insecurities is much greater. To learn to feel genuine love under such circumstances, devoid of any fears, would represent a huge stride forward in the enlightening process.

The entire question of multiple partners or promiscuity is a delicate one. There are many factors to consider, even if we disregard the pragmatic concerns of unwanted pregnancies and diseases. Even if we set aside all concern for social stigma, there are risks involved. From the sex magic point of view, there is a risk of 'losing energy' when having sex with someone you don't fully know and can't fully trust. There is also the risk of 'diluting your essence'. Whenever two people unite in sex, there is a co-min-

gling of energy patterns, so that one gives up a part of one's own pattern and takes on part of one's partner's pattern. It seems wise, therefore, to be sure one actually desires a particular pattern before allowing it to become a part of oneself. In other words one might ask oneself, "Do I really want that person's energy as part of me?"

Other than these risks, I don't see anything innately wrong with promiscuity. I don't believe that monogamy is written in stone for humanity. I don't believe it is encoded in our genes. (Many cultures are still polygamous.) I believe that we were once predominantly polygamous and that there's a good chance that we will be so again. I'm not referring to the patriarchal type—sultans with harems, etc—but rather to the type of arrangement whereby several individuals could live, love and have sex together.

I believe that, in this era of the 'quickening', as we move quickly toward collective enlightenment, toward the 'big shift', mankind will feel an expanded capacity to love. It will also bring a yearning for a more meaningful life, which will mean a yearning for more meaningful relationships. This will lead, and is leading, to confusion and difficulty with the current state of the institution of marriage. It is becoming increasingly difficult to find a suitable partner, a soul-mate, someone with similar values and goals. In the past, it was more common for one to tolerate a partner with whom they may have had little in common. In the past, people did not change so greatly throughout their lives. Today, in the era of the quickening, people are changing and evolving at a rapid pace. It is becoming more difficult for one to find a soul-mate who can meet all of one's needs, or who doesn't grow apart.

One of the tragedies of the modern era is the tendency for perfectly good marriages to fall apart because one of the partners commits an infidelity. Often such extra-marital affairs are the result of confusion or of an honest attraction to another human being. Such affairs could be great opportunities for growth, for new and unique experiences, and don't necessarily happen because of a lack of love between the two original partners. It seems a shame that such an infidelity should signal the end of the marriage. This is often due to pride or ego, to feeling hurt because of a betrayal of trust. These feelings are often based on some kind of fear. They are also based on the attitude that we can only truly love one person at a time. These same fears, and the social stigma attached to infidelity and divorce, often keep people 'trapped' in relationships that are stifling their growth.

I believe that this will change. We will become increasingly accepting of all forms of love, including homosexual love, recognizing that there is no such thing as 'bad' or 'wrong' love. Love is love. Ideally, we are all capable of loving everyone. Humanity is moving toward this ideal. In a more loving, liberal society in which polygamy was accepted, one would not necessarily need to totally abandon a beloved partner who does not meet all of one's needs for growth. According to Drunvalo Melchizadek, polygamy is common amongst other civilizations in the galaxy. On the third planet out from Sirius, the typical family consists of sixteen males and sixteen females and their collective offspring.

Using sex as a tool for reaching enlightenment seems a delicious idea to me. Like any tool, it would involve the overcoming of fears, the ability to see through illusion and the development of a greater capacity to love. This involves the use of the sex act as an opportunity to confront or address one's 'issues'.

If the practice of sacred sexuality is appealing, you could choose to delve deeply into the study of Tantra. To many, however, such a plunge could seem like a daunting undertaking, for which few of us have time. On a more practical level, it can be approached in a less overwhelming way, in a more playful way that is still effective. Please allow me to point out some simple yet effective methods.

First of all, it is essential to communicate with your partner before and after the sex act. Make sure you are both 'on the same page', that your intent is unified, that you know what you wish to accomplish. Some people find this very difficult. Remind yourself that it is okay to feel embarrassed or awkward. Allow yourselves to giggle or to blush. Tell each other secrets. What turns you on, what turns you off? Teach each other!

It is a good idea to do some kind of ritual whereby the bodies of the partners are worshipped or honored, with a conscious intent to alleviate the anxiety that many people feel regarding the way their body looks. Most of us are deeply indoctrinated by notions of what is beautiful and what is not. It is very useful to get past such imprisoning doctrine and to see beauty in a variety of body forms. Take turns expressing affection for each other's bodies. There are Tantric rituals that you could look up, or you could just make them up. They could include the creating of a 'mood setting' in the room, using candles, music, etc, followed by some sort of annointing. It could include some special food or drink. At some point it could include the systematic caressing of each body part, done with playfulness and love. This ritual may or may not end in sex. It is probably a good idea to remove any notion of 'sexual performance' from such a ritual, to feel no obligation to act or react in 'just the right way'. Just play and have fun.

Another very effective practice is the 'prolonged union', where the couple remains united in the sex act for an extra-ordinarily long time. The key to success in this venture is to remove the achieving of orgasm as the prime motive of the coupling. Make it clear to each other that the prime motive is more along the lines of experiencing unity, of breaking down the illusion that the two partners are separate individuals, rather than part of a cosmic whole. By removing the goal of orgasm, the male can let go of the feeling that he is responsible for bringing his partner to orgasm and just relax. The female can let go of the feeling that she should react in a certain way and just relax. That is not to say that the two partners cannot agree to have an orgasm eventually, just refrain from making it the dominating intent. Remember, intent is everything. For example, try to make the intent of 'feeling more love for each other' as the prime motive and forget any notion of how a 'real man' or 'real woman' should perform. Making love involves the heart more than it does the genitals.

After some foreplay and initial entry, try to relax, possibly by looking into each other's eyes. Allow yourselves to giggle or to be silly. Move very little, just enough for the male to retain his erection. Breath deeply. Try to get into a position whereby the chakras are aligned. Heart to heart, forehead to forehead, etc. After awhile, practice moving just enough to raise the energy in the genitals, and then 'breath' that energy up the spine. Visualize it rising up the spinal column. Do that over and over again, trying to feel sexual excitement all through the body. Allow whatever feelings might arise. Look these feelings in the eye, whether they are feelings of joy and bliss, or feelings of anger or sadness. Try to allow the boundaries that separate you from your partner to dissolve. Become one entity.

The first time a couple tries this prolonged union, a half-hour may seem like a long time. With a little practice though, a couple can easily stay united for one or two hours. Afterwards, talk about it. Be honest. Discuss any feelings you may have had, or may still be having. Acknowledge any buried memories that may have surfaced. Emotions and insights may continue to enter your awareness for days or weeks. Some such memories could be painful—help each other with compassion. Maybe the experience will be completely blissful and joyful. Possibly, among the memories that surface may be the realization that you are a beautiful, divine, loving creature with absolutely nothing to fear.

It seems obvious that, despite the fact that things are getting better, we still have a great deal of collective healing to do regarding sexuality. We feel a powerful confusion, a conflict between the inner knowledge that sex is a beautiful gift and the inherited indoctrination that sex is filthy and shameful—a conflict between natural urges and puritan restraint. The fears and imbalances associated with sex have led to some of the most hurtful actions, to behavior that is the furthest away from love and compassion. Rape and sexual violence, prostitution and degrading forms of pornography, brutal social stigma, predatory promiscuity and all manner of sexual exploitation— these social conditions are all due to twisted attitudes surrounding sex. Ironically, sex in the human animal seems to have been designed to foster love, yet these imbalanced attitudes often result in the exact opposite.

I believe that individuals, as well as collective humanity, will have a much easier time moving toward enlightenment if we can heal our sexual wounds. Compared to our attitudes toward sex in the recent past, I think it's clear that today's attitudes are changing. Despite what seems to be a continued confusion regarding sex, it seems clear that we are moving forward in this process.

In my opinion, humanity is experiencing a 'return of the goddess'. By that I mean a return to a state where the female aspects of human consciousness are valued and 'worshipped' once again. We are learning to value forms of intelligence other than the logical, reasoning, 'linear' thinking that is typical of the left-brain mentality. We are valuing intuitive, heart-centered, 'lateral' intelligence as well.

I don't believe, however, that we will return to a matriarchy. It makes more sense to me that we will soon become a 'neitherarchy', where neither type of intelligence predominates but where both types are honored as being integral to humanity. In other words, I believe we are moving toward a state of balance, toward a state of unity-consciousness.

ENDNOTES—PART SEVEN

1. Picknett, Lynn and Prince, Clive—*The Templar Revelation**, Bantam Press, 1997, London, p. 262
2. Allegro, John—*The Sacred Mushroom and the Cross,* Doubleday, 1970, New York, p. 80
3. Markale, Jean—*The Great Goddess*, Inner Traditions, 1997, Rochester VT, p. 4
4. ibid. p. 52—54
5. Camphausen, Rufus—*The Encyclopedia of Sacred Sexuality,* Inner Traditions International, 1999, Rochester, VT, p. 220
6. Allegro, John—*The Sacred Mushroom and the Cross,* Doubleday, 1970, New York, p. 77
7. Markale, Jean—*The Great Goddess*, Inner Traditions, 1997, Rochester VT, p. 2–3
8. ibid. p. 14—15
9. Cerminara, Gina—*Insights for the Age of Aquarius,* Quest Books, 1973, London, p. 243
10. Ibid. p. 245
11. Camphausen, Rufus—*The Encyclopedia of Sacred Sexuality,* Inner Traditions International, 1999, Rochester, VT, p. 205
12. ibid. p. 30
13. ibid. p. 34
14. ibid. p. 189—190
15. ibid. p. 88
16. Markale, Jean—*The Great Goddess*, Inner Traditions, 1997, Rochester VT, p. 10–11
17. Ibid. p. 19–20
18. Camphausen, Rufus—*The Encyclopedia of Sacred Sexuality,* Inner Traditions International, 1999, Rochester, VT, p. 160
19. Ibid. p. 91
20. Allegro, John—*The Sacred Mushroom and the Cross,* Doubleday, 1970, New York, p. 61–17
21. Camphausen, Rufus—*The Encyclopedia of Sacred Sexuality,* Inner Traditions International, 1999, Rochester, VT, p. 147–148
22. p. 223
23. Frater U.D.—*Secrets of Western Sex Magic,* Llewellyn Publications, 2001, St. Paul MN, p. 43
24. From an article in Time Magazine, Issue of Aug. 4, 2003—*Just Say Om,* Joel Stern
25. Sarita, M. A. and Geho, S. A.—*Tantric Love,* Fireside Books, 2001, New York, p. 6
26. Camphausen, Rufus—*The Encyclopedia of Sacred Sexuality,* Inner Traditions International, 1999, Rochester, VT, p. 139
27. Frater U.D.—*Secrets of Western Sex Magic,* Llewellyn Publications, 2001, St. Paul MN, p. 3
28. ibid. p. 11–12, 129–130
29. ibid. p. 179–186

BOOK 3

I BELIEVE
or
'I Think I Believe'

*I believe that my beliefs are transient. They do not define who I am. **Beliefs come and go, but I am forever**. Subscribing to a set of beliefs is a dynamic process by which my awareness moves toward absolute truth. The awareness of absolute truth requires no set of beliefs.*

I believe that, in this day and age, it is less useful and possibly detrimental to the process of enlightenment to adhere to a set of beliefs that belong to someone else. Although dogma and pre-set doctrine have played valuable roles at points in our collective evolution, I believe that it is becoming more useful to look inward, to listen to one's inner voice, to work things out for oneself. In doing so, it may be useful to assess some-one else's beliefs, weighing them to see if they have a place in one's own heart. I also believe that to cling rigidly to one's own beliefs would be to impair one's evolution toward truth.

I believe that amassing information such as that presented in this book in an effort to understand more clearly, is a useful tool. I also feel, however, that such an understanding would always be incomplete. True knowing can only come from experience, born of stillness. As mystics throughout the ages have told us, truth is ineffable, beyond words. A balance of head and heart is the best way to remember truth. If the process of amassing information assists in the process of letting go of fear and embracing love, then it is useful.

I believe that to move toward enlightenment is to move toward love. When one is capable of reacting to absolutely any situation or circumstance with love, compassion and gratitude, with a total absence of fear, and with the knowledge that we and all things are part of a divine whole, then one is enlightened. Once enlightened, one is ready to move into a new reality.

I believe that 'to awaken' is to come to a state of awareness whereby one begins to consciously work towards enlightenment.

*I believe that there are countless ways/paths/tools to assist one's 'healing', and thus, one's evolution toward light. Yoga, crystal-therapy, chanting, aroma-therapy, meditation, prayer, Reiki, following a guru, canoeing, making love with your partner, working on your car, gardening, all are possible ways/paths/tools to assist one's healing. **Joy brings light—light brings joy.***

I believe that writing this book is a way/path/tool for me. It helps me to evolve toward the light. It is the only reason I am writing this book. If reading this book also helps you,—bonus!

*I believe that **life is a great 'mystery school'** in which each and every circumstance is an opportunity to remember one's divinity, to choose compassion over fear. Our 'higher selves' steer us toward these opportunities. The energy that we emit in* *reaction to these opportunities brings further circumstances. This is one of the ways in which we create our own reality.*

I believe that our physical reality (and perhaps all levels of reality) is by design, an illusion. I believe that behind what appears to be a chaotic universe, there is an intelligent order. Someone capable of seeing through the illusion would see that there is no right or wrong, no good or bad, no matter, no time, no death, etc. **The process of recognizing more and more of the illusion is a 'fun game'** *by which we experience all there is to experience, and thus remember our own divinity, which is not an illusion. This 'fun game' often feels like something quite opposite to 'fun', i.e. misery and suffering. This also is an illusion. To a soldier watching his friend being blown apart on the battlefield, or to someone watching a loved-one wasting away with cancer, it is very difficult to see this as a 'fun game'. It can be infuriating to be presented with the idea that those loved ones have somehow chosen those horrible experiences. As energy/divinity evolves through all its stages, it seeks to experience all that can be experienced. In the process, somewhere along the way, it must experience pain, misery and death.*

Our current level of experience, the third dimension, the physical plane or whatever else you would like to call it, is that evolutionary phase in which energy has chosen the opportunity to learn these, and many other lessons. Thus, as individual parcels of the totality of divine energy, we chose to forget that divinity when we agreed to come to Earthschool. One cannot experience misery, which is based in fear, when one is aware of one's own divinity. We chose to forget that suffering and death are only transient experiences, micro-seconds in the grander scheme of things. We chose to forget that there is no right or wrong, no good or bad. We chose to forget that we are enormously powerful beings capable of creating any reality we desire. We chose to come here. We chose to partake in that stage of the game whereby, in the process of remembering, we get to partake in those experiences that correspond to life at the Earth-school of hard knocks. We all get our turn at some point in our many incarnations, to partake in the entire gamut of these experiences, whether they entail misery or ecstasy. A strange, inexplicable yearning is part of the human condition because, at a deeper level, we all know that there is more than what meets the eye. We yearn to get on with the game. Once we get past this more difficult phase, which involves seeing through illusions, it becomes much easier to view it as a fun game.

I believe that certain cerebral exercises are useful tools in seeing through illusions. The study of numerology, sacred geometry and 'magic', for example, are ways of seeing the order that underlies all of creation. Seeking to understand the 'laws of the game' which are themselves, by design, part of the illusion, constitutes walking toward truth. We have sought such understanding in our recent history largely via the scientific method, attempting to isolate and define various natural laws and to put them into categories such as physics, biology, geology, etc. Science has often been called the 'new religion'. Although it has been a very useful tool, science is not the only way to glean valuable information. Other non-scientific 'evidence' acquired by such methods as intuition, channeling, dreaming and otherwise accessing altered states of reality, is also valid. 'A priori' knowledge should be respected in conjunction with empirical knowledge. The longer we cling to the idea that the scientific method is the only method, the longer it will take us to move toward truth. The best scientists, those with open minds and hearts, know this.

I believe that humanity would more readily move toward the light if we chose to seriously question the ruling paradigms. I believe that we would gain greatly by reexamining the many mysteries with a more open mind, with less arrogance. I believe it would be useful to take a new look at our origins, our religions, our attitudes about sex, etc. We could ask ourselves, "Are these bodies of knowledge, these belief systems, helping or hindering our progress toward the light?" I believe we would benefit greatly by trying to understand why certain groups are invested in and continue to promote these paradigms.

I believe that many of our paradigms and larger belief systems are based on lies, deception and opportunism. At the core of most belief systems there is a seed of truth that has been distorted, manipulated and exploited—turned into an opportunity for certain factions of society to benefit at the expense of others. In other words, whenever a 'new thing' has come along throughout the course of our history, there have been those who have thought, "hmm, how can I profit from this new thing". In this way new 'power elite' groups come and go. For example, opportunists in the past have distorted the work of Jesus and other great teachers to create an elitist position for themselves. The best intentions of such philosophies as democracy, communism, capitalism and many other 'isms' have given way to distorted versions, which end up putting power in the hands of very few. This phenomenon has happened to scientific developments as well. Darwin's ideas were distorted and used to justify a ruthless form of capitalism. Innoculation with vaccines was used to erradicate some diseases, but it was also exploited to create enormous profit for drug companies. Even trade union movements, which at one point were of great benefit to mankind, have been manipulated to create a new power elite. Opportunists in the present continue to manipulate the latest developments, which end up benefitting small elite groups instead of making life easier for greater mankind.

I believe that almost all of what we perceive to be 'going on' in the world, i.e., governments, institutions, and most of what gets reported in the media, is another kind of illusion. I believe that most 'news events' such as wars, domestic policies, foreign affairs, matters of commerce, government initiatives, religious doctrine, etc., are orchestrated to keep the masses from knowing what is really 'going on'. I believe that there are (and have always been) secret bodies that govern from behind the scenes, busily promoting and arranging their own elitist agenda by various means, not the *least of which is public manipulation. Here is an incomplete list of names of various clandestine elitist groups; the Freemasons, Rosicrucians, Knights Templar, Illuminati, Priory of Sion, etc.; as well as an incomplete list of various not-so-clandestine elitist groups; the CIA, the WTO, the Tri-Lateral Commission, the World Monetary Fund, NATO, the Vatican, the FBI, the banks, the Rothschild family, the Rockerfeller family, etc.*

I believe that it is futile to attempt to discern whether these elitist groups are 'good guys' or 'bad guys'. It is not that simple. At various points in history various groups have gone through periods of relative clarity as well as periods of relative density. I believe that they, just like everyone else, are subject to the properties of this dimension, this level of learning/remembering. In most cases they, in their ignorance, believe they are doing the right thing. Hitler, in his imbalance, believed he was doing the right thing. Many modern corporations rationalize their predatory actions by believing that such actions will ultimately benefit mankind. Distorted thought, imbalanced attitudes—such is the nature of 'evil'.

Sometimes the motives of elitist groups can be interpreted as being noble, i.e.; protecting from distortion sacred information such as Hermetic, alchemical and other secrets, guiding the rest of us hapless peons and keeping us on the strait and narrow, protecting us from other predatory elitist groups, etc. Sometimes their motives can be interpreted as ignoble, i.e.; hoarding sacred information, wealth and power for themselves, suppressing and oppressing the masses, feeding off the negative emotions or energy of the masses, stopping at nothing including war and genocide to further their elite agenda, etc. Although they have shown themselves to be very clever, usually in a left-brained way, they are by no means unified and are constantly squabbling amongst themselves, jockeying for position and trying to manipulate each other. They are entities of the third realm, making mistakes, learning and remembering, just like the rest of us.

I believe the ruling elite groups are aware that their control over the masses is waning. New measures of control, such as the various 'free trade' agreements (the failed MAI, NAFTA, etc.) are acts of desperation. The Chinese government's attempted ban and persecution of the Falun Dafa movement, which has millions of people meditating daily, is an acknowledgement that traditional dogmatic controlling devices are becoming ineffective. Compared to the way it was only a few hundred years ago, when we were securely under the thumb of religious doctrine as well as other controlling devices, today's free-thinking society poses a threat to their power. In other words, internal power is threatening external power. In the days of the Inquisition, the price for freethinking was death.

Our collective consciousness is evolving, progressing. It may not seem that way to us as we are continually being fed negativity via the media. The media reports the events that are the direct result of the actions of those beings in the world who are *still caught up in the pursuit of external (false) power. In most cases these beings, because they have a distorted image of what constitutes 'real' power, are the ones most likely to seek to pull the strings of 'power', controlling world events, governments, economies, etc. The media is not interested in reporting the subtler manifestations of an awakening consciousness, the growing interest in things spiritual, the increasing awareness that our old paradigms just aren't cutting it. The popular notion that the world is going to hell, is yet another illusion. I believe that things are going perfectly, according to Plan. We are evolving; **things are getting better**.*

*I believe that we must resist the oppressive, deceptive methods of the power elite. The question is—how? I think most of us agree that war is not the answer. I believe that no form of anger/hatred/fist-shaking is the answer. I feel that better forms of resistance would be to protest in a peaceful and loving way, and to adjust our own lifestyles to reflect a higher awareness. There is some talk of an ultraelite who fuel turmoil and conflict in all forms, ultimately taking sides with whatever faction will cause further negativity. It is said that they are interested in wealth and power only to the extent that it allows them access to what they really want—negative energy. It is said that they actually feed from our fear-based negative energy. This sounds far-fetched, and yet all feeding, for all varieties of creatures, is some form of energy exchange. I believe that there is a good degree of truth to this, that somehow they have a vested interest in keeping us fearful and disempowered. They are left-brain imbalanced in a big way. If it is true that they are feeding on our negative energy, on our fears, then the best way to resist would be to starve them. To say it another way, perhaps we could convince them that **love is a better banquet**.*

I believe that it is not useful to view the power elite as any particular race or group, even if it may be true. I believe that any group is equally capable of behaving like the 'good guys' or like the 'bad guys'. There is some talk amongst well-meaning individuals that the 'real' power elite, covertly manipulating world affairs for their own gain, is actually a group of 'reptilian' extra-terrestrials. I can think of no useful reason for promoting this notion, but I can think of several ways in which it could be counterproductive;

1. This could be interpreted as a racist viewpoint. To label an entire group of beings in this way is a form of bigotry. 2. This notion could generate even more fear, which would further fuel the imbalance. 3. It is likely that the greater population is not 'ready' for such startling information and are thus not likely to take it seriously. 4. Even if there is a good deal of truth to this assertion, it is probably based on an oversimplistic view of things. I believe that the identity of the ruling elite is irrelevant. What is important to me is that, whoever they are, they are highly imbalanced, to the point that they are willing to perpetrate the most fiendish crimes against humanity in order to further their elitist status. What would benefit them the most, and thus all of humanity, is a great outpouring of love.

I believe that the power elite represents the most extreme negative aspect of the collective human consciousness. Thus, as the collective consciousness moves toward the light, so too will this negative aspect. We must learn to stop pointing the finger of blame. We are all responsible for our problems, for the dire situation in which we currently find ourselves. Even if we are victims of some group's predatory tendencies, we are responsible for allowing them to exploit us. **We are responsible**.

I believe we must resist the efforts of the dark forces as we battle for the light. In every way possible we must protest and resist actions that threaten human rights, that endanger lives and lifestyles, that exploit the world's resources to the detriment of the planet's ecology. To fight for our rights and the rights of others is a compassionate act. We must continue to demonstrate, to hold rallies and wave placards, to write letters to politicians, to seek information and to spread it to others. We must organize. We should keep doing all the things that activists do. However, I feel that it is very important to do these things in the right frame of mind. I believe that, in the grander scheme of things, it is useless and possibly detrimental to resist the dark forces in a spirit of anger and hatred. We cannot fight the darkness with more darkness.

I believe that spiritual types and activist types should unite in their endeavors to resist the darkness. Most activists see themselves as pragmatic, no-nonsense dissenters with little time for spiritual hocus-pocus. They are not aware of the dynamics of energy, the power of human consciousness to affect change at a vibrational level, etc. Many of them feel it would be a waste of time to pray for peace. Many spiritualists, on the other hand, see themselves as being 'beyond' marching in a peace rally, especially if there is anger or violence. They are less likely to get involved in the pragmatic aspects of resistance. I would be very happy to see these two groups come together, to recognize each other's methods as being very worthwhile, to set aside differences and realize that we are all fighting a common battle. The greater the numbers in a resistance movement, the greater the power. I firmly believe that, if a good percentage of the population put out the same intention at the same time, it would represent an irresistible force. It would be the type of force that could not be defeated by any type of weaponry. It would resist the darkness by changing it into lightness.

I believe that fear is linked with ignorance and love is linked with knowledge. To know the true nature of reality is to have no fear. It is relatively ineffective to say to oneself, "I hereby resolve to have no fear". It is easier to gain the knowledge that the premises on which the fears are based have no foundation in reality. It is very difficult to have no fear of death unless one realizes that there is no such thing as death. One would have no fear of loneliness if one knew that we are all cut from the same cloth, all part of the cosmic oneness. If we were aware of the illusion of duality, then judgement would be seen for what it is and we would no longer fear it. The more we could see 'the Game' with clarity, the more we would learn to enjoy it.

I believe that there is much confusion around the concept of humility. Most people feel that to be humble means to bow down to the over-whelming power of God, to admit that one is nothing compared to God. In the Catholic Church there is a prayer that is recited just before the receiving of communion. It goes something like this: "Oh Lord, I am not worthy to receive you. Say but the word and I will be healed." This prayer is an example of a general teaching that I have trouble with. It seems to be saying that God is something separate from me, that I am not worthy of God and that I am not in control of my own healing process.

*I believe that to be humble is to acknowledge that I am no better than anyone else, and to also realize that that means that **nobody else is better than me. We are all equal**. Every manifestation of energy is an essential component, an indispensable part of the totality that is God. Therefore, we are all God. There is no separation between us and God. Humility has nothing to do with being 'unworthy'. It has nothing in common with subservience, to God or to any entity. Rather, it is an acknowledgement of unity. Separateness is the root of weakness. To feel a part of the whole is to take ownership of the enormous power at hand; to take control of one's destiny; to be God. If I could be so bold as to rewrite the above prayer, it would go something like this; "As an equal part of the totality, I am worthy of the divine powers of the universe. If I say the word, I will be healed".*

*I believe that it is useful to one's quest for enlightenment to be of service to others. This may seem to contradict what was just said. But there is a great difference between being of service to mankind and being subserviant to the will of someone else. One can only be of service to mankind if it is also serving oneself. **It makes no sense to impair one's own path to enlightenment in order to serve others.***

I believe that we are all parcels of divinity. We are all a part of the same whole. It does not make sense to deny one's needs, desires and inner cravings in order to facilitate those of some one else. It does not make sense to hurt one part of the whole in order to help another part of the whole. Even from a more pragmatic point of view, it is easier to know what is joyful to oneself than it is to know what is joyful for someone else. Therefore, to sacrifice what one knows to be one's own happiness in order to facilitate what may or may not be the happiness of some one else, is not a winning proposition. However, if giving joy to some one else also gives joy to oneself, then everybody wins.

I believe that the best route to enlightenment is to follow one's joy. If you're doing something that 'makes your heart sing', you are probably assisting your own healing process. Such a statement often begs the question, what if your circumstances are such that it is impossible to do what makes your heart sing? I would argue that, within any set of circumstances, there is a range of choices that can be made—even if the circumstances are so severe that the best choice would be death.

I believe that the beliefs I have today are not the same as the beliefs I will have tomorrow.

I believe that …

In closing, I would like to share, once more, my seven core beliefs:

1. **Most of what we refer to as reality is an illusion.**
2. **We are not just clever naked apes designing better mousetraps—humanity is much more than we tend to believe.**
3. **An incredibly glorious, beautiful and exciting destiny awaits us all.**
4. **We are the creators.**
5. **We, and all things in all universes, are one.**
6. **There is absolutely nothing to fear.**
7. **Love is the master key to all doors.**

BIBLIOGRAPHY

Alford, Alan—*Gods of the New Millennium*, Hodder and Stoughton, 1997, London
—*The Phoenix Solution*, Hodder and Stoughton, 1998, London
Allegro, John—*The Sacred Mushroom and the Cross*, Doubleday,1970, New York
Alexanderson, Olof—*Living Water, Viktor Schauberger and the Secrets of Natural Energy*,
    Gateway Books, 1976, Bath UK
Arewa, Caroline Shola—*Way of Chakras*, Thorsons, 2001, London
Arguelles, Jose—*The Mayan Factor*, Bear & Company, 1987, Santa Fe, NM
Arguelles, J. and Nidle, S.—*Galactic Human Handbook, Entering the New Time*, Altea
    Publishing, 1995, Scotland
Baigent, Leigh and Lincoln—*The Holy Blood and the Holy Grail*, Corgi, 1982, London
—*The Messianic Legacy*, Dell, 1986, New York
Baigent, Michael—*Ancient Traces*, Penguin Books, 1998, London
—*The Dead Sea Scroll Deception*,
Bell, Art and Strieber, Whitley—*The Coming Global Superstorm*, Simon and Schuster, 2001,
    New York
Bentov, Itzhak—*Stalking the Wild Pendulum, On the Mechanics of Consciousness*, Destiny
    Books, 1977, Rochester VT
Braden, Gregg—*Awakening to Zero Point ***, Radio Bookstore Press, 1993, Bellevue, WA
—*Walking Between the Worlds*, Radio Bookstore Press, 1997, Bellevue, WA
Bramley, William—*The Gods of Eden ***, Avon Books, 1990, New York
Bronowski, J—*The Ascent of Man*, British Broadcasting Corporation, 1973, London
Camphausen, Rufus—*The Encyclopedia of Sacred Sexuality*, Inner Traditions International,
    1999, Rochester, VT.
Capra, Fritzof—*The Tao of Physics*, Harper Collins, 1976, London
Castaneda, Carlos —*The Teachings of Don Juan, A Sperate Reality,Journey to Ixtlan, Tales of
    Power, The Second Ring of Power, The Eagle's Gift, The Fire From Within*, Simon and
    Schuster, 1970 to 1984, New York
Cerminara, Gina—*Insights for the Age of Aquarius*, Quest Books, 1973, London
Childress, David Hatcher—*Extraterrestrial Archaeology*, Adventures Unlimited Press, 1995,
    Stelle, Ill.
Churchward, James—*The Lost Continent of Mu*, Ives Washburn Inc., 1931, New York
Clow, Barbara Hand—*Liquid Light of Sex*, Bear & Company, 1991, Santa Fe, NM
Collier, Joy—*The Heretic Pharaoh, The Life of Akhenaten*, Dorset Press, 1970, New York
Cotterell, Maurice—*The Tutankhamen Prophecies*, Headline Books, 1999, London
Danelly, Richard—*Sedona: Beyond the Vortex ***, The Vortex Society, 1995, Sedona AZ
Desroches—Noblecourt, C. and Kenett, F.—*Tutankhamen*, George Rainbird Ltd., 1963,
    London
Donnelly, Ignatius—Atlantis, the Antediluvian World, Rudolph Steiner Publications, 1971,
    New York
Doreal, M.—*The Emerald Tablets of Thoth the Atlantean*, Alexandrian Library Press
Drosnin, Michael—*The Bible Code*, Simon and Schuster, 1997, New York
Dunn, Christopher—*The Giza Powerplant*, Bear & Company, 1998, Santa Fe, NM
Freke, Timothy and Gandy, Peter—*The Complete Guide to World Mysticism*, Judy Piatkus, Inc.,
    1997, London
Feuerstein, Georg—*Sacred Sexuality*, Inner Traditions, 1992, Rochester, New York
Finkelstein, I. And Silberman, N. A.—*The Bible Unearthed*, Simon & Schuster, 2002, New
    York
Frater U.·. D.·.—*Secrets of Western Sex Magic*, Llewellyn Publications, 2001, St. Paul MN
Frissell, Bob—*Nothing in This Book Is True, But It's Exactly How Things Are ***, Frog Ltd., 1994,
    Berkely, CA
Furlong, David—*The Keys to the Temple*, Judy Piatkus, Ltd., 1997, London
Gass, Robert—*Chanting, Discovering Spirit in Sound*, Broadway Books, 1999, New York
Gardner, Laurence—*Genesis of the Grail Kings*, Bantam Press, 1999, London

George, Leonard—*Alternative Realities*, Facts On File, Inc., 1995, New York
Good, Timothy—*Above Top Secret*, William Morrow and Company, 1988, New York
Goodwin, David—*The Truth About Cabala*, Llewellyn Publications, 1994, St. Paul MN
Greene, Brian—*The Elegant Universe*, Vintage Books, 1999, New York
Hancock, Graham—*The Mars Mystery*, Crown Publishers, 1998, New York
   —*The Sign and the Seal*, Doubleday Canada, Ltd., 1993, Toronto
Harner, Michael—*The Way of the Shaman*, Bantam, 1980, New York
Haselhoff, Eltjo—*The Deepening Complexity of Crop Circles*, Frog Ltd, 2001, Berkely
Heseman, Michael—*The Cosmic Connection*, Gateway Books, 1996, Bath UK
Hoagland, Richard C.—*The Monuments on Mars*, Frog, Ltd, 1996, Berkely, CA
Hogue, John—*The Millennium Book of Prophesy*, HarperCollins Publishing, 1994, New York
Hope, Murray—*Atlantis, Myth or Reality?*, Penguin Books, 1991, London
Horrowitz, Leonard and Puleo, Joseph—*Healing Codes for the Biblical Apocalypse*,
   Tetrahedron Publishing Group, 2000, Sandpoint, ID
Hurtak, J. J.—*The Keys of Enoch*—The Academy of Future Science, 1975, Los Gatos CA
Icke, David—*The Robot's Rebellion**, Gateway Books, 1994, Bath U.K.
   —*The Biggest Secret*
Judith, Anodea—*Wheels of Life*, Llewellyn Publications, 1995, St. Paul, MN
Kaltreider, Kurt—*American Indian Prophecies*, Hay House Inc., 1998, Carlsbad CA
Krupp, E. C.—*Echoes of the Ancient Skies*, Harper and Row, 1983, New York
Laurence, Richard (translated by)—The Book of Enoch the Prophet, Adventures Unlimited
   Press, 2000 (orginal edition—1883), Kempton, IL
Mahr, Douglas—*Ramtha, Voyage to the New World*, Ballantine Books, 1985, New York
Marciniak, Barbara—*Bringers of the Dawn**, Bear & Company, 1992, Santa Fe, NM
   —*Earth**, Bear & Company, 1995, Santa Fe, NM
Markale, Jean—*The Great Goddess*, Inner Traditions, 1997, Rochester VT
Mavor, James—*Voyage to Atlantis*, Park Street Press, 1969, Rochester VT
Melchizedec, Drunvalo—*Flower of Life Workshop*—28 hours of video
Mookerjee, A. and Khanna, M.—*The Tantric Way*, New York Graphic Society, 1977, Boston
Moon, P. and Nichols, Preston—*Pyramids of Montauk*, Sky Books, 1994, New York
Moon, Peter—*The Black Sun, Montauk's Nazi—Tibetan Connection*, Sky Books, 1997 New York
Morford, M. and Lenardon, R.—*Classical Mythology*, Longman Inc., 1971, New York
Myss, Caroline—*Anatomy of the Spirit*, Harmony Books, 1996, New York
   —*Sacred Contracts*, Harmony Books, 2001, New York
Ouspensky, P.D.—*In Search of the Miraculous*, Harcourt Brace Jovanovich, 1977, New York
Picknett, Lynn and Prince, Clive—*The Templar Revelation**, Bantam Press, 1997, London
Ranke-Heinemann, Uta—*Eunuchs for the Kingdom of Heaven*
Ravenscroft, Trevor—*The Spear of Destiny*, Samuel Weiser, Inc., 1982, York Beach, ME
Redman, James—*The Celestine Prophecy**, Warner Books, 1993, New York
Sarita, M. A. and Geho, S. A.—*Tantric Love*, Fireside Books, 2001, New York
Scallion, Gordon-Michael—*Notes From the Cosmos*, Matrix Institute, Inc., 1987,
   Chesterfield NH
Schlemmer, Phylis V.—*The Only Planet of Choice*, Gateway Books, 1993, Bath U.K.
Schroeder, Gerald M.—*The Science of God*, The Free Press, 1997, New York
Shanks, Herschel—*The Dead Sea Scrolls*
Sheldrake, Rupert—*A New Science of Life*, Park Street Press, 1981, Rochester, VT
Simpson, Liz—*The Book of Chakra Healing*, Sterling Publishing, 1999, New York
Sitchin, Zecharia—*Genesis Revisited*, Avon Books, 1990, New York
   —*The Twelfth Planet*, Avon Books, 1978, New York
Spence, Lewis—*The Encyclopaedia of the Occult*, Bracken Books, 1994, London
Stearn, Jess—*Edgar Cayce on the Millennium*,
Szekely, Edmond—*The Essene Way*, International Biogenic Society, 1989, Nelson BC, Canada
   —*Biogenic Living*
Tansley, David—*Subtle Body*, Thames and Hudson, 1977, London
Temple, Robert—*The Sirius Mystery*, Destiny Books, 1976, Rochester, VT
Thompson, Richard—*Alien Identities*, Govardhan Hill Publishing, 1993, Badger, CA
Thiering, Barbara—*Jesus the Man*, Corgi Books, 1992, London

Von Däniken, Erich—*Chariots of the Gods?*, Bantam Books, 1970, New York
Walsch, Neale Donald—*Conversations With God**, Book 1, G.P. Putnam's Sons, 1995, New York —*CWG, Books 2 and 3**, Hodder & Stoughton, 1997, 1998, London
Watson, Lyall—*The Secret Life of Inanimate Objects*, Destiny Books, 1990, Rochester VT
White, John—*Pole Shift*, A.R.E. Press, 1996, Virginia Beach VA
Wilson, Colin—*From Atlantis to the Sphinx*, Virgin Books, 1997, London
Yogananda, Paramahansa—*Autobiography of a Yogi*, Self-Realization Fellowship, 1946, Los Angeles
Zukav, Gary—*Seat of the Soul**, Simon & Schuster, 1990, New York
—*The Dancing Wu Li Masters*, Bantam Books, 1979, New York

*—These books are recommended as a good place to begin. They are also relatively easy to find at a reasonable price.

WEBSITES

For updates and additional info related to the topics in this book, please refer to our website: **www.whyislife.com**

Websites arranged by topic. (Many of these researchers belong in multiple categories)

MISCELLANEOUS

Altered States—lots of interesting info and links—**www.altered-states.co.nz**
Ancient American Magazine –ancient archeology—**www.ancientamerican.com**
Art Bell—an amazing assortment of 'alternative info'.—**www.artbell.com**
Buckminster Fuller Institute—a true genius—**www.bfi.org**
Bushby, Tony—author of 'The Bible Fraud'—**www.thebiblefraud.com**
Chaos Theory and Fractals—**www.mathjmendl.org/chaos/**
David Icke—**www.davidicke.com**
Deoxyribonucleic Hyperdimension—weird stuff—**www.deoxy.org/deoxy.htm**
Dr. Karen Ralls—**www.ancientquest.com**
Drunvalo Melchizedec—special info from this amazing teacher.—**www.drunvalo.com**
Earthchanges—prophecies and observations by G. Michael Scallion. —**www.matrixinstitute.com**
For 'skeptical' arguments countering 'alterinfo'—**www.thehallofmaat.com**
Greatmystery—the Prophet's Conference, etc.—**www.greatmystery.org**
Library of Halexandria—a wealth of alterinfo—**www.halexandria.org**
Matthew Fox—a priest with some very different ideas –**www.creationspirituality.org**
Nazarene Way, the—this website presents the Gnostic Gospels as well as other info that challenges official church doctrine—**www.thenazareneway.com**
Neale Donald Walsh—author of the 'Conversation with God' series—**www.cwg.org**
Nexus Magazine—the world's premier alternative info mag.—**www.nexusmagazine.com**
Parabola Magazine—myth, tradition and the search for meaning—**www.parabola.org**
Ram Dass—a great teacher—**www.ramdasstapes.org**
Source Books—a great way to buy related books and stuff.—**www.sacredspaces.org**
The San Francisco Tesla Society—info about Tesla and related things—**www.sftesla.org**
The Seven Ray Institute—**www.sevenray.com**
Thom Hartman—author of 'The Rise of Corporate Dominance and the Theft of Human Rights'—**www.thomhartmann.com**

BOOKSTORES
Discount New Age Books—www.discountnewagebooks.com
More Used Books—and new—www.abebooks.com
Used Books—as well as new ones—www.addall.com

SHAMANIC
Brooke Medicine Eagle—www.medicineeagle.com
Carlos Castaneda—www.castaned.org
Chamalu—www.chamalu.com
Hank Wesselman, PHD—www.sharedwisdom.com
Michael Harner, PHD—www.shamanism.org
Ralph Metzner—Green Earth Foundation—www.metzner-greenearth.org
Shamanism—www.deoxy.org/shaman
Terence McKenna—www.levity.com

THE BIG SHIFT
Barbara Marx Hubbard—www.consciousevolution.net
Doreen Virtue, PHD—www.angeltherapy.com
Gregg Braden—www.greggbraden.net

CONSCIOUSNESS and HEALTH
Judith Orloff, MD—www.drjudithorloff.com
Laurie Monroe—www.monroeinstitute.org

EXTRA TERRESTRIALS
Father Charles Moore—www.moordune.com
John Mack, MD—www.centerchange.org

ALTERNATIVE HEALING
Carolyn Mys—www.myss.com
Deepak Chopra, MD—www.chopra.com
Vasant Lad—www.ayurveda.com

SUFI
Coleman Barks—www.pirvilayat.org

NUMEROLOGY
Dan Millman—www.danmillman.com

MAYAN
Carlos Barrios—www.sacredroad.org
Humbatz Men—www.mayamystery.com
Information re: the Mayan calendar—www.experiencefestival.com
Judith Bluestone Polich—www.web-of-light.com

CONSCIOUSNESS and SCIENCE
Alex Shulgin, PHD—www.mdma.net
Arny Mindell, PHD—www.aamindell.net
Don Beck, PHD—www.spiraldynamics.net

Edgar Mitchell, PHD—**www.edmitchellapollo14.com**
Elisabet Sahtouris, PHD—**www.sahtouris.com**
Gary Schwartz, PHD—**www.openmindsciences.com**
Jean Houston, PHD—**www.jeanhousto.org**
John Demartini, DC—**www.drdemartini.com**
John Hagelin, PHD—**www.hagelin.org**
Kate Darling—**www.motherwave.com**
Matthew Fox, PHD—**www.mathewfox.org**
Michio Kaku, PHD—**www.michiokaku.org**
Peter Russell, DCS—**www.peterussell.com**
Rupert Sheldrake, PHD—**www.sheldrake.org**
Story Musgrove, MD/Astronaut—**www.spacestory.com**
William Tiller, PHD—**www.tiller.org**

ARCHAEOLOGY
Paul Devereux—**www.acemake.com**

SACRED GEOMETRY
Bruce Rawls—**www.intent.com**
Dan Winter—**www.soulinvitation.com**
Sacred Geometry—info provided by Jonathan Quintan—**www.sacredgeometry.com**
San Graal School of Sacred Geometry—**www.sangraal.com**
Stewart Swerlow—**www.stewartswerlow.com**

SACRED NUMBERS
A site dedicated to 'phi'—**www.goldennumber.net**
Arcane, esoteric,cosmic knowledge by Michael Joyce—**www.jufo.freeserve.co.uk**
Earthchanges, etc, by Dee Finney and Joe Mason—**www.greatdreams.com**
The Jupiter Project—**www.shaka.com/~johnboy**

SACRED SEXUALITY
Beings of Light—**www.fromthestars.com**
Catherine Yronwode—**www.luckymojo.com**
Tantra—**www.tantra.co.nz**
The Church of Tantra—**www.tantra.org**
Worldwide Tantra Teacher Directory—**www.tantra.com**

SOUND POWER
Don Campbell—**www.mozarteffect.com**
Jonathan Goldman—**www.healingsounds.com**

DOLPHINS
Ilona Selke—**www.livingfromvision.com**
Joan Phillips Ocean, MSW—**www.joanocean.com**

JUDAISM
Michael Lerner, PHD—**www.tikun.org**

INDEX

Would you like to order a copy of

WHY IS LIFE?

The easiest way to do so is to go to
the following website:

www.whyislife.com

You will also find up to date information
related to the topics in this book, dates and
locations of speaking engagements, links to
other authors and websites and much more.